A Theory of Minimalism

Also available from Bloomsbury

Reparative Aesthetics, Susan Best
Aesthetics and Architecture, Edward Winters
Aesthetics and Painting, Jason Gaiger
Expanded Painting, Mark Titmarsh
Aesthetics of Ugliness: A Critical Edition, Karl Rosenkranz

A Theory of Minimalism

Marc Botha

Bloomsbury Academic India
An imprint of Bloomsbury Publishing Plc

BLOOMSBURY

NEW DELHI • LONDON • OXFORD • NEW YORK • SYDNEY

BLOOMSBURY INDIA
Bloomsbury Publishing India Pvt. Ltd
Second Floor, LSC Building No. 4, DDA Complex, Pocket C–6&7,
Vasant Kunj, New Delhi 110070

BLOOMSBURY, BLOOMSBURY ACADEMIC INDIA and the Diana logo are
trademarks of Bloomsbury Publishing Plc

First published in India 2025
First published 2017

This edition published with permission from Bloomsbury Publishing Plc,
50 Bedford Square, London, WC1B3DP, UK

British Library Cataloguing-in-Publication Data
A catalogue record for this book is available from the British Library.

Library of Congress Cataloging-in-Publication Data
A catalog record for this book is available from the Library of Congress

ISBN: 978-93-61317-69-9

Cover design by Clare Turner
Cover image © Ellsworth Kelly

Typeset by Fakenham Prepress Solutions, Fakenham, Norfolk NR21 8NN
Printed and bound in India by Replika Press Pvt. Ltd

To find out more about our authors and books
visit www.bloomsbury.com and sign up for our newsletters

For my parents, Neville and Annette

Contents

Acknowledgements

I have benefited immensely from exchanges at various points of this research with, among others, Derek Attridge, Stephen Bann, Carrol Clarkson, Timothy Clark, Frances Colpitt, Alec Finlay, Daniel Grausam, Francisco-J Hernández Adrián, Ulrike Kistner, Liliane Lijn, Ulrika Maude, Nico Muhly, John Nash, Reingard Nethersole, Jelena Novak, Christopher Norris, Marc Schachter, Stuart Sim, Henry Staten, Jennifer Terry, Samuel Thomas, David Watson, Patricia Waugh, Andries Wessels, Russell West-Pavlov, Merle Williams and Heather Yeung. I am especially grateful to Pat, Maebh and Heather for their intellectual generosity and friendship. Also, to my former colleagues at the University of Pretoria, current colleagues at the University of Durham, and to numerous other interlocutors and friends from various conferences, symposia, lectures, reading-groups and publications with whom I have had the privilege of corresponding, formally and informally, my sincere thanks.

My thanks to Liza Thompson and Frankie Mace at Bloomsbury for their patience and assistance, to Simon Cutts from Coracle Press, and to Tate and M HKA Antwerp for permission to reproduce verse and image. Much of this research was funded by a Durham Doctoral Fellowship at Durham University and, subsequently, by a Postdoctoral Research Associateship on the Leverhulme Trust *Tipping Points* project. My thanks to both organizations for their support.

There are many friends outside of academia who have been tremendously supportive: you know who you are and just how much your friendship means to me. But my first and final and greatest debt of gratitude is to my family: to my parents, Neville and Annette, to whom this book is dedicated; to my sister Andrea and her family, Jake, Helen and Olivia; to my aunts Yvonne and Lorraine; to my godfather Walter and to Annelize.

Preface

As the title suggests, this work offers a theory of aesthetic minimalism. It is a general theory inasmuch as it addresses minimalist works as they manifest across a range of expressive media in the visual arts, music, literature, architecture and performance. It does not seek to fix a definitive canon of minimalist works, nor to prescribe a formula for approaching minimalism. Rather, it offers a theory in the sense of the Greek term *theoria*: a way of seeing or viewing. Since its object – minimalism – is comprised of works that vary considerably in conception, medium, execution and commitment, a theory of minimalism worthy of its name must necessarily be dynamic and capable of drawing out connections between often disparate works. In short, a theory of minimalism must offer not a single view of minimalism, but multiple views.

Studies of minimalism have tended to fall into two broad categories: historical accounts that focus on minimalism as a chronologically delimited movement, usually drawing attention to a central canon of works and occasionally its precursors and successors; and formalist accounts that concentrate on the properties or qualities of minimalist works and how these differ from or conform to other aesthetic categories. In some studies these two paradigms intersect, while in others they are kept largely apart. In other studies, greater attention is given to the economic, social and political complexities that frame the emergence of minimalist aesthetic works. Without sacrificing the many gains from these different approaches, the present work aims to broaden and deepen the study of minimalism by developing a conceptual vocabulary that is able to reground minimalism, and in so doing also to clarify connections between these often competing accounts.

My principal claim is that minimalism cannot be reduced to a set of works or stylistic markers no matter how inclusive or exhaustive. Instead, I suggest that minimalism is best grasped as an *existential modality*: a way of existing in the world. What connects different types of minimalism – aesthetic, linguistic, legal, computational, or lifestyle – is that their existence is entangled with and comported towards *minimum*. Minimum finds two principle expressions: the infinitesimal, or the *least possible*; and the parsimonious, or the *least necessary*. In this light, it becomes possible to define aesthetic minimalism, in appropriately minimalist terms, as the investigation of the least possible and the least necessary across a range of media and works. Yet, as soon as minimalism is grasped in such broadly existential terms, it becomes evident that it is a transhistorical phenomenon that seems to emerge in some form or another in every historical epoch.

Thus, drawing on a range of examples, I argue that minimalism is far more diverse than is often admitted. In this light, my wager is that a general theory, as distinct from a complete theory, requires an eclectic conceptual approach, since it must be equally responsive to often very different types of minimalism with distinct historical trajectories. The radical concerns that pervade minimalism span numerous conceptual paradigms, often placing these different paradigms in conversation. Although I examine the variety of these conversations, the overall commitment of my argument is to a type of realism. In particular, I am concerned with a minimalist species of realism that aims to delineate that which is most radical to every real situation without proposing any sort of dogmatic theory of reality. It is these minimal conditions of the real that I believe aesthetic minimalism exemplifies with particular force. In simple terms, what I try to offer is a realist theory of minimalism that is able to feed into a minimalist theory of realism. In essence, I am concerned with the type of realism that the phenomenologist, Roman Ingarden, conceives in terms of the convergence, rather than the incommensurability, of reality as it is arrived at through perception, and reality as it exists independently of perception. I argue that minimalism, understood broadly as an aesthetic modality, intensifies and clarifies access to the real.

This theory is advanced by developing seven distinct concepts – historical intermittency, the encounter, objecthood, the real, radical quantity, lessness and minimum – which together frame a dynamic approach to minimalist aesthetics as a transhistorical existential modality. Each chapter is further divided into sub-sections which together constitute a constellation of concepts, each tied to a specific example, or series of examples, of minimalist works – often canonical, but including more peripheral and unacknowledged expressions of minimalism.

The opening chapter, 'Intermittency: On the Transhistoricism of Minimalism', introduces the concepts of minimum and minimalism, making a case for the latter as an existential modality as outlined above, rather than simply as a chronologically delimited movement or a closed set of attributes. What I develop instead is a transhistorical theory of minimalist aesthetics. Minimalism, as with many other radical aesthetic modalities, is governed by the correlative logics of *return* and *intermittency*, adapted from Hal Foster and Andrew

Gibson respectively. The radical force of minimalist aesthetics lies not in a single, historical event, but rather in its capacity to return, and in returning to turn aesthetics towards its most radical possibilities. Minimalism constitutes an event which in the singularity of its eruption conserves the potential for its intermittent return. Far from diluting the historical singularity of the minimalist moment of the mid-twentieth century, poised as it was between the modern and the postmodern, this dynamic conception intensifies our understanding of what it in fact means for minimalism to occupy a threshold position, and the immense potentiality invested in many of its works as a result.

Having made a case for the transhistorical study of minimalism, the second chapter, 'Encounters: On the Politics of Minimalism', turns to the specificity of minimalist works themselves. Drawing on Althusser's concept of the *encounter* and Merleau-Ponty's insights regarding the constructive role of *perception*, it focuses on the ways in which minimalist works are encountered. It is precisely the contingency of the encounter – which is distributed between the work, the perceiver, and the context of the encounter – that invests a certain immanent force in the work, even as it opens the work to multiple interpretations. An encounter is at once the most banal and the most profound occurrence: it is simply what happens when subjects and objects interact, yet it effects a modulation of the intensity of reality that harbours a genuinely transfigurative potential. By careful exemplification, I show how the encounter is at the very heart of minimalist aesthetics. It describes the event of connection between subject and object, but also the forces that underpin this event. In this sense, the encounter exposes both the micro- and macro-political aspects of minimalism. Minimalism possesses a remarkable, and to many unexpected, capacity for reflecting and reflecting on complex political questions. Its prominence exposes important issues regarding the rapid commodification of art and the role of the artwork in public space; while on the level of structure, its transparency and emphasis on process clarify a great deal regarding the aesthetic coding of power and control, and the ethico-political aspects of aesthetic experience.

The third chapter, 'Objecthood: On the Materialism of Minimalism', turns to the material manifestation of minimalism. In fact, close attention to the range of minimalist works, reveals that objecthood manifests in diverse and at times paradoxical ways, necessitating the distinction between material, temporal, and conceptual objects, as well as the many ways in which these different aspects interact. Minimalist objects problematize their own objecthood, but also objecthood more generally, and as such I suggest that they be interpreted in terms of what Damisch and Bal term *theoretical objects* – objects that prompt theoretical speculation while also providing a means of *doing* theory. Minimalist objects habitually clarify questions of form, scale, and process, constituting works that evade the usual mimetic economy of art – the imperative to reflect or represent reality – focusing instead on immanence itself. Defining themselves in terms of the immanence of their own objecthood, minimalist works become icons of the real: they clarify the ways in which objects are able to enter, persist, and produce effects in the world in a sustained relation to minimum.

The fourth chapter, 'The Real: On the Persistence of Minimalism', develops the iconicity of minimalism with respect to the real, beginning with an overview of the disputed ground of realism that continues to divide contemporary thought. Minimalism, I argue, testifies to a radical shift in the conception of realism from the *alethic* and *mimetic* paradigms, focused respectively on truth and verisimilitude, to a *poietic* paradigm focused on the production of the real itself. Examined through the lens of Danto's and Lukács's thought, it becomes evident that even the frequent minimalist focus on representational precision is concerned less with the reproduction of reality, than it is with the clarification and intensification of the real. Following Meillassoux's recuperation of the absolute as the basis for a contemporary realism, I examine, through exemplary works of minimalist aesthetics, the conditions under which a realist account of minimalism and a minimalist account of realism prove confluent. At this point of confluence, minimalism instantiates a sort of *transfiguration*: although there is no material shift in the constitution of the work, it comes to exist at an increased intensity, marking a minimal shift between the mere thing and the artwork. Such transfiguration is not dramatic, but is rather marked by the persistence of the minimalist work in the face of contingency.

The fifth chapter, 'Quantity: On the Radicality of Minimalism', presses towards the radical ontological ground of the real. It argues that although minimalism is first encountered in terms of its particular qualities, it is radical quantity that lies at the heart of the minimalist enterprise. In particular it draws on the thought of Badiou – and principally on his assertion that multiplicity, as pure quantity, is the stuff of being itself – to investigate the ontological moorings of minimalism. As with its remarkable capacity for clarifying the real, minimalism proves adept at intensifying the aesthetic apprehension of radical quantity itself. I identify two principal quantitative expressions of minimalism: *continuity*, which manifests principally in terms of sustained sound and silence, monochromatic works and unvaried repetition, and self-referential condensation; and *calculation*, which manifests principally in terms of seriality, incremental repetition and self-referential expansion. Existence, for the most part, is constituted by contingent entities that have no particular valences; entities that are counted, but which may not count for anything specific. Here minimalism proves particularly apposite to the task of presenting and representing, reflecting and reflecting on, the subtractive and cumulative processes that underpin the quantitative being of the everyday. Minimalism generates an aesthetic field in which the quantitative dimension of the work emerges as its most persistent quality.

The sixth chapter, 'Austerity: On the Lessness of Minimalism', turns to the minimalist pursuit of clarity through processes of reduction and simplification. This search proves closely allied to the transhistorical and transcultural manifestation of ascetic practice, marked by various processes of discipline, abstinence, renunciation, privation, and denegation. Much as the path of the religious ascetic leads towards minimum, so minimalist aesthetics often lead towards an ascetic path. This synergy is as much evident in the austere architecture of the monastic cell as it is in the austere processes that underpin the work of numerous prominent minimalist composers, painters and poets. Such *holy minimalism*, as it is often called, is sometimes expressed in iconic terms, as a contemplative lessness, while at other times it instantiates a theurgical or ritual urgency, repetitive and insistent. In both cases, what lies at the heart of this aesthetic is the recognition that transcendence is not external as such, but emerges from within the transfigurative immanence of the work itself. Yet, in holy minimalism, the transfigurative aesthetic is generally marked by an inward turn that is also a return to the universal. In this process, its works often appeal to an aesthetic of the sublime, attempting to uncover something primal at the heart of every expressive medium, pointing towards the archaic nothingness often intuited by the most austere minimalism.

In the final chapter, 'Minimum: On the Extremes of Minimalism', the focus falls precisely only this nothingness. Coming full circle, I return to the opening question of this work – *what is minimum?* – but now with a fuller understanding of minimalism's conceptual moorings and consequences in order to press towards a region only cursorily touched on by the majority of critics: the questions of negation, nothingness and disappearance. Yet, even in probing the void, minimalism retains a curious and radical positivity. To take account of this phenomenon, the discussion progresses through Hegel's conception of *sublation* or determinate negation, and the various modulations of *nihilation* that emerge in the thinking of Heidegger, Sartre and Nancy. A great deal of minimalism takes place at this sublime limit, probing the minimal distance between form and formlessness, appearance and disappearance, something and nothing. At the limit of existence, as the minimalist work seems to pull irreversibly towards inexistence, it is useful to recall Levinas's formulation of the *il y a* – the irremissible presence that is discovered at the heart of every negation – together with Agamben's conception of *taking-place*, which recognizes that there is a radical part of every entity that is immanent, prior to any external relation; it is *just as it is*. These concepts provide the tools with which to reconceptualize liminal minimalisms in terms of a persistence in the face of overwhelming odds to the contrary, and it is in this sense that the considerable existential significance of minimalism begins to come to light, also pointing towards the importance of future minimalisms.

In general, this study aims to open new vistas onto the field of minimalism while also reopening doors which, in some cases, were prematurely closed, very often on account of the narrowness which disciplinary formations of knowledge sometimes involve. My hope is that this work will be as useful to students and enthusiasts of minimalism across all media who are aiming to come to grips with the often under-articulated conceptual and theoretical aspects of minimalism, as it will be to critical theorists and aestheticians who are looking to come to grips with the significance of minimalism to their various fields and approaches. It makes no claim to be a complete work, or to offer the last word on minimalism. On the contrary, it is only a first word in a new register, aiming to consolidate existing approaches to minimalism and to hold them to intensified conceptual scrutiny and new constellations of thought. My hope, in this light, is to inaugurate new ways of thinking about minimalism, whether they are in agreement or disagreement, and to deepen our collective regard for a remarkable and still developing set of works.

1

Intermittency: On the Transhistoricism of Minimalism

1.1 Minimum

Minimalism as existential modality: Frans Vanderlinde's *Elimination/Incarnation* (1967)

Minimum names the absolute: it is the *least possible*, but also the *least necessary*. It is both an ending and a beginning, the terminus of patient processes of simplification, reduction, exposition, intensification and clarification, but also the site of sudden, transfigurative events and explosions of novelty. Minimum establishes a limit beyond which things lose coherence, disappearing into nothingness, returning to undifferentiated multiplicity. But minimum also marks a radix from which things acquire coherence, subtracting form out of nothingness, proceeding from pure multiplicity. Minimum constitutes an ontological threshold: on one side, being is expressed in terms of existence – the multiple configurations of real entities; on the other side, minimum gives way to pure being – multiplicity without configuration. In this sense, minimum clarifies the real by naming the point at which every given reality comes into or departs from existence, marking the passage between undifferentiated *being* and differentiated *existence* by revealing the least that is possible and the least that is necessary in a given reality.[1] In terms of human experience, we encounter minimum most forcefully at the two instants that frame our existence: birth and death. Perhaps because of its existential significance, minimum captivates us, marking a point of emergence and withdrawal, a moment of appearance and disappearance, an event of creation and destruction.

Minimalism, defined in minimal terms, describes all those objects and processes which provide access, however fleeting or intermittent, to minimum. Minimalism is best understood as an *existential modality*, or a way of existing in the world. Since minimum resists direct representation, minimalism often takes the form of a speculative search for the least possible and the least necessary.

Nowhere has this search found more hospitable ground than in the broad field of aesthetic practice – in the works of visual art, music, literature and performance in which the existential paradoxes of minimum, its simultaneous entanglement with foundation and finitude, have been the subject of sustained experimentation. A fine example of this sort of experimentation is found in Frans Vanderlinde's concrete poem, 'Elimination/Incarnation', a work that fuses word, image and concept to generate the conditions under which form and meaning are able closely to reflect one another in a poetic approximation of minimum.

The first and last lines of the poem consist of single capitalized words, 'ELIMINATION' and 'INCARNATION' respectively. In the sixteen lines which separate these, the poem takes shape first through a process of incremental subtraction – eight successive lines progressively eliminate the very marks from which the letters of the word 'ELIMINATION' are constituted, leaving the minimal unit, 'I', at the poem's centre – and then through a process of incremental addition – lines are progressively added to this minimal unit, 'I', giving rise to the word 'INCARNATION'. Thus the poem not only concretely reflects the meaning of its constituent words, manifesting first as elimination and then as incarnation, but does so by the pivotal relation each of these processes has to a minimal point. At minimum – the unstable centre of a restless dialectic of positive and negative – elimination and incarnation become generatively indistinguishable from one another: elimination, an approach to minimum, is generative of the work itself.

The material form of the poem reiterates the radical dialectic at its heart: its hourglass shape contracts and expands, executing the injunction of the two words which frame it at top and bottom, 'ELIMINATION' and 'INCARNATION'; it pivots on a narrow centre which acts as a minimal point of synthesis at which radix and terminus, beginning and end, are confluent, mediating between what might ordinarily be regarded as the apparently incommensurable processes of disintegration and reintegration. Indeed, this logic is concretely reinforced in lines four to fourteen at the poem's centre, which, although they lack any clear verbal content, are clearly made up of the remnants of a disappearing word and the elementary units for a new one. Here the *poietic* processes of subtraction and addition, unmaking and making, are shown to be both symmetrical and in an important sense equivalent, exposing the force of the poem at its most minimal. Simultaneously, the act of reading the poem, tracing the disappearance and reappearance of letters and words as material signifiers, is productive of a type of subjectivity. The 'I' at the poem's centre is not only the minimal mark of inscription, but also a cipher for the poetic subject: the finite, human subject, which ordinarily exists in the interval between birth and death, is suspended here between death and birth, elimination and incarnation, making room for the emergence of an infinite, generative subject – the container of a radical productive potential which moves through the poem, so that even in the process of elimination, the overall drift of the work is generative, a process of 'INCARNATION'.

In 'Elimination/Incarnation', we encounter an emblem of the broader aesthetic programme of minimalism in its existential register, the poem granting several points of access to minimum. Minimum understood as the *least possible*, is expressed as a principle of the *infinitesimal*, which habitually manifests in terms of minimal means deployed to maximal effect, and is conveyed in the maxim *multum in parvo*, or much in little, which is often translated by the familiar phrase, *less is more*.[2] Minimum understood as the *least necessary*, recalls the principle of *parsimony*, memorably conveyed in a maxim traditionally attributed to William of Ockham, and known colloquially as Ockham's Razor: *entia non sunt multiplicanda praetor necessitate*, or, entities should not be multiplied beyond necessity.[3] Where the infinitesimal indicates intensity, parsimony provides clarity, and yet, in practice, minimalism habitually reveals that these two poles are in fact confluent; and at this crossing of intensity and clarity – the 'I' at the heart of Vanderlinde's poem – a universal poetic force emerges from the singularity of the minimalist artwork. Such works intensify and clarify minimum, rendering it more accessible, even as minimum points to what is most radical and most real in every minimalist work – the threshold at which the potentiality of pure being passes into the actuality of existence. In this sense, minimalism also intensifies and clarifies the real, since the real simply describes those things which exist, or, more precisely, which *persist* in existence.

1.2 Intermittency

The transhistorical register of minimalism: Dan Flavin's *monument 1 to V. Tatlin* (1964)

Yet the real always manifests in a specific reality, and every reality is expressed in terms of particular historical conditions. For this reason, it is necessary to supplement the existential register of minimalism with a consideration of its historical register. In its historical register, the term minimalism is most often used to describe an aesthetic style or movement prominent in the mid-twentieth century – first in the visual arts and music, and later in literature, architecture, design and fashion – characterized by a sustained exposition of the media and processes of aesthetic expression in their most transparent, uncomplicated forms. Although relatively short-lived in this narrow historical or canonical sense, the initial eruption and codification of minimalism as a movement significantly influenced the course of subsequent aesthetic endeavour, exporting techniques and insights into a range of aesthetic contexts. The logic of minimalism manifests well beyond the artworld, in fields as diverse as computer programming, systems design, linguistics, sociology, theology, law and philosophy.

While these vastly different discourses appear only obliquely related to aesthetic minimalism, and indeed to each other, it is nonetheless true that they all express a certain relation to minimum conceived either in terms of the infinitesimal or least possible, or in terms of parsimony or the least necessary. It is also evident that the term minimalism was available to these discourses, although it is unclear whether this availability resulted from the rapid adoption of the term into the lexicon of an art criticism which had itself acquired a new cultural capital through the rapid commodification of art in the mid-twentieth century,[4] or whether it emerged from a shared desire for an alternative to the 'spectacular culture of advanced capitalism'[5] which, from very different perspectives, converged on the term minimalism as an appropriate point of resistance. In either case, the prominence of the term minimalism is at least indicative of a situation maximally receptive to various practices of minimalism.

Understood as a chronologically delimited set of works and events – exhibitions, installations, performances and publications – minimalism remains a heavily disputed region of aesthetic history. While prominent critics such as Barbara Rose[6] and John Perreault[7] recognize in minimalism both continuity and progression, notable defenders of high modernist aesthetics, including Clement Greenberg[8] and Michael Fried,[9] contend the opposite, framing minimalism as an anti-art that poses a radical threat to the entire programme of modernity – a sentiment famously echoed in the context of music by Pierre Boulez,[10] and less famously, but with no less vitriol, by writer and literary critic, Joe David Bellamy.[11] Less partisan are the divergent accounts which centre on the ideological and broader cultural significance of minimalism – those of Arthur C. Danto,[12] Rosalind Krauss,[13] James Meyer and Wim Mertens[14] among them – and which regard minimalism as a polemical field upon which to articulate the historical specificity of the work in relation to, rather than in isolation from, the discourses which frame its production and reception.

Yet even these judgments remain coupled to a historicist scheme which, as Hal Foster notes, centres on 'the conflation of *before* and *after* with *cause* and *effect*'.[15] A more dynamic understanding of minimalism emerges only when its historical register is brought more fully into conversation with its existential one: minimalism occupies a position at once *ahistorical* – its works are icons of a persistent potential relation to the radical, minimal ground which is universal to existence[16] – and *transhistorical* – its works appear intermittently, 'sporadically but repeatedly',[17] distributed across the times and locations of different cultural histories. Suspended between the ahistorical logic of *persistence* and the transhistorical logic of *intermittency*, minimalism is invested with a dynamism which lends it a substantial and sometimes unexpected momentum, allowing it to move both within and across the increasingly prevalent, but also potentially restrictive, critical codification of aesthetic history in terms of period and movement.

In this light, while the most recognizably minimalist works are those produced at a particular historical moment that appears to have been maximally receptive to the minimalist aesthetic – Judd's serial sculpture, Glass's modular composition, or Carver's austere short stories are all products of aesthetic experimentation in the 1960s and 1970s – this fact owes at least as much to the critical context which frames these works as to the works themselves. A more expansive view of aesthetic history might suggest that numerous and intermittent expressions of minimalism have emerged and receded in the more distant past, and are likely to do so again in the future. There are, for example, distinctly minimalist literary forms that manifest transhistorically: the aphorism, the parable and the proverb are as old as literature itself, yet remain prevalent;[18] and the desire to make the material form of poetry mirror its content is evident not only in the amuletic inscriptions of antiquity, but also in the popularity of visual poetry in the seventeenth century and the flowering of concrete poetry in the twentieth century.[19] Similarly, the sparse abstraction of much Neolithic rock art resonates with a certain contemporary approach to minimum;[20] while repeated melodic or rhythmic fragments, or ostinatos, provide a distinctly minimal means of structuring music, from its earliest folk origins, through subsequent polyphonic developments, to the present, where ostinatos find a new prominence in contemporary minimalist composition.[21]

The radical force of minimalist aesthetics lies not in a single, historical event – a revolutionary rupture which severs present from past – but rather in its capacity to *return*, and in returning to turn aesthetic pursuit once more towards its most radical parts and processes, methods and media. Minimalism constitutes an event which in the singularity of its eruption conserves the potential for its intermittent return. The event proves incomplete, inexhaustible: '[o]ne event is only registered through another that recodes it',[22] as Foster notes, and herein resides the source of minimalism's intermittency and the inner logic of its return. Minimum constitutes a radical existential ground – persistent, and to this extent, ahistorical – yet manifests in terms of a radical practice of minimalism only intermittently because the discourse of aesthetic novelty is itself subject to a 'continuous process of protension and retension, a complex relay of anticipated futures and reconstructed pasts'.[23]

A transhistorical theory of minimalism aims to unsettle rather than overturn historicist accounts, adding nuance and context to situations which are often artificially bound by epistemic constraints regarding chronology and location, formalist constraints regarding style and structure, and journalistic constraints which tend to take artists and critics alike at their word, without thoroughly testing their claims. What made minimalism so radical an aesthetic turn, or perhaps return, in the 1950s was not, as Fried feared, its accession to the theatricality of an anti-art,[24] but its capacity to draw out its radical consequences in relation to other artworks, movements and epochs; to radicalize both the past and the future. Once minimalism is recognized in terms of its aesthetic radicalism, aspects of minimum, anticipations and reverberations of minimalism, become widely evident.

How then might a transhistorical study of minimalism affect the canonical list of artists, composers and writers sanctioned in terms of a chronologically delimited movement? While the familiar canon of minimalist painters and sculptors – Ad Reinhardt, Barnett Newman, Ellsworth Kelly, Kenneth Noland, Frank Stella, Robert Ryman, Brice Marden, Robert Mangold, Agnes Martin, David Novros, Paul Mogensen, James Tuttle, Jo Baer, Tony Smith, Carl Andre, Donald Judd, Robert Morris, John McCracken, Dan Flavin, James Turrell, Sol LeWitt, Anne Truitt, Larry Bell, Robert Irwin, Ronald Bladen, Richard Serra, Walter De Maria, Eva Hesse and Robert Smithson – provides an excellent inventory of minimalist techniques, processes and effects, the work produced a few decades in either direction reveals that a minimalist aesthetic underpins a great deal of abstract, environmental and conceptual art.

Certain works, and often series of works, by prominent artists not always associated with minimalism benefit from a close analysis grounded in the aesthetic concerns that run through the work of canonical minimalists, and reciprocally make a significant contribution to the transhistorical analysis of an expanded minimalist field. Kazimir Malevich, Piet Mondrian, Theo van Doesburg, Josef Albers, Robert Rauschenberg, Robert Motherwell, Hélio Oiticica, Yves Klein, Walter Darby Bannard, Mark Rothko, John McLaughlin, Cy Twombly, Jules Olitski, Morris Louis, Neil Williams, Gene Davis, Howard Mehring, Thomas Downing, Mary Corse, Robert Grosvenor, Joel Shapiro, Richard Long, Michael Heizer, Bruce Nauman, Rachel Whiteread, Jene Highstein, Ólafur Elíasson, Daniel Buren, Félix Gonzáles-Torres, Fred Sandback, Binky Palermo, Hanne Darboven, Dan Walsh, Irma Boom, Paulo Monteiro, Martin Creed, Gedi Sibony, Ai Weiwei, Andy Goldsworthy, Tauba Auerbach, Ron Gilad, Bernardo Ortiz Campo, Wade Guyton, Edith Dekyndt, Iran do Espirito Santo, Eva Rothschild and James Lee Byars are merely representative of a potentially much longer list.

Similarly, an understanding of musical minimalism which centres on canonical works by La Monte Young, Terry Riley, Steve Reich, Philip Glass, John Adams, Meredith Monk, Michael Nyman, Arvo Pärt, John Tavener and Louis Andriessen is greatly enriched by considering the ways in which a minimalist logic intermittently expresses itself distinctively and meaningfully in the compositions of, among others, Eric Satie, Jakob van Domselaer, Anton Webern, György Kurtág, Alan Hovanhess, John Cage, Yves Klein, György Ligeti, Lou Harrison, Colin McPhee, Morton Feldman, Pauline Oliveros, Jon Gibson, John Luther Adams, Charlemagne Palestine, Harold Budd, Yoshi Wada, Alvin Lucier, Brian Eno, Phil Niblock, Francisco Lopez, Toru Takemitsu, Simeon ten Holt, Howard Skempton, Graham Fitkin, Gavin Bryars, Michael Torke, Kevin Volans, Aaron Jay Kernis, Steve Martland, Julius Eastman, Terry Jennings, Angus MacLise, Rhys Chatham, David Borden, Ann Southam, Wim Mertens, Yann Tiersen, Hanne Darboven, Tom Johnson, David Lang, Michael Gordon, Julia Wolfe, Nico Muhly, Richard Reed Parry and Colin Stetson. Minimalist aesthetic concerns move through the rock music of the Velvet Underground, John Cale, Tony Conrad and Popol Vuh, the minimalist electronica of Kraftwerk, Tangerine Dream, Robert Hood, Jeff Mills, Larry Bell, Richie Hawtin (Plastikman), Surgeon, Ricardo Villalobos, Fennesz, Microtrauma, Marcel Dettmann and Ellen Allien, and the minimalist jazz of Mal Waldron, John Surman, Marilyn Crispell, Keith Jarrett, Terje Rypdal, Jan Garbarek, Giovanni Di Domenico, Trygve Seim, Arve Henriksen, Eberhard Weber, Richie Beirach, Susanne Abbuehl and Nik Bärtsch, among many others.

The case is no different for minimalist literature, where critical accounts are dominated by a canonical core of North American prose writers – Raymond Carver, Amy Hempel, Ann Beattie, Mary Robison, Frederick Barthelme, Bobbie

Ann Mason, Tobias Wolff, Jayne Anne Phillips and Richard Ford – with the occasional addition, in various combinations, of Lydia Davis, Alice Adams, Andre Dubus, James Robison, Gordon Lish, Joy Williams, Alice Munro, Jack Matthews, Robert Olen Butler, John Cheever, Joan Didion, Alice Paley, John Updike, Charles Bukowski, David Leavitt, Jerzy Kosiński, Chuck Palahniuk, Bret Easton Ellis, Jay McInerney and Tama Janowitz. Yet some of the most audacious experiments in minimalist writing are missed in a chronologically limited and geographically bounded canon. Most notable among these are works of Samuel Beckett, Ernest Hemingway, Anton Chekhov and Alain Robbe-Grillet, but also of Virginia Woolf, Gertrude Stein, Maurice Blanchot, Jorge Luis Borges, Gabriel Josipovici, Paul Auster, J. M. Coetzee, Richard Brautigan, Cormac McCarthy, Dave Eggers, A. M. Homes and Tao Lin, all of which reveal very different aspects of a broadened minimalist aesthetic.

Minimalism in theatre and film, although arguably dominated by the work of Beckett, is in fact diverse, as exemplified in the approaches of Jerzy Grotowski, Peter Brook, Michel Vinaver, Robert Wilson, Harold Pinter, Sam Shepard, Roy Hart, Alain Resnais, Andrei Tarkovsky, Carl Theodor Dreyer, Derek Jarman and Jonathan Glazer among many others. Likewise, in addition to poetry documented as minimalist by Aram Saroyan, Robert Lax, Ian Hamilton Finlay, Robert Creeley, Tom Raworth, Richard Kostelanetz, Geof Huth, Jonathan Brannen, Karl Kempton, Adam Gamble, LeRoy Gorman, Crag Hill, Michael Basinski, Karl Young and Betty Radin,[25] there are a range of poets and intermedia practitioners who express very different minimalist-inflected approaches to the poetic medium, including by Stéphane Mallarmé, Ezra Pound, T. E. Hulme, H. D., William Carlos Williams, Marianne Moore, Guillaume Apollinaire, Raoul Hausmann, Kurt Schwitters, Velimir Khlebnikov, Alexey Kruchenykh, Vladimir Majakovskij, Louis Aragon, Isidore Isou, Louis Zukofsky, George Oppen, David Ignatow, Gary Snyder, James Loughlin, Clark Coolidge, Bob Cobbing, Edwin Morgan, Ernst Jandl, Eugen Gomringer, Decio Pignatari, Haroldo and Augusto de Campos, Ronaldo Azeredo, Emmett Williams, Dom Sylvester Houédard, John Furnival, Ilse and Pierre Garnier, Seeichi Nīkuni, Dick Higgins, John Cage, Jackson MacLow, Alison Knowles, Charles Bernstein, Ron Silliman, Barrett Watten, Bruce Andrews, Susan Howe, Lyn Hejinian, Steve McCaffery, Robert Grenier, bpNicol, Kenneth Goldsmith, Christian Bök, Liliane Lijn, Kenelm Cox, Paul Lansky, Trevor Wishart, Vito Acconci, Jenny Holzer, Willem Boshoff, Lawrence Weiner, Joseph Kosuth, Stuart Moulthrop, Ingrid Ankerson, Mitchell Kimbrough and Andy Campbell.

It is necessary in this light to continue challenging, disrupting and expanding existing canonical formations of minimalism, diversifying the ways in which minimalism reflects and reflects on both the historical and contemporary situations. Indeed, even the most canonical of minimalists objected to being constricted by a label, and many situated their work within a genealogy of responses to what they regarded as transhistorical problems. Light artist, Dan Flavin, for example, was never absorbed solely with questions of form, medium, facture or space – the aspects of his work habitually highlighted at the expense of others – but also with the socio-political force of art[26] and with metaphysical problems of transcendence and immanence.[27]

Between 1964 and 1990, for example, Flavin produced a large number of *monuments* dedicated to the Russian Constructivist, Vladimir Tatlin. These works, constructed from various symmetrical permutations and rotations of the same basic elements – one 8-foot white fluorescent lamp, and then two 6-foot, 4-foot and 2-foot white fluorescent lamps – continue 'the quest to express revolutionary social and political attitudes in an equally revolutionary language of pure abstraction'[28] which drove Tatlin, even as they ironically sought to draw attention to the failed monumentality of the *Monument to the Third International* (1919–20), which was never built save as a model. The first of Flavin's series, *monument 1 to V. Tatlin*,[29] also makes clear visual allusion to the structures which Tatlin's *Monument* had sought to surpass, the Eiffel Tower and the Empire State Building in particular.[30] Within the historically charged space between Tatlin's *Monument* and Flavin's *monument* we might recall any number of monumental structures, from the step pyramids of antiquity, to the Leaning Tower of Pisa, yet all draw attention back to a single point: that the full significance of Flavin's work emerges as much from its intuition of historical intermittency – its conscious return to an unfinished project[31] – as it does from the aesthetic immanence of its form and medium. Here the transhistorical logic of intermittency is not merely thematic, but arguably the most singular mark of the work itself. The peculiar immanence of much minimalism emerges precisely from the manner in which the ahistorical persistence of minimum as existential radix, and the transhistorical intermittency of minimalism as aesthetic practice, are brought together in the singularity of the work. To ignore this co-emergence threatens not only to oversimplify the works currently accepted as part of the minimalist canon, but to force to the margins some of the most significant expressions of minimalism.

1.3. Margins

At the periphery of minimalism: Robert Hooke's *Micrographia* (1655) John Lee Byars's *The Book of the Hundred Questions* (1969)

A curious but powerful example of a distinctly minimalist practice which has remained virtually invisible to historicist accounts of minimalism, is the venerable and varied tradition of *micrographia* – miniature books and tiny writing – which, since ancient times, has probed the sublime extremes of minimal scale by habitually seeking to press the greatest amount of writing into the smallest space possible. Micrographic practice assumes numerous forms: remarkable examples of miniature tablets, parchments and books, together with more unconventional methods of condensed inscription and, more recently, digital encoding of text, are exemplary of works distributed across the full ambit of literary history. This ancient and abiding fascination with minimal material scale is closely tied to the philosophical and scientific intuition that it is both possible and desirable to penetrate beyond the world given to us by our senses. The impulse, shared by aesthetic and scientific inquiry, is to discover a world within the world. As Stewart recognizes, '[w]hile the miniature book reduces the world to the microcosm within its covers, the microscope opens up significance to the point at which all the material world shelters a microcosm'.[32]

The microscope proves a fitting symbol for the confluence of scientific and aesthetic discourse on the microcosm, nowhere more pertinently than in Robert Hooke's *Micrographia*, a collection of thirty years of microscopic observation published in 1665, and a work which enabled wide access to an understanding of the invisible composition of the world which had until then been inaccessible to all except specialists. *Micrographia* significantly influenced public perception of science and its relation to the everyday, intensifying the deep human fascination with the minimal, miniature and microcosmic. Not insignificantly, micrographic writing – and in particular a minuscule fragment onto which several prayers and religious verses have been painstakingly inscribed – is an object of Hooke's scrutiny, and although he not surprisingly finds it lacking in finesse, he certainly recognizes the considerable effort and energy which have driven its execution.[33] In this sense, the process of symbolically exposing the hermetically sealed world of the micrographic text does not evacuate it of significance, but rather clarifies the considerable force invested in a practice of writing which is comported towards minimum, or the least possible.

Hooke intuits that there is something intrinsically compelling in micrographic practice, an abiding fascination with writing on a minimal scale. Confirming its universality, Stewart and Foer identify several ancient precursors, most notably a celebrated copy of Homer's *Iliad* so minutely inscribed that it fitted, in its entirety, into an actual nutshell.[34] Although the tiny *Iliad* may well be apocryphal, it nonetheless serves as a prototype for a transhistorical range of tiny textual objects which are 'emblematic of craft and discipline'[35] and vehicles through which immense concentration and concrete labour are transfigured into symbolic force and invested with a certain theurgical or ritual significance, recalling the ancient religious association of inscription and power.[36] It is no surprise, in this light, that micrographic texts – tiny renditions of religious scripture alongside eclectic marginalia – remained a concern for medieval scribes, while the subsequent development of printing technology stimulated a popular fascination with 'the miniature catechisms and tiny hornbooks by which the children of the seventeenth and eighteenth centuries could keep religious knowledge in the hand, in the pocket or under the pillow'.[37] Returning to the period and subject of Hooke's inquiry, micrographia of this sort are indeed invested with an almost talismanic quality, one which is arguably intensified rather than dissipated by the increased precision and compression made possible by changing technologies in printing and microphotography.[38] Micrographic texts assume a more nuanced function – at one pole in the commercial production of collectible miniature books, at the other as the medium of an increasingly mobile and immediate regime of communication – which is decisively transformed by the advent of digital technology. In the digital realm, the material distinction of short from long texts is rendered increasingly redundant by the binary transcoding and compression of information, and by the virtual space of the internet, which attenuates any clear distinction between the infinite and the infinitesimal.

Micrographic writing generates an ambiguous space, a microcosm in which the 'infinite time … of the world [is] collapsed within a minimum of physical space'[39] – a striking point of access to minimum understood as the least possible. By probing the extremes of minimal scale, micrographic experiments consistently press the boundaries between the visible and the invisible,[40] the material and the immaterial, demonstrating, as Stewart suggests, that '[s]mall things can be sublime as readily as the grand material phenomena of nature and human making'.[41] A striking contemporary example is James Lee Byars's *The Book of the Hundred Questions* (1969), 'a three-inch column of microscopic gold writing on a sheet of black linen paper'[42] which is impossible to read without magnification. Byars aims for nothing less than 'a reinvention of the sublime ... with its espousal of emptiness and radical loss of presence'[43] – a 'present[ation of] the unpresentable',[44] to recall Lyotard – drawing to a concrete point the processes by which the legibility of existence becomes illegible and the illegibility of pure being becomes legible. Here, the minimal sublime as exposed in Byars's micrographic masterpiece, composed entirely of questions, many of them unanswerable, 'calls on what is absent and is the perfect synecdoche of all that is unknown and that keeps on having to be asked'.[45]

Despite his abiding concern with 'minimal hermetic forms, a reduction towards essence and absence, and an acute sense of the ephemeral'[46] – all characteristic concerns of a broadened, transhistorical definition of minimalism – Byars's work is seldom mentioned in accounts of the minimalist canon, not even for the purpose of comparison. Although the relationship between the miniature and minimalism has been occasionally noted – in terms of their compatibility by Ralph Rugoff, who recognizes in certain miniatures an intensification of the minimalist aesthetic logic;[47] and in terms of their incompatibility by Mark McGurl, who suggests that where the effects of minimalism rest on understatement, those of the miniature rely on overstatement[48] – it remains largely ignored. The very fact that miniatures from all media have been consistently consigned to the margins of minimalist criticism suggests the limitations of prevailing historicist accounts and their exclusion of more unusual approaches to minimum.

1.4. Movement

Minimalism as a dynamic movement: La Monte Young's *Trio for Strings* (1958)

Yet, a transhistorical theory of minimalism is not without problems. Most centrally, it harbours the danger of imposing a normative vision of aesthetics which is essentially modern and Western onto heterogeneous cultural practices. While remaining vigilant of these risks, it is clear that significant gains can be derived from a transhistorical approach as well. First, in exposing minimum as the persistent, existential ground to which a transhistorical range of minimalist work is comported, minimalism itself is exposed to numerous conceptual paradigms – ontological, theological, phenomenological, epistemological – which have been only cautiously addressed in much extant criticism.

Minimalism proves itself capable of clarifying the often muddy relation between aesthetic practice and such significant, yet evasive, concepts as potentiality, event, force, facticity, exemplarity, and the real, extending its significance into the realm of socio-political reality. Second, as suggested above, a transhistorical approach reveals that there are numerous works that clearly belong to a minimalist aesthetic trajectory, yet which are often not registered as such in strict historicist and formalist regimes of criticism. Attending to the intermittent emergence of such works not only augments the field of minimalist aesthetics, but also sheds light on the ideological dimension of minimalism,[49] revealing how broader cultural, economic and political concerns influence the processes of inclusion and exclusion which underpin canon formation, and are reflected in the movements that are often at the vanguard of novel artistic endeavour, yet habitually deployed as constraints in critical discourse.

The term *movement* is used in a wide variety of discourses to indicate a collective comportment towards a specific subject or field. Social, political and aesthetic movements are all exemplary in this regard. Movements are sometimes the organic outcome of shared ideas and practices, but at other times represent engineered limits. In the arts, movements offer epistemological stability to works often as different as they are similar, making comparison, and hence the precise articulation of similarity and difference, considerably easier. From this position, processes of change – whether the gradual formation of trends or sudden shifts in aesthetic attitudes, means of production and theoretical understanding – are rendered more comprehensible. Movements often contribute to historicist propositions regarding the causes and effects of aesthetic transformation. At the same time, movements serve a more radical function: they usher in novelty, as is habitually reflected in the manifestos through which avant-garde practitioners bind themselves to sustained, aesthetic goals, challenging existing norms and practices.

Movements become problematic when, passing from the sphere of practice to criticism, boundaries which were intended to elucidate the co-emergence of works, become confines that encourage oversimplification in order retrospectively to impose unity of purpose, or prospectively to prevent dissent. In the case of minimalism, disproportionate critical energy continues to be expended in debating which chronological limits are most appropriate, which minimalist canon is least objectionable, and how to deal with the fact that minimalist practitioners from every discipline and in every medium habitually eschew the minimalist label.[50] Seminal figures such as sculptors Robert Morris and Donald Judd, composers Philip Glass and Steve Reich, and writers Raymond

Carver and Amy Hempel are in fact united by their vigorous rejection of the term.[51] This rejection owes as much to the negative journalistic attention the term initially garnered, as it does to the incommensurable aesthetic positions minimalist works often occupy. Yet, recalling with Giorgio Agamben that 'terminology is the poetic, hence productive moment of thought',[52] and that at 'certain historical moments, certain codewords irresistibly impose themselves and become adopted by antagonistic positions',[53] the fact that minimalism emerges as a contested term is in fact a reflection of its appropriateness to the task of signifying a *dynamic* movement.

Demonstrating that this dynamism is also transhistorical is less straightforward. The pervasive misapprehension that a movement arises solely to bring about specific changes, binding it to a specific historical telos, is almost certainly at the root of this difficulty. Indeed, as Agamben argues, the most substantial attempt to come to grips with the dynamics of the movement itself, is offered by Carl Schmitt for whom every movement claims an exceptional status in relation to the situation in which it emerges. The force of a movement derives from its capacity to divide this situation, realigning its parts to include some while excluding others. Since 'the excluded elements … come … back as what must be decided upon',[54] the movement in Schmitt's formulation effectively turns the totality of the situation in which it emerges towards a single purpose. It is an act of enforcement which expends the potentiality the movement harnesses in producing the actuality of a new situation.

Strongly opposed to this conception, Agamben views a movement as a means of conserving rather than consuming potentiality – a process which in essence evades the strictures of cause and effect, and expresses itself instead as 'an imperfect act, without an end'.[55] Understood in this way, a movement strongly recalls what Badiou conceives in terms of *truth*: the potentially infinite, but often intermittent, consequences of an event which make 'it possible' – possible, but not imperative – 'to group the elements of a situation so that they all count in the same way'.[56] A movement is not simply an instrumental application of a force to a particular end, but also an exposition of force as force – an exposition of what *moves* a movement. A movement is therefore capable of producing change, but is itself subject to change. Although oriented towards the future, a transhistorical movement does not decide absolutely on the terms of the present, nor does it assign a strict causal significance to those of the past. A movement may as easily desist suddenly as persist indefinitely; it may disappear forever or return intermittently. As Danto notes, it is possible to discern 'movements stopping but not ending, ending but not stopping, ending and stopping, and neither ending nor stopping'.[57]

The potentiality of minimalism understood in these terms is inextricable from the play of persistence and intermittency which marks it as a transhistorical movement. Attempting to fix the emergence of minimalist aesthetics to a particular temporal location – 1958 is often put forward as a moment of particular poignancy, since a number of significant canonical minimalist works were completed in this year – or, indeed, to trace it to a particular event or work, threatens to miss the essential dynamism at its heart: that to discover the beginning of a minimalist movement is already to encounter its return. Although significant in its own right, the genealogical inquiry into the genesis of minimalism is unlikely to yield a concrete point of origin – an event or work – since these are essentially indices of a more radical existential advent of minimalism which appears only in its disappearing,[58] marked by fleeting and intermittent contact with minimum – the least possible and the least necessary; the persistent absolute.

A fine example of this indexical function emerges in La Monte Young's *Trio for Strings*. One of the most celebrated minimalist works, the *Trio* was completed in 1958 – the critically sanctioned moment at which minimalism supposedly came of age – and is often regarded as the foundational work of musical minimalism.[59] Despite its apparently radical novelty, Young's work draws heavily on traditions as diverse as Webern's austere serialism and the ancient religious chant of East and West. The *Trio* in particular is constructed entirely of sustained tones, exposing an 'apparent contradiction between an aesthetic still rooted in the dynamism of classical forms and a resulting music that was often essentially static'. Spanning approximately an hour, alternating sections of sustained pitch and silence are presented in a single movement that 'takes economy of material to … an etiolated extreme'.[60] By various permutations of minimal material, these sustained sounds 'seem to grow out of the silences and generate them in turn'.[61] In the opening section, for instance, a 'strict durational symmetry'[62] is established as pitches are systematically added to and then subtracted from a single sustained note to constitute an eminently transparent arch-form.[63] While the 'use of long notes is in itself no novelty',[64] Young's choice of sustained pitch as the sole material for a composition remains radical and, at that point in music history, unprecedented.[65]

It is symptomic of the often restrictive understanding of minimalism as a movement that a composition such a Young's *Trio*, which brings musical movement to a minimum, should so often be invested with the indexical force that makes it a foundational work for minimalism as a movement. Often the minimalist works most heavily invested with an indexical function – works that come to stand for minimalism as a whole – have transhistorical resonances that undermine their indexicality. Thus, while it is true the *Trio* largely evades the conventions of Western art music – it lacks rhythm or pulse, and it does not yield readily to conventional diatonic or serial analysis[66] – the work also sets up a field of resonances that move across specific moments and movements. External to the vertical tension of harmony and the horizontal pull of melody, its sounds are *ateleological*,[67] 'going nowhere, and not fast'.[68] Yet they are also sounds that can go anywhere.

The soundscape Young conceives is at once intermittent and persistent: it emerges from and recedes into silence, but at the same time any sustained encounter with the work reveals a peculiar and contained dynamism in the undulating sonic continuum of the composition as a whole. Thus, although the work reduces 'movement to the point of stasis',[69] there is a further distinction to be made between stasis understood as an absolute lack of movement – this would be nothing other than a persistent presentation of minimum – and stasis marked by a lack of *progressive* movement, which offers intermittent access to minimum. It is principally the latter that concerns Young: a stasis which is dynamic; divested of momentum by the structural symmetries of the composition, yet invested with a peculiar potentiality. Within and between these sustained pitches, there exists a force that produces significant effects, material and psychoacoustic, yet which finally proves to be nothing more than the immanent taking-place of the work itself.

In this light, *immanence* describes a situation in which stasis and movement intersect, offering a means of coming to grips with the force of movement itself. For immanence undoes both strict genealogy and teleology, revealing that movement is no more than the intermittent appearance and disappearance of events and entities across the persistent ground of time. One sense of movement flows into the other, and Young's *Trio* comes to act as a '[p]rosthesis of [o]rigin'[70] – a work that exercises the force of a foundational event, albeit an event which has never taken place, an '[e]vent without event',[71] since minimalism, in constituting a transhistorical movement, returns in emerging, continues in beginning.

1.5 Minimalism

Name as paradigm: Donald Judd's *Untitled (Stack)* (1967)

Movements do not emerge into critical consciousness fully formed as stable structures, established principles, or universal laws. They are the products of an ongoing, relational process marked by disagreement regarding inclusion and exclusion, examples and exceptions, the accumulation of similarities alongside differences. Minimalism, in this light, should be approached 'not as a coherent movement but as practical field',[72] in Meyer's estimation – 'a dynamic field of specific practices'[73] marked by 'critical debate'.[74] In practice, however, it is habitually regarded as a movement. The act of naming proves particularly significant in this regard. The name constitutes a type of paradigm within which aesthetic events and the works to which they give rise enter into meaningful types of relation to one another. Yet, in the case of minimalism, what does it mean to encounter a nameless yet iconic minimalist work such as Donald Judd's *Untitled (Stack)* – a sculpture of twelve large green lacquered metal boxes, together over five metres in height, set in relief in a gallery wall of the Museum of Modern Art in New York?[75] A great number of minimalist works are left nameless – untitled, or identifiable only by numbers or the most uninflected descriptions of their materials or parts. Yet this lack of a name is in fact a nominal marker of sorts: it points towards a dynamic that precedes the name, towards the generative event of the work itself, the fact of its taking-place as a minimalist work without pronouncing on what such minimalism means.

Thus, as John D. Caputo notes, '[n]ames contain events and give them a kind of temporary shelter'.[76] Far from empty rhetorical posturing, critical debate around names and naming often has considerable historical and ideological implications. In Caputo's estimation, '[n]ames belong to natural languages and are historically constituted or constructed'.[77] It is no surprise, then, to discover the significance of the name emphasized across the history of ideas, and, moreover, closely tied to conceptions of essence, substance and reality: the medieval nominalism of Ockham seeks to denominate reality in terms of discrete entities; Bertrand Russell's descriptivist theory of names aims to bring name, meaning, description and object into alignment; Saul Kripke's rigid designators, a criticism of Russell's view and an intensification of the logic of medieval nominalism, offers the rigid designator a name which 'designates the same object in all possible worlds';[78] Jacques Derrida's deconstruction undertakes a careful demonstration of the ways in which the name paradoxically exists both in excess and in deficit of the subject to which it applies;[79] and Agamben develops a complex reasoning which, returning to Plato and Aristotle, reconnects the name to the idea (*eidos*) in order to expose, obliquely, the force of language itself.[80]

The name participates in regulating the intelligibility and interpretability of those things to which it applies, mediating between the specific and the general, as well as the static and the dynamic. In the case of minimalism, the numerous labels advanced to describe the intensified experimentation with minimal means are indicative of the challenges this radical aesthetic posed to existing critical categories and to the critical establishment in the mid-twentieth century. Terms including ABC art, literalist art, reductive art, rejective art, structurist art, rationalized art and cool art in visual arts criticism;[81] repetitive music, meditative music, hypnotic music, pulse music, trance music, modular music and systemic music in music criticism;[82] and dirty realism, new realism, designer realism, extra-realism, tv fiction, white trash fiction and post-postmodernism in literary criticism,[83] all vied for recognition with one another and with the term minimalism, which would eventually come to dominate, albeit not without considerable resistance from certain quarters, including visual artists, composers and writers themselves.

The point at which a particular name achieves ascendency over its competitors invariably marks a significant moment in the canonization of an aesthetic movement. Yet the precise limits of a movement – its historical reach, its location, its particularities with respect to medium and style – and whether these should be regarded as dynamic or static, are seldom decided so simply. In this light, the apparently trivial debate which emerges around the use of the proper and common name – Minimalism and minimalism – proves of surprising significance, each bringing with it a specific set of ideological implications. Names accept or reject authority, they imply inclusion and exclusion, and they reflect and effect decisions regarding canonicity. Names also participate in a hierarchy of value and are invested with specific cultural capital, which they in turn invest in the works they gather together, a process which often translates into considerable financial worth.

A broad survey of prominent criticism reveals that the proper name – the upper-case *M*inimalism – most often indicates a movement that is chronologically delimited, with medium-specific criteria for inclusion, and that is geographically bound to North America, establishing a degree of stability and specificity from which historical judgments and stylistic generalizations appear justified. The common name – the lower-case *m*inimalism – most often indicates a movement that is chronologically open-ended, with more general criteria for inclusion, and which potentially manifests in multiple geographical locations. In simple terms, accounts of *m*inimalism are generally more hospitable to what the present work proposes in terms of a dynamic, transhistorical theory than those of *M*inimalism, albeit they are also potentially subject to contingency and flux, and if uncritically applied, a degree of vagueness.[84]

The proper name, Minimalism, was first applied in an aesthetic context in 1929 to describe the work of painter John Graham,[85] and subsequently by Graham in 1937 in relation to his own work.[86] However, it only enters mainstream critical discourse in 1965 through the work of philosopher Richard Wollheim, as a slight variation, Minimal Art,[87] and by then surrounded by a host of competing terms. Early critics, among them Greenberg and Rose, address a fairly diverse range of work under the term Minimal Art,[88] and a similar sense of provisionality and inclusiveness informs Gregory Battcock's epochal 1968 anthology, *Minimal Art*. The emergence of Minimalism as an authoritative term in the critical lexicon roughly parallels its codification as an historical movement, one replete with a canon of associated works, which initially arises in the visual arts and music, and subsequently in literature and the other arts.

By the time major comprehensive studies of minimalism began to appear, the correlation of the proper name with a strong, historicist notion of the chronologically specific movement was well established. This is reflected in different ways in the work of numerous critics and across all expressive media, including Suzi Gablik, Anna C. Chave, Daniel Marzona, David Batchelor and James Dishon McDermott,[89] but nowhere more clearly than in Kenneth Baker's injunction to '[t]hink of "Minimalism" as the name not of an artistic style but of a historical moment, a brief outbreak of critical thought and invention in the cavalcade of postwar American art',[90] or in Frances Colpitt's clarification, that 'Minimalism is not used here with a lowercase *m*. It is restricted to those artists who shared a philosophical commitment to the abstract, anticompositional, material *object*.'[91] A relatively stable canon of works is pivotal to establishing *M*inimalism as an historical movement. In this light, it is no coincidence that the critically sanctioned, canonical minimalism of the visual arts and music should habitually adopt the proper name, while the more tentatively defined minimalism of literature favours the common name. Albeit for different reasons, and although several dispute the efficacy of the name to begin with, literary critics Warren Motte, Cynthia Whitney Hallett, Kim A. Herzinger, Wil Verhoeven, Diane Stevenson, Joe David Bellamy and John Barth all prefer the common name. Transhistorical studies of minimalism are perhaps of necessity more ambiguous as regards canonicity, and whether their task in this respect is to supplement, extend or disrupt the sanctioned canonical formations. Edward Strickland's *Minimalism: Origins*, which is both transhistorical and transdisciplinary, is for the most part concerned with supplementing the Minimalist canon, an approach that is also reflected in the work of K. Robert Schwartz, Sofía Cheviakoff and Pilar Bonet. Other transhistorical approaches – Robert C. Clark's to literature and Robert Fink's to music – are more concerned with extending than with supplementing the canon, and thus with reinvesting minimalism with a certain dynamism. Indeed, Keith Potter explicitly connects the lower-case *m*inimalism to a more open and dynamic understanding of the aesthetic movement.[92]

Finally, it is via the passage it generates from the particular to the general that the common name leads beyond the notion of minimalism as movement, and towards the understanding of minimalism as an existential modality. Minimalism itself acquires and benefits from a greater conceptual currency. In Foster's *The Return of the Real* and Walter Benn Michaels's *The Shape of the Signifier*, minimalism is framed by a conceptual complex of considerable nuance. Similarly, Mertens, Meyer and Fink all emphasize minimalism as a dynamic system in which art interacts, often polemically, with a mosaic of ideological, economic, and socio-political forces. Extrapolating to the sociological sphere, Christopher Lasch's *The Minimal Self* regards minimalism in terms of a zeitgeist rather than as a movement, and it is this broader sense of a minimalist culture which, amplified by the pervasiveness of minimalism in everyday life via architecture and design, conditions the emergence of often opportunistic brands of contemporary lifestyle minimalisms that bear little relation to minimalist aesthetics proper. These include various manuals by, among others, Joshua Fields Millburn, Ryan Nicodemus, Brian Night, Regina Wong, Francine Jay and Simeon Lindstrom which maintain in common that a path to simplicity is also a path to prosperity and happiness, taking on the various contemporary roles of life coach, financial guru and apologist for the austerity politics dominating an increasingly precarious global economy.

Minimalism, understood as a transhistorical modality, manifests intermittently, yet nowhere more clearly and with greater intensity, than in the mid-to-late twentieth century. As a dynamic movement it mediates between a closed chronology and an ahistorical continuum, drawing together a familiar canon of works central to historical Minimalism, while remaining open to the works of more distant minimalisms, both past and future. The logic of intermittency lays bare the contingencies that underpin even the most stable historical configurations, revealing that the internal logic which binds a movement to its name is one born from the same 'violent gestures with which aesthetic systems seek to exorcise their inability to ground their claims'.[93] Yet these gestures disguise rather than eliminate contingency, and it is finally the return of these contingencies to critical consciousness that makes it possible to grasp a movement in truly dynamic terms.

1.6 Transition

Between modernism and postmodernism: Ronaldo Azeredo's *VELOCIDADE* (1957) Ai Weiwei's *A Ton of Tea* (2007)

Reserved in the transparency, simplicity, austerity and immediacy of minimalism's objects is a remarkable capacity for transformation. As argued above this capacity is transhistorical and transcultural, emerging intermittently in the institutions and practices that define culture. It is perhaps most clearly felt and critically disputed, however, in contemporary ideologies of art and its institutions. In particular, minimalism opens into a polemical field[94] where the financial, cultural and political value of aesthetics becomes a vexed question. This is reflected most emblematically in the dispute between so-called high and low culture that marks the passage from a broadly modernist to a postmodernist conception of culture, and more schematically in the so-called *science wars* where disputes between realists and constructivists led to a broad reparsing of the relation of knowledge and utility.

There are emblematic examples of the former in all spheres of aesthetic production that reflect how minimalism is initially exiled from the institutions of high culture: composers are forced from concert halls into lofts, artists are ignored or condemned by the critical establishment, and writers initially publish their works solely in popular magazines. Yet, not surprisingly, as minimalism comes to be regarded as a coherent movement, codified by critical literature and represented by a canon of works, it also find itself appropriated by the institutional expressions of high culture and converted into cultural capital. Perhaps more significant than this fact, though, is the particular place canonical minimalism occupies with respect to the increasing translation of cultural capital into financial terms; or, in short, the commodification of art and the redefinition of the artworld as an art market. This is particularly evident in the case of visual art, where the rise of canonical minimalism is almost co-extensive with the rapid commodification of art and the exponential expansion of its market.

Viewed historically, this transition is not in itself surprising at an aesthetic level either. If minimalism presents the apotheosis of abstraction, this occurs in the space of ruination that follows the Second World War. As Adorno and Lyotard recognize, the history of mimesis is decisively disrupted by the horrors of this war, and particularly the Shoah. In his commentary on Lyotard, Rancière notes that

> [t]he absence of any common measurement [between art and life] is ... called catastrophe ... If modern art must preserve the purity of its separations, it is so as to inscribe the mark of this sublime catastrophe whose inscription also bears witness against the totalitarian catastrophe – that of the genocides, but also that of aestheticized (i.e., in fact anaesthetized) existence.[95]

In this situation, extreme forms of abstraction appear to take on different intensities, distinguishing modern abstraction from postmodern abstraction, a difference which is codified in terms of an increased reflexivity in the case of the postmodern, where abstraction increasingly relinquishes its mimetic mooring to the world, and becomes a radical form in its own right. Minimalism presents the apotheosis of this process. As Hal Foster notes, 'only with minimalism does this understanding become self-conscious. That is, only in the early 1960s is the institutionality not only of art but also of the avant-garde first appreciated and then exploited'.[96] The general field of intensified reflexivity that Lyotard identifies with the regime of the sublime – the negative pleasure which arrives when, in the face of an aesthetic stimulus which initially overwhelms us, we are able to affirm our mastery and the final ascendency of mind over phenomena[97] – becomes the mark of postmodern abstraction. Stated schematically, while 'modern art ... devotes [itself] to present[ing] the fact that the unpresentable exists',[98] 'postmodern [art is] that which, in the modern, puts forward the unpresentable in presentation itself'.[99] Thus, where modernist abstraction offers itself in pursuit of the transcendental conditions that make representation possible – Fried terms this *presentness*[100] – postmodern abstraction rejects the transcendental, focusing instead on the immanence of the work itself, released from its representational burden, or, in other words, on *presence*.[101] Critics tend to emphasize this distinction as a decisive shift: from a spatially dominated modernist vision in which the epiphanic experience of time presents the possibility of transcendence – almost an existential exit strategy within the legislation of aesthetic experience – to a stress on time as the concrete and sequential passage of moments, albeit moments with indeterminate content, within which an artwork is perceived.[102]

Canonical minimalism occupies a singularly ambiguous position with respect to the threshold between the modern and the postmodern. Its works in every medium are as frequently concerned with autonomy, a hallmark of modernist aesthetics,[103] as they are with their contingency. This ambiguous disposition is exemplified with some subtlety in the work of the Brazilian Noigandres poets – Haroldo de Compos, Augusto de Campos, Decio Pignitari and Ronaldo Azeredo among them – who are responsible for numerous striking works of minimalism. Among the first and most prominent practitioners of concrete poetry – the term used to gather a number of generative strategies that explore the ways in which visual, sonic, linguistic and conceptual elements of the poem are reciprocally amplified by their intersection in a single work – the Noigandres poets belong to what Perloff suggests is an aesthetic arrière-garde. '[W]hen … an avant-garde movement is no longer a novelty, it is the role of the arrière-garde to complete its mission, to insure its success',[104] she suggests, and in the case of the Noigandres group, this takes the form of a subtly ironic return to the vast synthetic ambitions of high modernism.

Adapting the intermedial concept of the *verbivocovisual* from James Joyce, these poets pursue what might tentatively be called the minimalist *Gesamtkunstwerk*. Works of limited scale, yet which are often pregnant with etymological, historical, social and political significance, expose dynamic poetic situations in which the word, the voice, and the visual sign are mutually implicative. Azeredo's *Velocidade* provides a compelling example. Beginning with 'VVVVVVVVVV', each subsequent line of the poem subtracts a single 'V' from the left while progressively adding the letter from the word *velocidade* from the right, until in the final and tenth line 'VELOCIDADE' is spelt out in full. The visual acceleration is matched sonically. Beginning with the extended fricative 'VVVVVVVVVV' the poem invites the reader to sound not ten separate lines, but rather the word *velocidade* itself, accelerating across its four syllables as the eye moves down, to converge, visually and semantically, on the final line: 'VELOCIDADE' – *velocity*. On a conceptual level, the poem occupies an historical threshold: on the one hand, it revisits the accelerationist logic of the historical avant-garde, particularly conspicuous in Marinetti's Futurism; on the other it anticipates the velocity of postmodern intermedia and especially digital poetry, as exemplified in works such as *poema-bomba* by Azeredo's Noigandres associate, Augusto de Campos.

Exemplary of an 'arrière-garde [that] is synonymous neither with reaction nor with nostalgia for a lost and more desirable artistic era [but] on the contrary, [with] the "hidden face of modernity",'[105] this species of minimalism occupies a threshold between the modern and the postmodern not by historical accident but because it actively seeks to transpose specific aesthetic ideas into new contexts. This is true of a great deal of canonical minimalism, which retreats rather than rejects the aesthetics of the past, and so positions itself at the cusp of the two great contemporary epistemes of the modern and the postmodern. Minimalism constitutes the 'historical crux in which the formalist autonomy of art is at once achieved and broken up',[106] returning once more to the dynamic understanding of *movement* exposed above.

Minimalism at once 'completed and broke with [modernist aesthetic practice]'.[107] According to Rosalind Krauss, minimalist art, by its formal austerity, effects a scission with 'the styles that immediately precede it',[108] yet on 'another level[109] can be seen as renewing and continuing the thinking'[110] of high modernism. According to Foster, Krauss 'projects a minimalist recognition back onto modernism so that she can then read minimalism as a modernist epitome [in which case] minimalism is an apogee of modernism, but it is no less a break with it'.[111] In this light, aesthetic modernism appears to harbour the final figure of its transfiguration *by* abstraction, and yet in minimalism this abstraction appears precisely through the instantiation of the radical, nonreferential work. As Frank Stella famously proclaimed, 'only what can be seen there *is* there ... What you see is what you see'.[112] Neither intrinsically meaningful nor nihilistic, minimalism aims to produce immediate effects and affect;[113] the affirmation of an immanence that echoes Lyotard's claim that the 'task of art remains that of the immanent sublime, that of alluding to an unpresentable ... which is inscribed in the infinity of the transformation of "realities".'[114]

Yet, regardless of the effects of minimalist art, it would be deeply problematic to suggest that the historical threshold that canonical minimalism occupies is in itself an unproblematic one. As one of its fiercest critics, Anna C. Chave, suggests, 'Minimalism forms the terse, but veracious last word in a narrowly framed argument about what modern art is or should be'.[115] Chave raises to critical consciousness the tremendous asymmetries of power that frame the emergence of canonical minimalism. Indeed, among the most pressing questions facing the study of minimalism today arise from these asymmetries, and the fact that, for the most part, they reflect an artworld that in the mid-twentieth century endorsed a predominantly white and Western inflection of heteropatriarchal capitalism, giving it a particular shape that habitually fails to register, let alone redress, domination with respect to gender, race, sexuality and class.

Yet it should be noted that minimalist composers – Glass, Reich, Adams and Monk among them – have often sought to shed new critical light on questions of gender, force, violence and justice. Even in the visual arts, works by, among others, Eva Hesse, Agnes Martin, Felix Gonzales-Torres, Iran do Espirito Santo and Ai Weiwei constructively complicate Chave's view. Ai's *A Ton of Tea* appears at first to mimic the formal concerns of minimalism, yet closer inspection reveals a work that undertakes an incisive and deeply political interrogation not only of the contemporary politics of art, but of the colonial and postcolonial economies to which the existence and exhibition of the artwork often silently attests. The sculpture consists of a cubic metre of compressed tea leaves weighing approximate a ton, making clear visual reference to Donald Judd's cubic sculptures of similar dimensions and Smith's celebrated *Die*. Although of modest scale, the work has an imposing presence: its deep brown, uneven surfaces are clearly organic, and its dynamism is intensified by the strong aroma of the compressed tea. Here the minimalist concern with objecthood is transformed, the sculpture reinvested with a peculiar agency that emerges not only from its material composition, but also from the complex historical and cultural resonances it detects and amplifies. The minimalist object, historically remarkable for its apparent nonreferentiality, becomes the vehicle for a complex engagement with the colonial roots of global capitalism: the tea trade was central to the East–West trade routes of the colonial past, and by travelling to the West, this object imports a still incomplete history of conflict. It becomes a decolonial intervention waiting to be uncovered; the next event in an intermittent, transhistorical trajectory that has all too often been artificially limited by critical overdetermination.

2

Encounters: On the Politics of Minimalism

2.1. Threshold

Between art and non-art: Carl Andre's *Venus Forge* (1980)

In 2007 I spent several hours observing visitors to Tate Modern in London interact with Carl Andre's minimalist sculpture, *Venus Forge* (Figure 1).[1] Like much of Andre's work, it consists of a series of flat metal tiles – a narrow central band of polished copper flanked by rows of larger and duller steel tiles – 'laid … so low that they mimic … the floor's flatness',[2] 'squeezing out sculptural space to the point of two dimensionality'.[3] The sculpture, despite being centrally situated, was easily missed. Many visitors, their attention firmly focused on the abstract paintings and drawings displayed on the wall of the room, paid *Venus Forge* no attention at all. A few, crossing from one wall to the other, appeared suddenly to become aware of the work – some by looking down as they walked, and others by catching the toe of their shoe on its edge, and then looking down. It was difficult to tell how many recognized *Venus Forge* as sculpture at this point, and how many assumed that these tiles had been laid as part of the design of the gallery.

Others seemed immediately to identify *Venus Forge* as an artwork. Doubtless some knew Andre's work before encountering the sculpture, yet there was still a detectable hesitation in gauging how best to approach it. Was *Venus Forge* something to be stepped on or stepped over? Was it to be viewed up close or from a distance? Was it best apprehended from multiple stationary positions, from a central position from which multiple perspectives can be gained, or was it to be retraced by walking its perimeter? Despite being familiar with Andre's work and writing – aware that, since he 'trust[s] a great deal to the tactile tact of the spectator'[4] it was perfectly permissible to walk on this type of hard metal floor piece – I found myself doubting my initial decision to make my way down the very centre of the sculpture, and it was this hesitation which prompted me to return to observe the responses of others.

To complicate matters, the sculpture – which is 1.2 metres wide and 15.5 metres long – was situated so that it ran between two rooms. There was no way of passing from one room to the other without walking over, or very awkwardly sidling past, it. Other than by reversing course entirely, the gallery visitor had no choice but to encounter the artwork, to coincide in a particular space with the work. This was a clever, if somewhat authoritarian, decision on the part of the Tate Modern curators, intended, perhaps, to call into question precisely those habits of perceiving, interpreting and interacting with artworks which so often dull the effects of aesthetic experience. Alternately, they may have sought to restage the famous objections which Michael Fried raises in his epochal essay, 'Art and Objecthood', regarding what he interprets as the minimalist attack on the interconnected modernist values of autonomy and authenticity:

> Someone merely has to enter the room in which a literalist [minimalist] work has been placed to *become* that beholder, that audience of one – almost as though the work in question has been *waiting for* him ... And once he is in the room the work refuses, obstinately, to let him alone – which is to say, it refuses to stop confronting him, distancing him, isolating him.[5]

Of course, what Fried regards here as a flaw of minimalism, might as easily be taken to be one of its strengths. Yet in either case, *Venus Forge* reminds us that there are many exceptions to the idea that minimalist works exercise a certain theatrical demand. For it is still perfectly conceivable that even at this very material juncture, *Venus Forge* might be missed – not only in terms of its status as an artwork, but even in terms of its physical presence as an ordinary object. Indeed, Andre himself describes an exhibition at which, paying attention to a painting, he failed to notice his own work: 'I had to walk the whole length of my piece one way and back the other way and then up, and I had not seen it myself!'[6] Yet, as Andre also proceeds to note, the capacity to miss or to misrecognize an artwork – which frequently involves mistaking it for a regular artefact or a utilitarian object – is in fact one of the principal accomplishments of minimalism: although its works are remarkably, and to some critics surprisingly, diverse in terms of medium, style, genre, purpose and effect, the minimalist aesthetic remains closely rooted to a sense of its own contingency.

When Rosalind Krauss remarks that engaging with minimalist sculpture 'is a matter of repeated encounters, no single encounter seeming to reveal anything more or significantly different from any other [and] no single moment, eclipsing all others',[7] she arguably threatens to consign minimalism to a blank determinism, effectively curtailing the contingency at the heart of the work which ensures that every encounter, no matter how apparently unremarkable, retains an aleatory element and hence the potentiality to produce remarkable effects in the world. Returning to *Venus Forge*, a fairly substantial number of people who seemed not to have paid attention to the sculpture prior to this very physical encounter now took a moment to look back and to trace the work through to the next room before stepping tentatively onto the steel and copper tiles. Others spent some time with the work. In my case, this involved what had become something of a checklist when first encountering minimalist sculpture: weighing the qualitative and quantitative elements of the work against one another; examining its surfaces and materials; trying to determine whether the work should be apprehended as a whole or analysed into the units of which it is composed. Indeed, the formal aspects of the sculpture are striking: in relation to one another, its parts reveal patterns and sequences, a fixed ratio of small to large tiles, and a serial composition which might, in principle, extend indefinitely. At the same time, although in apprehending *Venus Forge* our attention is drawn forward along the length of the sculptural plane, the work still communicates a strong and dynamic sense of unity – a sense of its immanence and singularity, which, as Merleau-Ponty notes, is the 'fundamental manner of being'[8] of the artwork in which 'the spatiality of the thing and its being as a thing are not … distinct problems',[9] and in which 'expression is indistinguishable from the thing expressed'.[10]

To encounter *Venus Forge* is to discover in a single work and its environment many of minimalism's most exemplary aspects, traits which are as pervasive in the various media and intermedia of minimalist literature, music and performance as they are in minimalist visual art. Andre's sculpture interrogates the most fundamental questions regarding the material constitution of the artwork: questions of quantity and quality; of spatial extension and duration; of form, material and scale. It radicalizes notions of medium and mediation, presence and representation: it mediates nothing other than its bare qualities and quantity, disrupting the mimetic economies of representation and external reference in favour of immanence, of presence, to itself and to the viewer, rendering maximally apparent the fact of its taking-place as an artwork. It interrogates various problems of process in aesthetics – processes by which the work is generated, exists in itself, is perceived, and is translated into various descriptive and interpretative discourses – and so also exposes the significance of place and placement, movement and environment, to aesthetic experience. Perhaps most significantly, however, the ambiguities and uncertainties which accompany an encounter with this work raise what Danto recognizes as the most pervasive problem in a contemporary ontology of art: the situation in which art and non-art are no longer easily distinguished; a situation in which despite 'radically distinct ontological affiliations'[11] it is no longer possible to tell 'which is an artwork and … which is not'.[12]

This disputed threshold of art and non-art becomes central to aesthetic theory and practice with the advent of Dadaism. A self-conscious positing of this threshold – most famously instantiated by Duchamp's readymades and amplified by Cage's sustained exploration of the aesthetics of indeterminacy – feeds directly into the interwoven trajectories of a number of the so-called movements of the 1960s.[13] Fluxus, Pop Art, Concrete and Minimalism – the last referring to the canonical expression of minimalism – although they diverge on numerous conceptual and aesthetic points, and are internally diverse as well, share a commitment to polemicizing the distinction of art from non-art, and re-examining the media through which this polemic is staged. Membership of these loosely defined movements was often multiple, with Morris, Oldenburg, Young, Higgins and Riley, among others, associated with several simultaneously. Similarly, there is a strong case for suggesting that the Concrete poets are, in fact, literary minimalists, despite the fact that they never formally aligned themselves with the Minimalist movement, such as it was. Indeed, it is perhaps the disparity between the discourse surrounding canonical minimalism as a movement – often vehemently disputed by practitioners and critics alike – and the mute insistence and intensity of minimalist works, regardless of whether or not they are recognized as such – that makes minimalism, in its broadest sense, an exemplary vehicle for examining the limits of what might legitimately be regarded as art. It is not surprising, then, that critics such as Greenberg[14] and Fried[15] – both resolute defenders of the modernist aesthetic, and particularly abstract expressionism – should have raised the alarm regarding what they *then* perceived as the minimalist attempt to misrepresent non-art as art. Similar misgivings characterize a number of critical responses to musical and literary minimalism, fuelled principally by the dubious conviction that minimalism constitutively involves an attack on the best practices of every aesthetic tradition.[16] In this light, although Danto's discussion centres on visual art, the problem to which it addresses itself is pertinent to the *artwork* in its broadest sense, and not as restricted to a particular medium.

In *Venus Forge*, Andre executes a work in which the threshold between art and non-art is not only at its most minimal – this is, after all, a work which might as easily be mistaken for a series of metal tiles as for a sculptural masterpiece – but also in which this minimal threshold between art and non-art is essential to our encounter with the work. This is not to undermine the view, shared by most minimalists, that their best works 'just are',[17] and that in this immanent facticity, minimalist art is finally a species of radical realism which is about the 'properties of materials'[18] and 'perceptible processes'.[19] Indeed, the threshold between art and non-art becomes visible precisely because we encounter in minimalism a realism so radical that it unsettles the established parameters of aesthetic judgment. Upon this threshold the distinction of artwork from artefact, of literary text from a utilitarian sequence of words, of music from a collection of sounds, and of performance from an everyday act is pressed to a point of near indistinction. Upon this threshold the many techniques of minimalist artists, composers, writers and performers direct the minimalist work towards the radical question of its own existence as an artwork rather than as an artefact. Applying Agamben's perceptive description of the *threshold* as 'the experience of the limit itself, the experience of being-*within* an *outside*',[20] minimalism appears to occupy a liminal zone in which its works belong most radically to the sphere of art precisely because they might be mistaken for non-art. If minimalism does indeed occupy such a threshold, it becomes necessary to determine whether *Venus Forge*'s specific arrangement of metal tiles is sufficient to qualify the work as a sculpture; or, for that matter, whether Steve Reich's *Four Organs* contains enough melody, harmony or form, and Mary Robison's *Why Did I Ever* enough unity, character development or plot, to be recognizable respectively as a musical composition or a novel.

2.2 Encounter

Minimalism and the sustained encounter: La Monte Young's *Dream Houses* (1966–70)

The radical recognition which Andre's *Venus Forge* brings regarding the threshold between art and non-art arrives not in *deciding* between the two, but in the naked fact that any decision in this regard arises, in the first place, from an *encounter* with the work. This is perhaps the most significant insight of Fried's 'Art and Objecthood', one which holds regardless of how much credence is given to its corollary claims. Many of the contours of this encounter, and the potential avenues of aesthetic experience it initiates, are described above. It is clear, at least, that any act of interpretation, however elaborate or minimal, presupposes an encounter of some sort – a 'fusion of horizons'[21] between works and interpreters, and the discourses through which they meet and negotiate,[22] revealing that 'understanding belongs to the encounter with the work of art itself'.[23] An encounter is at once the most banal and the most profound occurrence. It is simply what happens when entities interact in a particular situation, yet in this minimal event is harboured a radical, transfigurative potential.

In his late essay, 'The Underground Current of the Materialism of the Encounter',[24] Althusser proposes a radical and somewhat controversial theory of the encounter, developed from the fundamental ontological claim that 'for a being … to be, an encounter has to have taken place'.[25] While an encounter does not generate a world *ex nihilo*, it does 'confer reality' on elements which would otherwise be undifferentiated, unrelated and unreal.[26] Predicated on a 'rejection of all philosophies of essence',[27] Althusser identifies a concealed genealogy of thought, a 'materialism of the encounter',[28] invisibly running alongside the dominant metaphysical trajectories of Western philosophy – traceable to Presocratic atomism, but discovering its decisive orientation in the thought of Epicurus and Lucretius. The dominant Platonic and Aristotelian lineages against which this suppressed trajectory is counterposed, insist that reason and meaning, and thus also necessity and teleology, are radical to reality[29] in what is finally a deterministic vision of a world in which 'everything is accomplished in advance'.[30] By contrast, Epicurean cosmology asserts the pre-eminence of chance and contingency.[31] It asserts that there is no essence prior to the emergence of a real world, only a void in which a parallel fall, a laminar flow, of isolated elements exists. Within this disordered situation, for unknowable reasons, a fundamentally indeterminate event arises. Emerging from within the void, this event constitutes 'an infinitesimal, aleatory variation of nothing'[32] – an absolutely minimal swerve within invariant flow, which Lucretius terms *clinamen* – that brings some of these undefined elements into minimal contact, constituting an *encounter*.[33]

Althusser turns to Epicurean atomism not for its physics or the factual accuracy of its account, but for the paradigm it establishes regarding the radical contingency of existence and the emergence of novelty under these uncertain conditions. An infinitesimal displacement and a resultant encounter are the minimal conditions for the 'birth of a world',[34] for the appearance of radically contingent novelty subtracted from the void. 'Every encounter is aleatory, not only in its origins … but also in its effects',[35] in Althusser's judgment. 'In other words, every encounter might not have taken place, although it did take place [and] nothing in the elements of the encounter prefigures, before the actual encounter, the contours and determinations of the being that will emerge from it.'[36] The force of the encounter – its capacity to confer reality on the undifferentiated multiplicity which occupies the void – resides precisely in the way it transfigures 'transcendental contingency'[37] into fact: 'the fact of contingency, the fact of the subordination of necessity to contingency'.[38] Simply put, the force of every encounter resides in the fact that it can be missed, even in the very midst of its taking-place. It is this sense of contingency which an encounter with *Venus Forge* and many other minimalist works so clearly conveys: it is grasped by some and overlooked by others; for some it 'take[s] hold'[39] with remarkable aesthetic effect, while others recognize the encounter only to dismiss the artwork as artefact. In every case, the fact of the encounter's contingency constitutes the radical and immanent condition 'which thinks the contingency of necessity as an effect of the necessity of contingency'[40] – a difficult but crucial proposition which recognizes that even though it is the encounter that brings the elements of reality into relation, there is nothing which dictates that this particular configuration of the real *must* persist. Althusser is clear on this point: 'every accomplished fact is only a provisional encounter … there is no eternity in the "laws" of any world or state.'[41]

While the encounter cannot be predicted with any precision, this does not mean that it cannot be anticipated, or, indeed, actively sought. The strategic pursuit of encounters proves equally pivotal to political, scientific and aesthetic discourse, since it constitutes a radical means of stimulating the emergence of new configurations. Returning specifically to the works of minimalism – since minimalism characteristically renders both medium and process as transparently as possible – the encounter seems implicit to their very structure. This is evident in Andre's *Venus Forge* by the manner in which the artwork occupies space. Drawing the viewer around it, onto it, and along its surface, the sculpture invites the encounter which will affirm the immanence of its objecthood and the position it occupies at the threshold between art and non-art. At the same time, the work is constituted by an internal encounter between its parts which coexist in a specific ratio to one another, and an encounter of its parts with external objects in the intermediary space they occupy, upon a physical and conceptual threshold between rooms.

The aesthetic encounter – and indeed the aesthetic properties of the encounter itself, which are often of considerable significance to minimalist works – is by no means limited to the sphere of the visual arts. Indeed, it is a sustained perceptual encounter with sound that is most central to the work of minimalist composer La Monte Young. His remarkable extended drone compositions – works constituted by single or multiple sustained pitches sounded in physical environments that are designed to enhance the emergent frequency patterns – exemplify the paradoxical situation in which the artwork is intended at once to be radically independent of its perception, yet simultaneously to depend on an extended encounter and engagement for its many nuances. This species of existential ambiguity manifests in Young's pursuit of aesthetic autonomy through 'extensions of time and alterations of space'[42] which are simply unimaginable in conventional music, reflecting his ambition of creating an artwork which 'ultimately exist[s] in time as a "living organism with a life and tradition of its own"'.[43]

Such autonomy is always conditional, however: these minimalist drone compositions are tied to the singular architectural spaces of *Dream Houses* – the term Young and his partner, the light artist Marian Zazeela, prefer for their carefully constructed performance environments. In the specific conditions of the *Dream House*, Young and Zazeela are able to trace the effects of extended exposure to sustained sound, a process they think of as 'tun[ing the] nervous system to vibrate harmoniously with the frequencies of the environment'.[44] There are significant somatic and psychoacoustic effects that result from Young's various extended pitches, which might include 'enhanced attention spans and increased sensitivity of differences within apparent sameness'.[45] Yet to understand the full force of Young's minimalism, it is necessary to return to the *Dream Houses* themselves. Through an emptying of material space, whether of a single room or series of rooms, Young and Zazeela seek to generate a sort of atopian void, an indeterminate space within which events and encounters potentially arise. In this sense, the *Dream House* offers aesthetic expression to the radical logic which, according to Althusser, 'begins by evacuating all … problems … in order to set out from nothing'.[46]

The sonic substance of the more recent *Dream House* environments is habitually provided by drones set up to sound independently of the presence of performers or an audience. Exemplary among these are Young's *Drift Studies*, an ongoing series of electronically produced drone compositions constituted by '[f]requencies tuned to the harmonic series'[47] which serve to expose the inherent but often inaudible overtones that furnish specific pitches with their singular sonic qualities. Although radically minimalist, these drone compositions point to the fact that even when it appears most invariant, pitch is in fact multiple, complex, contingent, changeable. Indeed, it is tempting to recognize even in the title of Young's *Drift Studies* the echoes of the 'transcendental contingency'[48] which marks a materialism of the encounter. Is the *drift* to which they refer not the same minimal deviation that disrupts the laminar flow of elements in the void, giving rise to the encounter? Pursuing this analogical field, is it not possible to rethink the *Dream House* as an instance of the void enframed – walled in, rendered contingently stable, receptive to encounters and responsive to aesthetic events. In its most minimal instantiations, a solitary drone sounds in the void space of the *Dream House*. No sooner is the drone sounded, than it drifts. By encountering spatial limits in the bare walls of the empty *Dream House*, a complex series of reverberations are set in motion through which the drone gains sonic potentiality: apparently uncomplicated sound reveals the intrinsic complexities of the harmonic series of which it is constituted through 'the combination tones brought about by the interaction of the harmonically related sine wave frequencies themselves'.[49]

This subtle agglomeration of differences gives to the apparently inert drone a minimal momentum, one which gains force through the fusion of the insistent sound and Zazeela's dense fluorescent lights, revealing the *Dream House* as a space which is at once empty and full: it is a void space, but a void replete with the drift of encounters which constitute an atmosphere thick with latent aesthetic potentiality. A further drift, perhaps the most significant one of all, is marked by the encounter between the near-reified atmosphere of the *Dream House* and the perceiver. Although Young and Zazeela habitually describe their aesthetic ideal in the technical terms of the work itself – 'sets of chords and lighting mixing and meeting in hallways and alcoves to create new and more complex intersecting sets of frequencies in sound and light'[50] – this does not negate the fact that 'the emphasis is finally always firmly placed on the experience' of the work.[51]

While Young's capacity 'to create something potentially dramatic out of the apparently static'[52] rests, in the first instance, on the existence of the drone environment – on its sheer facticity and persistence – it is the 'extended contemplation'[53] of the work – the fact that it involves an 'encounter [which] must last'[54] – that accounts for its aesthetic effect. The free movement of the perceiver in the *Dream House* results in encounters through which acoustic phenomena gain specific perceptual properties. Depending on the position of the perceiver, 'both pitch and volume [of sustained drones] vary',[55] and interference patterns between approximate but non-identical frequencies or pitches are experienced as an unmistakable pulse.[56] In this light, the encounter is transfigurative: not only is the indifferent facticity of the drone transfigured into an exemplary minimalist artwork, but, through this transfigurative encounter, the *Dream House* comes to exist at a new intensity. Minimalism exposes a paradoxical but important aspect of its own persistence: the more things stay the same, the more they change.

2.3 Perception

Embodied perception as a generative process: Robert Morris's *untitled (3 Ls)* (1965–70)

Here, where a physical encounter with minimalism reveals in fundamental terms the significant role which perception plays in determining the material and affective totality of the artwork, it is particularly useful to recall the claim of Merleau-Ponty's *Phenomenology of Perception* regarding the generative role of embodied perception in constituting reality. 'Every external perception is immediately synonymous with a certain perception of my body, just as my body is made explicit in the language of external perception',[57] according to Merleau-Ponty. '[The body] is an expressive unity which we can learn to know only by actively taking it up' through the activity of perception, and it is this activity which makes it possible 'to reawaken our experience of the world as it appears to us in so far as we are in the world through our body'.[58] In this schema, art fulfils a very specific function: it clarifies the process of perception and so, too, the parameters of the world as determined by perception. Thus, Merleau-Ponty's principal concern with art lies not in conventional mimesis, but in its capacity accurately to represent the activity of perception itself. The painters which interest Merleau-Ponty 'make salient or perspicuous something that is part of visual experience, but [do] not *recreate* that visual experience'.[59] Art exists in the world in a way which clarifies perception even as it offers a novel point of access to the perceptual field.[60] In this light, abstract art continues the work of clarifying and intensifying the universal conditions of reality, 'attempting to find new systems of equivalences for the transhistorical features of human existence they disclose'.[61]

It is not surprising, given the radical vision which underpins Merleau-Ponty's philosophy of art, that it should prove a significant influence on minimalists, and particularly early minimalist sculptors. Yet, the centrality of perception to minimalism is not confined to material encounters, but extends also to representations of embodied perception. Indeed, it is difficult to overstate Merleau-Ponty's significance to a range of minimalist visual artists and writers. Central innovations in the work of literary figures such as Samuel Beckett and Alain Robbe-Grillet exemplify numerous of Merleau-Ponty's central arguments regarding the pivotal role of embodied perception in establishing the parameters of reality. Robbe-Grillet's 'In the Corridors of the Underground' – a short story that prefigures the striking phenomenological realism of his early novels – offers unambiguous testimony to the manner in which the motility of the perceiving body generates a coherent sense of the world.[62] Textually tracing the multiple perspectives which mobile embodied perception synthesizes into perceptual reality, Robbe-Grillet offers in a distinctly minimalist prose a disarmingly accurate aesthetic account of the situation which Merleau-Ponty describes as 'the body in movement [which] actively assumes [space and time] … tak[ing] them up in their basic significance which is obscured in the commonplaceness of established situations'.[63] The negative corollary to this position is found in much of Beckett's later prose, which involves the inner-dialogue of highly self-reflexive embodied consciousnesses – textually encoded presences rather than characters – which find themselves in restricted or closed spaces. Struggling both physically and imaginatively to move beyond these limits, their incessant monologue brings to light the disturbing extent to which spatial restriction imposed on the body reduces the total perceptual field, resulting in a radically impoverished reality.[64] These works are marked by a progressive diminution of external or hetero-reference, as the world recedes into an entropic self-referentiality in which imagination, memory and immanent experience grow increasingly indistinct from one another, marked textually by recursive patterns of repetition.

A great deal of visual minimalism emerges from a particularly productive dialogue with Merleau-Ponty's phenomenology. The proto-canonical minimalism of the colour field and hard edge painters – Barnett Newman and Mark Rothko among the former, and Kenneth Noland and Ellsworth Kelly among the latter – explores the central Gestalt principle, taken up and developed by Merleau-Ponty, that perception, as generative process, takes place in the distinction of a *figure* against a *ground*, or an *object* against an *horizon*.[65] The uniform surface of colour field painting offers a significant aesthetic site with respect to this distinction: against a monochromatic ground, the precise point at which a figure emerges is most clearly apprehended. At this minimal point of maximal clarity the totality of the aesthetic situation is transfigured. Exemplary among such instances are the bright zips which transect Newman's monochromatic fields in works such as *Cathedra* (1951) or *Midnight Blue* (1970), announcing the minimal but sublime fact of the artwork – that there has been an eruption of form from the very midst of formlessness.[66]

Less dramatic and more ambiguous – but no less pertinent in illustrating many of the essential precepts of Merleau-Ponty's theories of perception – are the paintings of Rothko, in which the relation between figure and ground is often less clearly defined, subject to a transitional zone of the sort found in *untitled (yellow, orange, yellow, light orange)* (1955) or *Red on Maroon* (1959), in which there are more graded changes in depth, density and focus which accompany defined chromatic shifts. It is precisely to these ambiguous zones that hard edge painting sought an antidote, attempting to bring the gestural and overtly painterly elements of late abstract expressionism under strict control. Clean lines mark the clearly defined and often highly contrasting colours of vertical, horizontal, and diagonal linear bands, and concentric circular bands, which constitute the hard edge paintings of Kelly and Noland, for example. At the same time, these works represent a shift in emphasis from ground – the implicit concern of much colour field painting – to figure. Indeed, it might be argued that we discover only a series of figures in the juxtaposed vertical bands of works such as Kelly's *Spectrum IV*,[67] the ground having been displaced from within the pictorial plane to the outside, the horizon of the wall, and the gallery more generally.

Minimalist sculpture translates the figure–ground or object–horizon relationship into three dimensions, clarifying that perception must finally be grasped as an embodied practice. Works such as Robert Morris's celebrated *untitled (3 Ls)* of 1965[68] – an artwork constituted of identical L-shaped units arranged in various orientations, combinations and contexts – demonstrate the potential disjunction between knowledge of reality as constituted by objective measures and the reality communicated by perception. Encouraging viewers to move around and between the units,[69] these sculptures gather definition precisely to the extent that they are 'seen from everywhere'.[70] Yet the objects that emerge are deeply ambiguous: although the L-beams are identical in measurement and uniform in the material from which they are constructed, the various arrangements of the units – lying flat, standing on one of the arms of the L, or standing on the points of the arms so as to form an inverted V – result in their being perceived as non-identical. Morris characterizes this phenomenon as a pull between 'the known constant and the experienced variable',[71] placing his work in unambiguous dialogue with Merleau-Ponty's thought. This characteristic tension pervades much minimalist sculpture from Ronald Bladen's and Richard Serra's monumental sculptures which demand an irregular mode of perception by interposing themselves between the body and its environment, to the light art of Dan Flavin or Daniel Buren in which the sculpture is at once located at the source of the light and distributed in various ways throughout the space of the exhibition, prompting the viewer to hold together distinct yet simultaneous instantiations of the work through the process of a dynamic but sustained perceptual encounter.[72]

The significance of minimalism in this light resides in its capacity to clarify the disjunctive relation, central to Merleau-Ponty's phenomenology, between 'absolute objects [which] consist of an infinite number of different perspectives compressed into a strict co-existence'[73] and objects as they are given to perception to be discovered 'at the very centre of our experience'.[74] Although in Merleau-Ponty's estimation the absolute object has no material counterpart, it has nonetheless been understood historically as providing consistency to both the empiricist and transcendental regimes of thought regarding the purportedly stable relationships between objects that constitute external reality. For Merleau-Ponty, the realist insistence on the individuation of an object that persists independently in space and across a specific duration of time has considerable consequences: 'the absolute positing of a single object is the death of consciousness',[75] since it decisively 'exceeds perceptual experience'[76] by asserting an objective realm in which the body, time and the world are external to one another, rather than the correlates of perception and experience.

As tempting as it may be to follow Merleau-Ponty in this regard, his argument finally rests on a single, sweeping assumption that perceptual and hence experiential knowledge of an object is correlative to the being of an object.[77] By limiting being to the perceptual knowledge of being, and existence to the perceptual knowledge of existence, it becomes possible for Merleau-Ponty to claim that positing an object is invariably an act of absolute positing when, in fact, contingency has always been and continues to be the touchstone of the realist understanding of the persistence of objects. The resultant conception in much of Merleau-Ponty's work is of the world as a complex set of relations – the predicate of a 'metaphysics of relations', in Harman's terms[78] – which can be given determinate content and consistency solely by the constitutive processes of perception. According to Merleau-Ponty, our encounter with an object presupposes perception: the object is given to perception in a manner which makes it appear to transcend or precede its perception,[79] but in reality this appearance is merely an operation of the immanent and world-making activity of perception itself. Accepting this argument, the apparently transcendental character of the world – that which allows the world to be apprehended as an independent collection of entities and relations between entities which precede and hence are given to perception and cognition – is given solely in the immanent situation of perception. Merleau-Ponty regards the transcendental as an aspect of immanence, and immanence as nothing other than the activity of the body as a 'general medium for having a world'.[80]

Although the formulation is compelling, it remains implicitly riveted to the inescapably anthropocentric understanding of the world as a predicate of perceptually acquired knowledge noted above. By foregrounding the necessity of perception in the constitution of this knowledge, Merleau-Ponty significantly subverts both the empiricist insistence on the acquisition of these facts by induction as well as the idealist understanding of facts as correlative to concepts. However, in offering an account of the world which is in equal measure anti-realist and anti-idealist, little attention is given to the many elements of existence which are unavailable to perception but are nonetheless active in constituting and shaping the world. Relegated to a pervasive but intrinsically undifferentiated horizon, even fairly dramatic events, processes and objects such as volcanic eruptions lack intrinsic interest in themselves. Thus, despite the dynamism of Merleau-Ponty's understanding of perception, the objects of the world it delineates remain curiously static. Undermining any simple opposition of chance and necessity, they reflect the 'fundamental contingency'[81] of existence in the unexpected terms of facticity: 'the fact that [objects] are in a world … appears as necessary to this world.'[82] For such objects to persist in a determinate world, they could not have been otherwise; had they been otherwise, the world too would be otherwise. In this way fundamental contingency and absolute necessity are manoeuvred into a curious symmetry.[83] The object, which has been divested of any independent agency, is subject to the constraints of a determinate constellation[84] in which it exists 'in-itself-for-us'.[85] It is an object waiting to be encountered, to be activated by perception, and to be recognized as a figure of order against the horizon of indifference.[86]

The challenges this ambiguous position poses for thought are exemplified with particular clarity in considering the field of minimalist aesthetics in which the artwork is 'caught in the contradictions of its moment',[87] in a field which must demonstrate how the work of art is simultaneously autonomous and responsive to context. Defined in its most minimal terms, the particularity of any artwork resides in an encounter between the interpreter – a viewer, listener, reader – and a specific constellation of quantitative and qualitative properties which contingently cohere in and as the artwork. Returning to Morris's L beams, we might say that the work is persistent with respect to its quantitative dimension – its constituent quantities are measurably stable – but only contingently stable with respect to its qualitative elements. The activity of perceiving the artwork reveals a work in flux: both the internal relation of parts to one another, and the external relation of parts to the work as a whole, and to the environment in which it is situated, shift depending on the perspective from which the work is perceived.

That the constituent units of the sculpture are still interpreted as equivalent to one another, despite the fact that they do not look identical, owes to the fact that perception, although an immanent and continuous process, involves provisional syntheses of disparate data. Yet, the fact that contemporary theories of perception are able to account for both the 'objective and changeable'[88] aspects of minimalist objecthood, does not simply obviate the need for working through the realist argument regarding the persistence and autonomy of objects. Since disbarring realism is accomplished not by any metaphysical necessity, but by a decision – the decision that the object is identical with actively acquired knowledge of the object, and that the qualitative aspects of the object have a greater determining factor in the constitution of the object than the quantitative – what might the consequences be if this decision is placed in doubt, or even reversed? Much of the present work interrogates this possibility, identifying in minimalist aesthetics an exemplary field upon which a modest but radical realism can be traced when close attention is given to those aspect of artworks that belong to the object and that are not determined by perception.

2.4 Disruption

Minimalism and the politics of public space: Richard Serra's *Tilted Arc* (1981)

To suggest that minimalist artworks are deeply invested in their own realness does not negate the importance of perception to the total significance of minimalism. It does, however, question Merleau-Ponty's assertion regarding the primacy of perception. To the extent that an object persists as a discrete entity, there remains some part of its constitution which is independent of any specific act of cognition or perception. Precisely how this independent element is interpreted – in terms of radicality, anteriority or primacy; as a material aspect or metaphysical condition for the emergence and persistence of an object or a situation – and whether or not it is accepted or rejected, depends in large part on the understanding of reality which underpins a given formulation of the object. The particular significance of minimalism in this respect resides in the fact that its finest works habitually articulate the terms of their own objecthood.

In this sense, the minimalist object is encountered as an aesthetic threshold upon which disparate conceptions of reality are brought into alignment.

A great number of minimalist works point to the encounter as a threshold event. The encounter with minimalism, which radicalizes the distinction between art and non-art, similarly problematizes any easy distinction between the realist conception of the object as an independent, persistent entity, and the understanding that the object is determined by its perception, a view shared, albeit in different registers, by the phenomenology of Husserl and Merleau-Ponty and the idealism of Berkeley. It is precisely because the encounter instantiates a threshold – an 'experience of the limit itself',[89] to recall Agamben's formulation – that we are not compelled to decide between the realist and the perceptualist paradigms of the object, but instead are able to recognize in the minimalist artwork a field of *continuity* between the two. As the work of philosopher Roman Ingarden clarifies, opposing accounts of reality rest less on a fundamental dispute as to whether or not the real exists than they do on how the real is articulated – how it is expressed in the epistemological terms of fact and knowledge.[90] In this light, the capacity of minimalism to hold together competing accounts of the real in the singularity of its objects exemplifies what Ingarden envisions in terms of a *phenomenological realism*,[91] and which the present work recognizes as the *persistence of the real.*

To encounter the minimalist artwork at its most radical is to encounter an object in the very medium of its facticity – not as an accomplished fact, but as an entity which persists in a manner which is open to perception and conceptualization, allowing it to be translated into factual terms. The encounter *confers* reality[92] in the sense that what is encountered is not merely an object, but an exemplary instance of the persistence of the real; and the encounter lasts[93] precisely because it apprehends the object in terms of its persistence, as an entity which both precedes and exceeds the event of the encounter. It is tempting in this sense to refer to the primacy of the encounter, rather than of the percept or concept, since it is the encounter that apprehends the singular intensity, or the real quantity, of the object as it exists within an existential situation in which the exact distribution of the qualities which describe the objects of reality is ambiguous. The singularity of the artwork resides not in some occulted essence, but in the manner in which it opens itself to the possibility of the encounter; and the encounter, as Althusser recognizes, relates 'not only [to] the essence of reality but, above all, [to] the essence of *practice*',[94] which is to say to 'the reality of politics'.[95]

How, then, might the reality of politics express itself in an encounter with the radical aesthetic of minimalism? Are minimalism's ethical and political dimensions implicit or explicit? Young's *Dream Houses* are instructive in addressing these questions: emptied of all but their aesthetic substance – sound and light – Young and Zazeela envisioned these environments as utopian spaces in which art and life would be indistinguishable. Their intention was to bring existence to a new intensity, aiming for what is 'universal and all-encompassing'[96] by recognizing in art the 'source of a heightened state of consciousness that brings both the performer and viewer/listener into a transcendent state of being'.[97] The search for an aesthetic encounter capable of granting access to what Young and Zazeela regard in terms of a universal consciousness, no matter how utopian or unattainable, remains an eminently ethico-political one to the extent that it culminates in a singular way of existing together – of encountering the work, and encountering one another in our relation to the work. Baker recognizes a similar potential in the minimalist sculpture of Morris and Smith: the multiple perspectives from which these works are perceived in any sustained encounter requires an extension of the perceiver towards the externality of the artwork. Arguing that 'shifting one's own physical standpoint promotes tolerance of the disparate vantage points on reality that other people embody',[98] Baker suggests that minimalism intensifies our awareness of the fundamental ethical relation of self to other.

This intensification can, of course, take a positive or negative form. For example, while works such as Flavin's celebrated light installation on the rotunda of the Guggenheim Museum in New York, *untitled (to Ward Jackson …)*, invite viewers into novel perceptual relationships with one another, other works such as Richard Serra's infamous *Tilted Arc* (1981) – a sculpture which, before its controversial removal, bisected Foley Federal Plaza in New York, obscuring views and limiting movement – have been judged by many to be essentially coercive. In both cases, it is the immediacy with which the minimalist artwork strikes us, and the manner in which it structures our perception, that accounts for its capacity to expose the implicit ethical and political dimensions of the aesthetic encounters. Such encounters readily give rise to more explicitly political situations, however. In the case of *Tilted Arc*, a petition signed by members of the public working in the sculpture's vicinity led to a protracted legal dispute that culminated in its being dismantled and stored. '*Tilted Arc* was not destroyed because the sculpture was uncivil', according to Serra, 'but because the government wanted to set a precedent in which it could demonstrate its right to censor and destroy speech'.[99] Furthermore, subject to an unambiguously economic logic, the decision codified the wholesale commodification of art from its conception to its destruction, assigning the intellectual as well as material property of the work to those who commissioned it, and in the process affirming 'the government's commitment to private property over the interests of art or free expression'.[100]

Serra's *Tilted Arc* offers an important point of access to the knot of socio-economic and political complexities that emerged in the mid-twentieth century so-called developed world. In a situation marked by an unprecedented expansion in the production and consumption not only of commodities and services, but also of information, and the archives and media through which this information is encoded, communicated and stored, the insistence of the minimalist project on parsimony and transparency seemed conservative if not regressive to many contemporary critics, among them Greenberg and Fried.[101] For minimalists, however, the obduracy of the artwork – its eschewal of the most pervasive markers of value and meaning, and its indifference to the dogmatic imposition of historical aesthetic norms – constituted a viable if 'oblique political gesture',[102] a form of resistance to the commodification of the aesthetic. However, it is clear from a short piece written by Judd in 1969 – only a few years after the exhibition of the first minimalist works and the first wave of manifestos, reviews and analyses which accompanied or immediately followed these – that the subversive potential of minimalism was almost immediately undermined through its domestication by professional curators and critics. Judd bemoans the obsession in the artworld[103] with closure – with demarcating and assigning fixed significance to 'a whole aesthetic or style; a half-aesthetic or movement; a way of working, history or development; seniority, juniority, money and galleries; sociology, politics, nationalism'[104] – expressing dismay at its capacity for impoverishing the singularity of the artwork by absorbing it into the normative nexus of gallery, museum, private collection, catalogue, review and critical journal.

In its initial fervour, the minimalist defiance of capitalist hegemony emerges through an often ironic use of anonymous procedures of industrial design and fabrication to produce artworks which, in a pointedly political manner, refuse any particular utility despite their frequent superficial resemblance to utilitarian objects.[105] It is not surprising in this light that critics at the time often failed to grasp that the formal and procedural choices which gave rise to such sculpture were simultaneously aesthetic and practical, and that the two remain intricately interwoven at every point of the minimalist object's genesis and emergence. The precision and scale demanded in the design, production, transportation, assembly and replication of many of these works required resources often only available in an industrial setting, making the conception of objecthood pursued by many minimalist sculptors inconceivable outside of the mechanical processes of industrial design. However, the suggestion, voiced by a number of critics, that the interpenetration of art and industry amounts to the subjugation of the technical skill and creative genius of the artist to the machine-culture of automated late capitalism,[106] is every bit as naïve as the claim that the objects of minimalism are free-floating, autonomous forms with no intrinsic connection to either the political or economic conditions in which they arise.

Similar critical vitriol was directed towards the heavily amplified minimalist compositions of Glass and Reich, once more stemming from an unwarranted prejudice which took it for granted that the supposedly unholy alliance of technology and performance would inevitably undermine the integrity of Western art music, effecting the mass emigration of attentive and restrained audiences to chaotic arenas and clubs where they would be overcome by the sonic and libidinal excesses of popular music.[107] The fact that this didactic, moralistic narrative belonged to the anachronistic, elitist fantasy of civilizing society at large by the imposition of norms of taste – norms which are themselves often as mutable as the popular cultural trends to which they are habitually opposed – went largely unremarked. Similar prejudices emerge in the widely held misconceptions that minimalist literature is uncritically populist, generally acquiescent to the neo-conservative, capitalist worldview, and opposed to the gains of the avant-garde[108] resulting in its marginal position within academic criticism, despite the fact that its remarkably diverse stylists remain among the most influential writers of recent decades.

Returning to the visual arts, later critics, tracing the remarkable rapidity with which minimalist works were acquired by leading collectors and galleries, came to regard the minimalist claims of resistance to the hegemony of capitalism as exaggerated, disguising the tacit complicity of minimalist visual artists in the systems they claimed to subvert. Chave, in particular, identifies in minimalism a 'cool display of power' which, far from ironizing the dominant ideologies of political economy, 'perpetrat[es] a kind of cultural terrorism'.[109] While many minimalists viewed the eschewal of mimetic reference and symbolic content as a means of opening the artwork onto a situation which either transcended or offered oblique critique of the dominant ideological conditions in which the work arises, Chave recognized in minimalism a vulnerability, if not acquiescence, to the same ideologies it purportedly sought to circumvent: '[w]ith closer scrutiny … the blank face of Minimalism may come into focus as the face of capital, the face of authority, the face of the father'.[110] Chave's argument is forceful, the ironic rhetorical mirror of the 'control and force'[111] she imputes to minimalist art. In seeking to expose in minimalism an aggressive formalism which often expresses a violent and patriarchal normativity with distinct proto-fascist proclivities, Chave's polemic remains among the most provocative ethico-political investigations of minimalism's complicity in obliquely reinforcing rather than undermining the teleological drive of aesthetic modernity. Yet, perhaps necessarily, it remains difficult to disentangle Chave's criticism from the critical norms of the artworld in relation to which it articulates itself. As a result, it arguably fails to acknowledge the genuinely radical force which moves through the finest minimalism, transcending any specific context into which it emerges, and quite irrespective of the intentions of either creator or critic: a force that is properly *poietic*; radically generative, radically immanent; an aperture to the encounter itself.

2.5 Force

Micro-political apertures to macro-political events: Frank Stella's *Arbeit Macht Frei* (1967)

Minimalist art is implicitly concerned with the generation of micro-political apertures – local encounters with artworks which call for decisions; decisions which align thought within larger ideological constellations; ideological constellations which drive political actions towards specific *teloi*. Yet, at the same time, minimalism also resists any straightforward incorporation into teleological sequences of historical purpose or utility: while its works incorporate fundamental shapes, patterns, harmonic possibilities and gestures, these are for the most part non-mimetic and thus disconnected from any external prototype. In cases where the minimalist work plainly participates in a representational economy – the verisimilitude of much minimalist fiction and the elaborate mimetic machinery of minimalist opera cannot be interpreted otherwise – it does so not merely to generate a believable world, but to lay bare the patterns upon which this, and every other, world depends for its coherence. Its concern, in other words, is not with measuring one species of reality against another to decide which is more or less real, but with intensifying the real.

Thus, while the title of perhaps the most celebrated work of Stella's series of twenty-three black paintings, *Arbeit Macht Frei*,[112] makes direct and provocative reference to Auschwitz, the political significance of the work emerges less from this reference itself than from the sense of immanent force it evokes – its chevrons converging at the centre of the black canvas, so that 'what begins as arbitrary design comes to develop its own existential dynamics, and perhaps its own ontology', in Altieri's estimation.[113] 'As these paintings break away from submission to external expectations', he goes on, 'they seem to create fresh possibilities for how we might understand processes of choice, and hence orientations of desire.'[114] The charged contingency of Stella's design effects a subtle reaffirmation of political subjectivity through the way in which the immanent facticity of the work itself comes up against the fundamental instability of our encounter with it. Yet, the hermeneutic steps which might lead a viewer to regard the painting as endorsing a specific political message – perhaps as a mute work offering silent witness to a crypto-fascist agenda,[115] or otherwise as a moral admonition to those who fail to recognize in current configurations of power the seeds of future fascism – arise from a contingent set of events and encounters, of which only one is with the work itself.

There can be little doubt, for example, that the socio-economic and political particularities of the United States in the late 1950s, the period during which Stella executed the black series, finds an oblique expression in these works. The political and social complexities of the Eisenhower years unfolded in the long shadow of the Second World War and the growing nuclear threat that dominated Cold War politics of the period, and which was complicated further by growing divisions over policy regarding how best to counter Communist expansion, and disagreement over continued military engagement in foreign territories. Domestically, the pervasive cultural mood was one of a cautious optimism that only thinly veiled the pervasive racial, gender and socio-economic inequalities and growing frustration at the slow progress of civil rights legislation, a reality all too easily glossed over by a conservative vision of prosperity which was animated in large part by burgeoning consumerism and commodity-driven capitalism. In a significant sense, the disjunction to which Stella's black paintings witness – insisting on the nonreferential autonomy of the artwork, that 'what you see is what you see',[116] while also situating these autonomous objects in relation to overtly socio-political situations through their titles – authentically translates into aesthetic terms the paradoxes of 1950s America.

As with all of his paintings of this period, Stella understood the inward-pointing chevron patterns of *Arbeit Macht Frei* as a means of limiting external relations while keeping contained something of the essence of work – the work of painting, the force of *poiesis*.[117] Yet, clearly, the work to which the painting points is also the terrifying work of its title: the work of death, of the extermination of the prisoners of Auschwitz; prisoners worked towards death, worked to death, be it through exhaustion, starvation, torture or mass-murder. Although Chave is deeply critical of what she views as Stella's opportunistic insensitivity to the political gravity which these titles exercise upon his black paintings, she does admit the possibility that this work exhibits an intuitive recognition that there is no adequate means of representing the intensity, scale and instrumentality of the violence and destruction of the Holocaust, a view which has been explored in significant and interconnected ways by, among others, Adorno, Lyotard and Agamben.[118]

As icons of presence which testify to the inadequacy of our ordinary economies of representation, Stella's black paintings gesture towards an aesthetics of the sublime – 'a sensory now [which] cannot be presented and [yet] which remains to be presented'.[119] Yet as Rancière recognizes, 'to assert an unrepresentability in art that is commensurate with an unthinkability of the event, the latter must itself have been rendered entirely thinkable'.[120] In this light, an encounter with Stella's *Arbeit Macht Frei* proves far more politically poignant than critics often admit, since the thought of the unthinkable revealed in this work is precisely that force is generic and eminently transferable. Force varies in its intensity, in how it is incorporated into or disentangled from situations, yet there is something terrifyingly banal about the absolute character of force itself. Force gives rise to events, the results of which it has no stable means of predicting or controlling. The moment at which force becomes tied to agency – constrained and directed – it is transformed into power. In this light, Stella's work poses a deeply unsettling question: is the force or power that imposes contingent order on a canvas really incommensurable with the force that underpins the imposition of order in other situations – social, political, legal?

To understand this absolute and transgressive aspect of force, it is necessary to interrogate the transition from potentiality to actuality as a generic process; one which underpins the emergence of every possible reality. Agamben is particularly instructive in this respect: he suggests that 'all potentiality to be or to do something is always also potential not to be or not to do … without which potentiality would always already have passed into actuality and would be indistinguishable from it'.[121] In other words, it is the possibility of a 'fundamental passivity'[122] – the possibility that the process of becoming by which potentiality becomes actuality might not take place – that constitutes the actual situations in which events, and hence change, can take place. A reality from which all impotentiality has been eliminated would exist as an immanent continuum, an absolute taking-place of force devoid of encounters.[123] Creation and destruction would become indistinguishable, interchangeable; and although this situation is improbable, precisely because this world is one in which pure force is spatiality distributed and subject to varying intensities, there exist terrifying approximations of this situation in the totalitarian exercise of power.

Art has historically constituted a field upon which absolute force can be examined and subjected to critique. As Schlegel recognizes, the work of *poiesis* 'continuously fluctuates between self-creation and self-destruction'.[124] This paradoxical situation is clearly evident when expressive gestures are presented at their most minimal: Isou's sound poetry destroys syntax and verbal integrity in order to resurrect the force of language through its most minimal phonemes; Metzger's action painting applies acid to canvas so that the very process of the canvas's dissolution constitutes the work. In Phil Chang's *Cache, Active*, Walter Benn Michaels identifies an important contemporary instantiation of this dual character of aesthetic force: 'expired photographic negatives … are exposed to light, the image very quickly fad[ing] … leaving instead a reddish brown monochrome'.[125] In being exposed to light, encountering the externality of world and perception, the photographic negative – the very means by which the representational verisimilitude of the photograph is rendered consistent, not to mention repeatable – becomes vulnerable to the same process of exposure and development upon which its mimetic capacity rests in the first place. As this destructive process gives rise to a new monochromatic work, we encounter art that is marked by the transposition of form and materiality into the processual terms of force. Thus, what is genuinely significant in Chang's *Cache, Active* is that it 'enforce[s] this shift … mak[ing] metaphor, meaning and representation itself into matter'.[126]

Plaiting together questions of aesthetic and political effect and, indeed, affect, the encounter with such artworks reveals how force, expressed in a radical and minimal form, transgresses the boundaries between apparently distinct systems. In Stella's *Arbeit Macht Frei* we encounter a work that, despite its title, is finally without a determinate subject. Its subject is force itself, ateleological to the extent that it exceeds the work to which it gives rise. Because the work is nonrepresentational, chromatic contrast and geometric pattern become the contingent vehicles through which this force makes itself felt. While an initial encounter tends to draw the attention of the viewer to its centre, a sustain encounter reveals far richer and more dynamic fluctuations of depth which emerge from interlocking patterns and quadrants. The *poietic* work of the painting – the force by which the internal parts of the painting produce effects within the external environment within which it is exhibited – requires, in turn, a surprising degree of perceptual work from the viewer, which extends further into the conceptual work of aligning the minimalism of the painting with the historical and political sequences evoked by the painting's title. It is precisely in this capacity to bridge the micro-politics of the aesthetic encounter with the macro-politics of the ideological or political encounter that minimalism offers an exemplary field for revealing the generic nature of force. Indeed, it is the capacity of minimalism to express radical force in the generative terms of *poiesis* – its capacity to harness the 'force to understand force from within itself'[127] – which clarifies how it persists as an existential modality, a radical way of existing towards minimum.

2.6 Anticipation

Unexpected epiphanies and the politics of the everyday: Raymond Carver's 'Fat' (1971)

The political stakes of minimalism become visible when its works clearly express forms and forces that are radical to existence itself, and hence likely to be regarded as universal to the human condition.[128] There are numerous instances where minimalists have sought to give expression to large-scale or macro-political ideas and sequences. Minimalist opera habitually addresses a range of major political issues and events: Philip Glass's *Appomattox* represents the last days of the American Civil War; John Adams's *The Death of Klinghoffer* recounts the hijacking of passenger liner, the *Achille Lauro*, in 1985 by the Palestine Liberation Front; the third part of Steve Reich's *Three Tales* deals with the controversial cloning of Dolly the Sheep and the social and ethical questions this raised. Equally, a good deal of minimalist land art is intimately connected to ecopolitical questions of climate change – sometimes rather forcefully, as in the case of Robert Smithson's iconic *Spiral Jetty*, which effected permanent changes at its site; while at other times, as with Andy Goldsworthy's remarkably delicate ice sculptures, with considerable subtlety.

Despite evidence to the contrary, the view that minimalism is essentially apolitical is a stubborn one, and owes in part to a sustained critical neglect of the everyday except as a means of symbolizing a sort of cultural inertia. Yet minimalism reveals that mundane, micro-political encounters matter. For, finally, do they not instantiate the same ideological and ethical problems which inform all levels of political praxis, but at a scale which is more immediately accessible? As Baker suggests, Morris's L beams not only possess aesthetic interest, but present an opportunity to extend ourselves towards the experience of others and their similar but non-identical perception of these sculptural units. Young's *Dream Houses* look towards a situation in which art and life are radically symbiotic, their sonic environment providing a continuum to bridge together the lives of those interacting with the work and each other for the sustained periods, and constituting in the process an innovative type of aesthetic community.[129] However, in the broad context of minimalism, it is perhaps literature, and particularly narrative fiction, that most effectively communicates the lived ethos which moves through the politics of the everyday.

This ethical capacity is encoded in the structure of narrative, but not 'because stories contain the thematic dramatization of ethical situations, choices, and judgments', as J. Hillis Miller recognizes, 'but because ethics itself has a peculiar relation to that form of language we call narrative'.[130] However, the ethical force of narrative language cannot be reduced to an intratextual distribution of formal functions, focalizations or frames, nor to an intertextual distribution of historical, social, political or ideological information which accompanies its genesis. Rather, the 'ethical moment'[131] of narrative literature is always an event, bound together by an act of reading: it arrives, encoded in the singularity of a literary style that makes a claim simultaneously 'on the author writing the work, on the narrator telling the story within the fiction … on the characters within the story at decisive moments of their lives, and on the reader, teacher or critic responding to the work'.[132]

How, then, is the act of reading which emerges from an encounter with minimalist narrative distinct from that which emerges from other types of narrative fiction? A principal technique of many minimalist writers is to eschew narrative omniscience, with its capacity to move freely between temporal and spatial frames, for a perspective that approximates the sense of time and place of the reader. Minimalist narrative time is marked by a strong sense of immanence, drawing both narrator and reader onto what appears to be a common ground. This is rendered with notable stylistic clarity, and a preference for a direct, realistic yet uncomplicated presentation of events, generally unhampered by interpretative interpolation of characters or narrative voice, sets this prose apart from the complexities which mark a great deal of contemporary fiction. It is not that minimalist narrative prose lacks richness or intensity, but rather that it encodes these in an unusually subtle manner. Indeed, subtleties acquire a certain power precisely to the extent that they are 'compact, condensed, and contracted',[133] offered in the lean, transparent prose, of 'highly crafted, pared down sentences',[134] pointing to the minimalist capacity for holding together affective force and expressive subtlety. As Raymond Carver, one of literary minimalism's most celebrated stylists, suggests, 'to write about commonplace things and objects using commonplace but precise language [can] endow those things … with immense, even startling power'.[135]

Carver's short fiction – often taken to be the model for the accelerated production of minimalist writing in the 1970s and 1980s by, among others, Hempel, Beattie, Robison, Wolff, Barthelme, Ford, Phillips, McInerney, Ellis and Janowitz – is exemplary in this regard, constructing storyworlds[136] which, on the surface, merely mimic a 'flat world of events',[137] but which, in fact, harbour a rich field of potentially meaningful encounters that produce 'narrative effects far more complex and diverse than they appear at first sight'.[138] As with much minimalism, these stories often begin *in medias res*,[139] evading a clear commitment to both causes and final outcomes. This sense of immediacy, of belonging to the present moment with 'no history to speak of',[140] contributes to the situation in which 'the political sphere as such … is all but invisible'.[141] These are stories about people at various life stages going about their everyday activities: eating, sleeping, going to work, doing their shopping, eating out, making mistakes, avoiding dealing with their problems, struggling financially, living with domestic strife, getting into arguments and fights, getting drunk or high, having occasional and mostly awkward sex, going on holiday and work trips, feeling bored and wasting time, indulging in inane hobbies, and trying to find ways of coping in general.

While few minimalist narratives engage discursively with political events, the tension between what minimalists choose to reveal and to withhold is itself of ideological significance, delineating the conditions under which politics is made present by its conspicuous absence.

According to McGurl, '[i]f there is a politics of minimalism … it would appear to be a negative politics, a politics of silence – a resistance, perhaps, to media overstimulation or maybe just the silencing … of the voice of the lower-middle class worker'.[142] Yet, if it is true that minimalism is written in 'the vernacular of the dispossessed, mainly white, lower middle- and working-classes',[143] it would be an error to assume that this implies a narrow field of concerns: '[e]ven within their collections', Clark points out, '[minimalists] write about the working class, college professors, teachers and a number of other people who do not seem to *do* anything'.[144] Still, despite a clear concern with individual and social vulnerability, and the economically precarious conditions of everyday life, minimalist fictions of the late twentieth all too often unfold in a conservative, white, hetero-patriarchal world with little sustained attention given to the politics of racial, cultural and sexual difference.[145]

Yet there is considerably more at work politically in this fiction than the reification through literary language of conservative norms; and to come to grips with the politics of minimalism it is necessary to return to the ways in which political and ethical possibilities are encoded in the forms and tropes of literary writing, intensified by the precise diction, transparent syntax and parsimonious style of minimalism, and actualized by the encounter of reading. Minimalist prose is remarkable for its capacity simultaneously to resist and to respond to the reader. In an initial encounter with a minimalist text, the reader is typically drawn very rapidly along the narrative surface, presented with a realism of considerable immediacy that seems to require little or no interpretation. Yet these texts are also punctuated by strategic interruptions – repetitions of words and phrases, dialogical non-sequiturs, and sudden shifts in tone – which suspend linear reading, functioning as ciphers for a multiplicity of potential meaning brought to the surface by a sustained encounter with the literary work.

For example, in Raymond Carver's short story, 'Fat' – an early piece, originally published in *Harper's Bazaar* in 1971 and later as the opening story of Carver's first major collection, *Will You Please Be Quiet, Please?* in 1976 – a waitress relates an encounter with a customer she describes as 'the fattest person I have ever seen'[146] to her friend, Rita. Her account is structured in one sense around the sequence of his ordering and eating a massive quantity of food, but in another by the parallel narrative of the abusive relationship (with Rudy) which threateningly shadows all her interactions, events which together act as ciphers for a deeply problematic gender and sexual politics on one hand, and for more implicitly political issues of conspicuous consumption and the dubious connection it claims to maintain between actual freedom and the freedom of choice on the other. Having given the customer 'plenty of time to make up his mind',[147] he chooses to order an unusually large number of dishes from the menu. As the man consumes course after course, it becomes clear that both freedom and choice have given way to compulsion. Carver uses the familiar minimalist technique of incremental repetition to emphasize this shift, gradually accumulating subtle details around the repeated verbal module *like this* to mark the shift: 'We don't often enjoy bread like this'[148] becomes 'Believe me … we don't eat like this all the time',[149] and eventually, 'Believe it or not … we have not always eaten like this.'[150]

In this way, Carver's measured exposition of the everyday reveals a micro-political situation in which the figure of the consumer has become so dependent on the cycle of production and consumption that need and superfluity, desire and satisfaction, pleasure and guilt, can no longer be told apart. The waitress finds herself equally bound by the economy of the situation: after all, her position as a waitress is defined by her ability to facilitate consumption, so it is not surprising that she is quick to reassure him that she 'like[s] to see a man eat and enjoy himself'.[151] Carver's minimalist fiction here offers itself as an early parable of the rise of neoliberalism with its concomitant recoding of the so-called free market in terms of the freedom of consumer choice.[152] Yet, choice proves illusory, paradoxical: there is no choice other than to choose *more of everything*. Yet *more of everything* in fact comes to signify *more of less*, and it is significant that food – so often regarded as a so-called basic commodity – should be at the heart of this broken calculus. Any sense of intrinsic value, determined in the first instance by hunger or need, is transformed into pure excess. Yet this excess no longer satisfies even basic needs, but rather intensifies the need it was intended to meet: it traps the customer, and more indirectly the waitress, in a cycle of compulsive consumption progressively stripped of function and offering not even the residuum of pleasure.

The posing of larger social, political or ideological questions through the dispassionate narration of apparently unremarkable events – and here again it is worth remembering that a very different analysis would emerge by focusing on the experience of heteropatriarchal violence reflected in the waitress's narrative – is characteristic of a great deal of minimalist writing. The invisible prison of gendered norms concealed in the routine of Hempel's miniature, 'Housewife', and the subtle indictment of inequality moving silently through the brief scene of pleasant country life in Davis's 'Workingmen', are two of many examples. Returning to Carver's *oeuvre*, 'Vitamins', 'Collectors', and 'Elephant' all address social and economic precarities of various kinds, focusing attention on the extreme and detrimental effects of a lack or loss of work on everyday lives, and the accelerated pathologies and strained relationships in which they culminate. There is an unambiguously ethical dimension to Carver's minimalism, which, recalling Miller's assertion that the ethical force of literature is located precisely in the event of reading itself,[153] is intensified by the formal transparency and stylistic austerity of his stories which provide an 'aesthetic framework of experience which allows readers a chance to come to ethical understandings of their own'.[154] It is precisely in their ability to evoke the everyday experience of the reader through the everyday experience of their characters, that the particularity of these stories is itself a species of the universal. As McGurl avers, 'literary minimalism finds its objectivity and universality [in the fact that everyone] want[s] to be fully human, prized for their very existence in the world and unalienated in the labor that enables them to survive in it'.[155]

In this way, minimalist fiction demonstrates that the disparity in scale between the micro-political sphere of the everyday and the macro-political sphere of ideology does not indicate an absolute rift between the two, but rather the necessity of the encounter in reconciling these toward the possibility of the universal. 'It is in the political *void* that the encounter must come about',[156] according to Althusser, and what bars Carver's characters, and by extension the reader, from exercising substantial political agency is precisely the missed encounter, the encounter which is not recognized as such.[157] In this light, anticipation takes on a particular significance. The force of anticipation directs itself towards the immanence of the encounter, yet it emerges from a relation to the imminence of a 'future-to-come',[158] to recall Derrida's celebrated phrase. It is in this sense that anticipation, like a spectre, 'presents itself only as that which could come or come back'.[159] Anticipation belongs to a tentative politics of hope, a 'pledge … given here and now, even before, perhaps, decision confirms it',[160] which steers the political subject towards the possibility of change. In the final lines of 'Fat', the waitress opposes her own sense of anticipation to the sense of expectation she detects in her friend Rita, who expects a decisive twist to the story of her encounter: '[s]he sits there waiting, her dainty fingers poking her hair. *Waiting for what?* I'd like to know. It is August. My life is going to change. I feel it.'[161] As McGurl notes, 'the usual disposition of Carver's characters, as of his narrators, is not one of hopelessness, exactly, but rather of wariness and waiting'.[162] Yet, here, Carver exposes two distinct species of waiting: where expectation directs the present towards a specific future, anticipation retains an indeterminacy, a receptiveness to an indefinite future. Anticipation is vigilance towards the possibility of the encounter; it is vigilance towards the possibility of a different future, and a political waiting for the transfigurative event.

This is not, therefore, merely a 'passive waiting for transformation',[163] as Saltzman would have it; nor an example of how '[v]erbal passivity is a close relative of passivity of action',[164] in Nessett's estimation. Rather, the 'hint of revelation'[165] that moves through the story – arising from the encounter, and subtracting from the indifferent inertia of the everyday a sense of anticipation – constitutes a minimal means of bridging the micro-political sphere of the alienated individual with the macro-political community. This subtle trajectory is opened up by the attention Carver draws to the customer's repeated use of the first-person plural, *we*, to describe himself, 'as though he needed to measure up verbally to his size',[166] yet which also 'evokes … a kind of complicity, a victimization common to the fat man and waitress both'.[167] *We* marks the manifestation of a minimal micro-political community, a shared but limited orientation towards events that transcend the limits of the present. *We* describes the situation in which consumer and labourer are knotted together by the dictates of the market. *We* outlines a world dominated by a vague yet pervasive determinism in which 'there is no choice'.[168] It is precisely in this mundane world, a world always veering towards stagnation, in which people are compelled to persist in cycles of meaningless and pleasureless production and consumption, and in which human interaction is marked by underarticulated resentments and automatic rituals, that the implicit politics of anticipation discovers its charge.

Yet anticipation here is not utopian. It is the beginning of a response to the ethical demand that the unassimilability of the customer to the regular order of things exercises on the waitress. It is no coincidence that, as their encounter continues, the waitress becomes increasingly aware that 'this is not the whole story';[169] that this face-to-face encounter has exceeded her initial expectation, giving rise instead to a sense of anticipation. By 'resist[ing] possession',[170] the 'epiphany of the face is ethical',[171] in Levinas's celebrated formulation; it constitutes a point of transcendence in the very midst of persistence, an encounter with alterity which is registered by the waitress as 'a feeling [which] comes over me'.[172] Although no material change is evident, the story emphasizes a shift towards potentiality: anticipation is the precursor of a transfigurative event which may arise, against expectation, in the generally eventless continuum of the everyday. To the extent that minimalism is able to evoke anticipation as ethico-political affect, it offers a tentative bridge between the micro-political sphere of the habitually depoliticized subject of neoliberal late capitalism and the macro-political sphere in which larger ideological questions of political subjectivity and agency might be interrogated. The insight that minimalist literature in particular seems to offer, finally, is that we always find ourselves at the threshold of potentially significant events, since there is no essential discontinuity between the remarkable and the unremarkable, the epiphanic and the everyday.

Once more it is necessary to consider the existential paradox that it is persistence that marks the possibility of change. The persistent movement of isolated individuals performing specific functions in clearly defined spaces – not unlike the laminar flow of particles in the Lucretian cosmology upon which Althusser draws – persists in a state of muted anticipation of encounters, crossings, accidents and events. For the epiphanic or transfigurative moment to arise, anticipation must itself be charged with a certain potentiality, lest the aleatory encounter, when it takes place, be reabsorbed into the undifferentiated continuum of everyday occurrence, as is so often the case. Although it is a vast exaggeration to claim that minimalism is invariably political, the specific vision of politics it makes possible is of a singular value precisely because it clarifies the taking-place of the political, while itself taking-place at the peripheries of what might normally be regarded as a political aesthetic.

3

Objecthood: On the Materialism of Minimalism

3.1 Objects

Minimalism and theoretical objecthood: Steve Reich's *Clapping Music* (1972)

Entities, things and objects are distinguished from one another by the increasingly complex relationship they have to the world in which they exist. While an *entity* simply describes a phenomenon that persists over a period of time, a *thing* describes an entity that exists independently in a particular world. An *object*, meanwhile, describes a thing that exists in a particular world in relation to a subject, or, according to certain views, in relation to other objects. As Heidegger notes, the thing 'stand[s] on its own … as something that is self-supporting, or independent … A self-supporting thing may become an object if we place it before us, whether in immediate perception or by bringing it to mind in a recollective re-presentation.'[1] Although this distinction has been repeatedly refined and contested, it remains compelling in its recognition that agency and relation are at the heart of objecthood: an object is 'what stands forth',[2] whereas as thinghood is marked by its 'presencing',[3] its coming into the peculiar intensity of its own presence in the world. In a significant sense, minimalism occupies the threshold between thing and object, between its own presence and its being made present to a subject. In this way, the minimalist object exists in a state of potentiality: it is not fully what it is. In being neither fully a thing nor fully an object, the minimalist work is able to exist in the world as both. It is autonomous and independent, yet always already woven into the context in which its autonomy is recognized as such. Minimalist objecthood does not offer a definitive response, but rather poses itself as question. While Heidegger is emphatic in his assertion that humans generate a world in which to dwell, that animals merely occupy a world, and that material objects exist in a world but are themselves fundamentally worldless,[4] numerous more recent thinkers, among them Bruno Latour, argue that objects participate in producing the world in which they exist,[5] '[t]heir action … much more varied, their influence more ubiquitous, their effect much more ambiguous, their presence much more distributed'[6] than is often admitted.

Objecthood is central to every form of minimalism, and manifests in diverse and at times contradictory ways. Although it is possible to distinguish between material objects such as sculptures, temporal objects such as musical performances, and conceptual objects such as Dadaist and Neo-Dadaist happenings, in practice a great number of minimalist objects exist in an intermediary state in which their material, temporal and conceptual elements implicate one another in a generative process. Minimalist narrative fiction, for example, clearly involves material text, the conceptual space of the storyworld and the temporal processes of writing and reading; and even massive sculptures such as Richard Serra's reveal considerable conceptual nuance and temporal intricacy in the various processes to which they are subject: conception, production, assembly, weathering, perception. Minimalist objects problematize their own objecthood, and it is for this reason that it becomes necessary to theorize objecthood itself alongside minimalism. These are objects that prompt theoretical reflection; objects in search of a theory. Indeed, Lyotard suggests that 'rules and categories are what the work of art itself is looking for',[7] and although this may be an overstatement in the case of minimalism, there is no question that many minimalist works belong to the category Hubert Damisch and Mieke Bal refer to as theoretical objects: objects that 'oblige [us] to do theory but also furnish [us] with the means to do it'.[8]

Recognizing that the process of interpreting an object begins the moment it is perceived,[9] the question arises as to how it might be possible to treat an object on its own terms,[10] to gain access to objecthood prior to perception and interpretation. Is it possible for a theory of objecthood to begin with the object rather than the subject? Theory, at its simplest, provides a way of seeing the world that emerges from the peculiar human capacity for self-reflexivity, for observing observation.[11] In this sense it is essentially a way of gaining perspective, of 'stand[ing] back … to form second-order judgements about the world and our own behaviour in it'.[12] The challenge, then, is to return to the object as the source rather than the *telos* of theory. The theoretical object, as explained by Bal, offers a particularly promising means of synthesizing the material, theoretical and meta-theoretical spheres.[13] Theoretical objects are ordinarily artworks or other cultural artefacts that provoke numerous and often contradictory responses.[14] In concert with Latour's actor-network theory,

Graham Harman's object-oriented ontology, and Bill Brown's thing theory, Bal's conception of theoretical objecthood calls for a sustained reappraisal of the role of objects in cultural politics and production.[15] Of particular interest is Bal's emphasis on theoretical objects as the carriers of cultural memory,[16] possessing the singular capacity to draw together apparently incommensurable transcultural and transhistorical narratives.[17] In this sense, the theoretical object leans towards the flexibility and adaptability that Wolfgang Iser terms *soft theory*, and that differs notably from the hard theory of laws and protocols, deductively formed and applied with the aim of prediction.[18]

In the case of minimalism, the soft theory of theoretical objects needs to account for works that habitually reject or limit referentiality, resist theorization,[19] and instead appeal to the blunt facticity of the real. A musical example, Steve Reich's *Clapping Music*, illustrates the problem well. Of all Reich's phasing compositions – his early works in which two or more identical musical fragments are repeated, and in the course of these repetitions, progressively displaced in relation to one another until they return to their initial position – *Clapping Music* is arguably the most minimal. Where earlier phasing compositions contained melodic material written for a specific instrument, here both melody and instrument are subtracted, leaving only rhythm produced directly by the human body, the act of clapping being perhaps the most immediate of all percussive gestures. Yet in the midst of almost transparent simplicity, this minimalist composition generates sufficient ambiguity to complicate efforts to impose order, to render it docile, its basic rhythmic material 'throw[ing] not only placement within the metre but metre itself into doubt … The listener can thus hear the complete pattern in a variety of ways.'[20] In this sense, the work exceeds the regulative framework that a formal analysis or theoretical account seeks to impose, and it is for this reason that writing elaborately on minimalism often proves prodigiously difficult. As this excess emerges, so it also becomes apparent that *Clapping Music* is a theoretical object, prompting speculation but resisting categorization – an object in search of a theory.

Two iconoclastic essays are particularly useful in addressing this aspect of minimalist objecthood: Susan Sontag's 'Against Interpretation', and Stephen Knapp and Walter Benn Michaels's 'Against Theory'. In a significant sense these essays, although very different, constitute a curious species of minimalism – a minimalist criticism advocating minimal intervention in the interpretation of works, and reinvesting faith in the autonomy of the work and its capacity to delineate the terms of its own interpretation. Targeting the manner in which interpretation becomes rapidly institutionalized and governed by normative protocols,[21] Sontag contends that the great error in critical practice lies in the reduction of art to content, since this content then encourages an univocal language of interpretation that 'impoverishes',[22] 'tames'[23] and 'violates'[24] art, preventing us from undertaking the real task of criticism, which is '*to show how it* [the artwork] *is what it is*, even *that it is what it is*, rather than to show *what it means*'.[25] Knapp and Michaels, on the other hand, target theory itself: 'the theoretical impulse … always involves the attempt to separate things that should not be separated: on the ontological side, meaning from intention …; on the epistemological side, knowledge from true belief'.[26] Theory should be abandoned because, finally, it amounts to no more than the set of strategies people have employed to evade their direct responsibility to the work itself.[27]

Despite numerous and possibly irreconcilable differences,[28] Sontag shares with Knapp and Michaels a common desire to radicalize our relation to art, allowing art to resonate on its own terms. They agree that it is theory, broadly speaking, that attempts to appropriate the objects of art. For both, resistance emerges through a vehement anti-institutionalism, a suspicion of method, and an affirmation of the ontological autonomy of art.[29] Art may have any number of effects, yet these are fundamental to its practice and not products of a theory that precedes and informs its practice.[30] In this light, it is not that the minimalist object obviates the need for theory, but rather that it is able to generate the conditions in which it is able to produce its own theory as a theoretical object. This claim rests on a simple recognition: to encounter a minimalist object as it is, affirms the fact that it is. To grasp an object in terms of the fact that it is, is to grasp it in terms of its facticity – the singular existential intensity that is its own – and such facticity gestures towards the essence of art, in Sontag's estimation.[31]

Minimalist theoretical objects seek to expose what Sontag recognizes as 'the luminousness of the thing in itself, of things being what they are'.[32] This is far from the abstract position that Greenberg famously described as 'too much a feat of ideation, and not enough anything else'.[33] In Greenberg's analysis, minimalism falls prey to its own 'ratiocination',[34] to the extent that we are confronted not with the sheer presence to which minimalist objects pretend,[35] but merely with the idea of presence, so that 'what they want to mean betrays them artistically'.[36] Yet if minimalism's objects are, for the most part, theoretical objects, it is precisely because their material, temporal and conceptual elements combine in a way that disrupts the imposition of any hard theory, to recall Iser's distinction. To grasp minimalist objecthood more clearly, it is necessary to interrogate that which mediates between theoretical abstraction and manifest objecthood: form.

3.2 Form

The architecture of objecthood: Sol LeWitt's *Incomplete Open Cubes* (1974) Frank Stella's *Tomlinson Court Park* (1967) Teju Cole's *Seven Short Stories About Drones* (2013)

Form is both immanent and transcendental: it describes that which has form and that which gives form; the structures that allow objects to cohere in existence, and the meta-structure that allows structures themselves to cohere.[37] Traditionally, form frames content, providing the means by which the material, temporal and conceptual aspects of a work are able to cohere as a singular object. The significance of form is intensified in the case of minimalism, since for many of its most characteristic works *form is content*. Sol LeWitt's *Incomplete Open Cubes*[38] is exemplary in this respect. A remarkable work, this serial sculpture exists in three forms exhibited together: a three-dimensional form in which 122 permutations of an open cubic structure are arranged in various series; a two-dimensional form in which photographs of these cubes are placed on the wall surrounding the sculpture's three-dimensional form; and in a conceptual form, as a book containing the overall conceptual scheme and design.[39] LeWitt's sculpture develops what Lippard recognizes as 'the intuitive side of mathematical thought, setting up order and then disturbing it into growth'.[40] In doing so, LeWitt's cubes significantly extend the logic of one of minimalism's central maxims: Frank Stella's claim that 'only what can be seen there *is* there'.[41] In *Incomplete Open Cubes* it is possible to see both less and more than what is there: these are, after all, incomplete cubes, and yet their incompletion in itself enhances the serial nature of the work, asking the viewer to retrace and to test LeWitt's permutation and patterning of a fundamental building block. The sculptural units themselves are notable for the way in which they systematically calculate, transform, and intensify ordinary sculptural space. Their form functions both to generate and to structure space.

A similar sense of formal intensification is evident in many of Stella's celebrated black paintings. In *Tomlinson Court Park*,[42] for instance, a series of thin, white rectangles on a black canvas reproduce the shape of the canvas, growing smaller towards the canvas's centre. Here, again, it becomes evident how canonical minimalism is poised between the formalist tradition of Bauhaus, *De Stijl* and Constructivism on one hand, and the colour fields of the monochromatic tradition on the other.[43] Stella's work constitutes a 'classicizing reaction'[44] to his immediate predecessors: place is abstracted to shape, the work containing itself in its most essential geometric and chromatic qualities. The central formal concern of the work is 'the relationship of [its] … internal structure and its bounding shape',[45] which, in this case, is the canvas. For Foster, by '[f]orc[ing] the picture (or depicted shape) into near coincidence with the picture support (or literal shape)',[46] Stella's work undertakes an uneasy negotiation of literalism, to recall Fried's term, and illusionism; a negotiation between the artist's desire to 'keep the paint as good as it was in the can',[47] and the fact that dynamic differences are revealed depending on which area, line or space of the painting the viewer's attention falls.[48] From one perspective the painting is marked by a sense of inward movement from the edge of the canvas towards the elongated central rectangle, exemplifying the formal property that Fried describes as 'deductive structure': it is from the shape of the canvas that the movement of the shrinking rectangular shapes towards the centre of the canvas is deduced. From another perspective, however, these rectangles race outward, pointing toward the corners of the canvas and beyond, thus perpetuating the disjunction between the pictorial plane and that of the wall, despite the absence of a frame. From yet another perspective, the expansion and contraction of these rectangles also acquire depth: the central rectangle at once draws the viewer towards an unspecified depth – an objectal[49] instantiation of infinite regress, perhaps – and also presents the apex of a pyramidal structure as viewed from above.

As a theoretical object, Stella's painting offers a number of ways in which its form might be perceived and interpreted, yet it does not comply with any particular view. That we 'understand the object better *on its* – the object's – *own terms*',[50] is central to the minimalist aesthetic vision; and what *Tomlinson Court Park* reveals in this regard, is that the formal aspects of minimalism, contrary to expectation, are both transparent *and* ambiguous. Finally, it is a commitment to objecthood that marks minimalism's drive to formal innovation. In the visual arts, '[t]he rejection of mimesis and reference, and concomitant emphasis on materiality, led artists and critics to the notion of objecthood',[51] observes Colpitt. 'To refer to the work of art as an object … meant that it was a nonrepresentational, concrete, and real thing existing in the world, without illusion or formal prototype.'[52]

Although objecthood often proves an ambiguous proposition, there are nonetheless certain formal concerns, processes, and techniques widely used or adapted across a range of aesthetic media in the pursuit of minimalist objecthood. Perhaps most ubiquitous among these is the simplification, reduction, or even elimination of relation: the relation between the parts that constitute an object, the relation between parts and the whole, and the relation of parts and wholes to the context in which they appear. Relation, in turn, is intimately connected to questions of scale, while scale – whether large or small – is one of the principal means by which minimalist objects seek to communicate a sense of their immanence or presence. Scale, in brief, is a relative measure of both spatial and temporal quantity – a relation of size and of duration that can apply to the object itself, as well as to the contexts of its production and reception. The external relation of parts or the whole of a work to other works or the context in which they exist, is the most common means of conceptualizing external scale, which can be defined in this light as the measure of an object in relation to other objects. The internal relation of parts to one another, or parts to the whole of a work, determines the internal sense of scale. This is often grasped in terms of proportion: a well-proportioned work is one in which the parts are arranged in such way that they offer minimal resistance to the work existing with a maximal intensity.[53]

In the visual arts, for example, the internal relation of elements involves the 'ordering of pictorial or sculptural parts'[54] within the work itself, including the relation of figure to ground and of the image or other content to the shape of the canvas or other type of support, and the relation of unit to unit in sculpture.[55] The emphasis in minimalism on nonrelational internal composition stipulates that 'individual parts and elements play a subordinate role to the overall form of the work. It is not that elements are necessarily eliminated, but rather that the idiosyncratic or dynamic relationships between them are expended'.[56] The most radical exposition of this principle arrives in monochromatic painting, exemplified most obviously in the invariant colour fields of painters such as Brice Marden, Robert Mangold, Robert Ryman and Jo Baer, or, indeed, the earlier generation of Yves Klein or Ad Reinhardt. Such fields of colour contain no parts as such,[57] except for slight shifts in chromatic intensity produced by minimal variations in the hues of pigment, retaining a subtle sense of tonal movement. They demonstrate the capacity for unified fields of colour to reinforce the sense of objecthood for which the minimalist work strives. Yet we might also consider a far busier minimalism with respect to nonrelational composition, exhibited in paintings such as Stella's *Delaware Crossing*, a work comprising a chevron design which, because it is deployed in perfect symmetry and pointing inwards, serves not to complicate the painting, but to focus the perceiver's attention on the centre of the canvas, reinforcing, indeed containing, the work in its singularity.

Judd claimed that in his work 'the parts are unrelational … [W]hen you start relating parts … you're assuming you have a vague whole … and definite parts, which is all screwed up, because you should have a definite whole and maybe no parts, or very few.'[58] Echoing these sentiments in concrete form, much canonical minimalist sculpture concerns itself with the creation of autonomous, self-contained objects.[59] Where works consist of more than one identical part – here we might consider Judd's serial sculptures which usually consist of repeated forms, mostly uniform in colour, size and material, but occasionally with variations – the object remains nonrelational in the sense that the relation of unit to unit is one of duplication emphasizing quantity rather than any particular qualitative dynamism. The case with sculptures that consist of multiple non-identical parts – some of LeWitt's serial works belong to this category, as do Morris's polyhedrons – of course involve a more ambiguous relation of parts or units.

Equivalent techniques can be observed in minimalist music. The extreme limitations of material in Young's *Trio*[60] give its parts, and the relationships that slowly develop between them, a sense of coherence – its form a carefully contained arch using the smallest number of notes possible. A similar observation can be made of Steve Reich's phasing technique: two or more melodic lines begin an identical melody in unison, then gradually shift out of phase at specific intervals, creating a series of unexpected and gripping melodic and pulse variations. Phasing distends time, stretching rather than containing the form as its internal parts move against one another. This processual torsion is cyclical and finally affirms, rather than undermines, the integrity of the composition.

Both minimalist poetry and prose radicalize the conventions of how literary parts relate to one another and to the work as a whole, converging to produce a sense of literary objecthood. This is especially clear in a great deal of concrete poetry, and the case is particularly well made by Aram Saroyan's celebrated poetic grapheme,[61] an untitled poster-poem that consists solely of an expanded letter *m* with four rather than three legs and three rather than two curves. Although it resembles a letter, it refuses to function as one, resisting incorporation in the regular economy of language in order to emerge with renewed visibility as an icon for the concreteness of writing itself. Focusing more closely on the internal relation of literary parts themselves, Claus Bremer's 'rendering the legible illegible' uses these four words of its title and opening line as its basic material, with its subsequent three lines formed as these same words are progressively overlapped until the poem achieves what it set out as its programme in its first line: illegibility. Yet despite the illegibility of the final line, the poetic process itself remain eminently legible, and so clarifies the relation of parts and the manner in which these converge to constitute what is readily recognizable as a theoretical object.

The condition of objecthood in narrative fiction is considerably more complicated. Of course it is possible to represent material objects with meticulous verbal detail, and to generate analogies between these textual objects and the objecthood of the text. Yet the fact that narrative, particularly in the realist mould of minimalism, ordinarily points outside of the text, means that regardless of how carefully coordinated its internal parts may be, objecthood will more often than not be a question of reference rather than self-reference. The preference in minimalist narrative for 'discontinuous devices, arbitrary and open endings, interplay of surface details,[62] narrative omissions, and anti-linear plots'[63] together represent a substantial departure from the norm that governs earlier realist fiction. This is evident in the eclectic routes to reduction followed by Chekhov, Hemingway, Robbe-Grillet and Beckett, alongside the canonical minimalism of Carver, Hempel, Beattie, Barthelme or Robison, and is continued in much blank fiction, experimental reductionism, neo-naturalism, and what is increasingly being termed *the new sincerity*. Such reduction should not carelessly be conflated with 'the quotidian, the utilitarian, and the non-artistic',[64] Foster emphasizes, but rather marks a 'reorientation'[65] and, as Alexander suggests, a 'mission of recovery'.[66] The everyday, far from an empty zone of existence, is a sign of the 'deep surfaces'[67] that move through minimalist writing, giving rise to a maximal realism pursued by minimal means.[68]

What distinguishes minimalist narrative prose from poetry is as much a question of scale as it is of style. Scale in Carver's writing, for instance, is determined not only by its brevity, but more especially by a sense of the unity of the work, by a careful arrangement of its parts achieved by a 'balance between inclusion and exclusion'.[69] This focus on unity expresses what Hallett identifies as a parallel poetics of minimalism and the short story[70] – recalling with Linda Hutcheon that a poetics in this sense describes a position that seeks to integrate theory and practice[71] – and is intensified even further in the most radical theoretical objects of microfiction. As a genre, microfiction is often excluded from the canon of minimalism,[72] yet its works consistently interrogate minimum, or the least possible, in terms of the extremities of scale, its effects, and their relation to a conception of literary objecthood. The term microfiction describes a diverse and transhistorical range of short forms – aphorism, parable, fragment, digression, epigram, fable, sketch, prose poem and miniature among them – connected by a shared commitment to minimal scale as a route to maximal intensity.[73] The precise point at which short fiction becomes microfiction, which is also the point at which quantity becomes the principal quality of the work, has proven stubbornly elusive. Definite quantitative markers – the number of words, pages, hyperlinks or screens – prove inadequate to this task. The degree of brevity, as Norman Friedman recognizes, rests on a principle of parsimony which stipulates that a story ought not 'exceed … the needs of [its] effect'.[74] A shift in scale is marked by a shift in intensity: microfiction is 'like most ordinary stories, *only more so*'.[75] One common technique is to write works in which the physical and temporal scale of the work are aligned, so that the duration of the narrative event represented in the story closely matches the time it is likely to take to read the story itself.[76]

More extreme still, are those microfictions that limit themselves to only a few words: Richard Kostelanetz's *Microstories* – 'Even the happiest love stories end in death',[77] for example – seldom exceed a single sentence; Jim Crace ends his cycle, *The Devil's Larder*, with the two-word miniature, 'oh honey';[78] while Lydia Davis is a master of enigmatic miniatures, such as 'Index Entry', which reads 'Christian, I'm not a'.[79] Teju Cole's twitter fiction, *Seven Short Stories About Drones*,[80] consists of a series of short tweets, each beginning with the opening line of a canonical novel, and continued in a sudden transposition to a contemporary setting in which the brutal futility of drone warfare is exposed. The tweet represents perhaps the smallest narrative unit in contemporary literary culture, and this technology is deployed by Cole to draw attention not only to the ever-increasing discontinuity between the Western cultural imaginary and the brutal geopolitical reality that supports it, but also to the ambiguous role of technology with respect to the understanding of literary objecthood. As N. Katherine Hayles recognizes, '[w]hen literature leaps from one medium to another … it does not leave behind the accumulated knowledge imbedded in genres, poetic conventions, narrative structures, figurative tropes and so forth'.[81] In this light, although conceived within the constraints of a social media platform that habitually devolves into a continuum of disposable thought, Cole's stories also enter into a complex dialogue regarding form and genre, intratextual tensions and intertextual connections, that transect numerous cultures and histories. Far from a vanishing verbal trace, these works are immediately distributed rather than dispersed – repeated, retweeted, anthologized – drawing attention to the many ways in which they complicate rather than negate questions of material, temporal, and conceptual objecthood. As their parts are at once localized and distributed, these miniatures mark a significant shift in emphasis from the internal relation of parts to one another, to the external relation of the work to the contexts in which it manifests.

3.3 Immanence

Presence and scale: Steve Reich's *Four Organs* (1970) Barnett Newman's *Cathedra* (1951)

Perhaps the most radical type of aesthetic object is one that not only eschews reference, but in so doing lays claim to absolute autonomy, a realness indifferent to its perception. Many minimalist works pursue this species of objecthood, yet it would be an error to mistake indifference for rejection: in practice, even the most apparently autonomous works are imbricated in complex processes of perception and interpretation. Indifference in this sense refers to a work that draws attention to the internal relation of its parts – to the work as an event of self-contained self-disclosure – rather than to the elimination of external relations. Few minimalist works fail to recognize, even to encode, the radically constructive role of perception in the constitution of objecthood. With respect to the visual arts, Colpitt suggests that minimalism reveals 'a new focus on relationships struck across and within the space between the spectator and the object of perception'.[82] The consequences of this relationship are by no means unambiguous, however. For Fried, the theatricality of minimalism is fundamentally detrimental to the fortunes of art,[83] a view that derives from his understanding that the literalist object deprives the perceiver of the capacity *not* to respond to it:[84] 'inasmuch as the literalist work *depends on* the beholder, is *incomplete* without him, it *has* been waiting for him.'[85] As Michaels notes, 'in Fried's account of Minimalism, the object exists on its own all right; what depends on the beholder is only the experience'. The act of perception does not negate the facticity of the object, as such, although, for Michaels, 'it is the *experience* instead of the *object* that Minimalism values'.[86] Yet to the extent that the general minimalist programme asserts that the aesthetic object is equal, rather than superior, to the perceiver, Fried's argument tends towards overstatement. Indeed, many minimalists 'consider … perception in phenomenological terms, as somehow before or outside history, language, sexuality, and power'.[87]

Objecthood and the experience of objecthood meet in the notion of presence, or immanence. The external relations of a minimalist work ultimately describe the conditions under which the work is immanent to a particular spatial and temporal situation – its environment or context – and, moreover, in relation to a perceiver. Colpitt holds that 'there are no exhibited, formal clues to signal the existence of presence, since it is felt, *responded to*, rather than *recognised*'.[88] Presence, in this light, offers itself as a measure of external scale – a contract between object, perceiver, context and environment[89] – that is at once a testimony to the radical, impassive, quantitative dimension of being – the real – and the manner in which the real renders itself intelligible in terms of minimalist objects that reach out into the experiential world. Colpitt recognizes that, '[l]ike presence, the ingredients of scale cannot be *pre*scribed'.[90] The most suitable scale for a minimalist work of any medium is the one that reveals the immanence of its objecthood with the greatest clarity. Indeed, as Fried notes, minimalists 'want … to achieve presence through objecthood, which requires a certain largeness of scale, rather than through size alone'.[91]

Historically, aesthetic judgments regarding physical and temporal scale have been predominantly anthropocentric, the human body or the human experience of time taken as the immanent ground for differentiating greater from lesser, principally in terms of size and duration in the visual arts and music respectively, and in terms of representation in literature. In minimalist aesthetics, these range from virtually microscopic works such as Hagop Sandaldjian's *Mt. Ararat on a Grain of Rice* to John Cage's *Organ²/ASLSP (As SLow aS Possible)* currently being played in a performance scheduled to last for 639 years, ending in the year 2640. Both extremes of scale are instantiations of the infinitesimal: the former, in terms of maximal material compressed into the smallest possible space – a mountain engraved on a grain of rice; the latter, in terms of minimal material sounded over a maximal duration – a few chords in eight sections spread over hundreds of years. Cage's work is an aesthetic example of what Timothy Morton calls a *hyperobject* – 'a very large finitude'[92] that is 'massively distributed in time and space relative to humans'[93] – and offers a vision of objecthood in which maximalism and minimalism are effectively indistinguishable.

This is often the case in works of extended duration, including the drone works and sound sculptures of Young, Oliveros, Budd, Eno, Maxfield, Niblock or López. In these works, the sonic continuum far exceeds the human capacity to deduce unity through any act or process of perception as such, and the sense of immanence that moves through these works seems to be precisely a question of immersion, making a case for a type of minimalist objecthood that is independent of the capacity of perception to deduce clear limits or structures. The sense of immanence that emerges from the music of Riley, Reich, Glass and Adams, by contrast – composers who make use of the techniques of repetition Fink collectively terms *pulse-pattern minimalism*[94] – involves a different type of immersion in sound. Where drone music gradually draws the listener into its presence, pulse-pattern minimalism confronts the listener with a charged, pulsating wall of sound. Repetition and variation are subtly interwoven into the formal architecture of these works, generating an immanent field of continuous transformation, reinforcing a sense of presence as a touchstone of much minimalism.

The minimalist concern with immanence relates closely to what in traditional aesthetics is recognized in terms of the sublime: an immediacy of experience which commands attention precisely by threatening to overwhelm the integrity of the senses.[95] Sudden shifts in scale are among the principal markers of sublime immanence. In much minimalist drone music, this shift occurs negatively in terms of the impossibility of deducing any sort of teleological structure from within the sonic continuum of a drone, and the sudden sense of diminished agency this often occasions. In phase-pattern minimalism, despite its formal and processual transparency, the very fact that process generally comes to determine form, coupled with the fact such processes often undermine conventional expectations regarding harmonic progression and resolution, produces what Fink recognizes in terms of a 'sublime excess of teleology'[96] – a restless sense of going somewhere without ever getting there. In this way phase-pattern minimalism calls into question the anthropocentric scale of conventional Western art music which is ordinarily structured according to the 'timescale of individual (or cumulative) arcs of tension and release'.[97]

This is evident not only in drone works, but also in works structured by repetition, and perhaps clearest in works of considerable or indefinite duration. Young's *The Well-Tuned Piano*, which is of indefinite variable length but seldom less than five hours, generates an often overwhelming cloud of sound through which to explore the composer's conception of just intonation; while Glass's *Music in Twelve Parts* is a three- to four-hour repository of the full range of Glass's compositional techniques from the 1960s and early 1970s, remarkable for its sustained intensity yet clearly operating outside of any regular music teleology. Even apparently smaller works exhibit a similar capacity, often ending abruptly or decaying to a point of stasis. In Reich's *Four Organs*, for example, 'four electronic organs repeat the pitches of a single chord, gradually extending them so that, while the pulse remains intact, the music gives the impression of slowing down'.[98] The scale of the work is distinct not so much for its pure duration, but for how it transforms the human experience of duration, effecting a gradual suspension of temporal passage. *Four Organs* is a minimalist theoretical object asking fundamental questions about temporal passage and suggesting new ways in which time might be perceived.

In the visual arts a sense of sublime immanence is marked both temporally and materially. For Strickland, it is the hard edge painting of Kelly, consisting of various sequences of contrasting, vertical bands of colour, that 'introduces the elements of objecthood and immediacy into Minimalist art [through the] overt formal regularity [of its parts]'.[99] A more dramatic expression of the sublime arrives in Barnett Newman's massive monochromatic canvases such as Cathedra Newman's *Cathedra* – a work now famous for being vandalized, but an exceptional example of the dramatic intensity of the artist's *oeuvre*. A vast expanse of blue, bisected by a stark, white central zip, and a dark zip toward the far right of the work, *Cathedra* demonstrates how the 'agonism of field and zip'[100] reveals both a material discontinuity – the interruption of an invariant field of colour and the emergence of a chromatic rhythm – and the eruption of an event – a sublime opening to the outside of the canvas and the world of external relations. According to Lyotard, '[l]ike a flash of lightning in the darkness or a line on an empty surface [the zip] separates, divides, institutes a difference, makes tangible because of that difference, minimal though it may be, and therefore inaugurates, a sensible world'.[101] The zip, the sublime disruption, serves not only to intensify and clarify the realness of the work itself, but also to intensify reality beyond the work.

3.4 Medium

On migratory objecthood: Dan Flavin's *untitled (to the real Dan Hill) 1b* (1978)

The relation of the work to questions of inside and outside is intimately connected to its medium. Defined simply, a medium refers to the means by which information is conveyed. In being mediated, information is transformed into a message, invested with a teleological drive, situated between a point of origin and a point of arrival. In this sense, mediation is at once a process of conveyance and of transformation. A medium can be transparent or opaque, something that withdraws as it conveys a message; or it can be something that insists on its materiality, transforming or even becoming the message it conveys. Thus, for example, while minimalist narrative seeks to close the distance between the reality of the storyworld and the reality of the reader by rendering the literary medium transparent – an example of what Rancière terms the 'medium as neutral means'[102] – minimalist drone music does the opposite, taking invariant sound as both material and medium. It is an example of what Rancière terms the 'medium as specific substance',[103] adding a certain existential weight to Marshall McLuhan's famous maxim, 'the medium is the message'.[104] Yet, as Garrett Stewart notes, 'we cannot know in advance the terms by which innovation will lay claim to the habits of a medium even as it contests and revises them'.[105] In this light, for art to remain responsive to the demands of its context, it must be able to transgress the medium-specificity first prescribed in Gotthold Ephraim Lessing's *Laocoon*,[106] and which discovers its theoretical apotheosis in the work of Clement Greenberg.[107] In the search for an objecthood that reflects immediate presence and access to the real, the media of minimalism are marked by an adaptability that invariably measures the concrete and conceptual against one another.

This is nowhere clearer than in the light art of Dan Flavin, whose work is exemplary of a medial migrancy, manifesting across multiple media simultaneously, both through and as a process of mediation, or rather, *transmediation*. Through this process, Flavin's work generates a paradoxical space that is at once placeless – migratory, fugitive, atopian – and yet inextricable from the specificity of place. Migrating between the physicality of the light fixture, the insubstantiality of light itself, and the environment with which the light interacts, these works effect a 'transformation of painting and sculpture into a third medium that both transgresses and transcends the first two'.[108] Effecting a significant shift in the traditional parameters of the gallery, Flavin's work is exhibited in five principal ways: wall-mounted fixtures, in which the lights effectively occupy the space traditionally reserved for painting; free-standing works, in which the fixtures are associable with sculpture; fixtures that lean against walls, and particular corners, offering a point of conjunction for the pictorial and the sculptural; fixtures situated in order to draw attention to specific architectural features of the environment; and large-scale installations where the light appears intrinsic to the architecture itself, such as the celebrated installation at the Guggenheim Museum in New York.

In each of these cases, the objecthood of Flavin's work is revealed as multiply located, imbedded in the very process of migration from the physical light fixture to the light itself as it irradiates and illuminates space, to the environmental boundaries it encounters in the architectural space in which the fixtures are installed, other objects in these spaces, and the body of the viewer which, through its capacity to perceive and conceive, synthesizes the distributed materiality of the work *as a work*. Ambiguity regarding the physical, conceptual and perceptual location of the work is intrinsic to migratory objecthood.

Indeed, Flavin's work is so effective and affective precisely because it poses a fundamental challenge to the synthesizing capacity of perception, a distribution of sense that exceeds any ready grasp, yet still converges as an artwork that conveys a profound sense of its own immanence. As Tiffany Bell recognizes, '[j]ust as you cannot really delineate the material boundaries of a Flavin installation, you cannot pinpoint the precise moment of its making. The lights shine in a continuous present'.[109]

The corner piece, *untitled (to the real Dan Hill) 1b* (Figure 2),[110] exemplifies the aesthetic intensity characteristic of even the most austere of Flavin's works. In a slight variation of the primary palette, Flavin uses four bunched fluorescent fixtures – blue, green, pink and yellow; two facing forward and two backward. With the gallery lights dimmed or completely switched off, the work takes on the force of an event, its objecthood the product of a tense merging of light and space with the dynamic process of perception. The forward-facing fixtures themselves pulsate with intensity, blue to the left and green to the right. The gallery wall to the left is lit an intense blue, a continuum of hues that curve away from the fixture towards a midnight blue edge. To the right, the wall is a more uncertain palette of greens, washed over towards its edges by the blue reflected from the facing wall. In the corner, at the heart of the work, an aureole of blended yellow and pink light glows from the back-facing fixtures, yellow on the left and pink on the right. The sublime intensity of the work is the result of a complex sequence of transmediations: from object to light, from light to wall, from wall to illuminated space, and from illuminated space, through a process of perception, back to a condition of objecthood. Flavin's work is simultaneously constituted and deconstituted by a dissipation of energy, the irradiance and distribution of light as a medium in a particular space. In a significant sense, minimalist light art belongs to an aesthetic of the sublime. Its objecthood arises from an encounter with a potentially overwhelming formlessness that is given form through a particular sequence of conceptual and perceptual considerations that emerge in the process of transmediation. Close attention reveals at least six distinct stages in this regard: the production of the light fixtures; the conceptualization of the work; powering the fixtures; the irradiance of the fixtures; the physicality and limitations of the environment in which the irradiance occurs; and the perception of the work.

Flavin's use of premanufactured, commercial fixtures for all of his work situates the first stage of transmediation, that of production, outside the field of either the artist or the work itself, and in the processes of industrial manufacture. The emphasis on eliminating artistic facture and on making use of industrial techniques of production and premanufactured objects as basic constituent elements of a particular work became a hallmark of much minimalist visual art.[111] Flavin insisted that these fixtures retain their union labels,[112] in part for legal reasons, but also to emphasize that they mediate between the worlds of everyday utility and art. Indeed, with the gallery fully illuminated, Flavin's 'proposal' – the term he preferred to artwork,[113] as he did 'situation' to installation,[114] and 'exposition' to exhibition[115] – simply leans in a corner, a forgotten object from the 'netherworld of dada … non-referential abstraction'.[116] The work thus retains a sense of its externality and autonomy even as it is subsumed within an aesthetic world. The second stage of transmediation involves the conceptualization of the proposal or work, an intervention of the imagination on the basic material of the fixture. Flavin affirmed the formal significance of conception in the work taken as a whole by executing draughtsman-like plans of all of his works which were issued as certificates, doubling the work in a sense. Flavin's own use of the term *proposal* to describe his work in general is suggestive of the significance of conception in the migrating objecthood of his light art. Irrespective of whether a fluorescent fixture is used in a commercial context as a source of functional lighting, or, through its conceptualization, formation and perception, as fine art, it requires a material activation – it needs to be powered, the third stage in the transmediation of Flavin's work. This is distributed between the intentional act of switching the fixture on, and the subsequent flow of electricity through sealed tubes containing aragon and mercury that glow as they are electrified, causing the coated tubing of the fixtures to fluoresce and give off light of a particular colour or hue depending either on the phosphors themselves, or the pigment which coats the tubes.[117] Through its irradiance – the fourth stage of transmediation – the work extends itself considerably and extremely rapidly. Although certain hues are directed – blue and green forward, yellow and pink backward – by its very nature this radiance cannot be neatly separated or absolutely organized. Yet this light does encounter limits, most obviously those that form part of the physical environment in which the fixtures are situated. It is this fifth stage of transmediation through which Flavin's work discovers its peculiar intensity, its capacity to alter the experience of space. The contingent form of the work depends significantly on the concrete, physical aspects of its exhibitionary environment – the shape of the gallery, the walls it encounters, the degree to which the space is enclosed – but also on the existing light in this environment. As Meyer notes, the light of these works 'does not cover the wall, but exposes it',[118] revealing how 'the actual space of the room c[an] be disrupted and played with'.[119] The point at which the activity of perception effects a contingent synthesis of the various stages of transmediation – the sixth and final stage – is also the point at which process is transfigured into an artwork.

A great deal of minimalist light art functions similarly, overwhelming the senses even as it summons them together to witness a species of immanent yet insubstantial objecthood. Immersive works such as Turrell's *Breathing Light*[120] or Elíasson's *The Weather Project*[121] are exemplary in this respect, although it is worth considering more unpredictable and explosive examples such as Walter de Maria's celebrated *Lightning Field* in which four hundred steel poles, each over twenty feet tall, act as lightning conductors arranged over almost a square mile in New Mexico, harnessing and distributing massive amounts of electrical energy.[122] The significance of scale, and particularly the capacity of light art to manifest across significant, even massive spaces or expanses, as is the case here, immediately reconnects it to questions of the sublime and the capacity of art to erupt as novelty within the world, without a stable point of reference.

3.5 Nonreferentiality

Mimetic economy and minimalism: Ellsworth Kelly's *Spectrum IV* (1967) Robert Lax's 'is' (1962)

The traditional mimetic economy that connects form and content to a world outside of the artwork – the proposition that the value of art is intrinsically tied to its capacity for representation and reference – is significantly undermined by minimalist aesthetics. The minimalist understanding of form and process as substance, and the manner in which questions of medium and scale are focused towards the immanence of the artwork itself, suggest that minimalist objecthood is not primarily concerned with its capacity for representation or reference to an external reality. For minimalists, aesthetic objecthood is in itself eminently real. This is not to suggest that minimalism is necessarily nonrepresentational, nor that its emphasis on objecthood is predicated on external reference giving way to self-reference, although the latter is common. The tendency towards nonreferentiality in minimalist music, poetry, visual art and architecture is connected to the pursuit of immanence, and even when minimalism relies on representation, as is often the case with narrative prose and performance, it functions not to reinforce but to problematize the mimetic economy; to press towards a more accurate measure of the real, a more intense access to the world.

The most radical minimalist works seek to eschew all external and mimetic reference: 'released from representation, they further remove themselves from allusion by their being new and unique objects, referring to nothing (except, some might argue, to the theories upon which they are based)'.[123] In early canonical minimalist visual art, and particularly sculpture, this ideal is pursued with considerable rigor. Theorizing their own work, artists including Judd and Morris seek to discard even the echoes of representation found in the progressive tradition of abstraction – an 'art whose forms have a basis in the real world'[124] – in pursuit of an objecthood that simply exists in itself, in a persistent and indifferent relation to the real. The material shape of their work arises from conceptual and formal deduction rather than a prototype that pre-exists the work. Similarly, anthropomorphism – the comprehension of parts and properties with reference to what is manifestly human – is 'displaced … by the nonanthropomorphic quality of "presence",'[125] discussed above and in relation to the complex question of scale. The condition implied by an ideal and dynamic combination of appropriate scale, presence and nonanthropomorphism is nonreferentiality – the artwork is free to exist in relation to its own objecthood.

Critics and artists disagree on the extent and desirability of minimalism's nonreferentiality, yet habitually acknowledge its significance: Fried proposes a deductive logic in minimalism in terms of which 'the shape *is* the object';[126] Wollheim asserts that 'the identity of a work … resides in the actual stuff in which it consists';[127] Robert Morris's *unitary forms* and Donald Judd's *specific objects* offer integral visions of nonreferentiality from the perspective of the object itself.[128] The unity and wholeness of such objects is pursued by various techniques of construction. In music, for example, both drones and repetitive modules draw attention to their limited means in order to render the work more transparent and thus effective in terms of its integrity and structural unity. 'Floe' from Glass's *Glassworks* is exemplary in this respect: having set out the basic harmonic progression to be repeated throughout, the rush of triadic melodic material and subtle polyrhythms merely fill in the existing structure – a powerful exposition of the way in which form and the audible process of its formation render one another increasing transparent.

Analogous techniques of repetition are observable in the serial sculpture of LeWitt and the modular sculpture of such artists as Judd, Andre, or the hard edge, serial repetition of such works as Kelly's *Spectrum IV*.[129] The painting, composed of thirteen repeated vertical bands, each a different colour of the spectrum, is at once an icon of chromatic containment and distribution, pointing inward and outward. Strickland highlights the unifying function of Kelly's repetition, which he associates with the immediacy evoked by the formal and chromatic interruption between these panels,[130] and their significance in exploiting the effectiveness of replication within modular patterns of structural uniformity.[131] Yet this same repetition, understood in terms of sequence, evokes a progressiveness, and a sense of temporal passage and continuity with the world beyond the canvas. Even as this work reflects an 'earlier purity [and] idealism'[132] according to Judd, it also offers 'an oblique but directly descriptive reference to nature'.[133] The spectrum, though radically imbedded in visual perception, and thus implicitly in every work of art, still points outward when it is presented as such – a minimal marker, a reminder, of the limits of nonreferentiality.

Repetition is similarly pivotal to the pursuit of nonrepresentational literary objecthood. It finds among its most intense expressions in Gertrude Stein's circuitous and cyclical writing with its emphasis on the immanence of language in itself – the 'satisfaction in language made present, contemporary; the pleasure/plenitude in the immersion in language, where language is not understood as a code for something else or a representation of somewhere else'.[134] Yet for the most part, rather than seeking to evade external reference altogether, techniques of repetition deployed in minimalist narrative seek to place the capacity of literary language for realistic representation radically in question. A fine example is Samuel Beckett's work, 'with its asymptotic approaches to zero', which, as Connor notes, instantiate a 'complex play between reduction and addition, in which to repeat oneself, and therefore to say progressively less, seems, uncannily always to involve saying more'.[135] Modular repetition – often replete with incremental additions and subtractions, and constructed from phrases making use of various techniques of contraction, elaboration, reversal, inversion or displacement – is central to the writing not only of Beckett, but also such writers as Robbe-Grillet and Josipovici. The 'voice … in the dark'[136] provides a central module in Beckett's 'Company', the permutations of which make it possible to trace a vigorous play of existential limits within the work – between internality and externality; active and passive voice; first, second and third person narrative[137] – as well as the recollection of largely traumatic childhood memories. In Josipovici's *The Inventory* entire passages are repeated,[138] reflecting on the manner in which conceptual chunking and repetitive narrative units often implicate one another. A stylistically similar use of repetition is observable in Didion's writing,[139] as well as in the writing of that 'stylistic genitor of contemporary minimalist prose',[140] Hemingway.

Repetition is more clearly integral to the structure and coherence of poetry, yet very often this repetition is used to strengthen rather than loosen the referential or allusive force of the poem. In the case of conceptual, concrete and L=A=N=G=U=A=G=E poetry, however, repetition becomes a means for pursuing non- or self-referential objecthood. A fine example is Robert Lax's poem, 'things into words', structured around the repeated alternation of two stanzas 'things/ into/ words' and 'words/ into/ things'. This alternation brings into focus a productive tension between the mimetic expectation that language is able accurately to represent external reality – 'things /into/ words'[141] – and the radical assertion regarding the materiality of language and its capacity to manifest the real – 'words/ into/ things'. In the poem, Lax works to affirm the force of radical *poiesis*: it is the transfiguration of 'words/ into/ things' that is its final emphasis, as the poem exceeds the referential gravity of its language, manifesting instead in terms of a language that affirms that it is real. Lax's work stresses the poetic taking-place of language as a real event at the heart of the work: the 'innermost exteriority'[142] by which minimalist objects are able to affirm their presence in the world. The startling simplicity of Lax's 'is'[143] – a work constructed solely from the repetition of the word *is* twenty-seven times over twenty-seven separate lines, divided into stanzas of seven, seven, three, three and seven lines – invokes precisely this sense of immanence. Lax seeks to draw the very force of being into a poetic pattern, a region of immanence in which the word is not only a thing, but also an act – the poem a pure instantiation without reference; 'is' after all, is the present tense of the verb *to be*, and asserting its presence without a definite predicate, the poem opens itself to the unspecified reality beyond it, revealing 'the potential for the simplest words and most common experiences to speak across our human separateness'.[144] The self-referential work retains a spectral connection to the referential world of relational meaning by the very absence of the latter in the former. It is the indifference of these works to the context in which they exist and are encountered that brings this context to a new clarity, emphasizing the considerable stakes of minimalism in bringing a new intensity of objecthood into existence that remains outside of the mimetic economy even as it produces effects in the world.

3.6 Process

Minimalism in motion: Ian Hamilton Finlay's *acrobats* (1964) Steve Reich's *Pendulum Music* (1968/1973)

The similarities Hallett traces between minimalism and the short story, referred to above, centre on their shared emphasis on a reduction of scale and means: 'both minimalism and the short story privilege the singular, focus on surface images, and speak sparingly'[145] presenting, in unadorned form, the 'concrete details which reflect complex states of being and which correlate with elements of the universal human condition'.[146] For Hallett, minimalist stories are 'containers of condensed meaning'[147] in which we are obliged to 'infer from the part exposed exactly what has been omitted, what lies beneath'.[148] The minimalist story, in other words, speaks of a simplicity arrived at through a disciplined process of reduction. Yet, as Colpitt notes, turning to the visual arts, there is an important distinction to be made between simplicity as the conceptual radix of the work, and simplicity arrived at through processes of reduction: 'while simplicity *implies* an intentionally reductive process … it does not demand it. For many artists there is a difference between the conception of a work of art as simple and the process of reducing from complexity to arrive at that simplicity'.[149] On a material level, there is also a difference between a simplicity that derives from 'using materials as they [are], without adulteration',[150] and a simplicity that reflects a transformation of materials or, indeed, of medium.

It becomes clear in this light, that the simplicity that often appears self-evident in minimalism is in fact the result of conceptual and material activity that shapes the production of the work, and perceptual and hermeneutic activity brought to the work when it is encountered. Therefore, although Colpitt is correct to assert that 'simplification or reduction are conceptual [so that] if elements were to be eliminated, they were done so in the artist's mind',[151] this conceptual reduction must be matched by the means and medium of the work in question, and in a sense repeated by the constructive activity of perception as formulated by Merleau-Ponty,[152] and the interpretative or hermeneutic processes this makes possible. Ian Hamilton Finlay's concrete poem, *acrobats*,[153] clearly demonstrates the ways in which conception, execution, perception and interpretation are confluent in the minimalist conception of simplicity. The poem consists of thirteen rows of repeated letters, alternating in rows of five and four letters, arranged so that the letters in alternating lines are aligned vertically, while those in the lines immediately above or below are displaced horizontally, and so aligned diagonally. Read from bottom to top, or from top to bottom, the letters spell out the word *acrobats*, meeting in the middle on the *s* that both words share. Yet, because of the repetition involved and the alignment of the letters, 'acrobats' also appears elsewhere – in part or whole, descending and ascending diagonally – in what is a typographic and semantic acrobatics of sorts; an acrobatics that sees the dynamic relation of concept, form, content, reading and meaning converge in its claim to minimalist objecthood.

These questions of where, of what, and of how an artwork is constituted – in short, questions of facture – are of considerable significance to the development of canonical minimalism, imbedding the significance of process in the constitution of minimalist objecthood. By abandoning the often metaphysical significance attributed to the writer, artist, or composer, minimalism also forgoes numerous of the outward signs of artistic facture such as technical irregularity, expressiveness, and gesture. Minimalists seek maximally stable and often impersonal techniques through which to produce their works. It is not that style becomes irrelevant, but rather that stylistic markers are displaced from the person of the artist to more impersonal processes. This is particularly evident in minimalist sculpture which, along with the mechanical, anonymous reproduction of Pop Art, 'rejected personal facture'.[154] Judd, Morris and Truitt all used unconventional media – sheet metal and plywood for example – often benefiting from outside experts involved in industrial fabrication who helped provide works with an increased 'sharpness and clarity of edge and surface'.[155] Thus at least some minimalism appears to move towards an aesthetic situation that 'evince[s] a "minimum" of artistic labour … purging … authorial feeling and demonstrable intention'.[156] The reasons for abandoning the physical labour of sculptural construction, preferring industrial fabrication and assemblage, thus seem quite as practical as they are aesthetic.[157]

This is evident in the work of numerous minimalist sculptors for whom the sheer scale of certain works and the incredible heaviness of their material – Bladen's monumental sculptures and Serra's infamous lead sculptures are exemplary in this regard – along with the use of prefabricated objects such as the fluorescent fixtures of Flavin's work,[158] require an unprecedented cooperation between artist, manufacturer, and various specialists in industrial construction and installation. That 'the artist functioned as conceptualizer; the factory as the actualizer'[159] provoked some dissent among critics,[160] with Hilton Kramer and Dore Ashton embarking on a protracted dispute on the matter.[161] A similar interest in impersonal techniques and the elimination of evidence of facture characterizes a great deal of minimalist painting.[162] Brush strokes, suggestive of human action, give way to instruments and techniques that ensure the even application of paint. Rauschenberg used a roller and house paint for his 'prototypical … series of six works composed of from one to seven panels of rolled white enamel paint';[163] Stella, too, used black house paint on unprimed canvas, generating a depth of blackness that remains a touchstone of minimalist painting;[164] while Robert Mangold famously used a spray gun to maximize the evenness of application.[165] Even though these works remain dependent on the effort of the artists, Colpitt stresses that 'the "look" of fabrication was evident in most paintings'.[166] Neutrality, impersonality and anonymity quickly became one of the understated yet striking hallmarks of minimalist painting.

Indeed, the minimalist preference for fabrication over artistic facture might be interpreted in more overtly historical terms as the point at which the utopianism of modernity tips into the scepticism of postmodernity: creative force appears to be displaced, first from genius to technique, then from technique to technology, generating a rupture in which the potential for true novelty is seen to collapse into a void of simulacra. Yet, in reality, minimalism resists this collapse, instead offering clarity on the manner in which various techniques of fabrication cross into art. Indeed, recalling that minimalism manifests intermittently, a similar migration of technology to art can be observed in micrographia and the art of the miniature over three centuries earlier.

Directly addressing new media and technological process, both composer and performer become invisible in much minimalist composition, including Steve Reich's *Pendulum Music*, a process work that derives its content from 'allowing four microphones to swing above four upturned speakers'.[167] Like many of the conceptual compositions of John Cage, La Monte Young, and various of the latter's Fluxus contemporaries, the musical process is notated entirely in regular language rather than musical notation and can be executed by anyone, with or without musical training, upsetting the conventions of musical facture. Having set the microphones swinging in a pendular motion, each to pass over a speaker turned to a volume that produces significant feedback, the composition is left to take its course, the gradual dissipation of energy being converted into a more or less continuous feedback. Initially, the microphones generate rapid, brief pulses of feedback, and a fair deal of rhythmic complexity; but these become progressively longer as the pendular trajectories lose momentum, the constantly shifting counterpoint of feedback pulses eventually giving way to an inertial union of continuous tone.

Notable in Reich's *oeuvre* for its distinctly Dadaist transgression of artistic convention and medium, embracing an aleatory process that clearly recalls the work of John Cage,[168] *Pendulum Music* uses a technological process in a way that challenges conventional definitions of minimalist objecthood in both conceptual and material terms. The work possesses an austere directness that is characteristically minimalist, incorporating repetition and drone in a singular manner. Repetition simultaneously dissolves, transforms, and reforms the work as the energy of the swinging microphones dissipates. The pulsing of sound is progressively transformed into a continuous drone, a process of transumption in which the constitution of the work involves the 'transference from one part or place to another, and marking this transference in a material way'.[169] *Pendulum Music* assists in clarifying the minimalist concern with impersonal physical or perceptual processes[170] and the way in which these constitute a significant species of minimalist objecthood. '[O]f all my pieces [*Pendulum Music*] was *the* most impersonal', claims Reich, 'and was the most emblematic and the most didactic in terms of the process idea [that process is impersonal and independent of its objects[171]] and also most sculptural … In many ways, you could describe *Pendulum Music* as audible sculpture, with the objects being the swinging microphones and the loudspeakers. I always set them up quite clearly as sculpture.'[172]

Minimalism seeks to clarify the processes through which objects emerge as artworks, and conversely, through which artworks define themselves in terms of their objecthood. In this respect, minimalist objects offer themselves as aesthetic icons of the real: they exit the mimetic economy in order to offer a radical vision of the manner in which objects are able to enter into the world, persist in the world, and produce effects in the world, all in a sustained relation to minimum. Far from uniform, the diverse expressions of minimalist objecthood reflect the entanglement of its theoretical and formal aspects, its pursuit of immanence in its migrations across media, and its eschewal of reference and embrace of process. The multiple configurations of minimalist objecthood interrogate the ways in which objects are able to speak on their own terms: speak of themselves in terms of their integrity; speak in relation to other objects and subjects, conceptual and existential situations; speak as examples of specific cultural contexts; speak as emblems of the force of generation itself – of *poiesis*. Yet the true promise of the minimalist object resides not in what it does in the world, but rather in what it is: the trace of a minimal difference between existence and the fact of existence; the aperture that reveals the heart of what is most real in every object. Here the entirety of being shudders imperceptibly.

4

The Real: On the Persistence of Minimalism

4.1 Verisimilitude

Competing realities: Raymond Carver's 'The Bath' (1981)

Reality – derived from the Latin *res*, or thing – might be defined, in minimal terms, as 'the totality of all real things',[1] and realism as 'a philosophical doctrine about the reality [of real things]'.[2] All species of realism share a radical, if minimal, positivity: for an entity to be real it must, first, exist; and, second, exist independently.[3] Thus, for a realist, 'at least part of reality is ontologically independent of human minds'.[4] The rejection of realism – which takes the form of various propositions regarding the anti-real, the non-real, the unreal or the irreal – must first of all assert that this autonomy is in fact relative, 'that there are no absolute and incontrovertible certainties available',[5] as Nelson Goodman maintains, and that reality is limited by some form of *access* to the real.[6]

The problem of reality – of determining what is real and what is not, and of what this means for thought – is intricately woven into the history of philosophical and scientific inquiry.[7] Presocratic cosmology, the classical theory of forms, the Scholastic conception of modality, the Enlightenment preference for scientific method, the Modern search for the transcendental conditions of knowledge, and finally the Postmodern pervasiveness of virtual reality[8] are all articulated against a particular understanding of what reality is. Yet, as Christopher Norris notes, relativism emerges when it is taken for granted that '"reality" *just is* coextensive with or restricted to the domain of known, verifiable, reliably vouchsafed, well-documented, adequately sourced, or at any rate sufficiently agreed-upon historical facts'.[9] He goes on to distinguish several species of this anti-realism: the 'trivial semantic variety', claiming that an intrinsic instability in signification is sufficient decisively to undermine reality;[10] the '"strong" sociological or cultural-relativist approaches' that derive their opposition to the real from a 'large investment in the idea of scientific "truth" or "reality" as relative to … some culture-specific discourse';[11] and formal arguments which assert that the loss of 'recognition-transcendent truths'[12] amounts to the loss of the real.

To understand the real as it manifests today, it is necessary first to recognize what Hilary Putnam identifies as a decisive shift in the conception of realism – from a pre-scientific realism grounded in intuition and common sense, to a scientific realism grounded in methods of induction and deduction[13] – occasioned by the claim, first formulated by Galileo, that the world operates according to a mathematical physics and can be approximated by mathematical formulae.[14] For Putnam,[15] '[t]he kind of scientific realism we have inherited from the seventeenth century has not lost all its prestige even yet, but it has saddled us with a disastrous picture of the world',[16] an understanding 'that denies precisely the common man's kind of realism, his realism about tables and chairs'.[17] How, then, might the real be restored to the everyday? To restore access to the real in the everyday, it is necessary to develop the means through which to think positively about different perspectives on reality, to formulate typologies such as the one developed by Ilkka Niiniluoto, which discerns six species of realism: *ontological* realism, which addresses the possibility of a mind-independent world; *semantical* realism, which attempts to establish reality in terms of an objective correlation between language or thought and world; *epistemological* realism, which formulates such correlation in terms of knowledge; *axiological* realism, which stipulates that at the heart of real being or knowledge is an axiom binding these to truth or non-truth; *methodological* realism which determines the most reliable means of arriving at knowledge regarding reality; and *ethical* realism which sets as its task the exposition of moral values.[18]

In practice, these types of realism cross one another at numerous points: what begins as an axiological realism is easily translated into semantic or epistemological terms. Yet, regardless of its precise rhetorical shape, the conflation of truth and reality – whether in terms of *aletheia*, the revelation of a withdrawn essence,[19] or in terms of a correspondence, correlation or convergence of cause and effect[20] – has profound consequences for the understanding of realism. Such correspondences may themselves be conceptualized in numerous ways: most significantly, for the present purpose, in terms of *verisimilitude* – that one proposition can be more true than others, without approaching absolute truth[21] – and *veridicality* – that propositions can be absolutely true given the hypothetical completeness of a situation, but, that as the completeness of a situation is itself only contingent, truth is always in the process of being completed.[22] The central proposition here, however, is simply that the majority of realist models are 'charted in terms of their attitudes towards truth'.[23]

Accepting that arguments regarding realism almost invariably return to evidentiary cases for the existence of reality, science and quasi-science retain considerable significance in debates around the real. Scientific realism is at once axiological and methodological, generally articulating itself in terms of an understanding that 'truth, realism and verisimilitude are all part of a single picture',[24] a picture that most often rests on descriptive models of truth.[25] Yet since descriptive language only approximates reality, these models tend to be provisional – 'the best account [of reality] currently available'[26] – resulting in significant doubt as to the completeness of any theoretical account. From this doubt emerges various 'half-realisms',[27] the entity realism of Cartwright, Hacking, Harré and Giere among them, which recognize that 'theoretical entities … play a role in causal explanation, but den[y] realism about theoretical laws'.[28]

In the face of a distinctly ontological turn, it becomes increasingly unclear whether the realist vocation lies in the faithful transcription through theory of existing relationships between entities, or whether it resides in the production of new entities themselves.[29] Nelson Goodman's irrealism, for instance, reconsiders realism in terms of generation: a real world is a world made of making; a world that 'always starts from worlds already on hand; the making is a remaking'.[30] Critical realism marks a different but equally compelling return to the world, offering robust criticism of both absolute reality and lack of reality, and is often invested with a political dimension, as in Roy Bhaskar's programme which advances '[c]ritical realism [as] a coherent account of the nature of nature, society, science, human agency and philosophy (including itself). Its intent is to underlabour for science, conceived as a necessary but insufficient agency of human emancipation.'[31] To this may be added a phenomenological realism, most persuasively articulated by Roman Ingarden, which suggests that 'our apprehension of a real object is based on our recognition that all the properties of which it is a carrier are appropriate to its nature in that they qualify the object as a concrete unity'.[32] Regardless of how an object is presented or presents itself,[33] there is no essential disjunction between how it is presented and how it is apprehended, but rather a consonance and continuity between the object as it is and the object as it is perceived. Hence, 'the real world is essentially connected with … the nature of the real individual object, since it occurs on the basis of their intertwining … as the possible form binding together their totality'.[34]

The aims of the present work are to a significant extent consonant with those of phenomenological realism, culminating in a minimal formulation of ontological realism encountered most clearly in the aesthetic objects of minimalism.

Autonomous, yet shaped by the generative processes of perception, these works persist in relation to minimum – the point at which a radically minimalist conception of realism and a radically realist conception of minimalism appear confluent. In this light, the confluence of a minimalist realism and a realist minimalism expresses the facticity of the real: the contingent taking-place of reality *as it is* despite a 'lack of reason for any reality',[35] as Meillassoux notes.

Inasmuch as it describes the relationship between the force of representation and the thing represented, *mimesis* clearly instantiates a type of realism, although the precise extent to which its reach is limited ontologically, epistemologically, semantically or axiologically – to recall Niiniluoto's typology – remains contested.[36] Indeed, pressing towards the dynamic heart of the real, it is necessary, as Raymond Tallis notes, to remain vigilant of the 'tendency to assimilate the iconic truth of a representational mode of signification to the referential truth of an expressive mode of signification'.[37] In short, to provide a point of access to the real is not the same as representing reality, and recognizing this distinction is crucial to understanding the force of *mimesis*. Historically, the question of aesthetic verisimilitude is coordinated by a mimetic rather than an aesthetic logic – by the set of techniques through which the world is represented[38] rather than the distribution of the senses to which it ultimately returns, precision habitually valued above beauty.[39]

In this context, periodic revivals of realism are less revolutionary than intermittently radical, an ongoing alternation of conservation and refoundation in pursuit of a field of immanence that, in a significant sense, has always been available. Realism succeeds to the extent that it exposes this immanence as the minimal but essential distance between the world and the *mimemata* – representational entities – generated through *mimesis*.[40] Danto's insights in this respect are instructive: first, that 'philosophy begins to arise only when the society within which it arises achieves a concept of reality … that can happen only when a contrast is available between reality and something else – appearances, illusion, representation, art';[41]and second, its corollaries, that 'one could not imagine, any more than one could a world made up just of shadows, a world made up solely of artworks. One could imagine a world without artworks … for such a world would be exactly that in which the concept of reality had not yet arisen'.[42]

For Danto, the difficult relation of thought and reality is at the centre not only of the *mimetic* enterprise, but of any attempt to come to grips with reality in itself. Historically, it is no surprise that the representational goals of aesthetic realism should correspond closely to the concerns of scientific realism.[43] Both aim for verisimilitude, and although the method and media of aesthetics differ considerably from those proper to the sciences, they similarly affirm that when realism fails to coincide with reality, it is not because of an intrinsic resistance at the heart of the real, but because mechanisms for perceiving and reproducing reality are limited and, as has been suggested, necessarily so if the coherence of particular entities is to be maintained. Aesthetic realism is in this sense the foil to an idealist transcendentalism – the view that what is at the heart of the real somehow transcends reality, and is thus not fully disclosed within this reality – motivated by the desire to express its own contemporaneity, as Nochlin notes.[44]

Turning to the political sphere, the thrust of Lukács's celebrated argument regarding realism is not dissimilar: although the efforts of modernism may be directed towards expressions of formalist autonomy,[45] desocialized existentialism[46] and denaturalized thought,[47] the principal exigency to which contemporary aesthetics returns is its capacity to exemplify a 'concrete potentiality [which] is concerned with the dialectic between the individual's subjectivity and objective reality'.[48] This concrete potentiality gives rise to the force of a contemporary realism – one which 'deliberately introduces elements of disintegration … to portray the contemporary world more exactly',[49] but which nonetheless returns aesthetics to the social and political present as an active participant in history.[50] Persuasive on its own terms, Lukács's case for realism situates, rather than negates, the multiple strands of avant-garde experimentalism that subvert traditional mimesis in order to intensify rather than abandon reality, discovering new paths towards an autonomy, often through austere abstraction, that is itself an instantiation of the real.[51] Thus, although many realists maintain 'that truth to observed facts – facts about the outer world, or facts about [the author's or artist's] own feelings – is important',[52] this commitment need not culminate in aesthetic works 'intent on arresting semantic play by insisting on the need of life-likeness and verisimilitude in representation'.[53]

Yet, as many minimalist works implicitly register, verisimilitude itself is complicated by the shifting intensities of reality: if it is clear that a central aim of minimalism is to provide transparent access to things as they are, it is also clear that things as they are, are marked by multiplicity. In this sense, verisimilitude, to the extent that it remains tied to the real, is often marked by ambiguity and incipient difference. Carver's short fiction provides an important vehicle in minimalist thought in this regard, exemplary of the ways in which the concern with verisimilitude that arguably drives the minimalist 'narrative economy',[54] to recall Barthes's term, evidences a shift from mimetic accuracy – the 'effective illusion of reality'[55] to which Winfried Fluck alludes – to mimetic acuity – an intensification of the real, as noted by Hallett and Alexander.[56] Thus, although according to Schechner, Carver's work acted as a catalyst for the realist revival in 1980s fiction,[57] expressing 'a capacity for seeing clearly and the power to create, in prose, the illusion of a sharply visualised world',[58] it is simultaneously concerned with a more ambiguous and ambitious social realism. Appearing to rest on the predictable 'reflex to lower-class exigency',[59] sustained examination reveals a prose of considerable subtlety in which '[f]undamental concreteness of detail and precision of expression'[60] is carefully combined with an understated but definite moral commitment, recognizable, in Wil Verhoeven's estimation, through 'the intensity of the artist's vision of life'.[61]

Daniel Just recognizes Carver's achievement in his turn away from the straightforward pursuit of verisimilitude[62] towards 'new forms of realism that … capture the essence of the changing world'.[63] By refusing narrative and semantic closure, Carver uncouples the precise language of description from the reality described: the 'referentiality of language is brought to the point of its breakdown, but rather than completing it, he suspends it for inspection'.[64] Thus the 'heightened realism'[65] that Just situates at the centre of Carver's aesthetic enterprise reflects the same minimal but radical distance between the world and the representation of the world that Danto recognizes as the necessary mark of every successful realism, and in light of which a great deal of conventional realism, insisting on absolute coincidence or convergence, appears to be hyperbolic and decidedly unreal.

For instance, 'The Bath' – a story recounting an accident in which a boy is run down by a car on the eve of his eighth birthday, and the vigil of his parents at his hospital bed – continues to divide critics on whether Carver's realism is adequate to the task of representing reality. Easily mistaken for a view of humanity so impoverished and devoid of empathy that it bars the intersubjective constitution of reality itself, Carver's stylized blankness – here famously shaped by the editorial intervention of Gordon Lish[66] – testifies to a more difficult conception of the real. His terse, dispassionate and fractured narrative captures with considerable subtlety the complex emotions and communicative disjuncture which might accompany traumatic experience. Indeed, Carver reflects the full distress of the incident in the devastating obliqueness of the mother's fragile story that she recites upon encountering complete strangers in a hospital waiting room:

> My son was hit by a car … But he's going to be all right. He's in shock now, but it might be some kind of a coma too. That's what worries us, the coma part. I'm going out for a little while. Maybe I'll take a bath. But my husband is with him.

> He's watching. There's a chance everything will change when I'm gone. My name is Ann Weiss.[67]

That the intensity of the situation is reduced to a series of flattened, factual statements should not be taken as evidence of minimalism's inability to convey a deeper sense of reality. Barely concealed beneath these faltering attempts to force some sort of narrative, however inadequate it may be, onto a chaotic sequence of events, is the almost overwhelming affective weight of unarticulated emotion. In this way, it becomes evident, by what the conventions of realism fail to accomplish, that a different realism is needed to give voice to those things which move beside, but not within, the prevailing mimetic economy.

4.2 Generativity

Approximating the real: Alain Robbe-Grillet's 'In the Corridors of the Underground' (1963)

Minimalisms of 'form, style, vocabulary, syntax, imagery, structure, plot, and characterization'[68] offer a radical reorientation of the medium of representation towards the world they seek to mediate and represent, shifting the emphasis of mimesis from the replication to the intensification of this world. The manner of this reorientation and intensification varies greatly. Modernist avant-gardes – often stylistically oriented towards minimum – frequently emphasize the role of objects in simultaneously instantiating and reparsing reality, from the Dadaist readymade, to the growing significance of objects in texts and texts as objects. In experimental narrative, Gertrude Stein and James Joyce are both deeply concerned with 'the objectivity and apartness of things';[69] and the Bloomsbury group, and Virginia Woolf in particular, adopted aspects of G. E. Moore's brand of atomism by way of a cognitive mapping of a realism that regards as central the constructive importance of sensation in its relation to externality.[70] In a proposition reminiscent of Stein,[71] Alain Robbe-Grillet considers literature subject to a mimetic exhaustion in which the writer 'has nothing to say, [retaining] merely a manner of speaking',[72] a style without substance. It is precisely the semantic evacuation of the late modern wordscape that gives rise to a new literary vocation: a new novel grounded not in the fast-failing *mimesis* of the past, but in the *poiesis* of the present, 'creat[ing] a world ... out of dust'.[73]

Through attention to infinitesimal detail, Robbe-Grillet's prose constitutes a literary phenomenology of particular intensity, seeking to recover the *poietic* or *generative* promise of literary language. The objects encountered in his storyworlds are exemplary in this respect: their reality is carefully distributed between sensation, perception, and the literary means of negotiating and relating these. It is intensified by the peculiarly self-reflexive, and arguably self-productive, character of the prose. For Robbe-Grillet, the problems of formal realism in literature 'completely lose … their meaning the moment we realise that not only does everyone see his own version of reality in the world, but that it is precisely the novel that creates this reality'.[74] If objectivity, understood as 'a completely impersonal way of looking at things … is only too obviously a chimera',[75] it is because writing has failed to integrate aesthetic self-reflexivity and representational precision – keeping in mind Danto's argument that representation does not of necessity require a formal prototype[76] – in a way that renders the distinction of artificiality and verisimilitude subsidiary with respect to questions of reality. The reality of the work is 'no longer … permanently situated elsewhere, but *here and now*, without ambiguity [and] no longer find[s] its justification in a hidden meaning … Beyond what we see … there would henceforth be nothing'.[77]

The strategies used to express this sense of immanence – familiar to much minimalism and here distinguishing Robbe-Grillet's phenomenological literature from its realist predecessors – are exposed with some clarity in the short prose work, 'In the Corridors of the Underground'. The first part of the work, 'The Escalator', offers a meticulous description of a group of people on an escalator in a Parisian underground station. To grasp accurately what simply *is*, Robbe-Grillet seeks first to defamiliarize familiar objects by suspending the language ordinarily associated with them, preferring disciplined description: the commonplace escalator is rendered in terms of its moving parts – 'a long, iron-grey staircase, whose steps become level, one after the other, as they get to the top, and disappear, one by one … with a heavy, and yet at the same time abrupt, regularity'.[78] By a curious inverse nominalism, the escalator is kept at an ontological distance from its passengers: its name is withheld, and its *haecceity* or *thisness* – the singular collection of properties that make it what it is – is divorced from its functionality.

The phenomenality of the objects in the text is heightened by a careful exposition of perception as a process constructive of reality, but essentially 'inexpressive'[79] in itself. Indeed, it is the neutral vision of 'a universe in which … most things are unsayable'[80] that, paradoxically, excites from this minimalist text a perceptible realness, reinforced by the redundancy and circularity of motion. Movement on the escalator is 'almost imperceptible',[81] or gives way to 'motionless[ness]'[82] itself, the group on the escalator 'petrified for the duration of the mechanical journey'.[83] Furthermore, what minimal movement exists is repeated,[84] is uniform in speed,[85] and preserves an indifferent equidistance between objects,[86] negating a dynamic sense of temporal passage. Such instances of inertia recall the deconditioning which Cela, following Barthes, sees as implicit in the self-reflexivity of this writing: '[f]ree of exterior ties, resistant to the attribution of a preconstructed meaning, the signs configured by Robbe-Grillet reactivate themselves with every new act of reading.'[87] To achieve this, Robbe-Grillet's phenomenological writing is built around particular generative units – initial ideas, signs, objects, or situations – subjected to various permutations, framed and reframed to approximate objective reality.

Of this creative procedure, Leach notes 'a strong inclination to allow the work to develop from a source outside of [it]'.[88] Refining this proposition, Morrissette identifies three principal types of literary generator: situational generators – occurrences, or sequence of occurrences, which produce a specific narrative course;[89] formal or linguistic generators – those parts of a text which operate at the level of plot and structure;[90] and serial generators, which involve a 'deliberate serial patterning',[91] guiding the development of the narrative, but not at the level of plot as such. Robbe-Grillet's 'In the Corridors of the Underground' makes use of serial generators: *motion*, as it relates to physical and represented movement on the one hand, and analogy with respect to generative process itself on the other. In the first part the reader encounters 'a motionless group'[92] on an 'interrupted journey',[93] which, by the second part, gains the uniform momentum of a 'thinly scattered crowd of hurrying people, all moving at the same speed,'[94] only to be 'brought to a halt';[95] and when these people attempt to board the train, 'they remain more or less stationary'.[96] The formal premises of generative fiction – the deployment of generative units as basic structural elements that produce works through processes of repetition, permutation and variation – resonate significantly with the units used in minimalist serial sculpture and in the incremental repetition of minimalist music. Generative fiction exists at the threshold of the mimetic economy: its language is representational, but the world it constructs is transected by ambiguities, external- and self-reference crossing one another repeatedly. The literary work takes on an immanence and intensity absent in more conventional narrative, pointing the way towards even more radical manifestations of minimalism; towards a minimal point at which there is no longer an easy distinction to be made between pointing inward and pointing outward. At this point textual objectivity passes into textual objecthood. As in the most exemplary cases of concrete poetry and prose, the symmetry of form and content envisions a new type of realism; not one in which reality is contained – a single unassuming work of concrete poetry may reach allusively to the remotest histories even as it remains rooted to the present – but rather one in which textual objects become icons of the real itself. This iconic function – the clarification and intensification of the real – marks the passage from a realist conception of minimalism to a minimalist conception of realism. Here it becomes necessary to begin again, not only with the real, but with question of being itself.

4.3 Transfiguration

A minimalism more-real: Marcel Duchamp's *Fountain* (1917)

Being does not begin. What we call beginning takes place within the pervasiveness of being. Being is pure multiplicity[97] and, as such, has no conditions to which it is tied. Being, without any conditions, is absolute. It has neither a nature nor natural limits. Its temporality is non-specific. Fluctuations occur in being[98] – events, occurrences, encounters – but these are not fluctuations of being itself.[99] The being of being, or the multiplicity of multiplicity,[100] constitutes the absolute horizon against which the real can be said to persist. The real describes the aspect of being that conditions the possibility of every reality, preceding any specific point of access, act of positing or interpretation of the particularities of reality. The real, which in a sense belongs to being, is nonetheless distinct from being by virtue of its temporality: the real describes the situation in which the non-specific temporality of being is grasped in the limited terms of the linear and irreversible temporality of reality.[101]

Being and the real constitute the horizon against which existence – entities, forces and the relations between them – is able to constitute a reality. For the real to manifest in terms of a reality, the contents of existence, or entities, must be able to emerge or desist, manifest or withdraw, appear or disappear.[102] In short, entities must persist contingently over a period of time. The radical contingency of existence – the fact that the only necessity in existence is its contingency[103] – is inherent to every reality, since every reality consists of entities which, although tied together in chains of cause and effect, could have been otherwise. Put simply, although every reality is made up of entities, forces and relations that exist within the real, it remains perfectly possible that these will cease to exist. Yet, when an entity ceases to exist, it does not exit being, or even cease to be real, but rather it 'inexists'[104] within a specific reality as the negative imprint or trace of its former existence. It is for this reason that reality is perhaps best conceived in terms of an existential field upon which entities or entites appear and disappear. For Badiou, 'being-there, or appearing, consists not of a form of being but of *forms of relation*'.[105] In this light, it becomes possible to recognize how the real intersects being and existence in a way that clarifies their relation to one another – existence describes the appearance of entities in terms of contingent unities subtracted from the pure multiplicity, or 'multiples of multiples',[106] that constitutes being – and, in turn, it is this relation that constitutes the ground for what is generally called reality.

Although mostly unremarkable, the appearance of entities in reality potentially reflects the eruption of something new in the world – an event – that cuts across both being and existence. In comparing the propositions of Deleuze and Badiou in this regard – arguably the two leading thinkers on the intersection of ontological multiplicity and the event – Sam Gillespie points to the fact that Deleuze's emphasis on becoming means that 'being continually produces itself anew',[107] and that 'everything new has its origin in an appearing or expression of being's innermost potential'.[108] In this case the event of novelty might be grasped in terms of a torsion internal to being itself. By contrast, Badiou understands the advent of novelty in terms of '[a]bsolute beginnings',[109] or events that 'derive from nothing',[110] emerging from the void and cutting across the entire order of being.[111] For Badiou, the event marks the advent of something rare in being – 'a point of rupture with respect to being'[112] – that introduces an axiom, prompting a decision, and thus occasioning a subjective fidelity to the process, or truth, that the event inaugurates.

The event transects being, but it does not belong to being:[113] '[i]n effect, an event is composed of the elements of a site [that belongs to the multiplicity of being], but also by the event itself, which belongs to itself'.[114] An event is an exception.[115] According to Badiou, it is strictly aleatory and transient:[116] an event erupts by chance, as an 'originary disappearance, supplementing the situation [of existence] for the duration of a lightning flash'.[117] As a consequence, it can only be known retroactively, from within a given existential field,[118] and in particular through its effects in shaping a historical situation,[119] or what Badiou terms a *truth*, precisely because it possesses the capacity to valorize what it encounters in a particular reality towards a universal position.[120] The corollary, as Latour notes, is that history and context become truly 'visible only by the *traces* [they] leave … when a *new* association is being produced between elements'[121] not intrinsically related.

The significance of entities, forces and relations in coming to terms with the emergence of novelty is thus considerable. This is nowhere more visible than in the field of aesthetics. While few artworks constitute events in the radical sense in which Badiou deploys the term, many offer novel access to the fact that an event has taken place, existing as the trace of this event and the trajectory of its consequences towards an indefinite future. At the same time, the artwork offers the possibility of an encounter, itself a species of event. In the most radical of these encounters – a radicalism to which much of the most characteristic minimalism aspires– the artwork seeks to approximate the event of *poiesis*, the force of generation, itself. The urgency of Glass's *Music in Contrary Motion*, the immersive aura of Flavin's Marfa installation, the ordering of bodies in space in Beckett's *Quad* or *What Where*, and the immanent experience of an imaginary *ur*-language in Isidore Isou's sound poetry, all point to the generative significance of the encounter to minimalist aesthetics. In this way minimalism intuits the generic nature of the event itself, and so also delineates the manner in which novelty erupts into the real, even if its works do not themselves constitute events in the sense Badiou reserves for the term. Rather, the event of minimalism belongs to the order of transfiguration – a change internal to existence, a shift in the intensity with which an entity persists, often triggered by an encounter with the work in the world, rather than the eruption of absolute novelty.

Transfiguration describes the process by which an event or encounter produces a shift in the way in which an entity exists but without a change in the material constitution of the entity in question. It is thus fundamentally a fluctuation in the intensity with which an entity persists in a particular reality, by which an entity becomes *more real*. In aesthetic terms, Danto employs the concept of transfiguration principally to describe the circumstances under which what in one context is judged to be non-art, in another is judged to be art. Paradoxically, aesthetic transfiguration reveals that transcendence is possible only as the result of an intensified sense of presence, an immanent reality. The exemplarity of minimalism with regard to an aesthetic of transfiguration derives in part from their shared emphasis on the problematic threshold of art and non-art, but more specifically on the capacity of the minimalist work to locate – through its clarity of form and process – the aspect of every entity that persists, recalling that persistence itself is the first mark of the real.

The transfigurative aesthetic is evident in a great number of minimalist works: Andre's floorpieces purposefully confuse the exhibited work and the space of exhibition; Flavin's light art effects a transfiguration of the gallery space as its iridescence becomes an environment in its own right; Young's drone compositions have significant effects on consciousness; Beckett's extended dramatic silences significantly alter the perception of dramatic time. Yet perhaps among the most interesting examples of aesthetic transfiguration are those in which what is transfigured in the first instance is not the relation of the work to its environment or perception, but in relation to itself. The iconoclastic self-reflexivity of Dada, and particularly of Marcel Duchamp's readymades, is exemplary in this regard, inaugurating a significant field of aesthetic possibility. Indeed, Dada operates as a kind of aesthetic stem-cell, a principle of continuity and persistence, that seeks to expose the anarchic core of reality. Dada adapts. Amid the dystopianism of collapsing empires and the failing politics of a hollow humanism, Dada was born – choking on, then spitting out the art of the past, and nourishing itself in the fervent belief that it was '*essentially* different'.[122] Yet Dada looks forwards and backwards at once. From Futurism it learns the lessons of *simultaneism* – the dynamic aesthetic situation in which traditional aesthetics cross into one another so that sensory information, and the forms and media which convey this information, are presented concurrently; a 'juxtaposition, within the same construct ... of different time frames',[123] and an 'interpenetrative spatial disruption [which] is supposed to represent the affective character of the spectator's perceptual experience'.[124] From Cubism it learns the lessons of '*psychovisual collage*'[125] – works that involve a 'synthesis or building up of separate objects on the picture plane'[126] – and the *calligram* – visual poems in which words are formed into a single icon or sign, 'lines of text ... ingeniously manipulated in order to imitate natural appearances',[127] their 'textual values ... read against the visual imprint of a shape whose referential frame inflects the entire text'.[128]

Yet even these familiar techniques become sources of instability and difference rather than recognition. Repetition in Dada is habitually transfigured into novelty, because Dada not only adapts, it also evades, 'behav[ing] more like a variable than a constant'.[129] Dada does not offer itself in terms of a stable set of objects, but rather as the radical marker of an anarchic, aesthetic disposition towards the world. 'Dada was a word, a brand new, meaningless and magic word',[130] one that drew sharp critical attention to the problematic nature of 'the accepted ... referential function of sign systems'.[131] In Tristan Tzara's own words, '[w]hat we wanted was to make a clean sweep of existing values, but also, in fact, to replace them with the highest human values'.[132] Dada reaches towards the radical point at which an aesthetics and politics coincide without simply reproducing the familiar categories of either.[133] To do this it must occupy not only a threshold between creation and destruction, but between art and non-art. This threshold is maintained by the contradictory way in which Dada asserts its own historicity by suspending its relation to history. As Sanouillet recognizes, 'Dadaism created while Dada was destroying',[134] producing the paradoxical situation in which '[t]he critic or the historian can only write or talk about *Dadaism* and the *Dadaists*, not about Dada and the Dadas'.[135] Yet, it is worth recalling, with Lyotard in his examination of the aesthetics of the most prominent of the Dadaists, Marcel Duchamp, '[i]nconsistency is not insignificance'.[136]

Indeed, this inconsistency is a strategic means of subverting laws of discipline and genre[137] and establishing in their place a 'self-referring law, a contract with oneself … From the fact that the law is itself not legitimate … comes the result that you have no guarantee of conforming to it'.[138] From this position, Dada is able to define itself in exceptional terms, which, to recall Agamben's formulation of the exception, describe 'a zone in which application [of the law] is suspended, but the law … as such, remains in force'.[139] It is through the suspension of norms, 'reinventing every discipline from within',[140] that Dada discovers the transfigurative event, the minimal displacement between art and non-art, that gives its efforts agency in the world. Duchamp's readymades are exemplary in this respect. These are everyday objects, identified and selected, divested of any functional significance, and then reinvested with aesthetic significance. In this sense, the aesthetic force of the readymade rests, in the first instance, on a choice: '[the artist] CHOSE it. He took an article of life, placed it so that its useful significance disappeared under the new title and point of view – created a new thought for that object'.[141] Duchamp anticipates the theoretical argument Danto subsequently frames in terms of the transfiguration of the commonplace. In Danto's terms, mere things are transfigured into artworks,[142] acquiring an ontological status different from their prototypes.[143] Although qualitatively indistinguishable from the commonplace objects,[144] these artworks exist at a greater intensity. The precise reasons for this shift in intensity remain disputed. Without denying the significance of context,[145] or of the formal sanction provided by the institutions of the artworld,[146] the transfigured works press beyond both the aesthetic question of representation and the contextual question of historical emergence.

There is, for Danto, an ontological distinction at the heart of the transfiguration of non-art to art;[147] a movement not only towards what Tristan Tzara termed an *art more art*,[148] but towards an *art more real*. The real becomes *surreal* – a term that 'has two meanings: more-real, and more-than real'.[149] This intensification of the real is exemplified with considerable clarity in arguably

Duchamp's most provocative readymade, *Fountain*,[150] a work submitted for exhibition under the pseudonym Richard Mutt that consists, in its entirety, of a urinal roughly signed on one side. Although materially identical, it is clear that a urinal as a mere thing, and a urinal as artwork, exist at different intensities. By this minimal ontological displacement – a small difference that makes all the difference – *Fountain* announces itself as more real precisely to the extent that it exemplifies the rules it prescribes for itself. '[E]ach example', Danto suggests, 'constitutes a sort of ontological argument in favour of its own designation.'[151] Furthermore, as Danto also notes, when '"real" is used in contrast with representation … [s]omething is "real" when it satisfies a representation of itself'.[152] It is the capacity of art to subtract *itself* from multiplicity – the ground of every reality – that marks it as more real.

The readymade reflects a radical shift away from a conception of aesthetic realism grounded in verisimilitude, or the faithful reflection of the natural world, to an art 'conceived as the way that semblance works out its proper distance from the real',[153] a change which resonates clearly in minimalist aesthetics and its emphasis on immanence and objecthood. In this light, the meaning and significance of the readymade lies not in its capacity for external reference, but in the contingency of its taking place as art. If *Fountain* represents anything it is the event and force of transfiguration itself. Although Duchamp recognizes that the readymade rests on an axiom – either it is an artwork or it is not – the force of transfiguration itself is a question of an internal difference, the threshold between an entity and itself, that expresses the most intimate aspect of its being in a significant sense prior to any sort of identity either as everyday object or artwork. Duchamp uses the term *infrathin* to describe the minimal distance between an object and itself, between a thing and its self-identity.[154] The infrathin constitutes a type of relational minimalism: the infinitesimal displacement that 'distinguishes the same from the same';[155] the minute delay[156] between the taking-place of the mere thing and the taking-place of the artwork; the invisible caesura between the real and the more-real.

Defining itself in relation to this threshold, the readymade evades any easy categorization in terms of medium or genre.[157] Nor can its particular intensity be fully explained with reference to form – 'the unmistakable "space" of … aesthetics'[158] that 'denote[s] the difference between determination and the determinable in general'[159] – or even concept. Indeed, the readymade reveals the conditions under which 'aesthetic judgment is [itself] an infrathin passage and an indifferent difference, something that does not have a name, and even less a concept'.[160] Here minimal differences have maximal consequences, the transfigurative aesthetic event generating an aperture to the intensified realism that remains at the heart of the minimalist aesthetic.[161]

It is difficult to imagine that the radical position adopted by the canonical minimalists could have taken hold were it not for the sustained challenge to the traditional mimetic economy central to the Dadaist and Neo-Dadaist enterprises. These debts are acknowledged by numerous critics. For Greenberg and Fried minimalism belongs to the Dadaist tradition of anti-art,[162] while Wollheim maintains that Duchamp's readymades and Reinhardt's monochromatic works are connected by their shared displacement of the evidence of physical work[163] to the realm of concept.[164] Rose confirms that minimalist art incorporates elements of both Dada and Constructivism,[165] a view echoed by Foster,[166] Meyer[167] – particularly in his discussion of Flavin and Andre[168] – and Perloff who, explaining theatricality in minimalism, juxtaposes Fried's essentially anti-Dadaist stance to the Constructivist position in which the work 'exist[s] only in relation to the environment and the viewer'.[169] Maurice Berger, meanwhile, identifies a bridging-figure in Morris, and particularly in works such as *Column*,[170] and a similar case could be made for the proponents of the 'vernacular realism'[171] that emerges from Neo-Dadaist installation art, events and happenings.

The various incarnations of visual, sound, concrete, intermedia and digital poetry represent another field of confluence for the Dadaist and minimalist aesthetic, manifesting in diverse ways in the Cubist, Imagist, Futurist, Vorticist, Constructivist, *De Stijl* and Dada experiments with image, typography and sound, but converging in the distinctly minimalist aesthetic of the international Concrete movement, still clearly felt in contemporary minimalist experiments. Similarly, the aleatory aesthetic that animates much of Dada and Surrealism – itself emblematic of a type of minimalism where aesthetic agency is reduced to chance – is revived in the Neo-Dadaism of John Cage whose influence is evident on the Black Mountain and Fluxus groups, including several of the leading figures in the first generation of canonical minimalists, Riley and Young among them.

Is it possible in this light to suggest that there exists a reciprocity between minimalism and the intensified realism of Dada? Certainly, the infrathin, as exemplified in the readymade, stresses that the transfiguration of object to artwork rests on a species of minimalism – an infinitesimal displacement that allows the object to enter into a relation of minimal difference with itself, and to emerge as more-real within the reality that frames it. In turn, this transfigurative aesthetic becomes central to minimalism, and one of the principal means by which it pursues the sense of immanence and persistence that marks its works not only as icons of the real, but as icons of a reality more-real.

4.4 Persistence

Contingency and absolute becoming: Eva Hesse's *Contingent* (1969) Steve Reich's *Piano Phase* (1967)

The real persists and yet every reality is defined by its contingency. It is this contingency that invests the most radical minimalist artworks with their peculiar intensity, and it is in response to their contingency that minimalist artworks are comported towards a reality more-real. Yet it would be an error to suppose that minimalism's intensification of the real – its search for a reality more-real – simply marks the ascendency of one realism over another. Instead, it points towards that radical part of every reality that can be grasped in terms of persistence; that part of contingency that is itself not contingent. For Meillassoux, this persistence is the force of contingency itself: 'contingency and only contingency, is absolutely necessary'.[172]

Minimalism clarifies the real precisely because the knot of persistence and contingency that manifests in its works generates the condition under which these works are able to exist as singularities – *just as they are*. Indeed, as Agamben recognizes in his work on potentiality, 'existence … is not the victorious struggle of a power to be against a power to not-be', but the capacity to 'allow … a contingency to be'.[173] What marks the minimalist artwork at its most radical is the facticity of its singularity, and the singular intensity of its facticity – *the fact that it is such as it is* – and at the heart of this transparent singularity is the recognition that things could have been different, yet are not. It is in this recognition that the minimalist artwork reveals itself as *more-real*, opening a path between the work and the facticity of the work, their shared contingency pointing to the particular contribution of minimalism in the elaboration of a contemporary realism: insisting that the instantiation and exemplification of the real are able to coincide in the singularity of the aesthetic work.

The insight that absolute necessity exists because of and not despite the fact that there is no entity that is absolutely necessary – either in itself, or as it is related within a set of determinate laws (of cause and effect) – is what reinvigorates realism. To construct a compelling case for the revivification of realism, Meillassoux explains his fundamental objection to what he terms *correlationism* – an idea that pervades intellectual modernity,[174] insisting that 'we only ever have access to the correlation between thinking and being, and never to either term considered apart from the other'.[175] In practice, the dogma that Meillassoux seeks to challenge is that it is impossible to conceptualize objects independently of subjects. The opponents of realism, that he, in turn, seeks to oppose, habitually claim that realism has no direct access to an objective world, because it 'always has to posit some more concepts to prove [that it] has accessed pre-conceptual reality'.[176] It thus slips into infinite regress, ostensibly making it impossible to formulate a convincing account of an entity that exists autonomously, or *in-itself*.[177] Reality is consequently reduced to a point of access to the real provided by thought and perception, so that the entity that exists does so not in-itself, but always, rather, *for-us*. [178]

Meillassoux seeks systematically to refute this position[179] by advancing a formal proof that this rejection of realism rests on an inaccurate dismissal of the absolute. A recuperation of the absolute requires accepting two principal points. The first asserts *ancestrality* – 'reality anterior to the emergence of the human species'[180] – which is indicated by the existence of *arche-fossils* or objects expressing the 'givenness of a being anterior to its givenness'.[181] Arche-fossils can be proven to exist independently, both by logic[182] and with respect to the laws of physics.[183] The second point involves the systematic reversal of the traditional opposition of necessity and contingency, arguing that the sole necessity in being is contingency itself.[184] From this position Meillassoux is able to argue that a minimal presupposition of absolute autonomy resides in every claim of interdependence: thus, the manner in which for-us, access-oriented correlationism exists includes some element of the *in-itself*. This demonstration requires the clarification of two further terms fundamental to Meillassoux's thought: contingency and fact. In Brassier's summation:

> [c]ontingency is empirical and pertains to phenomena: a phenomenon is contingent if it can come into or out of existence without violating the principles of cognition that govern phenomena. Facticity is transcendental and pertains to our cognitive relation to phenomena, and hence to the principles of knowledge themselves, concerning which it makes no sense to say either that they are necessary or contingent, since we have no other principle to compare them to.[185]

Meillassoux distinguishes between facticity and the factical on one hand, and factiality and the factial on the other. The latter refers to 'the speculative essence of *facticity*, viz., that the facticity of every thing cannot be thought as a fact. Thus factiality must be understood as the non-facticity of the fact.'[186] Meillassoux insists that there is no way of asserting the transcendence of the factial relation except through an ultimate self-contradiction, by falling back on an absolutization of facticity, of its being neither necessary nor contingent. Asserting an absolute, however, has the contradictory implication of deciding as to the necessity of contingency. In this case, what was meant to remain undecidable – that facticity could not decide between contingency and necessity – effectively asserts that 'the contingency or groundlessness of the *for-us* (the correlation) ... becomes *in-itself* or necessary precisely insofar as its contingency is not something which is merely *for-us*'.[187] In other words, fact, when absolutized as the condition of indecision, decides as to the necessity only of contingency. In the most direct terms possible, this compels the acknowledgement that there is a reality outside of the claim that reality cannot distinguish between subject and object.

It is necessary to retrace the most essential points of Meillassoux's argument. His first claim is ontological, derived from the Heideggerian position regarding the 'necessity for everything that is to be a fact'.[188] If something is, it is a fact in relation to some determinate principle or law which confirms that it is: it exists, and it is factual with regard to this existence. Facticity refers 'not [to] an objective reality, but rather [to] the unsurpassable limits of objectivity confronted with the fact *that there is* a world; a world that is describable and perceptible, and structured by determinate invariants'.[189] Meillassoux seeks to draw out the ontological consequences of facticity, resisting the reduction of facticity to the realm of knowledge – which, in framing contingent fact in the contingent terms of knowledge, would threaten to affirm the contingency of contingency itself, potentially leading to circularity and infinite regress[190] – in order to recuperate a pre-conceptual, ontological realism. Rejecting the idea that circularity and infinite regress are unfortunate but inevitable consequences of the search for a radical realism, Meillassoux insists on the persistence of the real against its possible reduction to any particular reality mapped out in terms of cause and effect.

To grasp the simultaneity of contingency and persistence, it becomes necessary to revisit the concept of the absolute. The absolute, the affirmation of the 'non-factual essence of the fact',[191] recognizes that there is something radically unstable at the heart of every fact, an instability that is not the result of any failure to articulate some spectral essence, but is the very basis of being and the real. Where facticity points to certain 'structural invariants'[192] of existence, the absolutization of facticity opens a path to 'grasping the "possibility" of that which is wholly other to the world, but which resides in the midst of the world as such',[193] or in other words, pure being or multiplicity itself. Rethinking contingency in terms of the absolute, and the absolute in terms of multiplicity, upsets conventional metaphysical schemes. It offers an alternate perspective on Meillassoux's claim that 'only the contingency of what is, is not itself contingent',[194] which is different from claiming that 'contingency is necessary'.[195] Indeed, the 'precise claim is that contingency *alone* is necessary – and only this prevents it from being metaphysical. For the statement, "contingency is necessary" is in fact entirely compatible with metaphysics'.[196]

The significance of this argument to the present work lies in the fact that it expresses the importance of determining the theoretical parameters of the real – the means of its communication, exemplification and effectiveness – with reference to objects that persist in the world. Where the majority of contemporary thought seeks to expose a rift between the real and realism, 'forbid[ing] any possibility of a conceptual discourse about the Real in itself',[197] Meillassoux advocates the reconnection, envisioning a 'realism that turns to the Real instead of turning *around* it'.[198] Persistence describes the ahistorical essence of minimalism – the part of every minimalist work that belongs not to the contingent reality of the work as such, but to the real. A powerful example is Eva Hesse's celebrated sculpture, *Contingent*,[199] which consists of eight rectangular sections of latex-covered cheesecloth, suspended in fibreglass banners from the ceiling. Since latex decays over time, darkening and becoming brittle, the work is able to embody the force and effects of contingency in a very concrete way. The reality of the work emerges through a continuum of change, and it is precisely this continuum that is indicative of the persistence of the real. The contingencies to which the work is subject, that define the singularity of the work, are themselves the markers of that which is not contingent: contingency itself – absolute, ahistorical, persistent.

Persistence is intimately tied to temporality, yet their relationship is often difficult and ambiguous, with different experiences of temporal passage often associated with competing accounts of realism. Here it is useful to recall McTaggart's distinction of A series, B series and C series in his epochal essay, 'The Unreality of Time'.[200] The A series is marked by relative temporal positions, 'from the far past through the near past to the present, and then from the present to the near future and the far future'.[201] The B series involves a more fluid progress 'from earlier to later'.[202] The C series, by contrast, 'is not temporal, for it involves no change, but only an order'.[203] Because aesthetics often involves exposing an implicit conflict between time as it is represented and time as it unfolds, the artwork often cuts across this understanding of temporal series. Minimalism, in particular, is concerned with immanence, and so with a temporality that is not easily reflected in a specific model of temporal passage. In this sense, the minimalist artwork often proves particularly appropriate to the task of exploring the ambiguities that the experience of temporal passage introduce to the understanding of persistence.

Among minimalism's most incisive examples in this regard is Steve Reich's *Piano Phase*. This model work of canonical minimalism turns the listener towards a temporally inflected phenomenology of the real, exposing how simultaneous and often apparently contradictory experiences of time still point towards a temporal continuity at the heart of obvious ambiguity and flux. *Piano Phase* exposes an apparent disparity between a chronological time that proceeds monodirectionally from past to future – which might be called intrinsic, irrefutable, consistent, objective, scientific, real, or ancestral time[204] – and a kairological time that expresses itself in subjective, experiential terms as singular moments or events, an 'infinite time … at once delimited and made present'.[205] *Piano Phase* is chronological inasmuch as it has a beginning and an end, both of which are part of a continuum of instants that constitute real time. It is kairological inasmuch as numerous of these instants are unstable, indicative of a temporal ambiguity captured in the rupture of the event, or, indeed, the cyclicality of the material from which the composition is constructed.[206] *Piano Phase* persists, suspended between chronological and kairological time, revealing a productive tension that does not force a choice between competing temporal models as much as it poses questions as to how these relate to one another.

As one of the defining compositions of musical minimalism, it goes without saying that much has been written on the technicalities of *Piano Phase* and what these accomplish aesthetically. It is a work of process music that witnesses a shift in emphasis to 'compositional process and a sounding music [as] one and the same thing',[207] as Reich himself suggests, and which is thus exemplary of the essential unity of form and content Mertens identifies as characteristic of minimalism in general.[208] *Piano Phase* employs very basic musical material: simple melodic units consisting of a steady, rhythmic flow of sixteenth notes and sixteenth note rests. A complex array of effects is produced when this material, played simultaneously on two pianos, is gradually shifted out of phase, one line accelerating while the other stays constant. *Piano Phase* was the composer's first purely instrumental attempt at phase-shifting or phasing, a process he had discovered in his earlier tape compositions.[209] Phasing, as it emerges in Reich's early *oeuvre*, refers to an essentially temporal process involving an acceleration and/or deceleration between two or more relatively short musical fragments which initially sound together. All phasing combines linear time and cyclical time. During the phasing process, the melodic lines making up short fragments or units move progressively apart until, at the point of greatest temporal distance,[210] they once more begin to converge until they have returned to their original relative positions, completing a cycle.[211] These cycles are arranged consecutively, constituting a linear temporal progression from beginning to end.

Structurally, *Piano Phase* consists of three full cycles, also called sections. The first and third consist of a single melodic fragment held by both pianists,[212]while the second consists of two distinct melodies: that of the first pianist reminiscent of the melodic material of the first cycle, and that of the second foreshadowing the material of the third cycle. Each cycle begins with a single piano repeating a particular melodic fragment a number of times (only guidelines are provided as to the specific number of repetitions). At an agreed point, the second player joins the first, either in unison (cycles 1 and 3) or counterpoint (cycle 2) and this new singularity is then repeated, followed by the first phase-shift, one pianist accelerating gradually in relation to the other, who continues playing the material at a constant pace throughout a cycle.[213] This process of acceleration results in what Potter refers to as a 'fuzzy transition',[214] a rapid rhythmic destabilization and melodic complexification, that continues until the phase-shift is complete, which occurs when the first beat of the stable line is coincidental with the second beat of the moving line. At this point the acceleration stops and a new singularity is evident, and is repeated a number of times, once again providing the listener and performer with a stable point of reference, before the phasing process continues. Various points of contingent stability are reached in this way and phasing proceeds until the first beats of both lines are once again coincidental, at which point an initial phasing cycle is complete.

The psycho-acoustic effects of the phasing process are considerable, and Paul Epstein's penetrative analysis is useful in this regard, tracing the perceptual fluctuations at various points of the phasing process and their effects.[215] Perceptual ambiguity is particularly evident in periods of fuzzy transition, giving rise to significant tension that borders on discomfort. As melodic material pulls apart, it creates the disconcerting sense that the musical lines are multiplying rapidly, first moving in two and then in multiple directions at once. It is almost instinctive for the listener to attempt to discern order in this flux and, equally, to anticipate the disorder of the next fuzzy transition during the periods of stability that punctuate the phasing process as a whole. The *restlessness* produced by the alternation of anticipation and resolution, invokes a specific tension, which is clarified only by carefully considering the temporal complexities at work in the composition.

Piano Phase involves three distinct temporalities: the chronological passage of real or ancestral time within which the composition piece begins and ends; the cyclical time that governs the different sections of the composition; and the ambiguous temporality that emerges within fuzzy transition. All three of these coincide in what Steven Savitt terms absolute becoming – a distinctly minimalist understanding of temporal passage as 'the ordered occurrence of events'[216] – in which competing temporal trajectories unfold simultaneously. To the extent that there is no intrinsic connection 'between this sort of passage and either freedom, spontaneity, and emergence on the one hand, or determinism, necessity, and reductionism on the other',[217] absolute becoming describes the real: neither banal nor profound, but persistent.[218] A tentative synthesis of these simultaneous but distinct temporalities occurs when the individual temporal trajectories of the performer and listener transect the field of absolute becoming on which the three temporalities proper to the process of *Piano Phase* – linear, cyclical, and ambiguous – coincide. Performance and perception introduce contingencies into the processes that define *Piano Phase* that were previously only potential, generating a restless simultaneity, a productive alternation between temporalities, that marks the finest minimalist process music.

The full sense of Reich's claim that the listening process 'always extends farther than … can [be] hear[d]'[219] now comes to light: the subjective time of experience, far from imposing a definite limit, represents a productive perturbation within the field of absolute becoming that greatly augments the minimalist work by effecting a provisional synthesis of multiple temporal trajectories within the work, including that of the performer or listener, without reducing any one to the others. The result is a restless simultaneity, an immanent imbrication of temporalities, in which persistence emerges not as the positing of a fact, but as the posing of a question: how does the time of the real accommodate the distinct times of multiple realities? It becomes clearer in this light how the temporality of persistence refers not simply to a continuum of instants, but to a field of tension between the continuity of chronological time – the ancestral time of the real – and the contingency of kairological time – or the experiential time describable in terms of a restless simultaneity. In this fragile and unstable way, minimalism comes to exemplify the persistence of the real.

5

Quantity: On the Radicality of Minimalism

5.1 Compossibility

One and many: Robert Barry's *[This work has been and continues to be refined since 1969]* (1971)

Quantity is what counts in the contemporary world. The historical assimilation of reason to various methods of quantification[1] has resulted in an understanding of reality as ordered by principles of equivalence and exchange, accounting for the ways in which entities are assigned particular values, rendered significant, and incorporated into various economies in a way that makes quantity itself a primary quality of being.[2] 'That number must rule, that the imperative must be: "count!" – who doubts this today?' asks Alain Badiou, confirming that 'under the current empire of number, it is not a question of thought, but of realities'.[3] Indeed, the task of clarifying the links between quantity, reality, and being may yet produce an effective means of resisting the reduction of existence to a mere set of numbers within the machinations of a global capitalist economy.[4] Without underplaying the worrying commitment in contemporary life to accumulation and acquisition, it is also true that a radical view of quantity provides a way of accounting for the emergence of reality from sheer multiplicity.[5] Arguably, it is only by working through this cumulative logic that it becomes possible to offer significant resistance to the numerical regime which dictates what is significant and what is not.

To challenge the reign of number it is necessary to show that what counts in existence is more than quantity alone. The Hegelian distinction of good from bad infinity,[6] the Marxist critique of capitalist accumulation,[7] and the Nietzschean struggle with the zero-point of nihilism[8] are all quintessentially modern strategies employed to undermine the domination of quantity understood as the ground of being. The opposition of many phenomenologists and ordinary language philosophers to this quantitative ontological order is also notable, as is the work of critical theorists. Indeed, Horkheimer and Adorno offer considerable critical resistance to the ways in which modernity has instrumentalized reason by bringing nature, justice, economy and knowledge under a supreme law of calculability.[9] By insisting on quantity as a radical ground, a 'substrate of domination',[10] philosophical modernity is, they claim, scarred by a strategic error that makes it possible for equation to become the master of the dialectic – the process through which it becomes apparent that 'each thing is what it is only by becoming what it is not'[11] – restraining the sheer 'abundance of qualities'.[12] The path through and beyond this impasse to this liberation must involve a progressive uncoupling of thought and quantity achieved through a negative dialectic process which, Adorno claims, 'change[s] this direction of conceptuality'[13] – the positive quantification of existence – through a 'turn toward nonidentity'.[14] The significance of aesthetics emerges through its capacity to assert its nonsummativity, its assertion of a non-identity that resists absolute quantification.

Although convincing on their own terms, the resistance of various qualitative discourses to the logic of calculation is only marginally successful. It is in this context that Badiou's conception of quantity proves particularly insightful – opposed to the tyranny of number, yet insistent that number is the proper medium for the species of thinking capable of grasping the fact that multiplicity, as pure quantity, is the stuff of being itself.[15] For Badiou, the challenge facing contemporary thought is to understand how multiplicity is able to constitute contingent unities that 'count-as-one'[16] without reducing or eliminating multiplicity as such. Conceived as an ontological ground, quantity reveals a radical vacillation between the one and the multiple.

Parmenides, the great philosopher-poet who was perhaps the first to theorize this fluctuation, distinguishes between unity as the truth of being which is 'ungenerated and indestructible, whole, of one kind and unwavering, and complete',[17] and the unreliable multiplicity of qualitative perception.[18] He arrives at arguably the most fundamental of all ontological axioms: the one 'must either altogether be or not be'.[19] From the perspective of existence, the decision in favour of unity, or *the one*, seems unavoidable; yet it is precisely the inconsistencies that emerge in its wake that Plato rigorously interrogates in his *Parmenides*. Here is established the principal axiom on which every quantitative ontology rests: 'whether one is or is not, it and the others both are and are not, and both appear and do not appear all things in all ways'.[20] Together, Plato's eight hypotheses probe the conditions under which the one and the many appear to be *compossible*,[21] existing simultaneously and providing existence with its particular charge.

For Badiou, however, 'the upshot of the aporias in *Parmenides* [reveals that] it is pointless to try to deduce the existence (or non-existence) of the One: it is necessary to decide, and then assume the consequences'.[22] In contrast to Horkheimer and Adorno, who reject quantity as ontological ground altogether, asserting in its place a qualitative model of dialectic becoming, Badiou affirms the radically quantitative ground of being, arguing unambiguously that the one does not exist, and that being is therefore irreducibly multiple.[23] As Hallward notes,

> the only coherent conception of Being as One ultimately depends on some instance of the One either as transcendental limit (a One *beyond* being, or God) or as all-inclusive immanence (a cosmos or Nature) ... [M]odernity and in particular modern science have demonstrated that ... the idea of a One-All is incoherent ... [T]herefore if Being can be thought at all, it must be thought as multiple rather than One.[24]

The present argument situates itself between the qualitative and quantitative poles, accepting the irreducible multiplicity of being, but resisting the suggestion that only mathematical procedure is capable of approximating the radical quantity at the heart of being.[25] The aesthetic sphere, for instance, resists the totalizing calculation of the one, holding itself open to the possibility of generating 'the world over again'[26] in a way that exemplifies the multiplicity that inheres in the contingent unity of the work. As with its remarkable capacity for clarifying the real, minimalism proves adept at intensifying the aesthetic apprehension of radical quantity itself. Its finest works provide minimal impediment to the accurate apprehension of the form, medium, substance, constitutive process and perception of the artwork in question. The task, then, becomes one of conceptualizing minimalism in quantitative terms in order to render being itself increasingly intelligible.

To examine this contention, it is necessary to show that minimalism can be quantitatively schematized – following the Parmenidean axiom of the one and the many – in terms of continuity (one) and calculation (many). Minimalism can then be revisited in quantitative terms without undermining the qualities of its objects. As regards *continuity*[27] – the chronological expression of the concept of persistence as already elaborated – minimalism reproduces in its objects a fundamental tension between immanence and absence. In minimalist music, this is particularly evident in the opposition of extreme loudness, amplification, and the duration of sustained pitch, to dynamic limitation and silence.[28] In visual art, it is largeness of scale and monochromatic density which might be opposed to miniature forms and sparseness or parsimony in exemplifying these poles of continuity.[29] Literary minimalism marks presence by various techniques of self-referential containment, semantic condensation, blank effusiveness, absence in works of extreme brevity, and narratives constructed of minimal material with only a fragile coherence.[30] With regard to *calculation* – the enumerative processes by which radical multiplicity comes to be represented – minimalism clarifies the quantitative ground of being when its objects are constituted by modular repetition and variation. Numerical symbols and sequences occur frequently in minimalist music, visual art and literature, offering concrete markers of their grounding in ontological quantity. Similarly, the addition and subtraction of material to the repeated modules which constitute certain minimalist works in all media, render their *autotelic* or self-directed generative processes and quantitative substance increasingly perceptible.

It is true that there is no neat separation between persistence and calculation, since, while the former refers to the actual substance of entities and the latter to the processes through which substance emerges and is sustained, the existence of any entity implies that substance is counted continuously. An interesting vehicle for this confluence, which nonetheless emphasizes the irresolvable tension between the one and the many, is Robert Barry's conceptual poem, *[This work has been and continues to be refined since 1969].*[31]

Pulling between simplicity and complexity, the one and the many, the poem consists of a sequence of eighty-six adjectives. Taken individually, each of these marks a specific event, a moment in which the ongoing process of poetic formation instantiates a new unity. Yet, read in sequence, or in various combinations, the words point to the irreducible multiplicity of the work, and the fact that every reading contributes to its growing complexity. The poem exists in flux: its constituent words point inwards, prescribing rather than describing the poem and becoming signifiers of the force of *poiesis* itself; but they also point outward, setting in motion multiple sequences of indefinite becoming. This antithetical movement is reflected even in the poem's title: 'this work',[32] affirming its unity, 'has been and continues to be refined',[33] gesturing towards its multiplicity.

Simply read from start to finish with a minimum of semantic reflection regarding the disjunctions that emerge as the lines progress, the reader might well take the sequence for a superficial, but nonetheless stable, unity. After all, it begins with the words 'It is whole, determined, sufficient, individual, known, complete'.[34] Yet there are clearly multiple routes of reading, numerous ways in which these modifiers might be aligned to make sense of the poem. If it is one – 'unified', 'isolated', 'harmonious', 'situated', 'limited', 'specific', 'uniform', 'particular' and 'restricted'[35] – it is at the same time multiple – 'dependent', 'varied', 'diverse', 'divisible', 'repeatable', 'complex', 'improvable', 'involved' and 'arranged'.[36] Upon closer reading, the poem offers compelling if indirect testament to the instability and indeterminacy that rapidly overshadow any attempt to claim the absolute ascendency of either the one or the multiple. This is the ambiguity that, for Badiou, compels a decision, framing radical quantity in axiomatic terms: either one, or many. Yet, as competing conceptual syntaxes emerge from the process of close reading, the minimal means of the poem reveal a rich field of compossibility – of one *and* many – echoing Perreault's sentiment that 'in the best [minimal] works … [the art] is maximal'.[37] Thus, even when a minimalist work so clearly suspends itself between the one and the many, its constitutive incompletion appears to point unavoidably towards multiplicity. For the sum of one and many is many, and one subtracted from many does not reduce multiplicity itself – simple calculations made possible by aesthetic intuition, that trace the contours of a radically quantitative ontology.

5.2 Quantification

Quantity as quality in minimalist aesthetics: Donald Judd's *Untitled (Six boxes)* (1974) Frank Stella's *Empress of India* (1965)

To grasp the full ontological weight of calculation it is necessary to examine more closely the fundamental premises of Badiou's quantitative ontology. Badiou argues that being in itself – the subject of ontology – is irreducibly multiple.[38] However, he also recognizes that the history of philosophy and thought is scarred by the misapprehension that being can be reduced to unity or the one: the contention that the one is, and all that is, is one.[39] Returning to the Parmenidean axiom of the one and the many,[40] Badiou seeks to recuperate an ontology of the multiple,[41] arguing that the conjunction of mathematics and philosophy reveals that the one is not, and that pure being is both thinkable and presentable in terms of pure multiplicity.[42] A problem immediately arises: if everything is multiple, how is it that things exist in any unified or substantive form, no matter how contingent this form may be? To account for this, Badiou distinguishes between consistent and inconsistent multiplicity, which corresponds to his differentiation of existence from being.[43] He claims that those things that can be said to exist, have consistency,[44] and that this consistency is subtracted from the inconsistency of multiplicity;[45] a subtraction that does not reduce multiplicity, since pure multiplicity, or being, is infinite and hence irreducible and inexhaustible.

Existence is therefore dependent on multiplicity being *counted as one*, a process Badiou refers to as the *count*.[46] However, as the count does not eliminate multiplicity from presentation, there necessarily remains some uncounted, inconsistent part in any presentation or existential situation: the *void*.[47] From the perspective of existence, the void operates as a sort of spectral ground – the unpresentable part of every presentation that is distributed everywhere but located nowhere; the part of every contingent unity that connects it to pure multiplicity.[48] Consequently, for the count to be guaranteed its consistency, it must be re-presented – literally presented a second time, or counted again.[49] So there are two principal processes involved in guaranteeing the persistence of existence: presentation, or the count; and re-presentation, or the count of the count. Presentation, or the count, provides structure to being; re-presentation, or the count of the count, generates the metastructure through which existence is subtracted from being.[50] Within these basic conditions, entities appear with varying intensities,[51] are subject to change,[52] and sometimes also disappear, become inconsistent multiples, or are destroyed.

Accepting that radical quantity grounds existence, which unfolds within various regimes of calculation, it becomes pivotal to pay close attention to the conditions under which these regimes are disrupted, opened up, clarified and reorganized. The most radical and rarest of these Badiou terms the *event*: an aleatory eruption,[53] a radical beginning,[54] a 'fundamental anomaly'[55] that cuts across both being and existence,[56] announcing the advent of novelty.[57] The event disappears almost as soon as it appears,[58] and what remains is a trace. In expressing a fidelity to this trace[59] – the minimal remnant of the event, the mark of its facticity – a new form of subjectivity is born, one capable of effecting a significant realignment of reality, and which is defined not by its finitude but rather by its potentially infinite progress set in motion by the event.[60]

In this light, access to the infinite – the calculation of multiplicity itself – is of considerable significance. For Badiou, overcoming the contemporary impediment to multiplicity, and hence to being itself, requires rethinking the substance of number with respect to at least three conceptual vocabularies: logical, formalist, and set-theoretical.[61] For Badiou, it is the capacity of set theory to account for infinity as a real quantity that sets it apart as the legitimate expression of ontological multiplicity. In short, a set is a conceptual entity founded on its capacity to distinguish itself from other entities which, by virtue of this very distinction, it groups together. Thus every set is defined by pure differentiation[62] – the void, which is precisely void of any qualities whatsoever[63] – in which case any of the entities it groups are grouped not solely by virtue of the qualities they possess, but by their difference from that which groups them. The corollary is that any entity can potentially found or belong to an infinite number of sets without exhausting its particular qualities or the force by which sets are able to group entities.[64] This force is none other than quantification itself. It is precisely for this reason that the contingent unities that are subtracted from the plenitude of the infinite – Badiou terms them 'one-multiples'[65] – are able to *exist* with a singular intensity while their being remains *multiple*. If being and belonging are demonstrably quantitative, the only quality shared by *every* entity is, in fact, its quantitative essence.

Erupting from the void, the event is of significance in this scheme because it establishes a new principle of calculation, and the aesthetic sphere emerges as one of the privileged sites for examining the event and its radical relation to ontological quantity, as well as for tracing its generative consequences in reality.[66] Yet the event is rare, an exceptional and aleatory supplement. Existence is, for the most part, constituted by contingent unties that have no particular valences; entities that are counted, but which may not count for anything specific. Here minimalism proves particularly apposite to the task of presenting and representing, reflecting and reflecting on, the subtractive and cumulative processes that underpin the quantitative being of the everyday. Minimalism generates an aesthetic field in which the quantitative dimension of the work emerges as its most persistent quality. The progressive alienation of the hard sciences from the cultural sphere – the former often incorrectly conflated with quantity, and the latter with quality – culminates with dismaying predictability in scientists quantifying cultural objects, and cultural critics qualifying scientific knowledge as self-justifying rhetoric.[67] Radicalizing this relation, the ontological accomplishment of some of the best minimalism lies in its depolarization of quantity and quality, intensifying the qualities of its objects by demonstrating how these are grounded in quantity.

Donald Judd's serial sculptures, most of them cubic or rectangular, are exemplary in this respect. Seldom measuring more than one cubic metre, with many lacking tops and thus perceptibly hollow, the singularity of these works resides not only in their qualities – their form and materials – but also in their quantitative dimension – their scale and the fact that they are conceived as part of a series. Particularly striking are the six polished brass cubes making up Judd's *Untitled (Six boxes)*.[68] The full significance of the work emerges only when it is grasped in terms of a serial logic, as a progressive tension between part and whole, unit and the contingent sum of units. It becomes evident that quantity grounds the qualities of these works, and that their qualities affirm this ground. Made from solid sheets of highly polished brass, the sides of these cubes mirror whatever is external to the work on their surfaces. By reproducing the world, these objects appear to draw it towards themselves, only to repel it. The point at which the surface and the world seem indistinguishable is also the point at which the work divorces itself from its mimetic function, revealing an irreducible ontological distance between this reproduction of the world on the surface of the cube and the cube itself. This distance is intensified considerably in the *mise en abyme* generated between individual units: each unit mirrors the capacity of other units to mirror, revealing that what is *reflected* in this irreducible gap is nothing other than irreducibility itself – quantity resisting its quantification or, in other words, quantity apprehended as an intrinsic quality. This exemplifies not only how the qualities of aesthetic objects frequently only *represent* the quantity which grounds their existence, but also how quantity is able to resist quantification to the extent that it constitutes the most radical quality of a work.

The serial nature of the sculpture is thus generatively complicated by its particular qualities, and these combine to mark its singularity as a work. What emerges is a type of dynamic and open-ended Gestalt marked by the relation between the unity, the series, the whole, and the processes which calculate the confluences and divergences between these. This ambiguity is more plainly revealed in the formal tensions that inhabit Stella's shaped canvases. In *Empress of India*,[69] for instance, the work is composed of four identical chevron-shaped segments of canvas in different shades of red, slotted together to form an irregular shape. For Fried, the work is apprehended as a Gestalt, exemplary of what he terms a deductive structure, 'demand[ing] to be seen as deriving from the framing edge ... as having been "deduced" from it'.[70] From another perspective, the work emerges through a constructivist process: in each segment, evenly spaced, thin white lines, characteristic of Stella's early work, reproduce the shape of the canvas and point towards its apex, while the apex itself points towards the outer segments, establishing a relation that anticipates the act of counting these segments together as a single or whole work.

Minimalist works give fragile clarity to the many ambiguities of calculation, demonstrating that, in the manifestation of real entities, the interrelationship of quantity and quality is a question of coordination rather than subordination. If quantity is radical to the minimalist enterprise, this does not imply a suppression of the qualities of the work, but is rather an exposition of the persistent quantitative ground on which these qualities emerge. When these qualities are themselves essentially quantitative, the effect is not to eliminate meaning as such, but rather to intensify the existential significance of quantity, and of the various process of enumeration and calculation through which reality is ordered. In this way, minimalism is able to offer an oblique critique of those situations in which identity is equated with number, and in which existence is reduced to value; situations in which number is instantiated as a destructive protocol which, as Badiou recognizes, threatens not only the political and economic spheres, but, equally, the institutionalization of knowledge acquisition and the arena of cultural representation.[71]

Indeed, there is no reason to presuppose an essential discontinuity between the insights regarding quantity and quantification gained from aesthetics and those that emerge from the scientific pursuit of knowledge or the unfolding of socio-political events. The quantitative dimension of reality may be concealed when entities are subtracted from multiplicity – or counted as one – but it can never be eliminated. It is often the concealment of, rather than the explicit appeal to, a quantitative logic that facilitates the reduction of quantity to a purely economic discourse. While an uncritical accession to the logic of calculation poses a significant danger, it is also true that an uncritical suppression of number fails to grasp that it is the quantitative force of ontology itself which stands against the absolute quantification of all existence. Thus, mistaking the radical quantity at the heart of being as just another number is itself an ideological reduction, one reflected in Badiou's lament that 'we don't know what a number is, so we don't know what we are'.[72] By exposing radical quantity as its principal quality, a great deal of minimalism resists this economy, interrogating what it might mean to perform a subtraction without reduction – which is reflected in minimalism's concern with persistence, as expressed in terms of continuity – and its corollary, an addition without accumulation – which is exemplified in minimalist works concerned with calculation. In this way, minimalism is able to maintain itself in a critical relation not only to the logic of capitalism, but to all regimes in which the reign of number is asserted in absolute terms.

5.3 Continuity

The logic of persistence: Yves Klein's *Monotone Symphony* (1949) Steve McCaffery's *Panopticon* (1984)

Persistence, to recall, describes the part of every entity that is most real; the continuous part that underpins every contingent manifestation of reality. Grasped in quantitative terms, persistence might be apprehended at the heart of the continuous process of structuration, of counting, that allows pure multiplicity to appear as the contingent unity of a particular reality. In this light, persistence describes the radical ontological capacity inherent in every entity to cohere with relative stability – although permitting quantitative and qualitative changes – for a continuous, if unspecified, period. An entity that persists is at once grounded by, yet indifferent to, its own persistence. This indifference distinguishes persistence from perseverance, endurance or resilience, all of which reduce radical quantity to a set of qualities. Persistence exposes the anteriority and interiority proper to every entity: the former insofar as every entity is persistent prior to its persistence being perceived or interpreted; the latter in the sense that persistence refers to the internal duration, or period of sustained existence, proper to every entity. Turning this durational aspect of persistence outward, moving from the temporality of the real to the temporality of reality, persistence comes to express a logic of *continuity*.

Grasped in terms of chronological continuity, the persistence of minimalism emerges from within a radical and essentially quantitative tension between immanence and absence. This is perhaps most conspicuous in minimalist music, particularly in the use of sustained tone and silence in monotonal and drone works. These are works which, by persisting, contain their own objecthood. The sustained presence or absence of sound, often undetermined by the composition itself, draws attention not only to duration as essential musical matter, but also to the manner in which sound emerges and persists. A plausible phenomenology of sound must account for the advent of sonic phenomena either by asserting a field of generative absence – silence – from which sound arises as a negation of the totality of a void, or by establishing noise as an archaic field of chaotic presence from which sound emerges as a subtraction or differentiation of contingent order from disorder.[73] In identifying sound as the negation of silence, the first conforms to the procedural contours of Hegelian sublation,[74] while the second, asserting sound in subtractive terms, recalls the Husserlian *epochē*.[75]

Where noise clearly affirms radical multiplicity as the essential stuff of being, silence is more subtle in its ontological allegiances, effecting a type of negative count, a contingent unity derived from absence rather than presence. Silence is thus an apophatic phenomenon, marking the 'unsayable limits to thought, rationality, even to the human imagination'.[76] Samuel Beckett, for example, conceives of silence upon a threshold of affirmation and negation, of emergence and disappearance, at the precise moment of its transmediation from a phenomenon to the *representation* of a phenomenon. This is an evasive silence. It is 'no such thing ... as sound',[77] which is approximated only obliquely by what it is not, and which reflects the polyvalence of being, 'the end, the beginning, the beginning again',[78] but also an ateleological essence since silence is in fact 'never left',[79] an unattainable constant which reveals in its place an irreducible 'core of murmors'.[80] Yet, even when silence is conceived positively in terms of an 'active human performance',[81] this performance is one of 'yielding'[82] to the field of silent potentiality of what is *to-be-said*[83] which precedes every affirmatory articulation of existence. By contrast, for the philosopher Michel Serres there can be no question that existence is subtracted from the noisy multiplicity of being: 'background noise never ceases; it is limitless, continuous, unending, unchanging ... So noise is not a matter of phenomenology ... it is a matter of being itself.'[84] A similar recognition arguably underpins the most minimal of all aesthetic works, John Cage's epochal *4'33"* – a composition which ostensibly instructs the performance of silence, but which in fact reveals, through the plenitude of coincidental noises which permeate every performance, that it is the noise of multiplicity that constitutes the fabric of being.

The complex relationship that persists between undifferentiated noise, sustained pitch, and silence is clarified by minimalism to the extent that it simultaneously exposes the ontological and perceptual properties of sonic objecthood. Theoretical constructs such as the *auditory filter*[85] explain how, through selective auditory attention,[86] contingently coherent sonic forms come to be subtracted from sensory multiplicity, reproducing at the level of perception what the present work claims in terms of the reality of sound itself. The minimalist use of sustained pitch and silence integrates subtraction and multiplicity in a singular manner: prolonged exposure to sustained sound, or to the genuine absence of sound, produces a curious and sometimes uncomfortable type of amnesia. As evidenced in the single- or multiple-pitch drone compositions of La Monte Young or Charlemagne Palestine, the longer an invariant sound is sustained, the more the sounds which precede the drone, or potentially follow it, cease to offer stable external points of reference from which the scale, acoustic qualities, or timbrel singularity of the drone situation can be judged. Drone music dominates perception to the extent that extraneous information is either missed or masked.[87] As a result, the scale and intensity of the work seem to increase exponentially the longer the drone is sustained, so that a sense of immanence – the *persistence* of temporal quantity as the basis of sonic objecthood – dominates the composition. The scale of a work is what enables it to 'hold its own space',[88] to express its singularity and produce its singular effect. Indeed, scale might be defined as the quantity proper to an artwork in order for it to persist at its singular intensity.

In the case of minimalist music, this intensity is conceivable in works of considerable duration and extreme brevity, as well as in those of indeterminate length. Arguably the earliest minimalist drone work,[89] Yves Klein's *Monotone Symphony – Silence*, consists of a single chord[90] held for an indefinite period, followed by an extended period of silence.[91] Returning to the fundamental possibilities of music itself, this 'two-part continuum of sound and silence'[92] reflects the quantitative basis of musical minimalism by demonstrating the confluence of duration and tonal presence or absence. Similarly, Young's first epic drone composition – *The Tortoise, His Dreams and Journeys*, a composition performed by his aptly named *Theatre of Eternal Music*, a work which, in principle, is ongoing[93] – effects a remarkably forceful sonic continuum. Minimal in conception and in performance, it consists of a variable number of unspecified sustained tones held above a continuous amplified drone. Young sets up this drone to sound for some time prior and subsequent to any performance of the work, intensifying its symbolic status as a 'primordial sonic vibration',[94] an ethereal continuum from which the quantitative 'sustenance'[95] or persistence of sonic being arises.[96]

Turning to the visual arts, the monochromatic lineage constitutes the most obvious visual analogue to drone music. The immediacy evoked by Newman's expansive fields of colour might be usefully contrasted to the introspective intensity of Reinhardt's and Stella's smaller black paintings. These work all demonstrate that the optimal scale of an artwork rests on its capacity to capture some sort of essential presence or immanence, rather than on the actual magnitude of the work in question. Similarly, Bladen's imposing *The X* – a massive wooden sculpture erected over two floors as part of *Scale as Content* exhibition at the Corcoran Gallery[97] – might be contrasted with Robert Morris's 'unitary forms' – eminently approachable irregular polyhedrons 'which do not reduce relationships [but] order them',[98] reinforcing presence through a more moderate scale, incorporating multiple perspectives into the definition of the object, strengthening rather than weakening its quantitative Gestalt.[99]

Where spatial scale is most significant to the visual arts, and temporal scale to music, the most notable capacity of minimalist literature resides in its ability to generate aesthetic constellations which explicitly incorporate spatial and temporal scale. The writing of Steve McCaffery, for example, self-consciously transgresses conventions of medium and genre in order to incorporate the immediacy of performance with the protracted engagement which is required by an avant-garde poetics that stresses complexity, hybridity and intermediality. Charles Bernstein situates this poetic capacity within a dialectical field which 'has as its outer limit, impermeability & as its inner limit, absorption'.[100] Where absorptive works seek 'not to represent the world … but to be the thing described',[101] anti-absorptive works make writing 'opaque to the point of repelling the reader'[102] emphasizing the quantitative materiality of the text by 'by maintaining its visibility & undermining its meaning'.[103]

In *Panopticon*, McCaffery develops a species of collagic textuality which, through a careful counter-point of techniques, radicalizes the relationship between the material, semantic and conceptual elements of writing. Illustrations on gridded drafting paper are incorporated within a range of typographical experiments, both reflecting and prompting rapid stylistic alternations between ornateness and sparseness. At some points several narrative sequences run concurrently, but there is also a more subtle alternation between blank, descriptive passages which recall Robbe-Grillet and Carver, and those reminiscent of the fragmented concision of later Beckett.

Remarkable in this respect, and with respect to persistence as describing an essential continuity between radical quantity and the real, is the 'Again and again' sequence through which McCaffery undertakes a substantial, performative exploration of the nature and significance of repetition. The sequence represents a relationship caught in a repetitive cycle which is patently as inescapable as it is destructive. A patently dysfunctional continuum is interrupted by partial accounts of arguments, sexual encounters and half-hearted resolutions to 'give it another try'.[104] Duplicating while simultaneously exceeding its semantic sense, formal repetition generates a pattern which is exemplary of both a progression and a sudden halt. Thus, the opening invocation – '[a]gain and again … once more … over and over'[105] – is almost immediately limited as – 'yet again not again'[106] and 'on and not on'.[107] Repetition promises what it cannot deliver – 'Moments anticipatory. Then cancelled'[108] – echoing Derrida's insight that 'once repeated … its identification with itself gathers an imperceptible difference'.[109]

This is especially clear in the nearly 400 consecutive repetitions of the phrase *and on* with which McCaffery closes the sequence. The visual effect of this repetition is startling, transforming text into a concrete pattern that clarifies the quantitative materiality of writing. Indeed, any actual reading or recitation of this final part of the sequence effects a similar recognition regarding fundamental quantity. The self-reflexive propulsiveness of the text – the fact that it is an icon of continuity, that it does indeed go *on and on* as it claims it will – is reinforced by the sheer number of repetitions. A similarly concrete expression of the significance of repetition in coming to grips with radical quantity is evident in Arrigo Lora-Totino's concrete poem, 'FINITEINFINITE'.[110] The work consists of a page almost filled by the repetition of the capitalized word 'INFINITE'. However each line begins with the word 'FINITE', indicative of the fact that what is 'FINITE' is, after all, part of the 'INFINITE', or that a 'FINITE' event has the capacity to produce 'INFINITE' consequences. In both cases, continuity and quantity are thus tied together through repetition.

Returning to McCaffery, distinct from the complex patterns of repetition and variation that dominate the earlier part of the 'Again and again' sequence[111] which function to draw attention to the form of the writing, is the final set of repetitions ('and on …') which seems to negate form, substituting pure quantity in its place. Each reiteration of 'and on' contributes to a curious and progressive amnesia, rendering more distant and vague the material which precedes it, while promising an immanence which it fails fully to deliver. Finally, this anti-absorptive writing has '[n]o means to gather',[112] is capable of fixing or confirming 'no fact',[113] and offers 'no frame'[114] within which its complexities could aggregate to constitute stable sense or meaning. What remains, then, is precisely persistence itself – the textual intuition of radical quantity as marked by '[r]epetition of the phrase'.[115]

However, persistence offers no easy distinction between more and less: scale, although a relative concept, remains singular to the work in question. It is in this precise sense – the communication of quantity without essential reference to proportion – that the 'Again and again' sequence moves beyond any straightforward distinction of minimalism and maximalism from one another. It is also such an indistinction that allows this terminal repetition to resonate in the precise sense that Nietzsche refers to as the eternal recurrence of the same, which imagines itself capable of rescuing difference from the very midst of indifference.

If largeness of scale indicates persistence in terms of the work's spatial, durational and conceptual continuities, then limited scale delineates the minimal conditions which are required for a work to persist as such. In this light, quantitative intensity is as central to minimalist works which are miniature as it is to those which are massive. Howard Skempton's *Lyric Study* for piano – less than a minute in duration – is as effective in exposing the significance of scale as is La Monte Young's *The Well-Tuned Piano*, which in most performances continues for several hours. Similarly, the minimalist poles occupied by Kenneth Goldsmith's *Soliloquy* – a transcription of every word uttered by the poet in a single week – and Ian Hamilton Finlay's one-word poems, reflect with equal force the poetic intuition of radical quantity.

Similarly, although the logic of persistence appears in much minimalism to be defined by stasis, close attention to these works reveals a field of considerable flux. In this light, it becomes apparent that the nonabsorptive impermeability of McCaffery's writing rests on an almost frenetic movement on its surface. Similarly, Young's drone compositions expose a significant tension at the heart of their apparently indifferent persistence by demonstrating that the effects of sustained tone are by no means uninteresting. Tying together the properly quantitative aspect of duration and the qualitative complexities of timbre, these works often expose the overtone series from which apparently stable pitches are composed, at first intensifying the dissonance that seems in fact to underpin consonance, but then clarifying how the intrinsic qualities of pitches relate to one another when sounded over prolonged periods.[116] The monochromatic tradition of minimalist painting effects a similar recognition: the considerable density of Reinhardt's black canvas becomes apparent through prolonged exposure to the work, and as the viewer is drawn beyond the surface of the work, into the being of colour itself, the multiple hues of black transfigure the painting into a dynamic field that reveals a great deal about the mechanics of perception.

Finally, the dynamism of minimalism remains rooted in its exposition of persistence as radical to quantitative ontology and its manifestation in realist terms. The fact that the persistence of minimalist objects is missed by some critics accounts for the manner in which the very same object can seem unremarkable to one person but deeply transfigurative to another. This is not, however, to undermine the active role of perception with respect to these works: in some cases, persistence involves the reader, listener or viewer literally spending time with them; in others it is tied to the immanence with which they communicate themselves as works. Much minimalism, on the other hand, seeks to integrate persistence and perception by drawing attention to the centrality of process in determining the parameters of the work. In such cases, form and formation are essentially confluent. The present contention is that this processual conjunction occurs according to a logic of *calculation*: whether by implicit or explicit evocation of number and quantity, the structure or form of these works is determined by processes of accumulation and subtraction.

5.4 Calculation

Autotelism and modular process:
Philip Glass's *Two Pages* (1968)
Samuel Beckett's 'what is the word' (1988)
Robert Lax's 'word' (1962)
Sol LeWitt's *Maquette for One, Two, Three* (1979)

Calculation, to recall Badiou, is pivotal to any situation that asserts the essential multiplicity of being,[117] yet which also recognizes that there is no way in which multiplicity in itself can be presented.[118] Distinguishing between consistent or structured multiplicity on the one hand, and inconsistent or unstructured multiplicity on the other,[119] Badiou maintains that all objects which exist, do so because there is a procedure – the *count* – by which inconsistent multiplicity is rendered contingently consistent.[120] Consistency is contingent for the very precise reason that there remains a foundational element in every situation which is necessarily unpresentable,[121] a *void* point without which consistency would be meaningless.[122] To encounter reality there is both presentation and re-presentation: the first, a *subtraction* without reduction – the *count*; the second a *calculation* of this subtraction and its remainder – the *count of the count*.[123]

Minimalism exemplifies this calculative logic both explicitly and implicitly. Explicit calculation is revealed in terms of the incorporation of numerical and alphabetical sequences, phonemic utterances, lists and series of various kinds. Implicit calculation is woven into the formal construction of minimalism through modular variation and incremental repetition, expanding or contracting sequences, and progressive displacements. Thus, if one type of minimalist calculation involves enumerative processes in which units added together or subtracted from one another, another consists of autotelic or self-directed processes in which initial material is subject to cyclical or open-ended processes of variation and elaboration.[124] As opposed to the deductivist Gestalt often pursued by minimalist visual artists, the logic of calculation is typically constructivist. In works such as Reich's *Four Organs* units are added together or taken apart in a specific and ordered way. In other works, basic material is subject to cyclical variation, as in Reich's phasing compositions, recalling the logic of Nietzschean eternal recurrence of the same; or is subject to open-ended elaboration, as in the case of Glass's early keyboard works, which often employ potentially infinite formal processes.

The logic of calculation does not yield easily to linear teleology precisely because its *telos* is distributed in the very processes through which the work takes shape. Minimalist calculation is typically autotelic, and in its self-directedness the quantitative implications of process are clarified. As already noted, *pulse-pattern minimalism* is the term Robert Fink proposes to account for process in minimalist music. It describes 'minimalism *as* repetition, particularly as repetition with a regular pulse, a pulse that underpins the complex evolution of musical patterns to alter listener perception of time and *telos* in systematic, culturally influential ways.'[125] In McCaffery's 'Again and again' sequence, a sense of persistence is communicated by the invariant repetition of phrases, whether they are distributed among other experimental techniques, as in the earlier part of the passage, or whether they constitute the continuous repetition with which the sequence ends. By contrast, pulse-pattern minimalism principally involves incremental repetition, the addition or subtraction of small melodic or rhythmic fragments.

In all media, repetition and process are fundamental mnemonic tools involved in providing cohesion at the level both of content and of structure.[126] '[R]epetitions make … up the structure of the work within itself … determining its multiple relations to what is outside it', as J. Hillis Miller recognizes.[127] Regardless of whether it is made possible by a radical unity or a radical distinction – fundamental sameness or fundamental difference – repetition might be interpreted as a means of guaranteeing continuity. Indeed, repetition appears to be a prerequisite for any teleological account of persistence. For a sense of direction and purpose to exist, the recollection of the past *must* imply the future, hence the cogency of Mertens's formulation of repetition in terms of a teleological imperative: '[r]epetition in the traditional work appears as a reference to what has gone before, so that one has to remember what was forgotten.'[128]

While the emphasis in minimalist music on process and repetition certainly provides a sense of motoric movement, even of propulsion, it is less certain that this propulsiveness is reducible to purposiveness or a substantial *telos*. In pulse-pattern minimalism, for example, the stable and predictable build-up and release of harmonic tension is not a predominant concern. Furthermore, it is seldom possible to determine any stable programmatic end from the music itself. Nonetheless, minimalism is highly affective, provoking intense and extreme reactions. These doubtless derive in part from the immanence and persistence described earlier, but are also related to the capacity of processual minimalism to intensify responses by subverting their teleological bias. Processual minimalism uncouples itself from the knot of representation and teleology which affirms that the relational aspects of art are expressed in their directedness towards meaning and significance. For minimalism, radical quantity – whether expressed in terms of persistence or calculation – is an end in itself. In this sense, processual minimalism is autotelic, instantiating a self-reflexive and self-contained teleology in which the purposiveness of its objects is determined by the internal relationship of their constituent parts.

Tracing the process of generation in real time, presenting a concrete accumulation of significant moments, music is particularly appropriate to clarifying these distinct species of teleology. According to Mertens, the representational or classical teleology of most music 'gives the listener a non-ambivalent orientation and … attempts to inform him of *meaningful* musical *contents*'.[129] For the classicist, '*telos* determines form'[130] by structuring sound in terms of an anthropic principle that matches the rhythmic, harmonic, and melodic tension and the release of the composition to a somatic experience of sound.[131] Many critics, Mertens among them, maintain that minimalism successfully subverts representational teleology, invoking a 'non-directed evolution in which the listener is no longer submitted to the constraint of following the musical evolution'.[132] Minimalist music does not compel the listener to follow any specific chain of reference or signification, and so makes it possible, to a significant extent, to experience the work in at least two distinct ways: as a generative process in itself; and as a generative process as a means of calculation or quantification.

Fink questions the possibility of ateleological music, suggesting rather that minimalism exemplifies a recombinant teleology: 'there is in fact no nonteleological experience of music in Western culture, only new recombinations of teleology not yet recognized as transformations of goal-directedness'.[133] Fink's recombinant teleology must be understood as an attempt to account for the inner-purposiveness of minimalist music in its indifference to anthropomorphic scale – the 'time-frames listeners can recognize'[134] – and to formalist protocols. 'Detach teleology from form, and an entire panoply of new arrangements opens up',[135] suggests Fink. Musical minimalism is not devoid of direction as such, but it subverts the conventional role that melodic repetition and isorhythmic patterns play in conventionally progressive diatonic harmony. Within the spare figures of minimalist process music direction is internally derived and limited. Nonetheless, pulse and rhythm, suspension and resolution, progression and cadence, persist indirectly in processes which are internally derived and bounded. A work is autotelic when its elements – whether sonic, verbal, visual or conceptual – establish that the generative force underpinning the work's progress is simultaneously self-referential and self-productive. The shape of such minimalism is determined by the fact that its initial material is expressed in terms of process, so that what drives the work – the evolving relationships of its elements, and the progressive constitution of its form – is also its most intimate potential.

Autotelic minimalism contains a structural and processual purposiveness sufficient to render external reference or relation non-essential. Terry Riley's epochal *In C* demonstrates how identical material, subjected to the non-identical conditions of performance, exemplifies that repetition is able to constitute an active, self-productive means of structuring a work. Players are given a steady pulse and the same fifty-three melodic fragments, but have significant freedom in deciding when to move from one fragment to the next. The effect is cumulative and paradoxical: the calculation which autotelic repetition instantiates produces a tensional arrangement, a hypnotic exuberance, which is quite singular to minimalism. This music integrates a clear pulse, propulsive rhythms, terraced dynamic, timbrel shifts and transparent melodic patterns into coherent modules and modular processes, clarifying the provenance of Fink's term, pulse-pattern minimalism.

Somewhat different, although no less significant, is the process employed in Steve Reich's *Piano Phase* which integrates linear and cyclical process.[136] Identical melodic lines gradually move out of rhythmic phase with one another, one line accelerating while the other remains stable, producing in the process periods of sonic instability, followed by unexpectedly complex singularities as the lines once again move into phase with one another. However, because the melodic material is strictly limited, the lines eventually move back into the initial position from which the composition begins.[137]

It is perhaps the early work of Philip Glass that most clearly illustrates the calculative logic of minimalist modularism, however. In *Two Pages* – which, in characteristically minimalist fashion, takes its name from the eminently material fact that its constituent modules were originally scored on two manuscript pages – the exposition of systematic and audible compositional process is expressed with an unmatched formal severity. It derives its structure from incremental repetition, or the use of additive and subtractive modules. In the case of additive modules, a sequence, consisting of a number of pitches in a specific order,[138] is repeated a number of times before being supplemented. Supplementation can either be by a single pitch[139] or by an additional series of pitches,[140] which is then repeated. For the structural systematicity of the compositional process to be transparent and thus maximally audible, such an additional series of pitches will normally be a variation on the first. These supplementary series can themselves be either additive – in which case they would present notes in addition to the original series[141] – or subtractive – in which case they would present fewer notes than the original series.[142] Properly subtractive variation, by contrast, involves the entire sequence contracting.[143] Of Glass's use of additive and subtractive modular repetition, Keith Potter writes the following:

> Each work is constructed from a Basic Unit … The scores simply notate the expansions and contractions of the Basic Unit that forms the structure of each work. They do this, though, by grouping sub-units and their expansions or contractions into figures of varying lengths … *Two Pages* represents Glass's first use of rigorous additive process in a composed-out score.[144]

For a work to be 'composed-out', its formal parameters must have been fully calculated with respect to a particular internally driven process of incremental repetition. In the case of *Two Pages* this involves straightforward addition and subtraction, but not the retrograde or inverted forms of its constituent module. Despite the composition's formal simplicity – being little more than a 'study in the elongation and subsequent contraction of a simple musical line'[145] – its transparency reveals an apparently fundamental complexity. This complexity is nothing other than the process of calculation apprehended in terms of its occurrence as a perceptible process.

Similar techniques are observable in minimalist literature and visual art. Modular repetition is central to many of the most provocatively austere prose stylists, from Samuel Beckett and Alain Robbe-Grillet to Raymond Carver and Bret Easton Ellis. However, it is in poetry that the full generative force of literary modularization and incremental verbal repetition is revealed. Where the one-word poetry of Finlay or Saroyan offers a nuclear account of verbal minimalism, works such as Beckett's 'what is the word' and Lax's 'word' demonstrate that verbal materialization is fundamentally linked to process.

In Beckett's final work, 'what is the word', the writer's familiar preoccupation with a profound, existential disappointment finds an especially austere expression. As with much of Beckett's *oeuvre*, thought and language prove equally inadequate to the task of coordinating a stable relationship to a reality, either internally or externally derived. A progressive 'lessness'[146] is inscribed as a loss of coherence and a highly reflexive incapacity to find the word which would render this absence concrete. The search itself is recognized as 'folly',[147] yet is pursued compulsively, the Beckettian project thus terminating in an incompleteness. Familiar modules appear in fragmentary form: 'for to', 'all this', 'this this here', and 'what where'[148] recall phrases which are encountered repeatedly in Beckett's writing. Incremental repetition of these modules concretizes the literary intuition of radical quantity and a quantitative ontology. For instance, 'this' is subject to the additive variation, 'this this', and subsequently 'this this here'.[149] However, while such modular variation literally compounds textual matter, its materialism destabilizes rather than stabilizes the traditional mimetic vocation of language which purportedly binds together objects and words, pointing instead to the concrete facticity of language itself.[150] Additive modular repetition in 'what is the word' generates a powerful recognition of a curious parataxis, ostensibly directed towards recovering the spectral word that haunts Beckett's final piece, but which recognizes in the process that every such attempt will invariably fall away into a laconic sequence. The em dash (–) which ends each line substitutes a mark for the absence of the word which would embody the coincidence of sign and sense, thus pointing to the familiar Beckettian intuition regarding the inadequacy of language to demands of thought, and of thought to the demands of being.

The remarkable insight of Beckett's final work does not regard the failure of language, however, but rather its facticity and persistence. In its failure to materialize, the absent word is transposed into a modular process through which it obliquely reclaims a degree of presence by a type of apophatic minimalism: the word is where it is not, and where it is not is intensified by the modular repetition which Beckett employs. In this sense, the minimal fact that language exists is conveyed negatively by the transfiguration of textuality into process, and this process is nothing other than a means of configuring ontological quantity. The initial access to sense promised by the 'glimpse'[151] of 'the word' is progressively diminished, first to an appearance of access, then to a longing for access, and then to a recognition that even to long for access is pointless: 'glimpse' becomes 'seem to glimpse', then 'need to seem to glimpse', then 'folly for to need to seem to glimpse'.[152] Formally, the module is additive, but semantically it is subtractive, and amidst this quantitative tension it is perhaps no surprise that a radically quantitative process is finally what is at stake.

In its processual failure to materialize, the non-appearance of 'the word' constitutes a field of potentiality precisely to the extent that impotentiality – the likelihood that 'the word' will never appear – is countered by the reiteration of this non-appearance in the interrogative module, 'what is the word'.[153] Posing the absent word as a question – 'what is the word[?]' – recalls how for Lyotard the sublime is characterized precisely by the anxiety which accompanies the 'possibility of nothing happening'[154] when existential presence is itself called into question. The very fact that there is no word capable of capturing 'the nothingness now'[155] – the most plausible response to the explicitly existential question posed by 'what is the word' – suggests that Beckett's question is autotelic in the precise sense that it recognizes itself as a prosthesis for this impossible, or absent, word. The only satisfactory answer to the question, 'what is the word[?]', is the question itself – modulated, reiterated, recalculated, and displaced in a process of quantifying absence without reaching a final quantity.

Where Beckett's 'what is the word' deals with the absence which haunts the materialism of language and text, Lax's 'word' aims to instantiate these in terms of a concrete immanence. The modular logic of Lax's work reveals considerable similarities to the pulse-pattern minimalism of Glass, and presents itself in terms of a four-line stanza flanked by three three-line stanzas, two at the start and one at the end, the second and the last being identical:

word
word
word

a word
a word
a word

one word
two words
one word
two words

a word
a word
a word[156]

The first stanza – 'word/ word/ word' – presents the initial module of the work. Here is an echo of the concern that Derrida famously identifies in terms of the triplicate logic of identity – 'There was immediately a double origin plus its repetition.'[157] Admittedly, Derrida's logic speaks not merely of the manifest, but of the very possibility of identity. Nonetheless, Lax seems also to be asking the question of how many times a word ought to be repeated to offer contingent stability to the void at the heart of identity. The answer appears to be three:

the first repetition marks the split and incommensurability between the lost unity of an idea and its presentation; the second repetition doubles the split, re-presents it, in order to stabilize presentation itself, also recalling Badiou's insight regarding this repetition or metastructure as the minimal necessity for existence to cohere.[158]

'Word' is clearly self-referential – it is the word 'word', and it traces, performs and encircles the performance of its content. Its reference is also external to the other repetitions of the module 'word' in the stanza, as well as a more general law of consecution that underpins the traditional order of language: that one word will follow another word. These concretize – indeed, quantify – the minimal conditions in which *poietic* force and poetic presentation are able to coincide with respect to process. By adding the indefinite article, *a*, the second stanza defines an expansionary supplement to the first: 'a word/ a word/ a word'. This increment further concretizes and predicates what in a sense remains ideal in the first stanza: 'word', hovering between the substantial and insubstantial, becomes '*a* word'. Simultaneously this predication is a subtraction, however, for there is a definite quality, or arguably a certain purity, retained in the idea, that is sacrificed through the addition of the indefinite article. '[A] word' hovers between the idea – the idea of identity and the reflexivity of the idea itself – and a definite instantiation: between 'word' and *the* word. Lax resolves the problem through a remarkable and, indeed, minimal manoeuvre, by shifting to the numerical realm of specific quantity.

The third stanza presents a more complex variation, the alternative 'one word/ two words/ one word/ two words', which is again both additive and subtractive in relation to the initial module, 'word'. It is additive, first, in several obvious senses: the addition of the plural ('word*s*'); the fact that these lines posit additional variations on the initial module; the internal variation of the stanza (the alternation of 'one word' and 'two words') is itself a type of addition; and most significantly, the alternating lines also present rudimentary counting and addition, 'one … two'. These lines also add definition: the indefinite article 'a' becomes alternately 'one' and 'two'. Interestingly, such definition is also subtractive in a significant sense, since specificity is shown here to be subtracted from non-specificity.

Interpreting *word* as a concrete poem – one in which the form and content of the poem reflect one another, the flow of language obeying its own meaningful prescription – we encounter the full sense in which this third stanza must be understood as deeply ambiguous. '[O]ne word' clearly is self-contradictory from the perspective of concrete reflexivity: it subtracts from its substantial, self-referential independence, since 'one word' is, of course, not *one* word, but *two* words. In this subtraction, however, it refers back to 'a word' of the second stanza, which, in turn, is a 'word', indeed *the* 'word' of the first stanza: a single word struggling for its conceptual and concrete singularity. So, in a sense, the developed module 'one word' subtracts from itself only to add quantitatively to the original module, while also affirming the intrinsic concrete value of 'word'. The alternate line of the third stanza, 'two words', presents itself without such contradiction.

Clearly, it is adding 'a word' to the initial module, 'word', and so is 'two words', a self-reflexive, affirmative performance. Simultaneously it makes oblique reference to the two words of its alternating partner – 'one word' – by providing an external point of reference for the latter. In returning to a repetition of the second module and stanza – 'a word/ a word/ a word' – the poem seeks to affirm the quantitative, cumulative, modular, and repetitive character of materialization, and, more specifically, materialization through language. Having begun with a self-referential idea, and proceeded through its indefinite and then numerical quantification, the final stanza suggests that the singularity of the poetic word lies precisely in its non-finality – it is *a* word, but not the final word; a contingent subtraction from an inexhaustible quantity.

In the visual arts, a parallel emphasis on serial and modular expansion is evident in Sol LeWitt's sculpture. The use of open cubes to expose the modular logic of geometric construction is evident in *Maquette for One, Two, Three,*[159] for instance. Here a 'numeric and geometric sequence of incremental units'[160] provides the sculptural analogue to the open-ended additive techniques of Philip Glass: a single, open cube constitutes a central axis, and is joined to a larger cube, made of eight of the original cubic unit (2x2x2), which, in its turn, is joined to a larger cube, made of twenty-seven of the original cubic multiple (3x3x3). The series, $\{1^3, 2^3, 3^3 \dots n^3\}$, describes a process as elegant as it is transparent. Presenting this series in three dimensions, LeWitt's *Maquette* literally renders an idea concrete, translating a mathematical process into a sculptural one – a process which, in principle, could 'extend out indefinitely'[161] in exposing the 'variations available within an original premise [and] within the basic cube and square form'.[162] To reinforce the conceptual substance of the work, the attention of the viewer is pulled simultaneously inward, along the central axis upon which it is aligned, and upward, along the diagonal line of its three progressive levels. The work transects space in a manner which is systematic, impersonal and pervasive: it 'set[s] art and reality on the same plane [since] the selection of a regulated scheme [results in] works that self-referentially stand for what they are without illusionistic deception'.[163] Yet, despite its formal simplicity and processual clarity, the symmetrical arrangement of the open cubes of *Maquette* reveal a complex lattice of visual superimpositions on closer examination. This is emblematic of how perception, description and interpretation often serve to complicate minimalist works. Arguably, however, this complexification is itself a type of clarification – a calculation even – of the ways in which minimalist sculpture is able to demonstrate that the quantifiability of matter in geometric terms emerges at the meeting of an indifferent autotelic process and spatial perception.

Elaborating minimalist materialism in terms of process, the logic of calculation seeks to intensify perception by clarifying the structure and structuration of the work, rendering it at once transparent and immanent. In this manner, processual minimalism reveals calculation as immanent to its objects, which, at their best, are simultaneously self-productive, self-structuring, and self-sustaining – in short, autotelic. In minimalism, systematic processes compete with the asymmetries of effect to establish an aesthetic position that exemplifies the relationship between repetition, additive and subtractive modularization, number, and quantitative ontology. In this, it becomes clearer what precisely is at stake in the instantiation both of the minimalist logic of persistence and of the logic of calculation: nothing less than the radical quantity which grounds every potential understanding of the real. Where the logic of persistence exemplifies radical quantity in terms of immanence and scale – duration, magnitude, sustenance, silence and invariance – the logic of calculation instantiates quantity with respect to autotelic process, incremental repetition, accumulation, subtraction, series and counting. Both paradigms demonstrate a way of marking a shift from the predominant assumption that the heart of the aesthetic can be apprehended only in terms of a complex set of qualitative criteria, to a reconsideration of the ontological vocation of the aesthetic in realist terms – a task which can only be grounded with respect to radical quantity.

5.5 Number

The consequences of counting: Dan Flavin's *the nominal three (to William of Ockham)* (1964) Philip Glass's *Einstein on the Beach* (1976) Nico Muhly's *Mothertongue* (2007)

Understood in quantitative terms, minimalism invokes a very specific tension between processes of enumeration, themselves potentially infinite, and the positing of number, the name under which these processes are contingently unified as a work. Badiou's ontology provides one means of unpacking this paradox, pointing to an understanding of infinity as immanent to existence,[164] rather than an abstract and always distant future – essentially unquantifiable. To make sense of this claim, it is necessary first to distinguish between ordinal and cardinal numbers which, together, inhabit every numerical expression. Ordinals, when sequenced by an act of counting, manifest in terms of a rule of succession – one is succeeded by two, by three, by four, and so forth – which is reflected in some of the most fundamental structures of thought: cause and effect, teleological processes, and various processes of calculation. The logic of cardinal numbers, by contrast, is not one of consecutive order or flow, but is rather tied to the singular quantity of the number itself. A number may be part of a particular count, but understood in terms of its cardinality, it might be taken out of the context of this count and substituted into an infinite number of similar counts without altering its fundamental quantity. A cardinal number is thus simultaneously part of a particular act of enumeration, but can also be substituted into other acts of enumeration, thus transcending the particular order to which it initially belongs and potentially giving rise to an infinite number of other acts of enumeration. Cardinality points to a sort of infinite metonymy – the possibility of an infinite number of infinities.[165]

In this light, the potential significance of number in even the most transparent of minimalist works is considerable. A striking example is Flavin's sculpture, *the nominal three (to William of Ockham)*.[166] The sculpture consists of six, bright, white fluorescent fixtures arranged against a single wall: a single fixture to the far left, two in the centre, and three on the right. Michael Govan goes as far as to suggest that it is '[o]ut of Ockham's *nominalism* [that] Flavin crafted his *minimalism*',[167] and there certainly is a parsimonious clarity to *the nominal three* that recalls the exclusion of extraneous complexity for which Ockham's is often remembered. In this work Flavin clarifies radical quantity by exposing an aesthetic situation in which the ordinal and cardinal logics of enumeration coincide. The nominalist affirmation of autonomous entities informs Flavin's search for 'primary figures'[168] that favour transparency and purity of form and medium over complexity.[169] Where ordinal logic is manifest in moving from left to right, in the sequence of one, then two, then three fixtures, a cardinal logic inhabits each group individually, being both part of an ordinal sequence and a singular quantity in its own right. Flavin's concern with number is supplemented by the corporeal experience of quantity. The substance of this work is finally inextricable from its luminescence, and its expansion in every direction emphasizes that any *account* of its phenomenology necessarily incorporates sensory and conceptual experience.

Equally concretized by somatic inference is the count that opens Glass's celebrated minimalist opera, *Einstein on the Beach*. Composed to be performed at high volumes, the deep bass of the electric organ that opens 'Knee-Play 1' consists of three notes which outline the entire harmonic structure of the composition. This sequence, one of the simplest of all harmonic progressions but with a strong sense of tonal gravity, is interrupted by the utterance of the number 'two'. Zero and one perhaps implicit, the count is already underway, although it is stilted, non-sequential, and irregular – continued by the recitation of random single-digit numbers by two female voices over the dominating presence of the organ. The arbitrary calling of numbers gives way to two voices reciting a poem by Christopher Knowles, its lines subsequently alternated with the numerical recitation. That this irregularity is framed by the powerful chordal progression, is strengthened by the entrance of the austere ascending line of the chorus sung in octaves which stabilizes the progression both in terms of its tension and resolutions.

There is something of the sublime in an encounter with this music, recalling that, for Kant, what marks an aesthetic of the sublime is precisely the manner in which reason is able to stabilize what is initially an overwhelming and discomforting sensory encounter with something that is 'absolutely large'.[170] The 'negative pleasure' that results from sublime experience is a clear extension of Edmund Burke's contention that '[w]hatever … excite[s] the ideas of pain, and danger … whatever is in any sort terrible, or is conversant about terrible objects, or operates in a manner analogous to terror, is a source of the *sublime*'.[171] More significant to the present discussion, however, is the Kantian distinction between the *mathematical* and the *dynamical* sublime. The former attempts to approximate sublime magnitude in spatial and temporal terms, by 'numerical concepts'[172] and the intuitive estimation of magnitude.[173] The latter more evidently emerges in the dynamics of thought and the imagination, which allow us indirectly to confront and overcome the fear-arousing objects and situations: 'we merely *think* of the case where we might possibly want to put up resistance against [an overwhelming magnitude], and that any resistance would in that case be utterly futile'.[174]

Kant does not, however, signal here 'that there are two kinds of sublime, the one mathematical and the other dynamical',[175] for 'mathematical synthesis and dynamical synthesis do not exclude one another'.[176] Indeed, in 'Knee-Play 1' the meeting of two languages of the infinite – mathematics and music – are clarified by these two dialects of the sublime. For where the pure quantity of these sounds – their scale, loudness and presence – refers to the dynamically sublime, the inclusion of numerical sequences by way of the explicit recitation of numbers and the implicit harmonic proportions of the music, recalls the mathematical sublime. It is precisely upon the productive tension of the two that the effect and coherence of the count rests. The recitation of numbers in 'Knee-Play 1', both aleatory and ordered, simultaneously indicates the spatial and temporal quantification of existence – the means by which fundamental material consistency and metrical regularity might be deduced. In other of his compositions, Glass prefers the fundamental pitch language of *solfège*, in which linguistic syllables (do, re, mi, fa, sol, la, ti) are substituted for sequential pitches. Significant echoes of this technique are discernible in John Adams's *On the Transmigration of Souls*, a threnody for those who died in the 9/11 attacks, which incorporates lists of names, addresses and telephone numbers as the haunting quantitative substitutes for those missing or dead immediately after the attacks. The cumulative and metonymic logics of sequences and lists are also explored to great effect in Nico Muhly's 'Archive' from the song-cycle *Mothertongue*. Number and listing together become the means of a fundamental musical language, but simultaneously interrogate number as a type of mnemonic cipher:[177] postcodes, addresses, telephone numbers, alphabetical lists and solfege syllables reflect not only on intrinsic quantities, but act as markers for place, identity, and the crossing of personal, interpersonal and cultural histories. Thus, the postcodes delivered with a growing urgency and intensity in 'Monster', the final movement of the *Mothertongue* cycle, might legitimately be interpreted as the markers for the reduction of humanity to numerical sequences – as identity- or social security numbers, the numbers assigned to prisoners, or in the most extreme case, the biopolitical tattooing of the Shoah.

The aesthetic of the archive often finds expression in minimalist works. At the heart of Gabriel Josipovici's novel, *The Inventory*, is an exhaustive list of the unspecified items of a deceased man's estate, a list which occasions the disturbing insight that human life is bound to a utilitarian, statistical abstraction. Equally, a great deal of Beckett's work reflects, and reflects on, the realization that existence is numerically quantifiable and approximated by a count, and the ways in which this calculation veers towards an absurd experience of existence. Perhaps the most comical of these calculations is Molloy's attempt to establish a 'mode of circulation'[178] through which he could evenly distribute and rotate his 'sucking-stones',[179] or the numerical rationalization of what he regards as his excessive flatulence, '[t]hree hundred and fifteen farts in nineteen hours',[180] reduced by a few simple acts of division to '[n]ot even one fart every four minutes'.[181] 'Extraordinary how mathematics help you to know yourself',[182] he observes. A more extensive calculation of greater existential seriousness emerges from the carefully weighted words with which 'A Piece of Monologue' opens:

> Birth was the death of him. Again. Words are few. Dying too … From funeral to funeral. To now. This night. Two and a half billion seconds. Again. Two and a half billion seconds. Hard to believe so few … Thirty thousand nights. Hard to believe so few.[183]

Yet it is continuity, rather than the discontinuity of death, however imminent, that fuels the count. Indeed, continuity as opposed to final calculation is central to Muhly's 'Archive' – a count within which number is replaced by the rapid recitation of the letters of the alphabet, a sequence which retains its ordinal and quantitative significance. Finally, as the complexity of musical information mounts, other verbal information is introduced – numbers, addresses, narrative fragments. However, the alphabetic litany which opens the work remains a powerful marker of radical quantity – both musical and linguistic – and the necessity of subjecting this to some sort of archival calculation in order to generate contingent cohesion.

Of a different, but no less provocative, species of alphabetic count is Aragon's well-known poem, 'Suicide', which consists of the full sequence of the alphabet laid out over five lines, the first four lines containing respectively six ('a' to 'f'), six ('g' to 'l'), six ('m' to 'r') and five letters ('s' to 'w'), and the final line, separated from others by a space, the three final letters of the alphabet ('x', 'y', and 'z')

> SUICIDE
> A b c d e f
> g h I j k l
> m n o p q r
> s t u v w
>
> x y z[184]

The poem self-reflexively consumes its poetic potential. Poetic language is reduced to its most atomic elements – 'letters of the alphabet spelled out in sequence'[185] – which are offered up for calculation, as an alphabetic sequence that seeks to expose both the 'finite and infinite possibility of the limited set'.[186] If in one sense language for the poet becomes the medium of perpetual, self-sacrificial exhaustion, indeed suicide, in another it retains its potential for being recharged, recalculated. Eric Andersen, for instance, offers a very similar poetic sequence – the full alphabet in both upper- and lower-case letters, followed by basic punctuation marks and numbers from 0 to 9 arranged from left to right over three lines – gesturing towards the inexhaustible possibilities of the poetic enterprise and captured with some force in the title of his work: 'I Have Confidence in You'.[187] Andersen turns the quantitative process outwards, passing custody of the poem from writer to reader in anticipation of the transfigurative encounter that invests the work with significance even as it reinvests in the reader that incalculable freedom that beats at the heart of aesthetic experience.

6

Austerity: On the Lessness of Minimalism

6.1 Asceticism

The austerities of the cell: The Carthusian monastery and monastic cell Samuel Beckett's 'For to end yet again' (1960/1975)

Minimalism begins and ends, yet it has no first or final work. Such is the wager of a theory of minimalism that expresses the logic of historical intermittency, but which remains grounded in the persistence of minimum, an existential modality which flows, inexhaustibly, through every manifestation of minimalism. Something ancient inhabits the most contemporary minimalism, just as its most archaic manifestations pulsate with an immanent sense of the present. Minimalism is always beginning again, intermittently but persistently articulating itself anew; and nowhere is this paradoxical phenomenon more evident than in one of the most pervasive and curious transhistorical minimalist phenomena – asceticism, or the systematic pursuit of existential austerity by various processes of discipline, abstinence, renunciation, privation and denegation.

Although particular ascetic practices are invariably shaped by the specific contexts in which they arise,[1] asceticism itself is a universal phenomenon, 'in evidence in ancient as well as modern societies',[2] and crossing 'boundaries of culture, religion, and chronology'.[3] Robert Thurman sees this ubiquity as an expression of 'the evolutionary impulse in human beings to attempt consciously to improve control over their habitual life processes';[4] while for Geoffrey Harpham, the universality of asceticism derives from the fact that it 'exceeds the ideological limitations of [any particular] culture; it may best be considered as sub-ideological, common to all culture [and that it offers] a fundamental operating ground on which the particular culture … is overlaid'.[5] In both cases, asceticism constitutes a species of minimalism: a minimal mode of critical self-relation in the former; a minimal ground supporting a way of life in the latter.

Although subject to considerable variation, at the heart of ascetic practice is an orientation towards minimum, traceable across vast spans of time and geographical distances. An ascetic logic moves through a great deal of ritual practice, from the trance dance of the San in Southern Africa, which aims through various bodily disciplines to facilitate the transition between the different planes of San cosmology, to the practice of continuous prayer as reflected in the hesychastic tradition of Orthodox Christianity, which aims, through the ceaseless repetition of a short verbal formula, to quiet the senses to generate the conditions necessary for an encounter with the divine. Equally compelling are the austerities of Śramaṇa in India and the abstinences of Stoics in ancient Greece and Rome; the renunciation of the desert fathers in the Scetes and the liturgical disciplines of the Carthusian monks of the Grande Chartreuse. Often the most radical instantiations of asceticism are identified with particular historical figures: the Buddha, who lived a life of extreme deprivation before advocating a more measured asceticism;[6] Porphyry, who illuminated the Stoic conception of privation as preparation for happiness;[7] Simeon the Stylite who inspired many by his life of radical austerity for thirty-seven years on a small platform atop a pillar or style;[8] or Francis of Assisi, who renounced all comfort and possessions to take up the penitential life of a mendicant friar.[9]

Yet, despite its persistence, Edith Wyschogrod recognizes that ascetic practice is marked by intermittent shifts. Asceticism is born into Western philosophy as an intuition of suspended access to a natural cosmological order.[10] Within the classical scheme, the human body is regarded as a 'disturbance'[11] which bars access of the soul to this order, and ascetic practice becomes a means of attaining the original simplicity of the cosmological order. In this sense, 'the body comes to function as a heuristic device for understanding the cosmos'.[12] Where the Stoic cosmos is 'good or indifferent', the Judeo-Christian emphasis is on the world in terms of 'vanity' or 'worthlessness'.[13] Thus, where ascetic practice previously sought clarification of and greater access to the world, it becomes increasingly tied to transfiguration: '[b]y denying the world', the ascetic 'brings the world that is being denied to the fore'.[14] This pattern of approaching minimum in order to discover the heart of the transfigurative process that is able to affirm through negation, is characteristic of asceticism as a whole. As Kalistos Ware has noted, 'by virtue of … self-transfiguration [the ascetic] also transfigures the world'.[15]

In this light, asceticism remains a significant means of transforming the subject in its self-relation, but also in its relation to the world and to others.[16] Indeed, Harpham identifies an 'ascetic imperative'[17] at the heart of contemporary existence – a 'primary, transcultural structuring force'[18] that is intimately tied to aesthetics and its capacity for knotting together representation[19] and production.[20] In aesthetic terms, asceticism habitually finds expression through an austerity that seeks to bring into alignment the transfigurative ambition of ascetic practice and the minimalist instantiation of the infinitesimal and parsimonious – the least possible and the least necessary. Like asceticism, austerity is a polysemic term with a long and vexed history. While some associate it with the admirable pursuit of simplicity and clarity, others regard it as an expression of a pathological zeal. For Florian Schui, austerity is intimately tied to historically contingent moral and political norms,[21] yet always manifests in terms of 'abstinence from consumption'.[22] Its logic is thus fundamentally quantitative, and it is in this light that its most debated contemporary manifestation, as a response to economic crisis, appears 'seductive in its simplicity'[23] yet has failed to accomplish its explicit aims.[24] Superficially, economic and aesthetic austerity seem to converge in their commitment to the dictum, *less is more*. Where economic austerity offers itself as a response to perceived shortage, aesthetic austerity is a response to perceived excess as an impediment to reality. Yet close inspection reveals that economic austerity, in its recent and current incarnations, is concerned less with shortage than with the fact that there is a shortage of economic growth – *less of more*. Its aim is finally more, not less, with less made a means to an end, and its logic not dissimilar to the great retail slogan, only here an imperative: *get more for less!* Austerity of this sort is almost diametrically opposed to the logic of aesthetic austerity, where the conviction that less actually *is* more makes lessness itself a plausible aim.

Although they intersect at numerous points, it is thus important to distinguish economic austerity from austerity as the aesthetic expression of asceticism. As soon as a way of life is understood in aesthetic terms as a means of representing the world that it simultaneously brings into being, then minimalism is convincingly able to identify asceticism, and its expression in terms of austerity, as one of its most important lineages. Much as the path of the religious ascetic leads towards minimum, so minimalist aesthetics often lead towards an ascetic path. This is exemplified not only in the austere works of minimalism, but often also in the austere lives of minimalists such as the poet Robert Lax or the painter Agnes Martin. The hermit, as ascetic minimalist, exposes the same conditions under which the familiar figure of the melancholic artist or poet, persisting in tense isolation, is able to thrive.[25] Austerity, whether secular or sacred, is always a site of struggle between presence and absence, immanence and transcendence; and it is precisely this struggle that marks the shared conviction of the hermit and the poet in the possibility of transfiguration – the discovery of transcendence at the heart of immanence. Thus, 'the epiphany of the unattainable'[26] that inspires the melancholic artist or poet reflects the same yearning for the sublime expressed by the hermit in turning towards solitude and silence.[27] As Ware notes, the ascetic abandonment of the world implicitly contains the possibility of return.[28]

It is within the interval between the two that austerity comes to comprehend itself in terms of radical receptiveness and perpetual preparedness: after all, it is in pastoral isolation that Hesiod's poet first encounters the Muses,[29] while in the *Rule of Saint Benedict* the monk sleeps in order to rise to *Opus Dei* or the Work of God.[30] By drawing out the tension between immanence and transcendence, the ascetic ideal is able to gesture towards an important tension in theological reasoning between cataphatic thought, which holds that knowledge is acquired through positive statements of what the phenomenon in question *is*, and apophatic thought, which holds that knowledge is acquired by negative statements of what the phenomenon in question *is not*. Quietism – the name given to a loose set of mystical practices in the seventeenth century – pursues a type of negative knowledge through a radical passivity and eventual negation of the self in order to become 'lost in God in an indistinct and objectless contemplation'.[31] The earlier concept of 'sacred simplicity'[32] is in some respects comparable, holding that at the heart of material austerity lies spiritual plenitude, presence being recovered through absence. Sacred simplicity crosses into the realm of aesthetics in numerous ways, but one of the most pervasive is in the tradition of the *vanitas* painting which habitually uses the skull as a symbolic vehicle to recall the strong historic connection of asceticism to the contemplation of death and the renunciation of the world as vanity.

In a different but no less poignant register, the skull is deployed in the opening of Beckett's 'For to end yet again', which uses the quintessentially minimalist technique of incremental repetition, to press beyond mere austerity towards the void:

> For to end yet again skull alone in a dark place pent bowed on a board to begin. Long thus to begin till the place fades followed by the board long after. For to end yet again skull alone in the dark the void no neck no face just the box last place of all in the dark void.[33]

From an anthropocentric perspective, the skull is a concrete reminder of minimal existential intensity: it is the remnant of the subject after death, anonymous yet peculiarly singular. At the same time it recalls the aesthetic logic of containment which often proves central to the minimalist aesthetic. The skull provides for our primary sensory organs and encases the brain. Although passive, it remains intimately connected to processes of perception and the consciousness through which a coherent reality is constituted. It is perhaps no surprise then that the skull should come to function as a peculiar type of minimalist icon. This is true for both the austere space of the hermit's cave as depicted in such paintings as El Greco's *Saint Francis Praying*[34] where the skull is contemplated from an external perspective, and the austere *atopia* or non-space of Beckett's prose, in which the skull is emblematic of the point at which consciousness discovers its own limits. In both cases, a deep engagement with a radically austere aesthetic makes it possible to understand the skull as a symbolic cell, and the cell as a space of potential transfiguration. Here it is instructive to juxtapose the austerities of the monastic cell with those of the prison cell in order to grasp how the experience or encounter with a radically minimalist aesthetic is transfigurative in some cases and not in others.[35]

Both the monastic and prison cells reveal their significance within 'complete and austere institutions'.[36] The interior of both types of cell, from which all inessentials have been subtracted, is shaped by function and marked by a lean, sparse intensity. In their contemporary layout, both contain little more than a bed, a desk, a shelf and basic ablution facilities. Both types of cell have evolved from communal cells or dormitories to spaces designed to contain a single body and life. While in the case of religious orders, this shift marks a return to the more ancient tradition of the desert fathers,[37] in the carceral system it represents a significant transformation in the logic of imprisonment from a historically retributive or punitive system to one focused on 'redemption through prolonged solitude'.[38] Drawing on the spirituality of the Quakers,[39] which places a similar emphasis on silence as traditional monastic orders such as the Carthusians, prison reformers believed that a limitation of sensory stimulation would result in an inward turn which would be beneficial to the rehabilitation of offenders. Yet, although the prison cell is often perceived as the locus of spiritual and moral transformation, it remains principally concerned with the 'technical transformation of individuals'[40] under the guise of reformation.[41] Attempts at thought and behaviour modification invariably align themselves to a larger regime of control which, as Michel Foucault recognizes, incorporates a range of 'procedures ... for distributing individuals, fixing them in space, classifying them, extracting from them the maximum in time and forces, training their bodies, coding their continuous behaviour, maintaining them in perfect visibility'.[42]

In this light, their shared aesthetic austerity aside, there is a clear conceptual and material distinction to be made between these two types of cell: life in the monastic cell is voluntary, based on a fidelity to an anticipated event, a transfigurative encounter with the divine; life in the prison cell is involuntary, reducing the prisoner to an object devoid of encounters or events. The frequent result of the latter is social death, or the 'exclu[sion] from belonging to any society whatsoever'.[43] Indeed, for Guenther, 'solitary confinement works by turning prisoners' constitutive relationality against themselves, turning their own capacities to feel, perceive, and relate to others in a meaningful world into instruments of their own undoing',[44] since 'interactions are vital for sustaining our most basic sense of reality and living personhood and for differentiating the void of empty and meaningless space from an experience of the world as open-ended context for meaning'.[45]

In the case of ascetics living solitary lives, 'though it might appear that they [are] "dead to the world," it is their conviction that they remain '"alive" to spiritual possibilities. The dark enclosures [of their cells], therefore, [are] spiritually luminous places'.[46] In such cases, the spiritual task of transfiguration is regarded as intimately connected to the austere minimalism of the cell's architecture.[47] In the case of the Carthusian order, the layout of the monastery or Charterhouse reflects a distinctly minimalist logic of repetition, contraction and containment:

> Layers of concentric circles wrap the monk in solitude, enclose him ... The first circle is the land surrounding the Charterhouse ... The exceptionally high walls around the monastic complex provide the next protective circle ... Within the exterior walls, the high walls of the monk's cell provide another layer of privacy, and finally, his ultimate privacy is the inner room in the cell, the *cubiculum*, where no one can enter without the monk's permission. He is entirely cut off from the world.[48]

Those who, by mutual agreement of the monastic community, choose enclaustration are immediately confronted by the unforgiving limits of the cell. '[B]ound by rule not to leave, there is no getting away from oneself. One has to live through it'.[49] Interrupted only by communal liturgy and a weekly walk, life in the cell centres on the cubiculum, which contains only 'a bed in the form of a cupboard with a straw mattress ... a stove, a worktable, and a small oratory with a ... built-in kneeler and bookstand ... some bookshelves ... and a small built-in dining table with a drawer'.[50] In this space the ascetic lives in search of a holy minimalism, an austere persistence, which promises a transfigurative encounter with the divine. The monk's life becomes the austere performance of a minimalist drama; an existential liturgy stripped of all its excesses and directed towards a stringent but luminous asceticism.

6.2 Clarity

The minimalism of waiting: John Adams's *Shaker Loops* (1978/1983)

The architectural austerity of the cell, with its transhistorical appeal to the silence and featurelessness which purportedly fuel contemplation, is the concrete marker of the broadly minimalist ideals of simplicity, transparency, and immanence which inform not only ancient ascetic practice, but also the more recent manifestations of the puritan and quietist[51] religious ethic. These, in turn, develop into various species of pragmatism which manifest aesthetically in terms of a functionalist or utilitarian approach to the design of the everyday – the spaces and objects that shape interaction – recognizing, with Jacques Rancière, that in 'drawing lines, arranging words or distributing surfaces, one also designs divisions of communal space [and] certain forms of inhabiting the material world'.[52] This pursuit of austerity – of the *tabula rasa* or blank slate which approximates minimum – thus extends beyond the cell to expose a field of social and political potentiality. This is nowhere clearer than in the case of the Quakers and Shakers.

The Religious Society of Friends, or Quakers, arose in seventeenth-century England as part of the protestant revival that gave rise to various, dispersed traditions which include several German Evangelical groups, Methodists and Baptists. Among the first of the Christian denominations actively to promote pastoral equality between women and men, [53] the Quaker emphasis on simplicity and silence is at once a continuation and an extension of the practice at the heart of traditional monasticism and cell spirituality. The ritualized silence of the Quakers is intended to enhance divine and interpersonal communion by eliminating those things that impede a patient attentiveness.[54] In the sense that it aims to gain progressive access to a reality by means of conceptual and experiential clarification, Quakerism legitimately describes a species of minimalism which marks itself in terms of the pursuit of potential universality by means of disciplined exclusion of excess. Thus it also promotes both internal and external temperance – simplicity of dress, speech and general life.

The charismatic and pentecostal revivals of the succeeding eighteenth century resulted in a tendency towards more extroverted practices among Quakers.[55] Known first as Shaking Quakers, and subsequently simply as Shakers – a term initially intended as derogatory – these individuals adopted a radical form of communitarian monasticism[56] as an expression of their millenarian beliefs.[57] Remarkable for their promotion of equality of the sexes without demanding absolute segregation[58] and despite advocating celibacy, the Shakers – 'simple, profoundly serious, deeply and religiously vulnerable, open to the winds of change and grace that swept the American frontier'[59] – established productive, self-sufficient[60] towns and communities in early nineteenth-century America as an alternative to absolute retreat from the world and society as such.[61] While Shaker rituals were markedly improvisational and elaborate, their aesthetic practice is notable for its distinct minimalism. Of particular renown with regard to a minimalist sensibility is Shaker furniture, which is noted for its simplicity, symmetry and functionality,[62] and for the manner in which it is integrated with Shaker architecture.[63]

For the Shakers, work was a form of prayer,[64] and prayer a search for perfection. As Merton notes, '[w]ork was to be perfect, and a certain relative perfection was by all means within reach: the thing made had to be precisely what it was supposed to be. It had, so to speak, to fulfil its own vocation.'[65] Focusing on the furniture for which the Shakers are most celebrated, it becomes clear that these are works of minimalism not only by virtue of their stylistic features – a 'rejection of ornament for an elegance born of optimum economy and practicality of design [that] has an unmistakable resonance with aspects of some Minimal art'[66] – but also by virtue of their concern with the work being an example of its own facticity, its own realness, with '[being] what it is meant to be'.[67] By persisting in relation to its own facticity, by being such as it is and no more than it is, the Shaker work points to transcendence as located in the immanence of the everyday. The typical Shaker chair, in this light, possesses a 'peculiar grace … due to the fact that it was made by someone capable of believing that an angel might come and sit on it'.[68] Made from carefully selected wood, the functional beauty of these chairs – their simple legs, woven or solid seats, and slatted backs undecorated yet elegant – have made them models of parsimony for subsequent designers.

Visually pleasing in its austerity, yet seldom decorative in the conventional sense, Shaker furniture seems to generate rather than to occupy space, and is readily portable, convertible and storable – for example, chairs were hung on walls – in a manner which anticipates the functionalist thrust of

Russian Constructivism and Bauhaus architecture and design.[69] The Bauhaus and Constructivist aesthetic resonates clearly in the work of *De Stijl* with its minimalist grids, chromatic limits (black, white and primary colours), and *Gestalt* forms, all of which are of considerable significance to subsequent canonical minimalist art and design.[70] It is thus worth noting certain continuities between the austere design of a typical Shaker chair, the parsimony of Gert Rietveld's *De Stijl* masterpiece, *Zig-Zag Chair* (1934),[71] and the 1991 *Chair 84/85*[72] by one of minimalism's most canonical sculptors and critics, Donald Judd.[73] Tracing a reductive line from the 'rudimentary, utilitarian elements introduced by the early settlers',[74] through the simplicity of Shaker design, to more contemporary expressions of this minimalist aesthetic, several critics draw attention to minimalism as an austere, transhistorical path that has as its destination a clarification of the real.[75] Echoing Merton's conviction that 'the Shaker vision was peculiarly and authentically American',[76] Kenneth Baker considers minimalism a 'distinctly American tradition of respect for plain facts and plain speaking, manifested in Shaker furniture and the pragmatist philosophy of Charles Sanders Pierce'.[77] Indeed, it should be clear that the pragmatic functionalism[78] of such austere design is no small part of minimalism's origin or legacy.

One of the most unambiguously minimalism explorations of Shaker austerity emerges in John Adams's *Shaker Loops*, completed as a string septet in 1978 and revised for string orchestra in 1983. Although its title is in part a reference to the rhythmic tremolos and trills which provide continuity to the composition,[79] it also makes clear reference to Shaker spirituality. In particular, *Shaker Loops* turns attention from the usual preoccupation with the Shaker's 'austere and disciplined life of renunciation and labor'[80] towards the prayer rituals during which 'these otherwise pious and industrious souls [got] caught up in the ecstatic frenzy of a dance that culminated in an epiphany of physical and spiritual transcendence'.[81] At the same time, *Shaker Loops* is something of a watershed in minimalist music, marking a shift in emphasis from audible process towards a more intuitive grasp of form[82] and an emotional language largely absent from the most systematic early canonical minimalism.[83] Its four movements trace this dynamic process, beginning with the pulsating, tense expectancy of 'Shaking and Trembling', discovering a more introspective plateau of 'Hymning Slews', moving onto the lyrical prayer of 'Loops and Verses' with its ecstatic culmination, subsequent exhaustion, and return to the excited, attentive atmosphere of the opening in 'A Final Shaking'. Drawing heavily on the minimalist proclivity for repetitive, tonal music, *Shaker Loops* is built on a series of modules, cells or loops that recur at different tempos across the composition's four movements, constituting the basic musical material of the entire work, and providing both continuity and variation, allowing each movement to evolve a distinct character that nonetheless resonates with the rest of the composition.[84]

'Shaking and Trembling' begins with a steady pulse, a trill or shaking between two notes, generating a shimmering musical surface on which events are able to unfold. The initial simplicity of the music is complicated as pitches are added, generating increasingly ambiguous harmonic relationships between pitches.[85] From within these tense and shifting fields of harmonic gravity – 'emerging overlapping, conflicting, fading'[86] – melodic fragments arise and recede in response to multiple tonal centres,[87] lending the oscillating continuum of sound a sense of urgency and propulsiveness. Initially in unison, but gradually accumulating difference through the combination of rhythmic displacements and rapid dynamic shifts, these melodic fragments pull unpredictably apart to expose canonical passages in which phrases imitate one another. Adams generates a subtle and dynamic group for the emergence of lyrical events – ephemeral but potentially epiphanic – that allows *Shaker Loops* to retain an improvisatory quality, much like the Shaker rituals to which it alludes.

Adams generates a curious sense of musical space, 'evok[ing] depth by employing varying levels of pulse … particular timbre and instrumental register',[88] and generating the conditions in which density and transparency are able to coexist. Indeed, there is an austerity that manifests in *Shaker Loops* that focuses not principally on simplicity, but on the search for clarity. This search is by no means easy: the anticipatory energy of 'Shaking and Trembling', the calm fluidity of 'Hymning Slews' and the sparse lyricism of the cello solo in 'Loops and Verses' eventually give rise to a series of cadential frenzies marked by dramatic dynamic shifts, accelerations and sudden halts and an exhausted, breathless pulse in the upper strings by its end, before returning to the shimmering recapitulation of 'Final Shaking'. Clarity is not continuous in *Shaker Loops*, but arrives intermittently in seeking to expose the same 'reality of things'[89] that Merton recognizes as central to the Shaker aesthetic. In this way, Adams reaches towards the heart of the minimalist enterprise: the transfigurative aesthetic encounter that clarifies the real.

6.3 Icon

Towards a holy minimalism: Arvo Pärt's *Spiegel im Spiegel* (1978) Robert Lax's *jacob & the angel* (1981)

The concept of transfiguration is central to understanding the transformative potential of minimalist aesthetics in their relation to ascetic, mystical and spiritual thinking. While it is true that proposing a mystical minimalism that leads to transcendence is fraught with internal contradiction, undermining the overriding minimalist concern with immanence, transfiguration, by contrast, emphasizes an amplification and intensification of the present that remains unambiguously rooted in the work itself. The transfigurative vision traced from Shaker spirituality through to Adams's *Shaker Loops* rests on a critical genealogy that often identifies minimalism as 'an indigenous American style',[90] obliquely connected to an indigenous American sense of spirituality. Yet, as argued above, there is considerable transcultural continuity in ascetic practice and its austere aesthetic, and clear evidence of a range of ritual influences on canonical minimalism. In her seminal essay, 'ABC Art', Barbara Rose connects minimalism to mystical experience through 'the state of blankness and stagnation preceding illumination,'[91] an experience she asserts manifests across cultures and histories, and is recognized by venerated European mystics including John of the Cross, Meister Eckhart, Miguel de Molinos and Evelyn Underhill.[92] Similarly, Mertens recognizes the significance of European, Indian, Balinese and Western African ritual music on the development of minimalism.[93]

The early music of Young, Riley, Glass and Reich belongs to a trajectory of Western composers, including John Cage, Colin McPhee and Lou Harrison, deeply influenced by non-Western music.[94] The influence of Indonesian *gamelan* music, frequently tied to formal ritual, is readily audible in Riley's *In C* and in a great deal of Reich's work, while Young and Glass both studied Indian classical music, which often has an explicitly spiritual, even devotional, dimension. Yet, while La Monte Young and Terry Riley considered their music fundamentally spiritual,[95] for Glass and Reich their early concerns were almost exclusively with form and process. Although today a practising Tibetan Vasjaryana Buddhist,[96] Glass's music tends to draw on the nuanced relationship of philosophical and socio-political questions rather than meditating on overtly spiritual themes. Thus, while the operas *Akhnaten* and *Satyagraha* draw on religious texts for their libretti – the former addressing the ultimately failed monotheistic reforms of the eponymous Egyptian pharaoh through the Ancient Egyptian *Book of the Dead*, and the latter Mahatma Gandhi's philosophy of passive resistance through the *Bhagavad Gita* – neither can be accurately described as spiritual works in the way Young's *Dream Houses* or Riley's *Salome Dances for Peace* might be. Similarly, although Reich's *Different Trains* (1988) and *Tehillim* (1981) draw in very different ways on the composer's interest in and study of Jewish history and music, especially psalm cantillation in the case of *Tehillim*,[97] the composer emphatically denies attempting to convey any direct religious message.[98] Meredith Monk's *oeuvre* occupies an interesting threshold between the secular and the sacred: it aims to 'break … down boundaries between the disciplines, an art which in turn becomes a metaphor for opening up thought, perception and experience',[99] drawing on religious themes and histories in a ritualistic music that itself often has a distinctly otherworldly quality. Monk's opera, *Vessel* (1971), recasts events from Joan of Arc's life;[100] *Dolmen Music* (1979) makes clear reference to a religious invocation,[101] and the film *Book of Days* (1985/1990) offers a startling vision of medieval Judaism that is at once historic and prophetic.

By contrast, those often termed *holy minimalists* – a term predictably contested by composers and critics alike,[102] and one almost entirely ignored up to now in the study of the visual arts and literature – are concerned with an inward turn: a turn not towards solipsism, but towards the soul; a 'quest for the … universal [in] human existence [mirrored by] the quest for the universally musical'.[103] Most prominent among these composers are Arvo Pärt, John Tavener, Henryk Gorecki and Sofia Gubaidolina. In their music, historical time itself becomes ambiguous and charged: they reach back to the musical modes of medieval Catholic Europe and the Orthodox musical legacy, yet with the purpose of creating a timeless, eternal music that, paradoxically, by virtue of its timelessness, is also able to inspire the transfigurative potential of the present – the capacity to imagine a different future. Tavener and Pärt explicitly conceive of these works as icons in sound that provide access to an intensified reality, at the apex of which is *theosis*, a type of union with the divine.[104]

The minimalist icon functions to clarify an idea – the accessibility of the real, configured in mystical terms as the divine – that might otherwise remain obscured or hidden. To this end, Pärt developed a minimalist compositional technique he refers to as tintinnabulation, named after the *tintinnabulum* – a small, framed ceremonial bell used in Roman Catholic basilicas. A well-crafted bell expresses a desire for perfection, for a sonic clarity and transparency that depends not only on the shape of the bell and the way it is struck, but also on the purity of its materials and the process of its casting, and on where it is situated and the way it is heard. Yet, despite all these markers of singularity, the bell is also universal. As Marguerite Botonia recognizes, 'a single bell retains a natural, unchanging tonal complex that is unbound by style conventions, which predates functional harmony, and which persists through modern times in its primitive manifestation'.[105] *Tintinnabuli* seek to expose 'musical archetypes'.[106] It is 'not just a composition technique but also a way of viewing the world',[107] a search for universality in the depths of individual experience, where 'we are all so similar that we could recognize ourselves in any person',[108] as Pärt himself suggests.

In pursuit of this vision, he develops a composition technique and style that synthesize objective and subjective music processes. Essentially modal, reflecting a strong gravity towards a root tone, *tintinnabuli* take shape through a simple and direct counterpoint of one or more melodic lines and an arpeggiated line called the *tintinnabulum*.[109] Although the melody itself is formed as the composition takes shape, the relationship between the pitches of the melody and those of the *tintinnabulum* is predetermined and objective, incorporating 'basic formal relationships such as mirroring, parallel motion, additions, and multiplications'[110] alongside specified pitch relationships. In this way, tintinnabulation is able to explore a difficult intersection of freedom and determinism that is charged with symbolic significance: a meeting place of the immanent and the transcendental, the temporal and the eternal, the human and the divine. It does not seek an absolute resolution,[111] but rather extrapolates tensions and unusual pitch relationships with a clarity that renders both melodic feeling and process transparent. These are icons of spiritual humility giving rise to a mystical search for the transfigurative heart of the work.

Exemplary of the aesthetic of the *tintinnabuli* style as a whole,[112] *Spiegel im Spiegel* (1978), a composition originally for violin and piano, but subsequently adapted to other stringed instruments, is among Pärt's most minimal works. As Leopold Brauneiss has noted of the work, explaining the significance of its title, 'if one holds two mirrors against each other, the two-way reflections show a picture … trail[ing] off endlessly … into [an] infinity, formed by a rational, technical arrangement'.[113] Yet this section of infinity is far from cerebral. Where compositions such as *Für Alina*, *Fratres* and *Tabula Rasa* reveal a certain severity alongside their crystalline, introspective purity, *Spiegel im Spiegel* is a lyrical work evoking tranquillity, sincerity and tenderness. The composition draws a transparent beauty of surprising emotional depth from its austere formalism and minimal musical means.[114]

Pärt's work constitutes an acetic practice in its own right – an austere opening of 'sublime anticipation'[115] through which it is possible to approach minimum as an inward turn that is also, finally, a return to the universal. Minimum moves across cultures and histories, finding expression in multiple ways and, in aesthetic terms, across multiple media. For instance, the unremitting density of Ad Reinhardt's black canvases – works that earned him the moniker 'the heretical black monk of Abstract Expressionism'[116] – invoke a spiritual intensity that often approximates the sublime. Likewise, the work of Mark Rothko and Barnett Newman manifest two opposing, but equally austere, aesthetic responses to an overwhelmingly religious sense of awe. Attempting to 'purge … their work of extraneous elements in order to develop an art of transcendental immediacy',[117] Rothko seeks to draw the religious into the aesthetic realm by means of its sheer chromatic density, while Newman, bisecting massive fields of colour with bright zips, attempts to generate a sense of the sublime encounter.[118] Other artists, perhaps most notably Agnes Martin, discover the sublime in withdrawal: the subtle grids, gentle palette, and extremely fine chromatic rhythm of her work step back rather than forward – the expression of a painstakingly ascetic ideal conveyed in Martin's claiming to 'paint with her back to the world'.[119]

Flavin's light art, meanwhile, seeks to problematize the distinction between materiality and immateriality, immediacy and mediation, and immanence and transcendence,[120] in order to gesture towards a more problematic experience of the sublime. In calling his early work *icons*, Flavin sought to ironize rather than exalt the idea of the icon as a vehicle for spiritual illumination: 'they are dumb – anonymous and inglorious … mute and indistinguished … They bring limited light'.[121] Flavin deflates any expectation that luminescence might lead to illumination, and yet there is little denying that many of his works effect a 'quasi-religious transport',[122] as Foster notes. This is nowhere more evident than in his final work, a large-scale installation at Chiesa Rosa, a parish church in Milan. Successfully transfiguring the space of the church, the work effects an ironic return to the religious spaces that had dominated Flavin's early life when he had briefly been a Roman Catholic seminarian, despite his persistent denial that his light art offers a path to religious transcendence.[123]

The position of literature with respect to the iconic logic of holy minimalism is far less certain. The heightened concern with a revivified realism that marks a great deal of canonical minimalism, amplified by the strong sense of secular disenchantment that moves through these works, habitually keeps the plots and characters of minimalist fiction anchored to an everyday world unaware of, indifferent to, or disillusioned with religion. Yet, despite this, much minimalist writing – from Carver and Hempel to Beckett and Davis – contains epiphanic, transfigurative insights and encounters, albeit often in the negative language of disappointment or even defeat. The brief, condensed and often fragmentary narratives of microfiction, the shortest of minimalism's narrative forms, regularly hinge on epiphanic moments, and although these are seldom religious they nonetheless reflect on the conditions under which secular forms of transfiguration might occur.[124]

Beckett's work, which itself is testament to an ascetic vision of considerable originality, contains frequent allusions to theological concepts and mystical insights, yet refuses any redemptive function. In works like the *Waiting for Godot* or 'For to end yet again' Beckett exposes different routes to an anticipation without expectation, a process of waiting that is potentially transfigurative precisely to the extent that it is devoid of any possibility of transcendence. These works are icons of an existential persistence through which Beckett draws to attention the point at which empty ritual and the ritual of emptying become indistinguishable from one another. In this respect, it is possible to recall another profound and poetic search for emptiness in the work of John Cage, which effects a 'renunciation of intention and the use of chance operations',[125] making extensive use of the *I Ching* and various techniques of Zen Buddhism to produce remarkable writing that moves between visual and conceptual poetry, exploring an aleatory space in which indeterminacy itself becomes an icon of possibility.

A much more gradual form of ritual emptying is reflected in the singular crossing of the poetic work and the poetic life in the case of Robert Lax, for whom '[w]riting simply about simple things'[126] was both a spiritual and aesthetic aim, and an iconic act precisely to the extent that it seeks to bridge these two spheres. As with many New York poets of the his era, Lax was mentored at Columbia University by the poet and pedagogue, Mark Van Doren, where he also became lifelong friends with artist Ad Reinhardt and writer, and later Trappist monk, Thomas Merton.[127] After various jobs in journalism, and a protracted period as part of a circus troupe, Lax withdrew to a semi-hermitic life on the island of Patmos where he applied himself to writing. For Lax writing was not simply an expressive act, but part of a search, framed by spiritual reflection, for the minimal elements of language, in the belief that these would reveal the poetic or generative act in its purest form.

Lax held to an essentially 'mystical experience of the world'[128] in which all that is needed, ultimately, is unmediated simplicity and poetic clarity. Making use of profoundly simple diction, repetition and subtle variation, space and silence, and through an almost complete abandonment of figurative conventions, Lax's sparse works habitually conceal the extreme precision and disciplined process of reduction that underpins them. There is a particular care for the poetic agency of single words, an agency often ignored or dominated by the forceful logic of syntax, that emerges in this poetry: numbers, colours, the auxiliary verb, and the infinitive point towards the force of the act itself – the poetic act as a pure act – distinguished from either agent or object. This lexical strategy is matched by an equally radical approach to form: Lax turns the poem on its side so that the horizontal lines of the conventional stanza become vertical columns,[129] often with only a single syllable per line, and with a single word comprising an entire section. At the same time, when these vertical columns are arranged parallel to one another, there is a pull between them, so that reading the poem is marked by a sense of movement in several directions at once, a vertical fall, a horizontal pull, and sometimes even a diagonal swerve.[130]

In 'jacob & the angel' – drawn from the Biblical tale of Jacob wrestling an angel, often interpreted as a theophanic encounter – the poem itself clarifies a symbolic struggle between humanity and the divine, immanence and transcendence, the finite and the infinite. Yet, as with Pärt's *tintinnabuli*, Lax's poem is concerned not with the reconciliation of opposites but with their capacity to persist in a state of tension. This tension is itself the mark of a spiritual struggle that yearns for the universality that grounds rather than emerges from opposition. The poem is constructed from only three phrases, broken down into syllables, and repeated in various orders and combinations: 'jac/ob/ said', 'an/gel/ said', 'ja/cob/ lift/ed', 'an/gel/ lift/ed', 'jac/ob/ fell', 'an/gel/ fell'.[131] These phrases constitute the thirty-six stanzas of the poem, arranged in three vertical columns of twelve stanzas each, or twelve horizontal columns of three stanzas each, depending on how it is read. In either case complex patterns of reading emerge, all of which hinge on the regular alternation of 'jac/ob/said' and 'an/gel/said', indicative of an argument between Jacob and the angel that escalates into physical confrontation, marked by the phrases 'ja/cob/ lift/ed', 'an/gel/ lift/ed', 'jac/ob/ fell', and 'an/gel/ fell' in various combinations, as one might legitimately expect of a wrestling contest where opponents are evenly matched. Yet this is clearly indicative of an internal spiritual struggle as well – a rift between the human and the divine that arises from the mythopoetic fall from grace, and which manifests in a conflict between the finite and infinite conception of the human being, the experience of immanence and the desire for transcendence.

Without seeking to resolve this conflict, Lax pursues a practice of poetic patterning through which 'both poles are seen as part of the whole',[132] merging significant metaphysical considerations regarding the realness and effects of the work with a contemplative, but also transfigurative, logic that marks the best icons of minimalism.[133] There are, of course, numerous other examples of conceptual and concrete poetry grappling with metaphysical, if not explicitly spiritual, problems: Ian Hamilton Finlay's work, which often finds expression on both the page and in three dimensional form, draws on sources from Heraclitus to Hegel in his transhistorical interrogation of the poetic and political paradoxes of mythology and metaphysics alike. Yet it is perhaps his one-word poems that reveal a concrete reinvestment of iconic power in the word itself. In 1968, Finlay published an international cohort of concrete and minimalist poets in a special issue of his journal, *Poor. Old. Tired. Horse.*, dedicated to this form. In a letter to Stephen Bann, Finlay suggests that 'a one-word poem consists of one word and a title of any length'.[134] Almost twenty years later, in a letter to Jessie Sheeler, his aesthetic resolve remains firm: 'I feel more and more that the purest poetry exists in single words or seemingly minute effects. These are what lodge in one.'[135] Indeed, it is by this logic that Finlay attempts to uncover in his one-word poem, 'Arcady', the very currency of a poetic utopia: 'ABCDEFGHIJKLMNOPQRSTUVWXYZ'.[136] As already witnessed in the poetry of Aragon and Andersen, the alphabet, in its infinite possible permutations, is both a single word and every word – an icon for the infinite within the finite. Seeking to present itself in terms of the most fundamental constituents of written language, this species of minimalism reveals its determination to uncover the fundamental stuff of *poiesis* – of production, generation.

6.4 Theurgy

Minimalist ritual: Velimir Khlebnikov's *Incantation by Laughter* (1910) John Cage's *Empty Words* (1974) Meredith Monk's *Facing North* (1990)

Yet to come to terms with this minimalist, iconic investment of force, it becomes necessary to press beyond the word and letter to even more fundamental parts of language, in the process revisiting the numerous and transhistorical attempts of concrete poetry to fuse the most radical conceptual, verbal, visual and sonic aspects of their media. If, as Wendy Steiner suggests, 'the attempt to overreach the boundaries between one art and another … attempt[s] to dispel (or at least mask) the boundary between art and life, between sign and thing',[137] then concrete poetry becomes far more than a field of experimentation, aspiring rather to nothing less than the aesthetic instantiation of reality itself. Here it is instructive to recall, with Perloff, that poetry as we understand it emerges 'from the Greek *poiesis*, a making or creation'[138] – one side of the 'ancient quarrel'[139] between philosophy and poetry, science and art, famously noted by Plato – reflecting the desire of the poem to reconstitute the true and perfect forms which, from a Platonic perspective, undergird every reality.[140]

Poetry is clearly more ancient than the discourse on poetry, however, and a long view of its aesthetic history reveals that the poem has always belonged to a more primal theurgical or ritual function. For instance, early calligramic texts in which writing is shaped into images functioned as amulets, invoking poetic language as both prescription and cure for various threats and illnesses.[141] This essentially talismanic use progresses to a more mystical view of calligraphy in which writing is 'connected not only with … technique, skill and art, but also with … spiritual and moral character'.[142] The venerable lineage of visual poetry, while not strictly separable from the 'magical and mystical impetus to shape texts',[143] attempts to integrate more fully the generative, aesthetic and symbolic aspects of text and form, drawing them towards a singular and distinctly minimalist expressive point. Such practices can be traced as far back as the third century BC and the Hellenistic *Technopaegina*, the egg calligram of Simias of Rhodes being the earliest known example, where the careful arrangement of poetic text to form objects, a technique adapted by the Romans in their *carmina figurata*.[144] Visual poetry, mostly of a religious nature, is fairly widespread across Medieval Europe – from Armenia and Turkey in the south-east, to Germany in the north-west. Of the finest religious calligrams are Hebrew massoeretic texts in which 'the massorah, which is the critical emendation found on certain pages [has been] shaped into patterns'.[145] In part as a result of religious prohibitions on pictorial representation, many medieval Arabic examples make use of an ingenious calligraphy, objects emerging from the careful reshaping of letters.[146]

It was only at the start of the seventeenth century, when, as Sloane suggests, 'the tendency to visualize ideas reaches its zenith',[147] that the first English calligrams of any poetic significance were produced. The vast majority of these poems have religious themes, as in the case of Robert Herrick's 'The Cross', or George Herbert's 'The Altar', among many others. The altar is in fact a favourite motif of visual poetry,[148] not only connecting the work to the formal rites of religion, but also connecting poetic inspiration to the surrender and sacrifice of the self to the divine.[149] 'The Altar' is a fine example of the visual poem as iconic symbol: its physical form reinforces the conceit that gives the poem its momentum – the heart as altar – while its true subject transcends either word or form, since the heart is finally a cipher for the human soul and its relation to the divine. Also significant is the rise of the emblem as a popular genre inherited from the Renaissance which combines a verbal motto, a symbolic illustration, and an epigrammatic exposition of these in formal verse, with many of these works gathered in Geoffrey Whitney's *A Choice of Emblems* (1586) and Francis Quarles's *Emblems* (1635).

The flourishing of sacred visual poetry in the seventeenth century – much of it distinctly minimalist in style and conception – was followed by a significant waning in its fortunes in the eighteenth and nineteenth centuries, as medium-specific aesthetic theories came to dominate, influenced in no small part by Lessing's influential essay, *Laocoon*. Where the point of comparison between painting and poetry historically rests on similarity – captured well in the Horatian maxim, *ut pictura poesis*, or *as is painting, so is poetry* – Lessing vigorously opposes this conception, insisting that a productive relation of the arts in fact rests on retaining a sense of their individuality and separation,[150] distinguishing dominantly spatial concerns of the visual arts from the predominantly temporal concerns of literature.[151] Although there is a resurgence of distinctly minimalist visual poetry among the avant-garde movements of the early twentieth century, for the most part the ancient theurgical function of poetry is displaced into the parallel field of experimental sound poetry, before these different trajectories finally converge in the emergence of concrete poetry in the mid-century.

The sounds of language have always been integral to the poetic enterprise itself. Its consonances and dissonances, its rhythms and repetitions, its tones and intonations, and its rhymes and resonances are central not only to its meaning, but also to its transmission. Critics, however, remain divided. Jacques Roubaud and Dick Higgins – respectively a founder of *Oulipo* and a pioneer of intermedia and concrete poetry – agree that sonic poetry is necessarily separate from music and song. According to Higgins, '[o]ne thing that sound poetry is not is music',[152] while Roubauld is unambiguous in asserting that '[a] song is not a poem and a poem is not a song'.[153] Both affirm the productive possibilities of a normative vision of genre, establishing the conditions in which their respective taxonomies of sound poetry are coherent.[154] By contrast, Steve McCaffery – himself a leading intermedia experimentalist – draws attention to the poetic significance of 'the many instances of chant structures and incantation, of nonsense syllabic mouthings and deliberate lexical distortions [and of] ludic strata … in the nonsense syllabery of nursery rhymes, mnemonic counting aids, whisper games and skipping chants, mouth music and folk-song refrain'.[155]

Although it may be true, as McCaffery suggests, that sound poetry belongs to a 'vast, intractable area of archaic and primitive poetries',[156] a distinct, if in parts fragmented, trajectory of experimentation can nonetheless be traced to the early cultic hymns of Ancient Greece which were used in public rituals[157] and adapted to almost every social situation, from political contestations to the alcohol-fuelled debates of symposia.[158] It was also these hymns that were elaborated in the iambic verse of parody that gives rise to comedy, and in the heroic narrative of epic poetry which sparks the genesis of tragedy.[159] The role of the chorus, the group of singers which offer both exposition of, and commentary on, dramatic action in tragedy,[160] is particularly significant: they recall the 'ritual poetic forms'[161] of tragedy's theurgical roots, singing or chanting in various metres, actively demonstrating the 'unity of poetry, melody, and gesture'.[162]

Much of this early ritual poetry is engaged in a distinctly minimalist pursuit of 'clarity and purity of tone, resonance, and coincidence with the accompaniment'.[163] In this art, simplicity and linearity are valued not as ends in themselves, but because they clarify the work, allowing poetry, music and performance to reflect and intensify one another. Although only a few fragments of notated music survive from classical antiquity,[164] the means of their accurate deciphering is contained in several theoretical treatises, produced by the Greeks and Romans in their attempts to work out the systematic elements of the acoustic universe.[165] These fragments – mostly didactic excerpts or choral prompts – were notated using letters adapted from the alphabet and inscribed above the poetic text. Rhythm, metre, duration and tempo were relative to the syllabic stresses of the poem,[166] a relation preserved in a great deal of religious chant across a range of periods and religious traditions,[167] while dialogic poetic structures are reflected in much medieval liturgy, and in many mystery and morality plays.[168] More significant still are the songs of the troubadours, whose aesthetic 'indissolubly interlaces a particular language to its music',[169] bringing rhyme to poetic prominence for the first time.[170] It is also to classical models of tragedy that the composer-poets of Renaissance Florence turned in pursuit of an aesthetic vision in which 'music shares integrally with the words in unfolding the drama',[171] giving birth to what today is known as opera.[172] Despite occasional flourishes, the aesthetic ambition of early opera is essentially minimalist, striving for rhythmic clarity, formal transparency, and an immediacy in relating poetic text to its sonic properties.[173] This is continued in later opera by the recitatives that connect lyric sections, as well as in Wagnerian *Sprechgesang*.[174]

Yet, arguably, the works closest to the theurgical roots of sound poetry emerge from the sustained period of experimentation with 'language's non-semantic, acoustic properties'[175] at the start of the twentieth century. Striking works of experimental sound poetry are produced by both the Russian and Italian Futurists, and key Dadaists from the Zurich and Berlin avant-garde scenes. Attempting to press to a linguistic point of origin that informs the rich rhymes, rhythms, alliterative and onomatopoeic potential of the Russian language, poets such as Velimir Khlebnikov, Alexey Kruchenykh, Ilia Zdanevich (Iliazd) and Vladimir Majakovskij are instrumental in uncovering a poetry which is 'spontaneous [and] instantaneous'.[176] Sound, in their estimation, is the element most capable of achieving the sense of dynamism that sought to propel these works into the future.[177] Kruchenykh's phonemic work is particularly minimal – brief, repetitive and entirely onomatopoeic[178] – an expression of the view that 'poetry must revert to a more primitive, more libidinal, outburst of organic orality'.[179] The patterns, permutations and reversals of 'zok zok zok'[180] press the phonemic constituents of poetic language to their most fundamental, not only pre-empting the processual approach of later minimalism, but also pressing the phonemic substrate of language to its most fundamental points in order to rediscover *explodity*, the generative potential at the heart of language.[181]

The radical poetics of Khlebnikov offers perhaps the most compelling case for a transhistorical theurgical minimalism. A mathematician by training, the poet's vision was driven by a search for the symbolic union of number and etymology with the aim of discovering and presenting the numerical basis of reality in poetic terms.[182] The implausibility of Khlebnikov's mathematical efforts are less significant than their affirmation of a super-sensible radix at the heart of language and poetry. For Khlebnikov, poetic language becomes what he terms a *zaum* language, a concept formed from the 'phonemic and morphemic play … beyond (*za*) mind or reason (*um*) … most persuasively translated by the neologism *beyonsense*'.[183] As Perloff goes on to stress, 'neologism is at the heart of this vision of *poiesis*, once again charging a poetic language exhausted by familiarity and which ignores is own strangeness'.[184] The task of the poet becomes one of uncovering the etymological radices of words from within the complex lattice of phonic similarities, and generating a genuinely novel poetic vocabulary, subtracted from history and utility.[185]

Sound is of particular importance to Khlebnikov, and in a striking anticipation of the concrete and minimalist problematization of external reference, 'the material form of the signifier is thus [regarded as] its meaning'.[186] The most celebrated example of Khlebnikov's 'elaborate etymology'[187] is the sound-poem

'Incantation by Laughter', which develops a complex set of permutations from the root, *sme*, of the word *laugh*, or *smekh*. Moving through various permutations – 'laughsters … laughters … laugherize … delaughly … belaughably … laughify',[188] among several others – the poem 'uses suffixes, for example, to turn the stem into plural nouns … verbs … or adjectives and adverbs. And stems are often joined to suffixes that don't go with them.'[189] Having grasped the fundamental lexemes, graphemes and phonemes of poetic language, it becomes possible to assert the universal poetic applicability of any number of etymologically derived and phonically coded neologisms. In these, 'every letter is letter perfect'[190] precisely because it enables us to move from the *letter as such* to the self-sufficiency of the *word as such*.[191] The patterning of reality which begins with the smallest poetic particles, empties the referential reserve of the sign so that we are left with a minimalist sonic object without specific meaning, but of considerable significance.

Khlebnikov's concern with origins finds notable resonances in the work of several Dada poets – notably Hugo Ball, Raoul Hausmann and Kurt Schwitters – who seek a 'pristine Adamic language',[192] an *ur*-language capable of capturing the most immediate and powerful sense of linguistic expression. The theurgical element of this work recalls the connection of sound poetry to the chant or hymnic tradition, clearly audible in the incantation of Hausmann's 'K'Perioum', and at various points of Schwitters's *Ur-Sonate*. Of more immediate interest than the theatricality of this work – its purposeful exaggerations, the ritualistic mannerism of its intonation, the self-conscious and often virtuosic patterning of its articulation – is its textual innovation in pursuing new ways of notating sound poetry, developing *optophonic* or *vocovisual*[193] scores designed to create a more immediate and accurate integration of letter, shape and sound.[194] Johanna Drucker explains that the 'concept of orchestrating verbal language through visual means became a mainstay of experimental poetics in the twentieth century',[195] and certainly points back towards an increasingly radical approach to poetic sound that, as Susan Stewart recognizes, has significant ontological implications.

While rhythm is an important aspect of sound poetry – a 'force in nature, indeed a force in the cosmos [which] may be a necessary, if not sufficient, condition of human life',[196] connecting the intimate experience of the body to the external world by 'mak[ing] a physical medium … seem to move with deliberateness though *time*'[197] – it is rhyme which best captures the minimalist poetic potentiality of the phoneme, the 'possibilities of chant and charm, *zaum* and word-magic'.[198] Rhyme constitutes an arrival or cadence which activates both memory and anticipation, pointing at once towards a past and a future from within the intensity of the present moment.[199] As Stewart recognizes,

> [r]hyme offers a particular kind of pattern, one that is only partly determinative. Unlike rhythm, which may exist as pure haptic or tactile feeling, rhyme comes with acoustical, if not always semantic, content; and unlike meter, which remains ideal, rhyme is always realized or manifested. There is a certain balance between the will and contingency which is effected in rhyming.[200]

Rhyme is no longer solely a question of homophony, or sounding the same, but becomes a marker of existential consonance, of the way in which similar but distinct entities come to resonate with one another. This transfigurative relation is contingent on various types of proximity – temporal, material, conceptual – but most of all it is indicative of a situation in which *seeming* similar shows itself to be an incisive measure of *being* similar. What rhyme brings to light is a site of struggle between the concrete being of objects and their 'being-in-language',[201] to recall Agamben: their possession of a name; the manner in which, through a simultaneously self-reflexive and signifying force, the name becomes appended to an object; the contraction of the name into the minimalist sphere of the phoneme.[202]

Agamben suggest that it is the force of exemplarity, the ways in which the example comes to be understood *as* an example, that presents the conditions in which seeming and being become indistinguishable.[203] It is possible in this light to suggest that the many works of minimalist sound poetry – the phonemic, morphological rhyme of Khlebnikov's 'Incantation by Laughter', for instance – exhibit this same exemplary force, and that this exemplary force is a fundamentally transfigurative one. In this case, the resemblance between two or more sounds proves sufficient to render the relation between these sounds so intense that it fundamentally transforms the work in question: rhyme describes the conditions in which seeming flows into being, appearance into essence; the vehicle for a type of secular magic. A different but not less compelling case is encountered in the work of Antonin Artaud, whose late idiolectic work Stecopolous describes in terms of 'glossolalia, magic spells, vocables or syllables,'[204] the 'debris … of words from 'natural' languages'[205] put to use in a 'visceral poetics [that] is always … seeking out language that could embody it as indeed all and nothing at once'.[206]

The transhistorical yearning for a primal language, itself a reorientation of existence towards minimum, is evident in a great variety of subsequent sound poetry. Only a few moments of Austrian experimentalist Ernst Jandl's 'Ode auf N' reveals its debt to the morphological experiments of the futurists. The ritualistic incantations of the Dadaists are similarly audible in works as diverse as the incantations of British concrete poet Bob Cobbing, the Brazilian practitioner of '[i]ntersign poetry',[207] Philadelpho Menezes, and the Romanian-French Lettrist, Isadore Isou, whose sound poems have an unambiguously ritualistic element. The poetry composed and improvised by Isou identifies the *letter* as the most minimal element of language: by 'always taking all the letters together; unfolding … the marvels brought about by letters … creating an architecture of lettric rhythms',[208] Isou believed he had discovered a means of presenting 'transitions between feeling and saying'[209] – a manner of 'concretizing silence; writing nothings'.[210] The primal, even brutal, force of Isou's work is clearest when it is performed: the voice, a precarious extension of the impermanent body, mediates the relation between language and silence, existence and nothingness.

As Agamben recognizes, the voice is '[*n*]*o longer* the experience of mere sound and *not yet* the experience of a meaning',[211] existing between 'the animal *phonē*',[212] and the production of linguistic meaning.[213] From the essential 'ungroundedness'[214]of being, the voice marks the 'event of language'[215] that makes it possible to delineate existence as a relation to finitude: '[v]oice signifies … becom[ing] capable of another death – no longer simply a deceasing, but a person's ownmost and insuperable possibility, the *possibility* of freedom.'[216] Exposing the relation between language and finitude, *voice* not only indicates the taking place of language *in* time, but also the 'taking place of language *as* time'[217] – language in itself,[218] an absolute where there is no 'difference between showing and telling, being and entity, world and thing.'[219] This pure occurrence of language is 'without any determinate event of meaning', pointing instead to the 'possibility of thought beyond meaningful propositions',[220] a poetic articulation of the archaic nothingness intuited by the most austere minimalism.

In the passage from verse to voice and voice to void, works such as Henri Chopin's 'Espaces et gestes' evidence the considerable struggle to apprehend the essence of language in poetic terms. Only the traces of vocal incantation remain, with the principal material of the poem taking the form of amplified atmospheric sounds of breath, unpitched whistling, unvocalized plosives and stops, and hard whispers. Invested with an unmistakably theurgical quality, these technologically altered precursors and remnants of the voice all gesture towards a minimal point – a precarious space, the threshold of appearance and disappearance. John Cage's 'Empty Words' echoes these concerns, reworking the journals of Henry David Thoreau through an aleatory process that progressively effects a decomposition of the voice by stripping language of its structural cohesion and dissolving it into minimal units. Although visually striking in its own right, the work is intended to be performed, enacting a liturgy of lessness in which solid syntax is decomposed to floating phrases, floating phrases to scattered words, scattered words to dispersed phonemes, and dispersed phonemes to drifting letters; until the work finally arrives at an entropic point, a minimal point – a silence in which poetry proves itself capable of 'making language say … nothing at all'.[221]

Yet the sheer facticity of language presses poetry beyond this silence, towards a 'language without Voice, a word that is not grounded in any meaning',[222] and which 'remains to be thought as the most human dimension'[223] of being. It is perhaps towards this radical possibility – the voice before *voice* – that Meredith Monk's minimalism inclines. Monk consistently pursues 'clear and simple structure[s] that would allow for primal yet transparent vocal qualities'[224] to manifest in a minimalist music centred on the embodied subject. For Monk the voice is a singular musical instrument invested with an affective intensity that ranges in its expression from the ritual severity of *Dolmen Music* to the fragile intimacies of *Facing North*. According to Martha Nussbaum, since 'all human experiences are embodied [it follows that] human emotions are finally embodied processes as well. However, the question is, are there any bodily states or processes that are constantly correlated with our experiences of emotion?'[225] The sheer range of expression that emerges from Monk's sustained exploration of the voice seems to intuit something more radical than language or the voice: pure affect in itself. Is this what is 'the most human',[226] to recall Agamben? In works such as 'Arctic Bar', a duet from the *Facing North*, the voice constitutes a simple, direct and exuberant evocation of the combination of 'fortitude and tenderness'[227] required to flourish in 'the elemental, bracing clarity of the northern landscape'.[228] Yet although it touches on the apparent unremarkability of the everyday, the affective force of the voice is immediate and unambiguous: this is an extroverted, joyful work, brimming with humour and tenderness. It reveals that the voice at its most vital is also the voice at it most vulnerable, a reminder that *Eudaimonia* – a human life of goodness, virtue, fulfilment and happiness – is one from which uncertainty cannot be eliminated.[229]

In practice contemporary vocal performance is increasingly mediated by technologies which deconstitute the human voice.[230] The voice can be recorded, transmitted, altered and combined without undermining its integrity, reflecting Steven Connor's theorization of the *vocalic body* as 'a projection of a new way of having or being a body, formed and sustained out of the autonomous operations of the voice'.[231] For Connor, 'the leading characteristic of the voice-body is to be a body-in-invention, an impossible, imaginary body in the course of being found and formed'.[232] Thus, although Bök is justified in noting that contemporary technology 'threaten[s] to overwhelm the organic coherence of any unified performer',[233] it simultaneously generates new possibilities for the poetic reconstitution of a posthuman voice. In works such as Paul Lansky's *Idle Chatter* and Trevor Wishart's *Globalalia* the technological mediation of the voice exposes the possibility of an alternate understanding of minimalism grounded not only in the deconstitution of the voice into its most essential sonic elements, or in the radicalization of the voice on conceptual grounds, but in the concrete translation of these into electrical or digital information, and the almost infinite possibilities for generative re-synthesis this process sets in motion.

7

Minimum: On the Extremes of Minimalism

7.1 Negation

Sublation and saying *no*: Ad Reinhardt's *Abstract Painting* (1957) Bruce Nauman's *Clown Torture* (1987)

While minimalism regularly aspires to render the qualities of its objects maximally visible through various processes of reduction, formal simplicity, repetition and processual transparency, in some instances it pursues minimum through the proscription of quality itself.

Ad Reinhardt, best known for his black, monochromatic paintings, also composed a strikingly militant manifesto, 'Twelve Rules for a New Academy', interrogating the limits of an aesthetic of negation:

> No realism or existentialism ... No impressionism ... No expressionism or surrealism ... No fauvism, primitivism, or brute art ... No constructivism, sculpture, plasticism, or graphic arts. No collage, paste, papers, sand, or string ... no '*tromp-l'loeil*,' interior decoration, or architecture ... No texture ... [Painting] techniques are unintelligent and to be avoided. No accidents or automatism ... No brushwork or calligraphy ... No signature or trademarking ... No sketching or drawing ... No line or outline ... No shading or streaking ... No forms ... No figure or fore- or back-ground. No volume or mass, no cylinder, sphere, or cone, or cube ... No push or pull. 'No shape or substance' ... No design ... No Colours ... Colours are barbaric, physical, unstable, suggest life, 'cannot be completely controlled' and 'should be concealed.' No white. 'White is a colour' ... White on white is 'a transition from pigment to light' and 'moving pictures' ... No light ... No space. Space should be empty, should not project, and should not be flat ... Space divisions within the painting should not be seen ... No time ... There is no ancient or modern, no past or future in art. 'A work of art is always present.' The present is the future of the past, and the past of the future ... No size or scale ... No movement. 'Everything is on the move. Art should be still' ... No object, no subject, no matter. No symbols, images,

> visions or ready-mades. Neither pleasure nor pain. No mindless working or mindless nonworking. No chess playing.[1]

By rejecting aesthetic quality as the determining property of an artwork's singularity, Reinhardt presses minimalism 'as far as, or farther than, it can go',[2] relentlessly challenging the 'fundamentally delusory enterprise of representation'[3] through works that abandon, if not actively negate, the traditional aesthetic concerns with reference, relation, imagination, and expression. Form and colour – the 'two primary elements of representation on canvas'[4] – are reconceived in radical terms as quantities singular to the work itself, and thus a means of escaping rather than fastening the chains imposed by mimesis and its accompanying compulsion to repeat the world, and the conviction that by repeating the world, it becomes possible to master it. As Yve-Alain Bois explains, extreme abstraction such as Reinhardt's,

> [f]reed from all extrinsic conventions … was meant to bring forth the pure *parousia* of its own essence, to tell the final truth and thereby terminate its course … [T]hrough its essentialism (its idea that something like the essence of painting existed …), the enterprise of abstract painting could not but understand its birth as calling for its end.[5]

In fact Reinhardt's most radically minimalist works – his celebrated black paintings – occupy an ambiguous threshold in this respect: from one perspective they represent a terminus – ending with the least possible; from another they are foundational – beginning with the least necessary.

Probing the limit between formlessness and form, Reinhardt's work offers a negative presentation of the generative process itself. It is through the elimination of qualities that the essential quantity of the work – its realness – is rendered radically immanent. Reinhardt's concern with negation paradoxically constitutes a significant point of *poietic* affirmation, one which arises from the least necessary required for an object to emerge and persist. This minimal point approximates the void, the charged nothingness that emerges in the tension between radical presence – recalling Reinhardt's assertion that '[a] work of art is always present'[6] – and absolute absence – the implicit end of Reinhardt's 'no[s]'.[7] Early biomorphic and collagic works give way to a monochromatic austerity that aims to pinpoint and contain the most fundamental elements of visual expression. The formal regularization progressively explored in terms of line and texture in his earlier work, is increasingly displaced into subtler gradations and tonal contrasts. Even the minimal vestiges of abstract expressionism – the visibility of gesture that reveals a concern with spatiality and depth that are still evident in the horizontal strokes of the lighter greys and whites in *Number 107*[8] – are practically invisible in the black monochromatic canvases of the late 1950s.

In black monochromes such as *Abstract Painting*,[9] which on first encounter appears entirely uniform, sustained exposure to the work reveals a masterful monochromatic weave of vertical and horizontal bands of subtly distinguished hues of black – a weave that renders practically indistinguishable stasis and movement, non-illusionistic flatness and dimensional fluctuation. The perceptual ambiguity of the work – the manner in which it keeps the eye unsettled and draws the viewer subtly and slowly into a complex relation with the canvas – points to a more nuanced understanding of spatiality and temporality as intrinsic markers of the work's immanence. Colour and illusion, pattern and space, temporality and gesture are condensed into a plain of remarkable intensity, revealing a generative negation as the heart of the work. What emerges is an unprecedented chromatic density and intensity, and a strong sense that the work is only just able to contain its considerable existential weight.

Pressing towards a region of absolute absence, Reinhardt's later black works, as also the encaustic experiments of Marden, reject all formal properties and relation in order to commit to the 'most austere reductivism imaginable'.[10] Yet, precisely at this point, where remnants of *something* seem to pass into the absence of *nothing*, the work returns as a sublime presence – a *now* that 'dismantles consciousness',[11] in Lyotard's estimation, since the 'art object no longer bends itself to models, but tries to present the fact that there is an unpresentable'.[12] The task, henceforth, becomes one of discovering the range of means by which minimalist negation seeks to fulfil its sublime vocation. Barret Watten recognizes that

> negativity is common to a range of concepts that include non-identity, antagonism, nihilism, revolt, defamiliarization, rupture, opposition, dissociation, conflict, delusion, void, emptiness. Negativity as it occurs 'in the field' so to speak, with the radical forms and interventions of the avant-garde, partakes of one or all of these modes – even as its final horizon, a denial of positivity, locates each instance as a potential of critique.[13]

There is an important distinction to be made between negation as a structural means to an end and negation as a protocol; or, in short, between *no* as resistance and *no!* as injunction. Often this distinction remains threateningly vague, even in the relatively transparent sphere of minimalist aesthetics. The minimalism of Serra and Smith, for instance, has been interpreted as authoritarian, their works judged vehicles of a coded hostility, and indifferent to their destructive potential.[14] In this light, the work of Bruce Nauman takes on a particular poignancy, spanning various media and regularly deploying broadly minimalist techniques in explicating the violence of negation, particularly as invested in the word *no*.

This is nowhere more forcefully exhibited than in *Clown Torture*,[15] a series of thoroughly disturbing video works combining projections with individual and stacked colour monitors, each with a separate soundtrack. If the first impression is carnivalesque, the cumulative effect is deeply discomfiting. As Schaffner recognizes, 'to watch *Clown Torture* is to participate in it: what is at first funny soon becomes unbearable'.[16] These works explore the tragi-comic figure of the clown in various of its visual, historical and allegorical manifestations. Clowns engage in activities that range from the absurd – propping up a goldfish bowl on a ceiling using a broom, upsetting a bucket of water propped on a door, or telling jokes that repeat indefinitely – to the invasive and violent – footage of a clown using the toilet, terrified kicking and screaming suggestive of torture, and an extended tantrum. Hyperbolic mannerisms and obsessively repeated words, phrases and catches of narrative are ceaselessly looped to effect a 'poetics of confusion, anxiety, boredom, entrapment, and failure'.[17] 'Whatever they do, they do over and over', [18]notes Danto, forced to 'endure what no right-minded person would tolerate'.[19]

Clown Torture is clearly allied to the Beckettian aesthetic of negation and failure as routine,[20] which through repetition becomes a type of negative accomplishment – a reflection of the radical meaninglessness of existence. As Schaffner notes, there is a 'clownish deliberation that … endlessly sidetrack[s] all of Beckett's characters',[21] rendering them habitually unable fully to make sense of or master the situations in which they find themselves thrown. Nauman's work amplifies this sense exponentially, intensifying and compressing Beckett's already austere vision into looping scenes of grinding repetition. Much as in Beckett's writing, the viewer is witness to the disintegration of conventional narrative language and the birth of a new language, more faithful to the *lacuna* at the centre of experience.[22] It becomes necessary to pass right through negation, often by way of the absurd, to arrive at a minimal positivity – the generative nucleus of negation.[23]

In *Clown Torture* the problem of witnessing is intensified by the almost invariably voyeuristic relation of the viewer to the work. While an initial response might be laughter, many viewers subsequently withdraw when confronted with the 'visceral sense of foreboding'[24] that emerges from the apparently interminable humiliation of the clowns. Others, however, linger in this voyeuristic relationship, attempting to decode the source of its fascination, but arguably also indulging in a perverse pleasure many appear to derive from witnessing the misfortune, even the physical suffering, of others. What emerges in this light is a particularly troubling aspect of subjectivity: the connection between a sense of self and the capacity of this self to exercise power and agency, in this case through a vicarious regulation and control of the body. The remarkable effect of *Clown Torture* – a work capable, in Brooks Adams's estimation, of 'blast[ing] just about any painting off the wall'[25] – resides in its terrifying ability to 'make … violence tolerable, turn[ing] torture into art, and the viewer into an accomplice of the artist … whose intent in the first place was to torture his audience with the truth of their own tolerance for cruelty'.[26]

Nauman deploys the familiar techniques of minimalism to generate a sense of immediacy, an intensified and contained experience of the dark gravity of violence. In the minimal terms of a self-referential, looping joke – 'Pete and Repeat are sitting on a fence. Pete falls off. Who's left? Repeat …' – the mounting frustration of the clown's performance peaks in rage, only to give way to growing despair and eventual resignation: the drama of existential depletion is laid disturbingly bare by distinctly minimal means. Particularly remarkable in the *Clown Torture* series are the two works that centre on Nauman's sustained interest in the word *no*. The first involves a clown retreating from the camera, collapsing on his back, kicking and repeatedly screaming the words, 'No! No! No! No! No! …' in clear anticipation of violence, or, indeed, torture. The second is *No, No, New Museum*, consisting of looped footage of two clowns dressed as traditional jesters, head to head on separate stacked monitors. Stamping violently, jumping up and down defiantly, each repeats its own litany of noes, generating an unsettling and asynchronous rhythmic counterpoint.

This gesture of negation, both verbal and physical, exposes with traumatic immediacy questions of violence, cruelty, frustration, anger, absurdity, redundancy and resistance. At the same time, it becomes clear that the verbal act of negation – the articulation of 'no' – in fact resists elimination. To say 'no' repeatedly is not inherently destructive, nor does its path necessarily lead to absolute negation or the void. Rather, it intensifies the tension in existence between persistence and finitude. In the case of *No, No, New Museum* it is impossible to know precisely what is being denied, resisted or refused. Yet it is certain that in the very act of this negation 'something is taking its course',[27] to recall a phrase that Beckett repeatedly uses in 'Endgame' to describe the sheer facticity of existence and its persistence in the face of ongoing negation. Another of Nauman's works – a minimalist concrete poem consisting of a wall-mounted neon light that flashes between two words, 'ON' and 'NO' – adds further nuance. Yet, as Schaffner recognizes, '[d]oubling "NO" back on itself, "ON" overrules resistance with action … But the line always switches back to: "NO"'.[28] In a similar manner, Maurice Blanchot – arguably the writer closest in spirit to Beckett in their shared concern with the subject faced by nothingness[29] – captures this sense of negative persistence with precision in his recognition that 'the work … is neither finished nor unfinished: it is. What it says is exclusively that: that it is – and nothing more. Outside of that, it is nothing. Anyone who tries to make it express more finds nothing, finds that it expresses nothing';[30] or, as Robbe-Grillet suggests, '[t]he existence of a work of art, and its weight are not at the mercy of an interpretative screen which may or may not coincide with its contours. A work of art, like the world, is a living form: it *is*, it needs no justification.'[31] In this light, anything the work means or could mean is measured with respect to its contingency, but the primacy of this contingency also means that the closest it is possible to come to an essence of the work is in the simple fact that it exists as it does.

It is possible here to recognize an aesthetic approximation of Meillassoux's position according to which facticity can no longer be understood simply in terms of the existence of facts,[32] since facts ultimately prove inadequate to the task of eliminating the fundamental contingency of all things.[33] Rather, facticity refers to 'the absolute necessity of the contingency of everything',[34] and functions according to a principal of *unreason* – 'that there is no reason for anything to be or to remain the way it is'.[35] In its most transparent examples, minimalism seems to mediate between the contentless facticity of Blanchot's aesthetic vision, and Meillassoux's conviction that 'it is the contingency of the entity that is necessary, not the entity [itself]'.[36] In short: minimalism persists; and this persistence manifests in the way that even its most nihilistic gestures resist the possibility of absolute negation. '[T]he writer will continue to remain dependent on the very language that is to be dissolved',[37] writes Weller of Beckett's essentially constructive relation to negation.[38]

The form of Hegel's conception of determinate negation[39] – that 'whatever individuates something distinguishes it from all others by contrast'[40] – moves unambiguously through this conception of minimalism. 'The "different" is just this', Hegel maintains, 'not to be in possession of itself, but to have its essential being only in an other.'[41] The inside is affirmed not only through its opposition to an outside, however. 'Spirit becomes object because it is just this movement of becoming an *other to itself*.'[42] That which is negative in relation to a determinate entity is also its innermost quality. Recognized as confluent, intrinsic self-contradictoriness and extrinsic differentiation effect the dynamic, positive calculation of the dialectic process Hegel identifies in terms of the negation of negation, or *sublation*.[43] As Franco Chieregin explains, '[t]he fact that in the affirmation of something we must also comprehend its negation does not constitute a contradiction that results in nothingness. It permits us to reach a higher content where both the abstract affirmation of something and the necessary relation to that which negates it flow together in unity.'[44] In the dialectic emergence of a determinate entity, the contraries that inhabit its identity are simultaneously preserved and abolished; modified through their interaction, 'render[ing] them no longer contraries, and therefore no longer self-contradictory in virtue of their reciprocal containment'.[45]

Although the Hegelian dialectic always seems to constitute finite entities predicated on a series of negative relations, it does not reveal a stable, independent, unmediated ground upon which such entities can be forwarded other than these relations of negation themselves. Every apparently stable entity exists simultaneously as a dynamic and infinite field of relations and negations. According to Badiou, in Hegel's system 'the point of being … *generates* out of itself the operator of infinity … Infinity becomes an internal reason of the finite itself, a simple attribute of experience in general.'[46] Norris argues convincingly that this decision stems from Hegel's suppression of the relation between quantity and concept: quantitative, bad infinity – a mindless law of quantitative repetition – is opposed to qualitative, good infinity – the infinity necessarily at work in any process that ends in determinate negation.[47] Sublation, in this light, is the predication 'that would finally transform the bad into the good, or the quantitative into the qualitative mode of infinity'.[48] Accordingly, the repetition of negation which emerges in Nauman's work presents the shift from a cumulative negation, which might indeed imply destruction or elimination, to the negation which marks good infinity – the sublation involved in the mere facticity of repeatedly saying *no*. Much minimalism is similarly composed of signifiers progressively emptied of specific meaning by negative means, but rendered significant by their persistence; works which demonstrate that '[b]eginning again and again is a natural thing'.[49]

Beckett's characters, almost invariably trapped in self-reflexive doubt,[50] add nuance to a minimalist understanding of sublation. Habitually, the most they can affirm is that 'something is taking its course';[51] that existence persists in the face of negation. Yet, even as it persists, existence veers, sometimes gradually but always irreversibly, towards inexistence. Thus it is that in 'Ill See Ill Said' the neutral phrase, 'neither more nor less',[52] is always followed by 'Less!'[53] Beckett's fatigued but unwavering delineation of existence points to an ideal minimalism in terms of the pursuit of lessness 'Less. Ah the sweet one word. Less. It is less. The same but less.'[54] Beckett's minimalism veers towards silence, the '[s]ilence at the eye of the scream'.[55] The disappearance of the voice which marks the incomprehensible moment of our own organic finitude, is countered in 'Texts for Nothing' by the persistence of the voice, a vocality as an affirmation of existence: for 'once there is speech, no need of a story, a story is not compulsory, just a life'.[56] Here it is possible to recall once more Agamben's conception of *voice* as that which calls us towards 'thinking language as such',[57] beyond the 'scission of voice and word'.[58] In this space, where the voice falls silent, existence as it is presented in language confronts death. Only by dwelling in pure language,[59] beyond any reference to time or persistence, is it possible to move past the radical trauma of being thrown into being,[60] escaping the condemnation of existence to a passive persistence stripped of activity and its valences with the infinite.

In this light, to *go on* – a phrase central to Beckett's existentialist aesthetic[61] – might be understood in terms of an ateleological persistence. In 'Footfalls' this persistence is experienced in atopian terms, 'neither here nor there where all the footsteps ever fell can never fare nearer to anywhere nor from anywhere further away'.[62] Existence in this light is simply *more of the same*, one foot after the other, over and over, indefinitely, as in 'Heard in the Dark I', where the narrator realizes that 'many more [footsteps] will be necessary. Many many more.'[63] Indeed, the compulsion to walk on, to pace backwards and forwards in various predetermined patterns, shapes the dramatic action of several of Beckett's most memorable works, reflecting repetition and cyclical movement as material markers of existence itself: 'motion alone is not enough, [one] must hear the feet however faint they fall'.[64] No matter how austere, minimalism finally remains anchored to minimum, and minimum to the material remainder at the heart of existence – the indelible trace of the real that makes it impossible never to 'have done … revolving it all',[65] in Beckett's terms.

7.2 Taking-Place

Something in nothing: Richard Serra's *Gutter Corner Splash: Night Shift* (1969/1995) Samuel Beckett's *Texts for Nothing* (1950–2)

In *The Coming Community* Giorgio Agamben offers an intriguing account of how the teaching of thirteenth-century theologian, Amalric of Bena, reclaims transcendence, and arguably the infinite itself, from within the immanent taking-place of existence, despite the almost overwhelming pull of existence towards limitation, finitude or even annihilation. According to this doctrine, subsequently declared heretical, it is in the most intimate moment of the present that we encounter infinite perfection: '[t]he transcendent ... is not a supreme entity above all things; rather, the *pure transcendent is the taking-place of every thing*'.[66] Accordingly, what is good 'is the taking-place of the entities, their innermost exteriority', while what is evil is 'the reduction of the taking-place of things to a fact like others'.[67] What is radically positive is that which habitually is taken for granted: the almost miraculous singularity of the fact of existence itself; *that* entities exist. Meillassoux, to recall, recognizes a similar existential positivity in his understanding of facticity, albeit from a realist perspective, as opposed to the pantheistic transcendentalism Agamben recognizes in Amalric's thought. The most intrinsic part of an entity is its *persistence* – its taking-place as a contingent quantity across a period of time, within and as the real. It is the facticity of persistence that renders existence always positively charged – potential, yet immanent.

What Agamben formulates in terms of a transcendental immanence – that which is 'not somewhere else [but rather] the point at which [entities] grasp the taking-place proper to them, at which they touch their own non-transcendent matter'[68] – constitutes a curious type of minimalism. What exists returns to itself: immanent, prior to any external relation; it is *just as it is*. By taking-place in this sense, entities come to count as singularities, the exemplars of a distinct realism that finds expression in an aesthetic minimalism which exemplifies what is immanent, prior to any relation yet open to future relations. Such a minimalism seeks to envision a type of *tabula rasa* on which nonrelational and independent works are able to exist just as they are. According to this view, the real persists in every entity through the radical quantity that defines its singularity as an entity. The particular qualities of the entity emerge from this radical ground, and are subsequently incorporated into elaborate, meaningful sequences and relations in order to constitute a particular reality.

Reparsing the negative instantiation of minimalism in terms of the taking-place of quantity, which is radically affirmative, also clarifies the problematic aesthetic region in which the difference between conceptual and concrete negation is easily overlooked. Minimalism frequently traces the extreme boundaries of this distinction, examining the often uncomfortable proximity of pure quantity and pure negation. It summons the viewer, listener or reader to a new vigilance: to an awareness of the existential simplicity of taking-place and its relation to the existential complexity of the act; to an awareness of persistence as a positivity at the heart of the real and the ways in which concrete works can elevate or negate this persistence.

Numerous of minimalism's most prominent works occupy a threshold between absolute negation and generation. Richard Serra's *Gutter Corner Splash: Night Shift,*[69] for example, makes use of molten lead, 'synonymous with weight',[70] hurling it at the intersection of a wall and a floor. Once the molten lead has solidified, it is lifted from the intersection, rotated and displayed, before the process is repeated. Six separate units, each weighing approximately a ton, are placed in front of the intersection, itself still marked by the final splashing. Reimagining the sculptural medium in 'chemically elemental'[71] terms, Serra's work stages the meeting of the expressionistic gesture of the artist, the concrete environment, matter at its most brutal, and natural forces such as gravity, Newton's third law (action-reaction), and the rate and manner of the solidification of liquid metals.[72] At this intersection, creation and destruction flow into one another. Molten lead is dangerous – toxic, heavy, and capable of inflicting serious burns – and even in its solid state the sculpture is shadowed by the vulnerability of the human body that encounters it.

The action of the artist unquestionably requires a particular degree of strength and physical force – much as in the acid action painting of Gustav Metzger – and critics have recognized in Serra's work something 'inherently more kinetic and menacing'[73] than earlier minimalism. Chave famously contends that 'it is more often the case with Serra … that his work doesn't simply exemplify aggression or domination, but acts it out'.[74] A similarly ambiguous position with respect to negation and generation is apparent in numerous works of concrete poetry: parts of Hanjörg Mayer's 'fortführungen'[75] present lines so densely overlaid that all sense is destroyed except the bare facticity that it is some form of typescript; an untitled poem by Heinz Gappmayr goes further still, almost entirely blocking out the poem's text by superimposing a large, black block over his writing, with only the minutest traces of script still visible around its edges.[76]

In Samuel Beckett's work, the difficult meeting of generative negation and destructive negation discovers a different intensity. His aesthetic conception moves beyond Hegelian sublation, towards the transcendental change central to Schopenhauer's conception of negativity, in which, as Weller notes, 'the very distinction between subject and object is overcome'[77] through a real abolition which exposes 'nothing other than nothing'[78] which can be overcome only by a type of ecstatic or rapturous quasi-transcendence.[79] Importantly, such quasi-transcendence does not actually leave the field of existence in relation to which it gestures its transcendence. Much as in the case of Agamben's conception of taking-place, transcendence is immanent to existence. Beckett remains particularly concerned with the most minimal intensities of existence: the moment of death, and those situations in which death seems imminent but in which we persist nonetheless.

These are moments of extraordinary self-reflexivity, although it would be an error to regard Beckett's work as conventionally metafictional. He is not generally writing about writing, although much might be implicit in this regard. Rather, Beckett writes about thought – recalling that thought provides both a point of access and a final barrier to the stuff of existence – and specifically about thinking about thought. More accurately still, Beckett, at his most acute, writes about thinking about the intense struggle between thought and the absence of thought as analogues for being and non-being. Language and its mediation through voice and writing might be our most obvious points of access to this opposition, but they are not necessarily our most immediate. This at least partly accounts for the significance of physical movement, theatrical staging and the mediation of the body and voice by sound recording, radio, television and film in Beckett's *oeuvre*.

As Meillassoux astutely notes, the phenomenological assertion that it is impossible to gain knowledge of the intrinsic nature of being, is predicated on the assumption that being is inextricable from thought:[80] the dogma that '[w]e cannot represent the "in itself" without it becoming "for us"'.[81] In many instances, Beckett's work reflects a radicalization of the relation of being and thought, yet it is only very occasionally that it loosens its phenomenological mooring in thought and perception to offer a poetic aperture to being in its generic state, or what Beckett gestures towards in terms of death or dying. Far from a straightforward deceasing, this understanding approximate what Agamben terms *whatever being* – 'what is most difficult to think: the absolutely non-thing experience of a pure exteriority'.[82] Although writing is itself subject to the weakness and transience of its own inscription of being, and so cannot ordinarily effect the fantasies of exteriority that it reports, in Beckett's case it traces the limitations of its powers with such patience and persistence that it becomes a strange source of consolation.

What this writing witnesses is the struggle of consciousness to render pure exteriority an object of knowledge by recognizing the minimal point at which the work expresses itself as a vanishing trace of its own existence. Yet the very taking-place of language – voice and writing – connects the persistence of the body to the material world, and tentatively conditions the possibility of a recuperative aesthetic gesture. In this light, Beckett's work addresses a transitional point between interiority and exteriority. Recalling Badiou's terms, it *subtracts* itself from between minimum and nothingness to reveal the point where disappearance and emergence can no longer be easily differentiated. In this light, Beckett's pursuit of the conditions of pure absence in works like 'Texts for Nothing' – '[i]s it possible, is that the possible thing at last, the extinction of this black nothing and its impossible shades, the end of the farce of making and the silencing of silence?'[83] – proves as futile as every other pursuit; just another instance of 'the screaming silence of no's knife in yes's wound'.[84] As always with Beckett, it is the existential facticity of the work itself – 'murmuring a trace'[85] – that disrupts the passage from existence to non-existence, and returns to the positivity of taking-place.

7.3 Nothingness

Approaching zero: Maurice Blanchot's *Death Sentence* (1948)

Nihilism arises from 'a failure to accept the world as it is',[86] according to Bülent Diken; a resentment of the 'fact that the world is devoid of a goal, unity or meaning',[87] making it necessary to discover ways 'to endure the meaninglessness, the chaos of the world'.[88] So entwined is nihilism with the emergence of philosophical reason, that its roots can be traced from Socrates through to the Stoics, and from the Stoics along the *via negativa* of apophatic theology to Scholasticism.[89] It was the German philosopher Friedrich Heinrich Jacobi who first employed the term *nihilism* to oppose what he regarded as a dangerous solipsism at the heart of the transcendental idealism of his contemporaries, among them Kant and Fichte, that would logically terminate in nihilism.[90] It was only in the mid-1800s that nihilism crossed from metaphysics to the field of political praxis, where it has an ambiguous heritage in Russia, reflected in the work of, among others, Cerhnyshevsky, Lermontov and Turgenev.[91] Transecting the transcendental and the immanent, the theological and the socio-political, this shifting understanding of nihilism discovers a new existential intensity in the work of Nietzsche, arguably the most penetrating thinker on the relationship of nothingness, thought and being, who claims that nihilism constitutes

> *[t]he new fundamental condition: our conclusive transitoriness* … Formerly one sought the feeling of the grandeur of man by pointing to his divine *origin*: this has now become a forbidden way … One therefore now tries the opposite direction: the way mankind is *going* shall serve as proof of its grandeur and kinship with God. Alas, this, too, is vain![92]

Insisting that religion is the cause of rather than the antidote for nihilism, Nietzsche holds that what were formerly considered the highest human values have been rendered inoperative by a pervasive 'will to untruth'.[93] Far from succumbing to a melancholic inertia, it becomes necessary to pursue the horizon of thought which seems 'again free, even if it is not bright'.[94] In this light it is significant to stress, with Vattimo, that '[n]ihilism is still developing',[95] and so cannot be regarded as an accomplished task, either in historical or in metaphysical terms. The ongoing redefinition of the relation of the subject to a world emptied of transcendental certainty, demands 'new categories and new values that will permit us to endure the world of becoming'.[96] The ongoing task of defining nihilism is thus intimately bound to the transformation rather than the destruction of value: a *trans-valuation*. According to Vattimo, '[n]ihilism does not mean that Being is in the power of the subject [but rather] that Being is completely dissolved in the discoursing of value, in the indefinite transformations of universal equivalence'.[97]

Approaching *nihil* or nothing in this light requires what Critchley recognizes as a patient delineation that 'keep[s] open the slightest difference between things as they are and things as they might otherwise be'.[98] In this sense, nothingness points to a space of potentiality rather than merely of negation. For Heidegger, nothingness is only conceivable through the overcoming of metaphysics, excepted from the ontotheological framing of being which brings both everything and nothing under the coordination of a transcendental unity.[99] According to Heidegger, almost all accounts of nothingness fail: the dialectic conception fails by pressing nothingness into the shadow of becoming;[100] science fails by rejecting nothingness simply because it cannot be observed and described by traditional methods;[101] logic fails because it restricts nothingness to a formal concept at the end of a process of negation.[102]

Heidegger's nothingness is more radical: 'the nothing is the nothing',[103] he contends, 'and if the nothing represents total indistinguishability no distinction can obtain between the imagined and the "proper" nothing'.[104] Yet nothingness cannot be the end of a process of negation, nor an accessible foundation. It is pervasive – recalling also Badiou's conception of the void – yet evasive, unlocated: 'nothing is more original than the "not" and negation'.[105] For Heidegger nothingness is intuited as a sort of radical pre-cognitive mood or *Grundstimmung* characterized by an 'indeterminate unease or dread'[106] which he terms *Angst*.[107] Heidegger believed he had uncovered a reliable point of contact between nothingness and the finitude of existence which brought definition to both: '[o]nly in the nothing of Dasein do beings as a whole, in accord with their most proper possibility – that is, in a finite way – come to themselves.'[108] As Sartre develops this position, 'only *Being* can nihilate itself':[109] nothingness is at the very heart of the process of identification in the form of this nihilation.[110] In aesthetic terms, the poet 'holds firm in the Nothingness',[111] so that *poiesis* itself becomes thinkable in terms of a 'nothing … growing as something',[112] in Jean-Luc Nancy's estimation. Indeed, since '[n]othingness can be conceived neither outside of Being, nor in terms of Being',[113] the aesthetic sphere takes on a special significance. What becomes evident is a paradoxical generativity at the heart of nothingness: 'the nothing itself nihilates'.[114]

Levinas's formulation of the *il y a* presses further still. An 'impersonal, anonymous, yet inextinguishable "consummation" of being, which murmurs in the depth of nothingness',[115] the *il y a*, or *there is*, is central to Levinas's philosophical conception, conditioning not only his early work but also his later thought on ethics as first philosophy.[116] The *il y a* recognizes being in general as a presence so relentless it cannot even be conceived in a dialectic relationship to absence. The *il y a* is the 'ambience of being',[117] the indefinite 'field of forces [that underpins] every affirmation and negation'.[118] The *il y a* is, paradoxically, filled with absence – 'the absence of any being'[119] which is experienced as a 'loss of world'[120] – and hence evades representation.[121] It is pre-conceptual, pre-reflective and pre-cognitive and hence defies equivalence.[122] The *il y a* can only be approximated in the oblique terms of an existential mood: a pervasive atmosphere of horror[123] which Levinas believes follows the threat of absolute existential anonymity;[124] the faint rumble falling towards the impossibility of complete silence;[125] the insomnia of an endless night in which exhausted vigilance is perpetual;[126] an experience of the immense weight of being and a dying within which there is no death.[127]

That existence is not simply consumed by the pure presence of the *il y a* – the 'nothingness of everything',[128] or the 'presence of absence [which] embraces and dominates its contradictory'[129] – can be traced to the capacity of the subject to adopt a position within and in relation to being. Much as Heidegger's poet 'holds firm in the Nothingness',[130] so Levinas's subject is affirmed '[t]hrough taking position in the anonymous *there is*'.[131] Levinas refers to this as *hypostasis*: an *instant*, an event of beginning,[132] through which a minimal subjectivity emerges by suspending the indeterminateness of the *il y a*, where 'anything can count for anything else',[133] in order to expose 'the indissoluble unity between the existent and its work of existing'.[134] As the proper ingression of an existent into existence, hypostasis marks 'the apparition of a substantive',[135] and since hypostasis is also a 'localization of consciousness',[136] this process is predominantly associated with a process of human 'subjectivization'.[137] Yet, as Harman notes, '[t]he anonymous work of existence occurs in the sheer labor of things at being what they are, and not in any supposed *access* we might have to this labor, not even a noncognitive sort of access'.[138] In this light, he contends that the *il y a*, 'however devoid it may be of specific features, already stands at an infinite remove from the infernal work of objects'.[139]

Yet, if the balance of existence always favours the plenitude of objects – 'to be in the world is to be attached to things';[140] since 'human life in the world does not go beyond the objects that fulfil it'[141] – it is also true that the instant of hypostasis and the minimal intervention of consciousness remain pivotal to apprehending this 'world [that] is given',[142] even as 'the fact of [its] being given is the world',[143] in a familiar recursion to facticity as ground. Still, as Harman notes, the 'improved status of concrete things'[144] is notable in Levinas's thought, reflecting an understanding of being as 'scattered across the full multitude of entities that inhabit the world',[145] 'defining each as being just what it is'.[146] The *il y a*, the persistent presence underpinning this distribution of being, names what is most real: the taking-place of every entity. The *il y a* cannot begin or desist, it cannot be accepted or declined, sought or evaded; it just *is* – absolute, ceaseless presence. The *il y a* recalls that it is '[n]ot grace but gravity'[147] that marks being, its immanence echoed in the depth, weight, and density of beings in their self-relation. There is no means of exiting being,[148] and the mark of existence – its essential quantity – emerges in its relation to infinity,[149] to the 'eternal futurity of death',[150] so that in existing we are fixed in perpetuity to the 'duration of the interval – the *meanwhile* [which is] never finished, still enduring'.[151]

This 'time of dying'[152] is a temporal expression of the fact that '[n]othingness is impossible',[153] particularly from the perspective of an existent. Consequently, 'death *qua* nothingness'[154] is simply a fantasy of no longer being bound to the immanence of being and its revelation of the bankruptcy of any future event of metaphysical redemption. Death is the most banal of all existential occurrences – this is above all the lesson of the *il y a* – and the *time of dying* becomes a marker for the manner in which an existent reaches for its minimal existential intensity. Critchley encapsulates the situation well in suggesting that 'representations of death are *misrepresentations*'.[155] The laconic prose of Maurice Blanchot – exemplifying a 'carefully constructed dynamic of eschewal and restriction',[156] the austere markers of a certain brand of minimalism which he shares with several prominent *nouveaux romanciers*[157] – offers a powerful vision of the time of dying.[158]

In the novella *Death Sentence,* for instance, Blanchot presents the apparently impossible scene in which a narrator, having witnessed the terminal decline of a friend, J., describes her eventual death and subsequent miraculous resurrection, followed by a second death two days later. The narrative time seems to remain bound within a nightmarish ambiguity, a persistent cycle of decline, death and resurrection.[159] The true terror of this interminability[160] – of this 'infinity of a timeless instant'[161] – is revealed in a growing awareness that J.'s prophetic utterance – 'soon you will see [death]'[162] – is directed not to the characters in the narrative, but to the reader. For where the time of narrative remains subject to a fundamental ambiguity, and hence the possibility of recurrence, the time of reader is irreversible, limited.

Yet precisely in its emphasis on interminability, *Death Sentence* also seeks to transcend human finitude, exposing the 'language of literature [as] a search for th[e] moment which precedes literature',[163] a quest for a 'literature [which] communicates an uncommunicating presence that is not quite self-presence and never quite posits itself but nevertheless stirs and persists'.[164] Writing affirms its materiality as the exact point at which the word supplants the concreteness of the world, annihilating the very thing it purportedly mimes, leaving in it its place a language bound both symbolically and actually to death.[165] Although the referents of language cease to exists, the force of language persists, generating a spectral world, a 'reawakening of the interminable',[166] the irremissible presence of the *il y* a. As Fynsk recognizes, 'the persistence of the word as word … becomes the indication or expression of the *il y a* … The self-reflection or self-offering of language becomes the showing of the *il y a*.'[167]

By a severe self-limitation, this language reflexively affirms its status as thing, and so interrupts its own participation in the economy of mimesis. With each repetition, each recursion, each return, language refers progressively less to an external world, and increasingly to the self-referential field of the work itself. In this way it provides an intensified access to the *il y a*, to the immanence of absence, to what is next to nothing. The force of writing effects 'existence without being, existence which remains below existence, like an inexorable affirmation without beginning or end – death as the impossibility of dying'.[168] This poetic comportment towards a nothingness that finally proves an impossible end prepares the ground for a difficult species of minimalism. It moves across the blank and black canvases of Rauschenberg and Reinhardt, behind the silence and sublimity of Feldman and Pärt, and through the repetitions and recursions of Beckett and Blanchot. The work moves infinitely towards minimum, and in this movement exposes the point at which the least possible and the least necessary are indistinguishable, and where possibility and necessity both consume and produce one another in the irremissible presence through which the approximation of nothingness comes to be understood as the ground of everything.

7.4 Atopia

Minimalism beyond minimum: Alvin Lucier's *I Am Sitting in a Room* (1969) Samuel Beckett's *Imagination Dead Imagine* (1965) Cy Twombly's *Arcadia* (1958) Ian Hamilton Finlay's *The Present Order* (1984)

It is clear in this light that while a great deal of minimalism is comported towards minimum, it is comparatively rare for a work to exist minimally in the most radical sense. At minimum the aesthetic work flickers with a curious intensity. It remains bound to being by the sheer gravity of existence, yet its singular quantity is one that emerges less in terms of immanence, than in terms of evanescence, as it leans away from presence towards absence. The peculiar impossibility that concerns such works is of a minimalism beyond minimum – an absolute disappearance. It is this sense of withdrawal from the aesthetic sphere itself that marks the tentative minimalism of Andy Goldsworthy's delicate ice sculptures, works formed from thin shards connected by dripping water, icons of contingency designed to disappear as the ice melts. Equally compelling is Alvin Lucier's legendary *I Am Sitting in a Room*, a work of sonic art which involves a recorded voice reciting a text being played into an empty room, resulting in a reverberation which is then recorded together with the original recording, looped, recorded again, and repeated until the original content has completely dissipated, and all that remains is atmospheric noise. As LaBelle notes, 'sound sets into relief the properties of a given space, its materiality and characteristics, through reverberation and reflection, and, in turn, these characteristics affect the given sound and how it is heard'.[169] Technologically mediated, reproduced, exposed to certain physical laws and properties of reverberation within limited spaces, what is finally audible is space itself, the minimal material having gradually conformed to the emptiness of the room.

Lucier generates a minimalist atopia, a non-space where the work in a significant sense crosses the threshold of minimum, moving from the contingent order of speech to the disordered multiplicity of noise. This same atopia is pervasive in Beckett's work. It emerges in the closed spaces in which his characters habitually find themselves trapped; a *space of dying*, not only empty but always emptying, in which they narrate their unlikely persistence in a state of interminable decline. It manifests on the stage as well, where the players of Beckett's drama perform ritualized repetitions of their final moments, their search for entropy effecting a gradual erasure of the space of performance, leaving in its places an atopian *space of disappearance*. The interminability of dying and disappearance perhaps exercises such force on the human imagination because it reveals the profound tension between the shocking ease with which death strikes every living entity and the inability of consciousness to master finitude.

The '[s]epulchral skull'[170] – invoked earlier in relation to ascetic practice – is a powerful minimalist vehicle in this regard, at once the tomb of fading consciousness and a monstrance of the incarnate imagination and its resistance to disappearance. The skull is also a cipher for the atopian closed spaces in which a great deal of Beckett's prose from the 1960s and 1970s is located, indeed contained.[171] These 'narrative ideograms'[172] centre on a single paradox captured with some clarity in the title of 'Imagination Dead Imagine':[173] to imagine the extinction of the imagination is itself a feat of the imagination. In fact, the closed space pieces test the capacity of the imagination to 'reconstruct … whole worlds out of minimal fragments'.[174] Written in a prose both emaciated and compressed, 'All Strange Away' and 'Imagination Dead Imagine' are set in enclosures of extremely limited dimensions. The former is '[f]ive foot square, six high, no way in, none out',[175] and 'gradually becom[es] smaller as memory diminishes'[176] in the failing coherence of its narrative. The latter is situated in a minuscule cylinder[177] containing two figures, back to back, immobile, and imperceptibly alive but for the condensation which would appear were a mirror held to their lips,[178] and the terrifying image of 'the left eyes which at incalculable intervals suddenly open wide and gaze in unblinking exposure long beyond what is humanly possible'.[179] If these spaces clearly recall the tomb or coffin, the dome-shaped setting of 'For to end yet again'[180] intentionally evokes the skull, the 'dark place'[181] within which consciousness is encased and from which consciousness attempts to dislocate itself in an attempt to transgress the limit even of minimum. Different intensities of light in each of these closed spaces reflect different stages of this struggle. The blinding white light which pervades 'All Strange Away', 'Imagination Dead Imagine' and 'Ping' is replaced in 'The Lost Ones' by an eerie, lifeless, yellow light as figures wander through an 'entropic abode',[182] each in search of 'its lost one',[183] while there is only a dark void in 'For to end yet again'.

Where external light sources appear dim, brilliant white light seems to have its source in the closed spaces themselves. Taking light as metonym for consciousness, a principal concern of these works is then the manner in which consciousness is at once limited, and yet rendered substantial, by the body. For it is the struggle of an apparently immaterial consciousness with its material substrate that lends force to these works, the embodied imagination testing itself against an infinity which marks a point of egress from existence, the impossible nothing beyond minimum. This ambiguity is clear in the post-apocalyptic futurity of 'Lessness': a '[l]ittle body little block beating ash grey only upright',[184] the persistent vertical presence of a person, 'face to endlessness',[185] in an infinite landscape which is revealed, the container in which this person existed having collapsed. The narrative shifts to the imminent future which, however close, remains potential only: '[h]e will curse God again',[186] '[h]e will go on his back face to the sky', and he will die.[187] 'Figment light never was', Beckett tells us; and illumination here evokes only the pathos of a tragic hope – the desistence of persistence in the face of actual infinity.

The unavoidability of our return to reality, to the nearside of minimum, is the painful price of consciousness in Beckett's estimation. As Kearney notes, imagination 'has ceased to operate as a human agency, of expression, will and creativity and become instead a mechanical pulse of repetition … But this entropic decline of imagination into emptiness [is] caught in the reflexive spiral of imagining.'[188] Existing in an atopia delimited not by the successes but by the profound failure of the imagination is 'less and less a matter of exercising the will and more and more a matter of waiting',[189] as Pilling recognizes. With fading intensity, these bodies persist against all odds in a space of diminishing hospitality, veering towards inexistence but halted at zero by the inexorability of the sheer insistence of consciousness, the proverbial figments of their own imagination. They remain suspended – waiting – in a zone at once lifeless and deathless.

Exemplary of this suspension is the minimal action of 'Rockaby', a short dramatic work in which a '[p]rematurely old'[190] woman in a rocking-chair interacts with a recording of her own voice – an inner-dialogue turned outward – through which she rehearses, perhaps even negotiates, the conditions of her death. The relationship of the embodied voice to its disembodied counterpart is somewhat ambiguous. It is uncertain whether the utterance, '[m]ore'[191] – the word with which the embodied woman punctuates the work, each time setting in motion the mechanical movement of the chair[192] and the description, by her uncanny double, of the eventless solitude of her existence – is offered as supplication or instruction, whether it is intended to provoke pathos or resignation. The occasional convergence of the two voices, repeating together the words 'time she stopped',[193] reaches towards the unknowable atopia beyond minimum yet is merely returned to the most banal[194] quantitative expression of being: 'more'.[195]

As the woman becomes increasingly dependent on her vocalic spectre[196] – the technologically mediated confluence of her imagination and memory – it becomes apparent that her refrain, 'more',[197] paradoxically marks a space of existential *lessness*,[198] fading to the bleak point of the work's final lines: 'fuck life / stop her eyes / rock her off / rock her off [*Together: echo of 'rock her off', coming to rest of rock, slow fade out*]'.[199] The woman dies – at least, this is suggested by the slow inclination of her head at the close of the work[200] – but, unsurprisingly, death is not a simple accomplishment here.[201] For finally, which is the real subject, the embodied consciousness or the disembodied voice, when it is the latter that prescribes the expiration of the former? In this way Beckett points to a situation that exceeds subjectivity, a time of dying which evokes the 'possibility of a future without me, an infinite future, *a future which is not my future*':[202] the atopia, the space which is not a space, of disappearance.

A different type of minimalist disappearance is sought by many not ordinarily described as minimalists. In works such as Cy Twombly'a *Arcadia,* for example, a reticent 'language of indiscernible writing'[203] becomes apparent. On paper stained unevenly with a translucent brown, Twombly has made scratches of various thickness and intensity, mostly in grey and black, that resemble writing yet resist easy recognition. Yet among these is a word vaguely and imperfectly traced that becomes evident with sustained attention, spelling out the word, 'Arcadia' – the name of a lost utopia, of the disappearance of perfection. In this carefully disintegrated calligraphy of letters, handwritten words, 'marks of measurement [and] tiny algorithms',[204] the moment of disappearance is marked by an increased intensity.[205] In the very act of disappearing, the work exposes the complex relationship of the minimalist aesthetic to historical time,[206] a 'tremor of communication'[207] comprised of 'archaic symbols'[208] that reach back to classicism, yet sacrifice none of their relation to the contemporary ruins that mark the present horizon of crisis. '[C]ombining the small and the smallest elements',[209] this is a writing that fills the space of language in an attempt to think its depths – not only transhistorically, but also in relation to a more pervasive nothingness. Yet in contrast to the sheer weight that marks the existentialist progress towards nothing, Twombly gesture towards an 'absolute spaciousness',[210] an echo of the thought of absolute absence.

Reflecting on Twombly's negotiation of matter and nothingness, Barthes offers a compelling metaphysical proposition: 'the essence of things is not in their weight but in their lightness'.[211] It is this sense of lightness that opens onto another minimalism still in its infancy: an atopian minimalism disconnected from the material conditions of objecthood, yet still marked by immanence; a minimalism in which disappearance on one level marks reappearance on another. This would be a minimalism responsive to the technogenesis of contemporary cultural sequences, that makes increasingly possible a digital minimalism that not only generates the archives and routes of access to encounter a transhistorical range of minimalist objects, but also opens the path to new conceptions of minimalist objecthood itself. Here it is useful to recall another arcadia – the concrete poem by Ian Hamilton Finlay, 'Arcady', which consists in its entirety of the alphabet in sequence. It instantiates an alternate vision of minimalist atopia: one in which the disappearance of the work is matched by the work yet to appear.

In a significant sense this atopian propensity of minimalism has always been anticipated, even in its most concrete works. In the far corner of Finlay's *Little Sparta* – the famous poetry garden associated with an arcadia of a different kind – lies one of the concrete poet's most iconic works. Backed by woodland and facing the ever-shifting landscape of the Pentland hills, this poem consists of eleven large granite slabs, each containing a single word and arranged in four lines that read: 'THE PRESENT ORDER/ IS THE DISORDER/ OF THE FUTURE/ SAINT-JUST'. [212] Finlay uses this celebrated maxim of the French

Revolutionary leader Louis Antoine de Saint-Just to indicate that beneath the semblance of natural, political and aesthetic order lies a world shaped by profoundly unpredictable forces, subject to aleatory shifts, and fundamentally turbulent and chaotic.[213] Within a fragile ecology, the aesthetic work offers itself as 'model of order',[214] albeit an impermanent one. And yet the work persists. Suspended contingently between appearance and disappearance, minimalism persists.

Illustrations

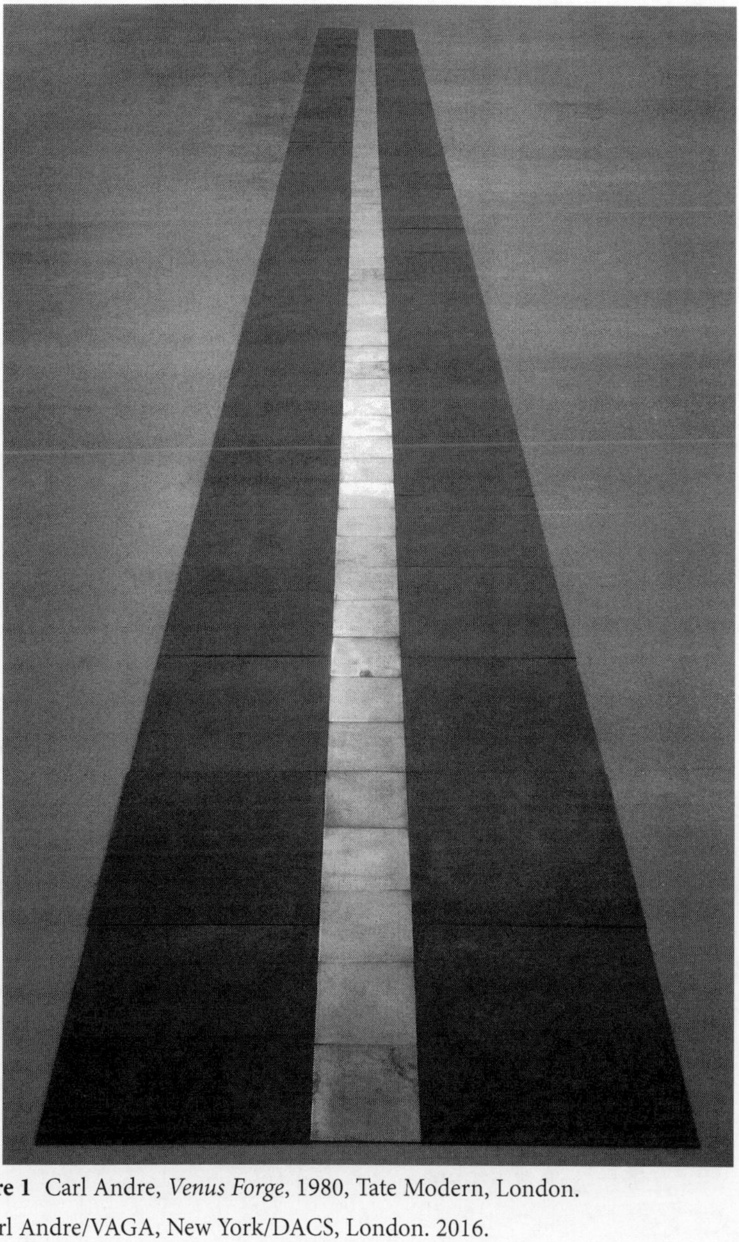

Figure 1 Carl Andre, *Venus Forge*, 1980, Tate Modern, London.

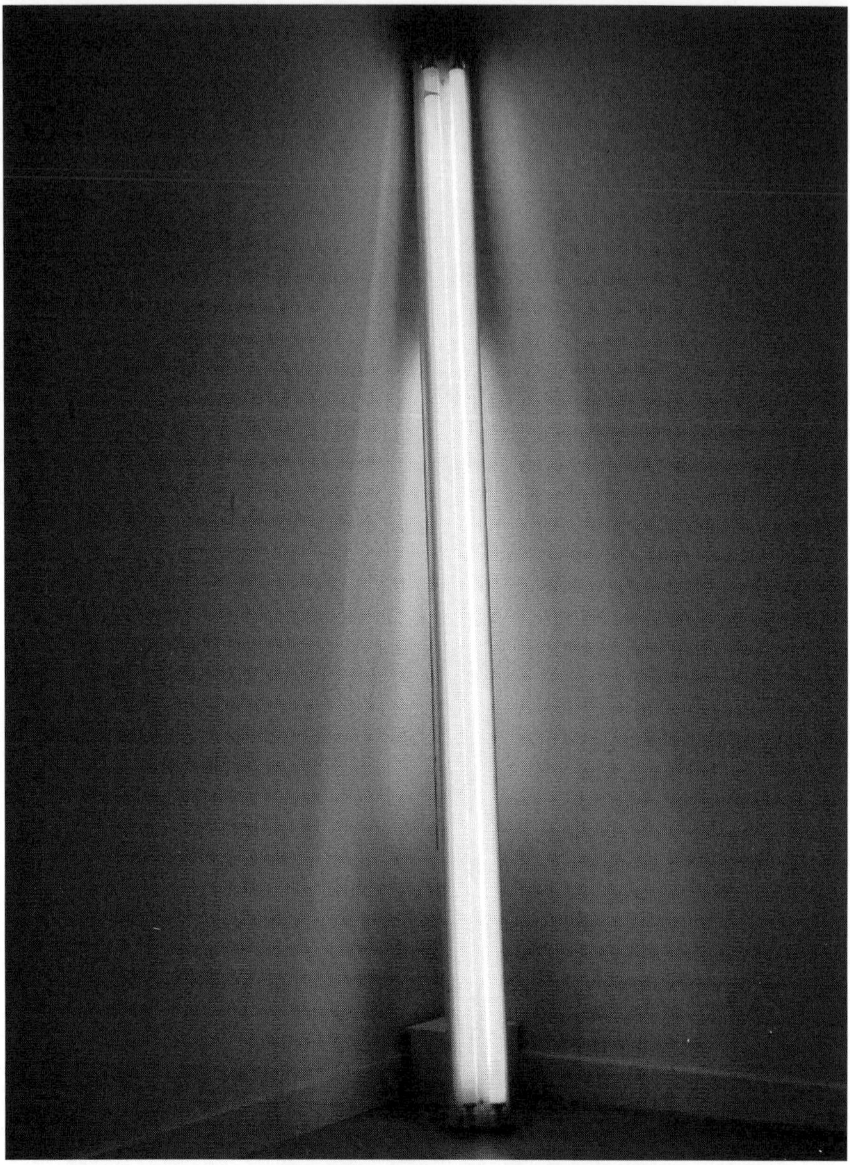

Figure 2 Dan Flavin, *untitled (to the real Dan Hill) 1b*, Collection M HKA Antwerp, 1978.

Notes

Chapter 1: Intermittency: On the Transhistoricism of Minimalism

1 The distinction of existence from being, the former drawn from the ground constituted by the latter, is made in the work of Badiou, who differentiates between being qua existence as distinct from being qua being (*Second Manifesto*, 43–4); Heidegger, who differentiates the ontic from the ontological (*Being and Time*, 31–5); and Levinas, who differentiates existents from existence (*Time and the Other*, 44), and is central to the argument developed in this book.

2 An example of *litotes* – the figure of speech in which emphasis is derived from understatement – the phrase *less is more*, often attributed to Mies van der Rohe, is an aesthetic dictum adopted to describe the principle of minimalist design exemplified in the work of Bauhaus architects such as Walter Gropius, László Moholy-Nagy and Mies van der Rohe himself, as well as *De Stijl* works of Theo van Doesburg, Piet Mondrian and Gerrit Rietveld among others (Cheviakoff, 'Minimal Art', 74–5). Its actual origin remains a source of contention, however. John Barth claims it is a remark 'first made in fact … by Robert Browning', although he nonetheless regards it as 'a memorable specimen of the minimalist esthetic' (Barth, 'A Few Words', 64).

3 Spade, 'William of Ockham'. http://plato.stanford.edu/entries/ockham/ (accessed 24 June 2017). Leff offers a concise explanation of the 'radical simplicity' (*Medieval Thought*, 288) at the heart of Ockham's work in relation to its broader philosophical implications (ibid., 281–91).

4 See Foster, *Return of the Real*, 62–8. Chave offers an important account of the significance of patronage to the flourishing of minimalism in the late twentieth century ('Revaluing Minimalism', 466–70, 478–9).

5 Foster, *Return of the Real*, 60.

6 Rose, 'ABC Art', 274–81, 296–7.

7 Perreault, 'Minimal Abstracts', 258–60.

8 Greenberg, 'Recentness of Sculpture', 182–3.

9 Fried, 'Art and Objecthood', 123–6.

10 Kennedy, 'Pierre, Prince of Darkness', 30.

11 Bellamy, 'Downpour', 31–9.

12 Danto, *Transfiguration*, 50–1; 'Learning to Live', 225; 'Art World Revisited', 41–51.

13 Krauss, *Passages in Modern Sculpture*, 198–9.
14 Mertens, *American Minimal Music*, 113–24.
15 Foster, *Return of the Real*, 10. Italics in original.
16 As is demonstrated subsequently, this contention regarding a minimal ground finds numerous philosophical correlates, from Democritus to Heidegger, but most notably in Badiou's conception of the void and its expression in the idea of a minimal existential state, the inexistent or the 'the minimal degree … [of existing] in the world but with an intensity equal to zero' (*Second Manifesto*, 58).
17 See Gibson, *Intermittency*, 44.
18 See Botha, 'Microfiction', 201–2; Oates, Afterwords, 246; Stevick, Afterwords, 242.
19 Among the many sources specializing in visual poetry of different eras, the two most notable for spanning the entire history of visual poetry across a range of cultural contexts are Berjouhi Bowler's *The Word as Image* and Dick Higgins's *Pattern Poetry*.
20 See Botha, 'Poetics of Remoteness', 25, 30, 35–40.
21 Yarmolinsky draws attention to the significant, and to many surprising, similarities between Baroque and minimalist music ('Minimalism and the Baroque', 72).
22 Foster, *Return of the Real*, 29.
23 Ibid.
24 Fried, 'Art and Objecthood', 125–8. In *Passages in Modern Sculpture in Modern Sculpture*, Krauss offers a detailed genealogy of the inextricability of theatre and sculpture that concludes with a brief but striking riposte to Fried's claims in this regard (242).
25 See Grumman, 'MNMLST POETRY', https://www.thing.net/~grist/l&d/grumman/egrumn.htm (accessed 24 June 2017), and Perloff, 'Minimalism', 886–7.
26 See Potts, 'Dan Flavin', 6–10.
27 See Chave, 'Revaluing Minimalism', 472–3, 476; Foster, 'Dan Flavin', 139–42.
28 Govan, 'Irony and Light', 42.
29 Dan Flavin, *monument 1 for V. Tatlin*, 1964. Museum of Modern Art. http://www.moma.org/collection/object.php?object_id=81337 (accessed 24 June 2017).
30 Govan, 'Irony and Light', 44.
31 See Foster, 'Dan Flavin', 137; Fer, 'Nocturama', 37; Govan, 'Irony and Light', 45.
32 Stewart, *On Longing*, 41.
33 Hooke, *Micrographia*, http://www.gutenberg.org/files/15491/15491-h/15491-h.htm (accessed 24 June 2017).
34 Stewart, 'At the Threshold', 76; Foer, 'Minor History', http://cabinetmagazine.org/issues/25/foer.php (accessed 24 June 2017).
35 Stewart, *On Longing*, 38.
36 See Bowler, *The Word as Image*, 7–9.

37 Stewart, 'At the Threshold', 77.
38 Foer, 'Minor History'.
39 Stewart, *On Longing*, 39.
40 Ibid., 37–9, 41–3.
41 Stewart, 'At the Threshold', 75.
42 Rugoff, 'Homeopathic Strategies', 17.
43 Powers, 'James Lee Byars', 109.
44 Lyotard, 'Presenting the Unpresentable', 64.
45 Powers, 'James Lee Byars', 109.
46 Ibid., 108.
47 Rugoff, 'Homeopathic Strategies', 43.
48 McGurl, *Program Era*, 376. See also Hall, Afterwords, 234.
49 A different critical assessment of minimalism and ideology is offered by Fried, who suggests that the theatricality of minimalism confronts its audience in a way that elevates the work's ideological substrate above its aesthetic properties ('Art and Objecthood', 116–17).
50 Batchelor, *Minimalism*, 6–7.
51 Strickland, *Minimalism: Origins*, 23; Hallett, *Minimalism and the Short Story*, 8–9.
52 Agamben, 'Movement', http://www.generation-online.org/p/fpagamben3.htm (accessed 24 June 2017).
53 Ibid.
54 Ibid.
55 Agamben, 'Movement'. As in much of his work, Agamben draws here on Aristotle's *Metaphysics*.
56 Hallward, Introduction, 9.
57 Danto, 'Style and Narrative', 247.
58 This formulation is adapted from the thought of Badiou.
59 Strickland, *Minimalism: Origins*, 9–10, 121–2; Fink, *Repeating Ourselves*, 117; Schwartz, *Minimalists*, 23.
60 Ibid., 29.
61 Strickland, *Minimalism: Origins*, 124.
62 Potter, *Four Musical Minimalists*, 35.
63 Strickland, *Minimalism: Origins*, 119. The pitches which make up this arch are distributed between violin, viola and cello, and expose a range of consonant and dissonant pitch relationships, all drawn from what Young terms the dream chord, composed of the pitches G, C, C# and D presented in various combinations, transpositions and inversions (Potter, *Four Musical Minimalists*, 37).
64 Mertens, *American Minimal Music*, 21.
65 Potter, *Four Musical Minimalists*, 34.
66 Ibid., 39. The term diatonic refers to seven-note scales and the harmonic tensions

and releases which constitute the basic material of most music, whereas seriality refers to a specific sequence assigned to the twelve pitches of the chromatic scale as an alternate way of structuring music and adopted by many composers in the mid-twentieth century.

67 Mertens, *American Minimal Music*, 17, 21.

68 Strickland, *Minimalism: Origins*, 129.

69 Ibid., 123.

70 This is the subtitle of Derrida's extended meditation on the relation of language, identity, ethnicity and ethics, *Monolingualism of the Other; or, The Prosthesis of Origin*.

71 Derrida, 'Before the Law', 199.

72 Meyer, *Minimalism: Art and Polemics*, 3.

73 Ibid., 4.

74 Ibid., 3.

75 Donald Judd, *Untitled (Stack)*, 1967. Museum of Modern Art, New York. http://www.moma.org/collection/works/81324 (accessed 24 June 2017).

76 Caputo, *Weakness of God*, 2.

77 Ibid.

78 LaPorte, 'Rigid Designator'. http://plato.stanford.edu/entries/rigid-designators/ (accessed 24 June 2017).

79 Derrida, *On the Name*, 12–13.

80 Agamben, *Idea of Prose*, 105–6; Agamben, *Coming Community*, 73–7; Agamben, *Remnants of Auschwitz*, 128–32.

81 Colpitt, *Minimal Art*, 5; Strickland, *Minimalism: Origins*, 17.

82 Ibid.; Mertens, *American Minimal Music*, 11.

83 Herzinger, 'Introduction', 8.

84 Fink, *Repeating Ourselves*, 19–21.

85 Strickland, *Minimalism: Origins*, 18–19

86 Baker, *Minimalism*, 17.

87 Wollheim, 'Minimal Art', 388.

88 Although Rose's epochal essay is entitled 'ABC Art', she makes use of the proper name, Minimal Art, in the essay.

89 McDermott similarly stresses precisely the distinction of upper-case *M*inimalism from lower-case *m*inimalism, albeit in somewhat different terms (*Austere Style*, 1–4).

90 Baker, *Minimalism*, 9.

91 Colpitt, *Minimal Art*, 1.

92 Potter, *Four Musical Minimalists*, 1.

93 Redfield, *Phantom Formations*, x.

94 Meyer, *Minimalism: Art and Polemics*, 6.

95 Rancière, 'Sentence, Image, History', 40–1.

96 '[O]nly with minimalism does this understanding become self-conscious. That is, only in the early 1960s is the institutionality not only of art but also of the avant-garde first appreciated and then exploited' (Foster, *Return of the Real*, 56).

97 Kant, *Critique of Judgment*, 98, 105–6; Lyotard, *Lessons*, 75–6; 112–14. See also Lyotard, 'Sublime and the Avant-Garde', 98; Crowther, *Kantian Sublime*, 80–3; Bennington, *Lyotard*, 165–9.

98 Lyotard, 'Answering the Question', 78.

99 Ibid., 81.

100 See Fried, 'Art and Objecthood', 146.

101 See Foster, *Return of the Real*, 50–2; Michaels, *Shape of the Signifier*, 88–9.

102 The 'minimalist work complicates the purity of conception with contingency of perception, of the body in a particular space and time' (ibid., 40).

103 Simon Critchley's recognition in the Beckettian aesthetic of a means of 'establishing the *meaning of meaninglessness*, making meaning out of the refusal of meaning that the work performs without that refusal of meaning becoming a meaning' is applicable to much of minimalism (Critchley, *Very Little*, 151). On minimalism's evasion of meaning see Foster, *Return of the Real*, 40. Fink presents the alternative of a minimalism with 'at least the theoretical possibility of unmeaning' (Fink, *Repeating Ourselves*, xiii).

104 Perloff, 'Writing as Re-writing', http://www.lehman.cuny.edu/ciberletras/v17/perloff.htm (accessed 24 June 2017).

105 Ibid.

106 Foster, *Return of the Real*, 54. See Batchelor, *Minimalism*, 8.

107 Foster, *Return of the Real*, 35. See also ibid., 53–4.

108 Krauss, *Passages in Modern Sculpture*, 279.

109 Krauss refers primarily to minimalist, abstract sculpture which retains an anthropocentric element as long as its effect is measured in relation to the human body and movement (ibid.).

110 Ibid.

111 Foster, *Return of the Real*, 42.

112 Stella in Glaser, 'Questions', 158.

113 Berdini, 'Similar Emotions', 43.

114 Lyotard, 'Representation, Presentation, Unpresentable', 128.

115 Chave, 'Minimalism and the Rhetoric of Power', 45.

Chapter 2: Encounters: On the Politics of Minimalism

1 Carl Andre, *Venus Forge*, 1980. Tate Modern, London. http://www.tate.org.uk/art/artworks/andre-venus-forge-t07149 (accessed 24 June 2017).
2 Colpitt, *Minimal Art*, 84.
3 Ibid., 39.
4 Andre, *Cuts*, 144.
5 Fried, 'Art and Objecthood', 140.
6 Andre, *Cuts*, 289.
7 Krauss, *Passages in Modern Sculpture*, 199.
8 Merleau-Ponty, *Phenomenology of Perception*, 174.
9 Ibid., 171.
10 Ibid., 175.
11 Danto, *Transfiguration*, 4.
12 Ibid., 6.
13 This is only one of many possible trajectories following the Dadaist explosion of the distinction between art and non-art. Another possible line might be drawn from the work of Tzara through to the Lettrism of Isou and the Oulipo group, for example.
14 Greenberg, 'Recentness of Sculpture', 182–3.
15 Fried, 'Art and Objecthood', 141–2.
16 Schonberg, 'Critic's Notebook', unpaginated; Bigeunet, 'Notes', 40–5.
17 Finlay, *Model of Order*, 16.
18 Andre, *Cuts*, 144.
19 Reich, 'Music as a Gradual Process', 34.
20 Agamben, *Coming Community*, 68.
21 Gadamer, *Truth and Method*, 305, 578.
22 Ibid., 370.
23 Ibid., 87.
24 For reasons of clarity, Althusser's italicization has been removed from quotations.
25 Althusser, *Philosophy of the Encounter*, 192.
26 Ibid., 169–70.
27 Ibid., 188.
28 Ibid., 167.
29 Ibid., 168.
30 Ibid., 200.
31 Ibid., 167.
32 Ibid., 175.
33 Ibid., 168–9.
34 Ibid., 169.

35 Ibid., 193.
36 Ibid.
37 Ibid., 170. There are notable similarities between Althusser's aleatory materialism in its emphasis on a transcendental contingency and Meillassoux's speculative materialism and its emphasis on contingency as sole necessity, which remain largely unremarked.
38 Ibid.
39 Ibid., 192.
40 Ibid., 187. Althusser paraphrases this point as 'the attempt to think not only the contingency of necessity, but also the necessity of contingency at its root' (ibid.).
41 Ibid., 174.
42 Duckworth and Fleming, Introduction, 18.
43 Young and Zazeela, 'Continuous Sound and Light', 218.
44 Ibid.
45 Duckworth and Fleming, Introduction, 17–18. See also Potter, *Four Musical Minimalists*, 52, 77–8.
46 Althusser, *Philosophy of the Encounter*, 174–5.
47 Potter, *Four Musical Minimalists*, 77.
48 Althusser, *Philosophy of the Encounter*, 170.
49 Potter, *Four Musical Minimalists*, 77.
50 Young and Zazeela, 'Continuous Sound and Light', 220.
51 Neill, 'Pure Resonance', 191.
52 Potter, *Four Musical Minimalists*, 69.
53 Ibid., 77.
54 Althusser, *Philosophy of the Encounter*, 169.
55 Potter, *Four Musical Minimalists*, 78.
56 Ibid., 77.
57 Merleau-Ponty, *Phenomenology of Perception*, 239.
58 Ibid., 239.
59 Gilmore, 'Between Philosophy and Art', 297.
60 Ibid., 299–302.
61 Ibid., 311.
62 Robbe-Grillet, 'In the Corridors of the Underground', 27–30.
63 Merleau-Ponty, *Phenomenology of Perception*, 117.
64 Guenther's *Solitary Confinement* offers a sustained examination of the phenomenology of confinement and its effects; see especially 77–81.
65 Merleau-Ponty, *Phenomenology of Perception*, 78–80.
66 Lyotard, 'Newman: The Instant', 84–6.
67 Ellsworth Kelly, *Spectrum IV*, 1967. Museum of Modern Art, New York. http://www.moma.org/collection/object.php?object_id=79739 (accessed 24 June 2017).

68 Robert Morris, *untitled (3 Ls)*, 1965/1970. Whitney Museum of American Art, New York. http://collection.whitney.org/object/1774 (accessed 24 June 2017).

69 Morris, 'Notes on Sculpture', 234.

70 Merleau-Ponty, *Phenomenology of Perception*, 79.

71 Morris, 'Notes on Sculpture', 234.

72 See Gilmore, 'Between Philosophy and Art', 312; Foster, *Return of the Real*, 43–4; Meyer, *Minimalism: Art and Polemics*, 160–3.

73 Merleau-Ponty, *Phenomenology of Perception*, 81.

74 Ibid., 82.

75 Ibid.

76 Ibid.

77 Since the present concern is principally with the radical, and often schematic, ways in which Merleau-Ponty's phenomenology is taken up by minimalists, the focus falls on these elements of his early work rather than on the many nuanced ways in which it is subsequently developed by the philosopher himself, as well as numerous exegetes and critics.

78 Harman, *Guerilla Metaphysics*, 50.

79 See Merleau-Ponty, *Phenomenology of Perception*, 73–4, 95. In this regard, it is necessary to distinguish between two principal paradigms of transcendentalism at work in modern philosophy. The first, tracing itself from classical philosophy and Judeo-Christian theology, finds its principal expression in the Kantian conception of the *a priori* as the necessity which precedes and grounds particular situations. The second, which is of considerable significance to the present argument, takes a more speculative form: the transcendental is in fact the mark of immanence, a pure presence which always exceeds itself in its orientation towards the future. Where the first paradigm grounds teleology – and hence also historical situations and causal relationships – the second is in an important sense ateleological, a situation of flux and becoming.

80 Ibid., 169.

81 Ibid., 256.

82 Ibid.

83 This formulation is diametrically opposed to the one advanced by Meillassoux, discussed elsewhere in detail, and which stipulates that contingency alone is necessary.

84 'The thing is that manner of being for which the complete definition of one of its attributes demands that of the subject in its entirety; an entity, consequently, the significance of which is indistinguishable from its total appearance' (ibid., 376).

85 Ibid., 375.

86 Merleau-Ponty's rhetoric is often characterized by an apparent relativism starkly at odds with much contemporary phenomenology or critical realism:

'what precisely is meant by saying that the world existed before any human consciousness? An example of what is meant is that the earth originally issued from a primitive nebula from which the combination of conditions necessary to life was absent. But every one of these words, like every equation in physics, presupposes *our* pre-scientific experience of the world, and this reference to the world in which we *live* goes to make up the proposition's valid meaning' (ibid., 502).

87 Foster, *Return of the Real*, 50.
88 Baker, *Minimalism*, 71.
89 Agamben, *Coming Community*, 68.
90 Ingarden, *Time and Modes*, 6–7.
91 Ibid., 11–12.
92 Althusser, *Philosophy of the Encounter*, 169.
93 Ibid.
94 Ibid., 187. Althusser uses the term *essence* rhetorically in this context, rather than in reference to a philosophy of essence, to which his work is unambiguously opposed.
95 Ibid.
96 Neill, 'Pure Resonance', 193.
97 Ibid., 194.
98 Baker, *Minimalism*, 74.
99 Serra, 'Art and Censorship', 188.
100 Ibid., 185.
101 Greenberg, 'Recentness of Sculpture', 184; Fried, 'Art and Objecthood', 141–2.
102 Baker, *Minimalism*, 77.
103 Danto proposed the term *artworld* to describe the network of creative, curatorial, interpretative and critical practices involved in the commissioning, production, preservation, sale and collection of art in contemporary capitalist societies. It is widely used today in context-driven studies of aesthetics, particularly by proponents of what has become known as the Institutional Theory of Art.
104 Judd, 'Complaints, part I', 197.
105 See Colpitt, *Minimal Art*, 9–19.
106 See Meyer, *Minimalism: Art and Polemics*, 262–4; Colpitt, *Minimal Art*, 21–2.
107 See Schwartz, *Minimalists*, 10–12; Strickland, *Minimalism: Origins*, 231, 246–7.
108 See Bellamy, 'Downpour', 36–7.
109 Chave, 'Minimalism and the Rhetoric of Power', 49.
110 Ibid., 51.
111 Ibid., 48.
112 Frank Stella, *Arbeit Macht Frei*, 1967. Museum of Modern Art, New York. http://www.moma.org/collection/works/61219 (accessed 24 June 2017).

113 Altieri, 'Frank Stella and Jacques Derrida', 193.
114 Ibid., 194.
115 Chave veers rather hyperbolically towards the view that the work itself, by virtue of its concern with power and force, contains a sort of fascist gesture ('Minimalism and the Rhetoric of Power', 47–50).
116 Stella in Glaser, 'Questions', 158.
117 See ibid., 149.
118 See Chave, 'Minimalism and the Rhetoric of Power', 48–50; Adorno, *Negative Dialectics*, 361–3; Lyotard, *Différend*, 87–90; Agamben, *Remnants of Auschwitz*, 33–9.
119 Lyotard, 'Sublime and the Avant-Garde', 103.
120 Rancière, 'Are Some Things Unrepresentable?', 138.
121 Agamben, 'Bartleby', 245.
122 Agamben, 'On Potentiality', 182.
123 In *State of Exception*, Agamben describes the effects of force in situations in which the rationale for exercising this force has been suspended, as one in which 'potentiality and act are radically separated' (Agamben, *State of Exception*, 39).
124 Schlegel, 'Athenaeum Fragment 51', 247. Schlegel's precise reference is to the Fragment as a literary genre, which, as Lacoue-Labarthe and Nancy note, is unique in its capacity to establish, as a singularity, the aesthetic paradigm within which incompleteness and totality are simultaneously instantiated: '[f]ragmentary totality…cannot be situated in any single point: it is simultaneously in the whole and in each part. Each fragment stands for itself and for that from which it is detached' (Lacoue-Labarthe and Nancy, *Literary* Absolute, 44).
125 Michaels, 'Meaning and Affect', http://nonsite.org/feature/meaning-and-affect-phil-changs-cache-active (accessed 24 June 2017).
126 Ibid.
127 Derrida, 'Force and Signification', 3.
128 Albeit with reference to a far narrower definition of minimalism, a similar point is made by McGurl in *The Program Era* (316, 319–20).
129 Potter, *Four Musical Minimalists*, 77–9.
130 Miller, *Ethics of Reading*, 3.
131 Ibid., 4.
132 Ibid., 8.
133 Hallett, *Minimalism and Short Story*, 4.
134 McGurl, *Program Era*, 300.
135 Carver, 'On Writing', 24.
136 David Herman defines a storyworld as a model of 'who did what to and with whom, when, where, why and in what fashion' ('Storyworld', 570).
137 Abrams, 'A Maximalist Novelist', 27.

138 Leypoldt, 'Epiphanic Moments', 532.
139 See Nelles, 'Microfiction', 93–4.
140 McGurl, *Program Era*, 314.
141 Ibid.
142 Ibid., 315.
143 Lainsbury, *Carver Chronotype*, 8.
144 Clark, *American Literary Minimalism*, 4.
145 See Lainsbury, *Carver Chronotype*, 2–5; Bellamy, 'Downpour', 31–9; Federman, 'Short Note on Minimalism', 57.
146 Carver, 'Fat', 13.
147 Ibid.
148 Ibid., 14.
149 Ibid.
150 Ibid., 15.
151 Ibid., 14.
152 See Harvey, *Brief History*, 42, 64–5.
153 Miller, *Ethics of Reading*, 4–8.
154 Lainsbury, *Carver Chronotype*, 150.
155 McGurl, *Program Era*, 320.
156 Althusser, *Philosophy of the Encounter*, 173.
157 Ibid., 172.
158 Derrida, *Specters of Marx*, 37.
159 Ibid., 48.
160 Ibid., 37.
161 Carver, 'Fat', 17.
162 McGurl, *Program Era*, 275.
163 Saltzman, *Understanding Raymond Carver*, 24.
164 Nessett, *Stories*, 17.
165 Carver, 'On Writing', 23.
166 Saltzman, *Understanding Raymond Carver*, 24.
167 Nessett, *Stories*, 15.
168 Carver, 'Fat', 16.
169 Ibid., 15.
170 Levinas, *Totality and Infinity*, 197.
171 Ibid., 199.
172 Carver, 'Fat', 15.

Chapter 3: Objecthood: On the Materialism of Minimalism

1 Heidegger, 'The Thing', 166–7.
2 Ibid., 168.
3 Ibid., 174.
4 Heidegger, 'Fundamental Concepts of Metaphysics', 177–8.
5 Latour, *Reassembling the Social*, 71–3.
6 Ibid., 85.
7 Lyotard, 'Answering the Question', 81.
8 Damisch, 'A Conversation', 8.
9 On this point thinkers as different as Hans-Georg Gadamer (*Truth and Method*, 306–7), Arthur C. Danto (*Transfiguration*, 124) and Paul Churchland (*The Engine of Reason*, 11–13, 21) agree.
10 Bal, *Travelling Concepts*, 8.
11 According to Eagleton, theory emerges from 'human activity bending back upon itself, constrained into a new kind of self-reflexivity' (*Significance of Theory*, 27). See also Culler, *Literary Theory*, 14–15.
12 Waugh, Introduction, 10.
13 Bal, *Travelling Concepts*, 185.
14 Ibid.
15 Ibid., 8–9.
16 Ibid., 177, 201.
17 Ibid., 177, 185.
18 Iser, *How To Do Theory*, 5–7.
19 In this regard it is worth recalling Paul de Man's provocative formulation: 'Nothing can overcome the resistance to theory since theory is itself this resistance' ('Resistance to Theory', 19). Theory's reflexivity regarding its own operation, revealed in its 'controlled reflection on the formation of method' ('Resistance to Theory', 4) culminates in the situation in which theory becomes increasingly reified, and thus structurally abstracted from the practice to which it purports to relate, undermining its own connection to practice. In this sense, '[j]ust as resistance of objects is a necessary condition of the possibility of knowledge', notes Culler, 'so resistance to theory may be seen as a necessary force, which calls theory to account' ('Resisting Theory', 80).
20 Potter, *Four Musical Minimalists*, 225.
21 Sontag, 'Against Interpretation', 15.
22 Ibid., 17.
23 Ibid.

24 Ibid., 19.
25 Ibid., 23. Italics are Sontag's.
26 Knapp and Michaels, 'Against Theory', 742.
27 Ibid.
28 Their views on intention, hermeneutics and style are radically opposed. Sontag is finally a realist while Knapp and Michaels are pragmatists.
29 The logical or epistemological autonomy of art is a more contestable arena.
30 Culler offers an interesting corollary to this position: theory does not evade its object; rather, 'the literary in theory … has migrated from being the object of theory to being the quality of theory itself' ('The Literary in Theory', 38).
31 Sontag, 'Against Interpretation', 23.
32 Ibid.
33 Greenberg, 'Recentness of Sculpture', 183.
34 Ibid.185.
35 Ibid.
36 Ibid., 184.
37 See Plato, 'Republic', 1128–32.
38 Sol LeWitt, *Incomplete Open Cubes*, 1974. San Francisco Museum of Modern Art, San Francisco. https://www.sfmoma.org/artwork/97.516.A-KKKKKKKKKK (accessed 24 June 2017).
39 See Lippard, 'The Structures', 24.
40 Ibid, 23.
41 Stella in Glaser, 'Questions', 158.
42 Frank Stella, *Tomlinson Court Park*, 1964. Museum of Modern Art, New York. https://www.moma.org/collection/works/61217 (accessed 24 June 2017).
43 Strickland, *Minimalism: Origins*, 24; Colpitt, *Minimal Art*, 1; Baker, *Minimalism*, 29–31.
44 Ibid., 13.
45 Meyer, *Minimalism: Art and Polemics*, 121.
46 Foster, *Return of the Real*, 78.
47 Stella in Glaser, 'Questions', 157.
48 This relation becomes particularly complex as Stella's work increasingly makes use of shaped canvases, expressing 'a desire to reconcile the materially sufficient surfaces and serial logic of Johns and Rauschenberg's pictorialized neo-dada with the ambition, scale and alloverness of the Pollock or Newman mural, whose surfaces also invited … a literalist reading', as Meyer has it (*Minimalism: Art and Polemics*, 124).
49 Where the term objective relates to objectivity, objectal relates to objects and objecthood itself.
50 Bal, *Travelling Concepts*, 8 (Bal's italics). As Bal recognizes, 'by selecting an object,

you question a field … [T]ogether, object and methods can become a new, not firmly delineated field' (ibid., 4).

51 Colpitt, *Minimal Art*, 107.

52 Ibid.

53 See Botha, 'Microfiction', 205–7.

54 Colpitt, *Minimal Art*, 41.

55 Ibid., 43.

56 Ibid.

57 Some monochromatic painters do vary the hues of the pigment they use, retaining thus a sense of tonal movement.

58 Judd in Glaser, *Questions*, 153–4.

59 This view is expressed by sculptor Robert Morris (Strickland, *Minimalism: Origins*, 267).

60 La Monte Young, *Trio for Strings*, 1958.

61 Saroyan, 'Untitled poster-poem', 28. As Alexander points out, this poem is formally recognized as the shortest existing poem (Alexander, *Minimalism*, 6).

62 In this context it is necessary to point out the potential differences between surface and deep structural relations between units.

63 Alexander, *Minimalism*, 16.

64 Foster, *Return of the Real*, 38.

65 Ibid.

66 Alexander, *Minimalism*, 8.

67 Simmons, *Deep Surfaces*, 2. As Simmons goes on to argue, 'minimalist fiction attempts to give mass culture a place in a new "deep surface", a new and problematic historical consciousness' (ibid., 107).

68 See Danto, *Transfiguration*, 9, 11–13, 21, 24–5.

69 Simmons, *Deep Surfaces*, 110.

70 Hallett, *Minimalism*, 20–1.

71 Hutcheon, *Poetics of Postmodernism*, 17.

72 McGurl, *Program Era*, 376.

73 Botha, 'Microfiction', 200–1.

74 Friedman, 'What Makes a Short Story Short?', 109. See Botha, 'Microfiction', 205–6.

75 Howe, Introduction, x.

76 Nelles, 'Microfiction', 93.

77 The following is one of Kostelanetz's microstories in full: 'Even the happiest love stories end in death' ('Microstories', 93).

78 Crace, *The Devil's Larder*, 194.

79 Davis, 'Index Entry', 713.

80 Cole, 'Seven Short Stories About Drones', *The New Inquiry*, 14 January 2013.

https://thenewinquiry.com/blog/seven-short-stories-about-drones/ (accessed 24 June 2017).

81 Hayles, 'Intermediation', 106.

82 Colpitt, *Minimal Art*, 67.

83 Fried, 'Art and Objecthood', 141–2.

84 Michaels, *Shape of the Signifier*, 88.

85 Fried, 'Art and Objecthood', 140. Italics are Fried's.

86 Michaels, *Shape of the Signifier*, 89.

87 Foster, *Return of the Real*, 43.

88 Colpitt, *Minimal Art*, 70.

89 Ibid., 75.

90 Ibid., 77.

91 Fried, 'Art and Objecthood', 126.

92 Morton, *Hyperobjects*, 60.

93 Ibid., 1.

94 Fink, *Repeating Ourselves*, 5–8.

95 Kant, *Critique of Judgment*, 115.

96 Fink, *Repeating Ourselves*, 44.

97 Ibid.

98 Potter, *Four Musical Minimalists*, 200.

99 Strickland, *Minimalism: Origins*, 73.

100 Ibid.

101 Lyotard, 'Newman: The Instant', 82.

102 Rancière, 'What Medium Can Mean', 35.

103 Ibid.

104 McLuhan, *Understanding Media*, 7.

105 Stewart, *Bookwork*, 44.

106 Lessing, *Laocoon*, 150–3. See Steiner, *Colors of Rhetoric*, xiii, 12–14.

107 Greenberg, 'Avant-Garde and Kitsch', 6–7.

108 Weiss, Preface, 10.

109 Bell, 'Fluorescent Light as Art', 127.

110 Dan Flavin, *untitled (to the real Dan Hill) 1b*, 1978. Museum of Modern Art, Antwerp. http://ensembles.mhka.be/items/untitled-to-the-real-dan-hill-1b?locale=en (accessed 24 June 2017).

111 See Meyer, *Minimalism: Art and Polemics*, 186.

112 There are a number of reasons for this instruction, largely legal, or related to the goodwill of workers involved in the assemblage of proposals or situations within the exhibitionary space.

113 Govan, 'Irony and Light', 71.

114 Smith, 'Recollections and Thoughts', 138.

115 Bell, 'Fluorescent Light as Art', 116.
116 Meyer, *Minimalism: Art and Polemics*, 106.
117 Govan, 'Irony and Light', 59.
118 Meyer, *Minimalism: Art and Polemics*, 102.
119 Ibid.
120 James Turrell, *Breathing Light*, 2013. Los Angeles County Museum of Art, Los Angeles. http://www.lacma.org/art/exhibition/james-turrell-breathing-light (accessed 24 June 2017).
121 Ólafur Elíasson, *The Weather Project*, 2003. Tate Modern, London. http://olafureliasson.net/archive/artwork/WEK101003/the-weather-project (accessed 24 June 2017).
122 Walter de Maria, *Lightning Field*, 1977. Dia Art Foundation, New Mexico. http://www.diaart.org/sites/main/lightningfield (accessed 24 June 2017). See Baker, *Minimalism*, 125–6.
123 Colpitt, *Minimal Art*, 102.
124 Ibid., 101.
125 Ibid., 70.
126 Fried, 'Art and Objecthood', 119.
127 Wollheim, 'Minimal Art', 391.
128 Colpitt, *Minimal Art*, 110.
129 Ellsworth Kelly, *Spectrum IV*, 1967. Museum of Modern Art, New York. http://www.moma.org/collection/works/79739?locale=en (accessed 24 June 2017).
130 Strickland, *Minimalism: Origins*, 73.
131 Ibid., 70–1.
132 Judd, 'Young Artists', 130.
133 Ibid.
134 Bernstein, *Poetics*, 143.
135 Connor, *Samuel Beckett*, 11.
136 Beckett, 'Company', 3.
137 Ibid., 7.
138 We might consider the *You're early* (Josipovici, *The Inventory*, 27–8, 35) and *the old man in the rocking-chair* sequences in this regard (ibid., 45, 55, 57, 58).
139 Didion's repetition reflects on the compulsive element of social interaction and dogma regarding decorum, and their link to what numerous writers depict as a notable poverty in much contemporary communication (Didion, *A Book of Common Prayer*, 30; Didion, *Play It As It Lays*, 28–30).
140 Hallett, *Minimalism*, 37.
141 Lax, 'things into words', 42.
142 Agamben, *Coming Community*, 15. The significance of Agamben's thought on facticity is developed subsequently.

143 Lax, 'is', 13.
144 Beer, Introduction, xviii.
145 Hallett, *Minimalism*, 20–1.
146 Ibid., 47.
147 Ibid., 11.
148 Ibid., 9.
149 Colpitt, *Minimal Art*, 114.
150 Ibid., 114.
151 Ibid., 115.
152 Merleau-Ponty, *Phenomenology of Perception*, 239.
153 Finlay, 'acrobats', 140.
154 Colpitt, *Minimal Art*, 17.
155 Ibid., 18.
156 Meyer, *Minimalism: Art and Polemics*, 3.
157 Ibid., 8; Colpitt, *Minimal Art*, 16–18, 20–2.
158 The vast majority of Dan Flavin's light art is constructed from prefabricated fluorescent tubes.
159 Colpitt, *Minimal Art*, 16.
160 Colpitt and Meyer agree that critics quickly accepted and assimilated the precepts of minimalism (ibid., 21–2; Meyer, *Minimalism: Art and Polemics*, 3), although Meyer suggests that the sale and purchase histories of various works suggest that the hostility of the general public was more long-lasting (ibid., 271).
161 Colpitt, *Minimal Art*, 21–2.
162 It is important to emphasize that minimalism retains a remarkable technical heterogeneity within and between its various media (Strickland, *Minimalism: Origins*, 7; Baker, *Minimalism*, 9, 13, 20).
163 Ibid.
164 Strickland, *Minimalism: Origins*, 26.
165 Ibid., 52, 75, 113–14; Colpitt, *Minimal Art*, 23; Marzona, *Minimal Art*, 70. Benedikt refers to Mangold's 'disarming … pastel, matt-surfaced wall-slabs' ('Sculpture as Architecture', 74).
166 Colpitt, *Minimal Art*, 23.
167 Schwartz, *Minimalists*, 68. See Reich, 'Pendulum Music', 31–2.
168 In a celebrated interview, Reich draws out these connections: 'where [Cage] was willing to keep his musical sensibility out of his own music, I was not' ('Excerpts', 33). Reich, instead, sought 'music … that was completely personal … but that was arrived at by impersonal means' (ibid.).
169 Bann, 'From Place to Place', 34.
170 Foster, *Return of the Real*, 36–42; Fink, *Repeating Ourselves*, 157; Meyer, *Minimalism: Art and Polemics*, 178–83.

171 'I compose the material, decide the process it's going to be run through – but once these initial choices have been made, it runs by itself' (Reich, 'Excerpts', 33).
172 Reich, 'Second Interview', 95.

Chapter 4: The Real: On the Persistence of Minimalism

1 Niiniluoto, *Critical Scientific Realism*, 1.
2 Ibid.
3 Noal and Irzik, *Philosophy, Science,* 286.
4 Niiniluoto, *Critical Scientific Realism*, 10.
5 Goodman, 'On Starmaking', 144. See also Lawson, *Closure*, xxix.
6 Harman, 'Speculative Realism', 375-6; Meillassoux, 'Speculative Realism', 412; Meillassoux, *After Finitude*, 5, 19–20.
7 Indeed, as Russell famously contends, science and philosophy are initially indistinguishable from one another, and similarly focused on the question of reality and the real (*History of Western Philosophy*, 15).
8 With respect to the ascendency of the virtual as a sign of the failure of traditional realism, Baudrillard goes as far as to claim that the real 'is no longer really the real', and that the real will '[n]ever again … have the chance to produce itself' ('Precession of Simulacra', 2). He argues that there has been a wholescale ruination of the first order of simulacra – the mimetic processes which, in aiming to reproduce the world as it is, commit it to a naive realism – leading to the burden of representation shifting to second- and third-order simulacra. The second order simulates, through the construction of fictions, the things that the first order fails accurately to represent, encouraging speculation regarding possible futures. The third order, to which the second gives way, involves the 'simulacra of simulation' (Baudrillard, 'Simulacra and Science Fiction', 121), enforcing a distance between the real and representation by installing 'the model … [as] an anticipation of the real … leav[ing] no room for any sort of fictional anticipation … or imaginary transcendence' (ibid., 122). Baudrillard recalls a time when '[r]eality could go beyond fiction: that was the surest sign of the possibility of an ever-increasing imaginary. But the real cannot surpass the model … And, paradoxically, it is the real that has become our true utopia – but a utopia that is no longer in the realm of the possible, that can only be dreamt of as one would dream of a lost object' (ibid., 122–3). Although the current work largely circumvents questions of representation, and hence is only obliquely concerned with the specific problem to which Baudrillard draws attention, his thought in this regard remains pivotal in weighing the claims of new species of realism.

9 Norris, *Re-Thinking the Cogito*, 212.
10 Norris, *New Idols*, 117–19.
11 Ibid., 117.
12 Norris, 'Reply', 358–9.
13 Putnam, *Many Faces of Realism*, 3–4.
14 Ibid., 5.
15 Norris views this as a 'retreat…from a robust realism to an 'internalist' perspective on issues of knowledge and truth' (*New Idols*, 1–2).
16 Putnam, *Many Faces of Realism*, 8.
17 Ibid., 7.
18 Niiniluoto, *Critical Scientific Realism*, 2. Niiniluoto's exposition is limited to formal models of realism. Aesthetic realism is examined below.
19 Heidegger, 'Question Concerning Technology', 11–12; Norris, 'Reply', 362.
20 Aronson, Harré and Way, *Realism Rescued*, 123.
21 Niiniluoto, *Truthlikeness*, xi-xiii, 160–3; Nola and Irzik, *Philosophy, Science*, 65; Newton-Smith, *Rationality of Science*, 54–6; Psillos, *Scientific Realism*, 252–3.
22 Badiou, 'Truth', 130–1.
23 Niiniluoto, *Critical Scientific Realism*, 10. See also ibid., 3–4; Losee, *Historical Introduction*, 253–6; Ridley, *On Science*, 43. Regarding the conflation of truth and reality, it is possible to further distinguish pragmatists and neo-pragmatists such as Dewey, James and Rorty (Niiniluoto, *Critical Scientific Realism*, 11–12), semantic anti-realists such as Dummett, who systematically decouple truth and reality (ibid.), internalists, such as Putnam, who resist relativism by promoting internal consistency (ibid.; Bhaskar, *Reclaiming* Reality, 155), and constructivists such as Stengers and Latour (Niiniluoto, *Critical Scientific Realism*, 12).
24 Aronson, Harré and Way, *Realism Rescued*, 123.
25 These include empiricism (Bacon, Berkeley, Locke and Hume), positivism (Comte), logical positivism (Neurath, Schlick and Carnap), logical atomism (Russell and Wittgenstein) and, more latterly, instrumentalism (Nagel, Stegmüller and van Fraasen).
26 Bhaskar, *Reclaiming Reality*, 143.
27 Niiniluoto, *Critical Scientific Realism*, 12.
28 Ibid.
29 Feyerabend, *Realism, Rationalism and Scientific Method*, 6.
30 Goodman, *Ways of Worldmaking*, 6.
31 Bhaskar, *Reclaiming Reality*, 191.
32 Falk, *Poetics of Roman Ingarden*, 114–15.
33 Ingarden identifies the Absolute, Real, Ideal and Purely Intentional as the four principal or highest modes of being (Thomasson, 'Roman Ingarden').
34 Tymnieniecka, 'Beyond Ingarden's Idealism/Realism Controversy', 283.

35 Meillassoux, 'Speculative Realism', 428.

36 Although in terms often quite different from those of the present discussion, René Girard's *Deceit, Desire and the Novel* and *Violence and the Sacred*, along with Philippe Lacoue-Labarthe's *Typography*, remain seminal analyses of the cultural and ontological significance of *mimesis* and its relation to truth and reality.

37 Tallis, *Defence of Realism*, 195. Danto similarly draws attention to the ongoing philosophical dispute regarding whether representation is intensional, extensional or relational (*Transfiguration*, 68–70). See also Goodman, *Languages of Art*, 34–9.

38 Danto offers several significant arguments regarding the fact that imitation, inasmuch as it is intensional, does not necessarily require an original (*Transfiguration*, 68–71).

39 Sörbom, 'Classical Concept of Mimesis', 19–21.

40 Ibid., 22; Tallis, *Defence of Realism*, 195; Danto, *Transfiguration*, 13, 79, 82. It is worth keeping in mind Goodman's argument that it is '[s]urely not … any sort of resemblance to reality … [that] constitutes a realism of representation' (*Languages of Art*, 34), but an adherence to a similar means of presentation (ibid., 39).

41 Danto, *Transfiguration*, 78.

42 Ibid., 83.

43 Livingston, 'Why Realism Matters', 143–5, 150; Beer, 'Wave Theory', 193–4.

44 Nochlin, *Realism*, 103, 105–6.

45 Lukács, *Meaning of Contemporary Realism*, 19, 25.

46 Ibid., 19–24.

47 Ibid., 27, 31–3, 38–9.

48 Ibid., 24.

49 Ibid., 39.

50 Ibid., 34, 36. This is similar to arguments in many broadly Marxist analyses of the opposition of modernism and reality, including those by Adorno, Benjamin and some of the later Frankfurt School (see Morris, *Realism*, 17–23). Bruce Robbins makes a convincing case for reconsidering the relation between representation and realism as determined by social rather than epistemological criteria ('Modernism and Literary Realism', 225–31).

51 Foster, *Return of the Real*, 127.

52 Fraser, *Modern Writer*, 21.

53 Fluck, 'Surface and Depth', 69.

54 This is the term Barthes deploys to describe the complex relation of parts in his structural analysis of narrative ('Introduction to the Structural Analysis of Narrative', 97).

55 Fluck, 'Surface and Depth', 69.

56 Hallett, *Minimalism and the Short Story*, 15–17; Alexander, *Minimalism*, 136–7.

57 Schechner, 'American Realisms', 40.
58 Ibid., 43.
59 Hilfer, *American Fiction Since 1940*, 182.
60 Verhoeven, 'What We Talk About', 53.
61 Ibid., 55.
62 Just, 'Is Less More', 308–9.
63 Ibid., 304.
64 Ibid., 312.
65 Ibid.
66 An earlier version of 'The Bath', published only subsequently as 'A Small Good Thing', is considerably longer and narratively and emotionally more complex than its successor. Yet it is debatable whether the fuller version of the story is in fact the affectively more nuanced one, as often claimed.
67 Carver, 'The Bath', 219.
68 Verhoeven, 'What We Talk About', 43–4.
69 Bergonzi, *Situation of the Novel*, 25.
70 Rosenbaum, *Aspects of Bloomsbury*, 4. This prefigures Merleau-Ponty's identification of sensation as the basic unit of perception (*Phenomenology of Perception*, 3–12).
71 Similar propositions are offered by Beckett and Sontag.
72 Robbe-Grillet, 'On Some Outdated Notions', 73.
73 Ibid.
74 Robbe-Grillet, 'From Realism to Reality', 156.
75 Robbe-Grillet, 'Path for the Future Novel', 52.
76 Danto, *Transfiguration*, 69–70.
77 Robbe-Grillet, 'On Some Outdated Notions', 68–9.
78 Robbe-Grillet, 'In the Corridors of the Underground', 27–34.
79 Ibid., 34. See also ibid., 28, 33.
80 Hallett, *Minimalism*, 25.
81 Robbe-Grillet, 'In the Corridors of the Underground', 27.
82 Ibid., 27. See also ibid., 33–4.
83 Ibid., 27.
84 Ibid., 28-30.
85 Ibid., 29-31.
86 Ibid., 34.
87 Garcia Cela, 'Hearing in Robbe-Grillet', 453.
88 Leach, 'Parallel Methods', 11.
89 Morrissette, 'Generative Techniques', 27. Importantly, Morrissette maintains that 'there is no such thing as a pure situational generator, and … there is no situation which does not already occupy a number of forms' (ibid.).

90 Ibid.
91 Ibid., 31.
92 Robbe-Grillet, 'In the Corridors of the Underground', 27, 30.
93 Ibid., 27.
94 Ibid., 31.
95 Ibid., 33.
96 Ibid., 34.
97 Badiou, *Being and Event*, 40–8. See also Hallward, *Badiou*, 61–3; de Beistegui, 'The Ontological Dispute', 46–7, 49.
98 See Prigogine and Stengers, *Order out of Chaos*, 7–8; Badiou, *Second Manifesto*, 29; Badiou, 'On Subtraction', 109–10; Serres, *Genesis*, 13–14.
99 According to Badiou, 'being is … multiplicity plucked from the void' (*Second Manifesto*, 29).
100 Badiou, 'Question of Being', 47–8.
101 On the likelihood that the universe – the taking place of time and space – is ultimately the becoming of an essentially entropic process, see Prigogine and Stengers, *Order out of Chaos*, 7–8.
102 Badiou, *Second Manifesto*, 30–2.
103 This is an adaption of Meillassoux's formulation: 'contingency alone is necessary' (*After Finitude*, 80).
104 Badiou, *Second Manifesto*, 60.
105 Ibid., 31.
106 Badiou, 'Question of Being', 47.
107 Gillespie, *Mathematics of Novelty*, 5.
108 Ibid., 2.
109 Ibid., 8.
110 Ibid., 3.
111 Badiou, 'Event as Trans-Being', 103.
112 Ibid., 100.
113 The event is something 'which is not being *qua* being … which subtracts itself from ontological subtraction' (ibid.; see also Badiou, *Being and Event*, 189–90).
114 Badiou, 'Event as Trans-Being', 103.
115 For Badiou, whose entire ontological schema is derived from the mathematics of set theory, this exceptional status can be substantiated in set theoretical terms. According to the axiom of foundation in Zermelo-Fraenkel set theory, a multiple – a set that coheres in existence – cannot be founded on its own elements, since in every multiple there is a founding element which is not part of the multiple in question (ibid., 103; Badiou, *Being and Event*, 186). According to Badiou, the sole exception to this rule is the event, which is founded on an element that is also its essential constituent.

116 Ibid., 191, 193.

117 Badiou, 'Truth', 124.

118 Badiou, *Being and Event*, 178.

119 Ibid., 179.

120 Badiou, 'Truth', 127; Badiou, *Manifesto*, 85.

121 Latour, *Reassembling the Social*, 8. Latour's Actor-Network Theory (ANT) – 'a type of momentary association which is characterized by the way it gathers together into new shapes' (ibid., 65) – similarly emphasizes contingency and provisionality.

122 Sanouillet, 'Dada: A Definition', 21.

123 Perloff, *Futurist Moment*, 174.

124 Butler, *Early Modernism*, 147.

125 Bohn, *Visual Poetry*, 17.

126 Butler, *Early Modernism*, 167.

127 Bann, Introduction, *Concrete Poetry*, 11.

128 Drucker, 'Visual Performance', 134.

129 Welchman, 'After the Wagnerian Bouillabaisse', 60.

130 Sanouillet, 'Dada', 21.

131 Hutcheon, *Poetics of Postmodernism*, 142. See also Caws, *Poetry of Dada and Surrealism*, 110–11.

132 Tristan Tzara, qtd in Dachy, *Dada*, 34.

133 The polemical use of the manifesto 'counter[s] any purely aesthetic interpretation of their work[...]' (Dachy, *Dada Movement*, 8), pointing to an active resistance to the 'delusions of politics' (Dachy, *Dada*, 33). Although Ades maintains that the geographical and stylistic diversity of the artists suggests 'no real unity' ('Dada and Surrealism', 113), according to Sanouillet, Dadaists actively 'banded together their talents and energies to wage an excruciating war against society as a whole' ('Dada', 23).

134 Ibid., 20.

135 Ibid., 25.

136 Lyotard, *Duchamp's TRANS/formers*, 12–13.

137 According to Welchman, Dada 'militated against the divisionism of nineteenth century practices: divisions of labor, divisions of academic and other disciplines, down to the divisions between the arts and the dividing of art from non-art'. ('After the Wagnerian Bouillabaisse', 61).

138 Lyotard, *Duchamp's TRANS/formers*, 22, 24.

139 Agamben, *State of Exception*, 31. Although to a significant extent generic, this definition is formulated in the context of legal theory rather than aesthetics.

140 Dachy, *Dada*, 14.

141 Marcel Duchamp, qtd in Dachy, *Dada*, 71. Richard Wollheim offers an interesting

discussion of the manner in which this emphasis on decision redefines the concept of the artwork ('Minimal Art', 396).

142 Danto, *Transfiguration*, 149.

143 Ibid., 99.

144 Ibid., 6, 43, 143.

145 Ibid., 39, 47.

146 Ibid., 5, 91–5.

147 Ibid., 99.

148 Dachy, *Dada Movement*, 8.

149 Albright, *Modernism and Music*, 319.

150 Marcel Duchamp, *Fountain* (1917; replica 1964). Tate Modern, London. http://www.tate.org.uk/art/artworks/duchamp-fountain-t07573 (accessed 24 June 2017).

151 Ibid., 190.

152 Ibid., 81.

153 Badiou, *The Century*, 49.

154 Perloff, *21st Century Modernism*, 116; see also ibid., 109–10.

155 De Duve, *Pictorial Nominalism*, 160.

156 See Perloff, *21st Century Modernism*, 87–8.

157 'The readymade … renders the act of naming … undecidable' (De Duve, *Pictorial Nominalism*, 159). Joselit recognizes a similar 'alienation between words and objects [that] occurs in virtually all of Duchamp's readymades' (*Infinite Regress*, 87).

158 Gasché, *The Idea of Form*, 10.

159 Ibid., 12.

160 De Duve, *Pictorial Nominalism*, 160.

161 Compare, for example, the varied responses in this regard of Wollheim, 'Minimal Art', 395–7; Rose, 'ABC Art', 278; Foster, *Return of the Real*, 4; Perloff, *Futurist Moment*, 110; Greenberg, 'Recentness of Sculpture', 183–5.

162 Ibid.; Fried, 'Art and Objecthood', 139–42.

163 Wollheim, 'Minimal Art', 395–9.

164 Ibid., 399.

165 Rose, 'ABC Art', 278. Gregory Battcock, a leading early anthologist of minimalist and conceptual art, devotes a full study to the close relationship between minimalist art and constructivism, *Constructivism and Minimal Art*.

166 Foster, *Return of the Real*, 4.

167 Meyer, *Minimalism: Art and Polemics*, 145.

168 Ibid., 106, 111–12, 190.

169 Perloff, *Futurist Moment*, 110.

170 Berger, *Labyrinths*, 6, 22, 34.

171 Haskell, *Blam!*, 19.

172 Meillassoux, 'Speculative Realism', 432.
173 Agamben, *Coming Community*, 32.
174 See Meillassoux, *After Finitude*, 5–8.
175 Ibid., 5.
176 Meillassoux, 'Speculative Realism', 422.
177 Meillassoux, *After Finitude*, 3–5. The terms *in-itself* and *for-us* are most famously developed in Sartre's existentialist project.
178 See Meillassoux, 'Speculative Realism', 409, 416–17, 426–8; Brassier, *Nihil Unbound*, 64–7.
179 It should be recalled that there are numerous species of anti-realism, and that Meillassoux's tactic of gathering several of these under the term correlationism is not beyond dispute. A realist phenomenology, for instance, might emphasize a convergence rather than correlation of subject and object, introducing a different set of implications for the understanding of realism.
180 Meillassoux, *After Finitude*, 10.
181 Ibid., 14.
182 Ibid., 10–19.
183 As Meillassoux notes, '[d]ating became 'absolute' with the perfection of techniques…that allowed the scientist to determine the actual duration of the measured object' (*After Finitude*, 9).
184 Ibid., 78–81. According to Harman, Meillassoux is 'doubting the Principle of Sufficient Reason while keeping the concept of non-contradiction and he's thereby doubting necessity' (Harman, 'Speculative Realism' 385–6).
185 Brassier, *Nihil Unbound*, 66.
186 Meillassoux, *After Finitude*, 79. The present work follows this distinction, although since its primary concern is with existence as it is presented to thought, its sphere of reference is for the most part to facticity, and hence the factual and factical.
187 Brassier, *Nihil Unbound*, 67.
188 Meillassoux, *After Finitude*, 79.
189 Ibid., 40.
190 Meillassoux, 'Speculative Realism', 437.
191 Meillassoux, *After Finitude*, 79.
192 Ibid., 39.
193 Ibid., 40.
194 Ibid., 80.
195 Ibid.
196 Ibid.
197 Meillassoux, 'Speculative Realism, 434–5.
198 Ibid., 435. The italics are Meillassoux's.

199 Eva Hesse, *Contingent*, 1969. National Gallery of Australia, Canberra. http://www.nga.gov.au/EXHIBITION/softsculpture/Default.cfm?IRN=49353&BioArtistIRN=15232&MnuID=3&ViewID=2 (accessed 24 June 2017).

200 McTaggart, 'The Unreality of Time', 457–74.

201 Ibid., 458.

202 Ibid.

203 Ibid., 460–1.

204 Meillassoux offers the term *ancestrali*ty to counter correlationism and discusses its temporal aspects in some detail (*After Finitude*, 10, 14–17, 20–2).

205 Agamben, 'Critique of the Instant', 111.

206 While a composition may be formally cyclical so that a continuous displacement of its elements will result in a return to the original position of its material, it is problematic to claim that the experience of time is itself cyclical. In an important sense cyclicality only presents the illusion of temporal return or recurrence, since performers and listeners follow distinct and continuous temporal paths of their own (see Botha, 'Evental Distension', 276–7).

207 Reich, 'Music as a Gradual Process', 35.

208 Mertens, *American Minimal Music*, 89.

209 Potter, *Four Musical Minimalists*, 167–8; Strickland, *Minimalism: Origins*, 186–7.

210 Ibid., 184.

211 Ibid; Epstein. 'Pattern Structure', 495.

212 For a detailed discussion of the melodic structure and its effects see Epstein (ibid., 495–8) and Potter, *Four Musical Minimalists*, 183–5, 187.

213 The anchoring role is taken by the first pianist in the first two sections of the composition and exchanged in the third, with the second pianist holding the rhythmically stable melody.

214 Ibid., 180.

215 Epstein, 'Pattern Structure', 494–502.

216 Savitt, 'On Absolute Becoming', 160.

217 Ibid., 165.

218 Ibid., 165–6.

219 Reich, 'Music as a Gradual Process', 35.

Chapter 5: Quantity: On the Radicality of Minimalism

1 Horkheimer and Adorno, *Dialectic of Enlightenment*, 19–20.

2 Elden, *Speaking Against Number*, 147–8.

3 Badiou, *Number and Numbers*, 1.

4 Badiou asks: 'Isn't another idea of number necessary, in order for us to turn

thought back against the despotism of number?' (ibid., 4). See Smith, 'Badiou and Deleuze', 91–3.

5 With respect to the relation of absolute multiplicity and real infinity, Badiou contends that mathematics proposes 'a vertigo of an infinity of infinities distinguishable within their common opposition to the finite' (Badiou, *Being and Event*, 146).

6 As opposed to a dialectic understanding of infinity – 'finitude and infinity … each already possesses within it the moment of the other' (Hegel, *Science of Logic*, 190) – bad infinity, according to Hegel, 'persists in the determination of the beyond of the finite' (ibid., 192), insisting on the realness of the infinite.

7 For Marx, 'the antagonistic character of capitalist accumulation' (*Capital Vol. 1*, 799) culminates in the situation in which 'accumulation of wealth at one pole is, therefore, at the same time accumulation of misery, the torment of labour, slavery, ignorance, brutalization and moral degradation at the opposite pole, i.e. on the side of the class that produces its own product as capital' (ibid).

8 The principal form of this resistance comes with the recognition of the eternal recurrence of the same within existence – 'the eternal yes to all things' (Nietzsche, *Ecce Homo*, 131) which 'affirms the return, the re-beginning, and a certain kind of reproduction that preserves whatever comes back' (Derrida, 'Otobiographies', 20).

9 Horkheimer and Adorno, *Dialectic of Enlightenment*, 4.

10 Ibid., 6.

11 Ibid., 11.

12 Ibid., 6.

13 Adorno, *Negative Dialectics*, 12.

14 Ibid.

15 Badiou, *Being and Event*, 28–9, 43.

16 Ibid., 93.

17 Parmenides, 'Of Nature', 83.

18 See Russell, *History of Philosophy*, 55.

19 Parmenides, 'Of Nature', 83.

20 Plato, 'Parmenides', 397. See Brumbaugh, *Plato on the One*, 185–6.

21 This concept is developed in the modal thought of Leibniz with the purpose of accounting for situations in which a possible world, 'while remaining numerically one and the same…is capable of admitting contradictory possibilities' (Jolley, 'Leibniz: Truth, Knowledge and Metaphysics', 354). Every possible world is marked by 'a maximum set of compossible individuals' (Jolley, *Leibniz*, 171. See Deleuze, *Logic of Sense*, 1712; Madarasz, Introduction, 19–20), each intrinsically distinct, but not in a manner which contradicts the distinctness of the others.

22 Badiou, 'Platonism and Mathematical Ontology', 60.

23 Badiou, *Being and Event*, 23.
24 Hallward, Introduction, 3–4.
25 Badiou, 'Philosophy and Mathematics', 22, 30–3.
26 Horkheimer and Adorno, *Dialectic of Enlightenment*, 13.
27 Sections of this chapter appear in an article, 'Why Minimalism Matters', which prefers the term *persistence* to *continuity*. However, subsequent work has suggested the usefulness of distinguishing the two, although the latter remains essentially an expression of the former, and both are used in this way in the present context. See Botha, 'Why Minimalism Matters', 746–72.
28 The music of Young or Niblock might be opposed to that of Feldman or Skempton.
29 The painting of Reinhardt or Stella might be opposed to that of Martin or Ryman.
30 The writing of Carver or Beckett might be opposed to that of Cage or Lax.
31 Robert Barry, '[This work has and continues to be refined since 1969]', *The Ubuweb Anthology of Conceptual Writing*, ed. Craig Dworkin. http://www.ubu.com/concept/barry_this.html (accessed 24 June 2017).
32 Ibid.
33 Ibid.
34 Ibid.
35 Ibid.
36 Ibid.
37 Ibid.
38 Badiou, *Being and Event*, 23.
39 Badiou reminds us of 'the stubbornness of the […] residues of the One's empire' (*Manifesto*, 57). See also ibid., 103-4; Badiou, *Number and Numbers*, 7–8, 10–11, 14. For Badiou, 'ontology has built the portico of its ruined temple out of the following experience: what *presents* itself is essentially multiple; *what* presents itself is essentially one' (Badiou, *Being and Event*, 23).
40 It is, after all, Plato's version of Parmenides that furnishes our knowledge of the one.
41 Badiou, *Being and Event*, 23–4, 31, 36–7; Badiou, 'Platonism and Mathematical Ontology', 60; Norris, *Badiou's Being and Event*, 39.
42 Badiou, *Being and Event*, 40-1, 44–5, 48. See Hallward, Introduction, 3–4.
43 Badiou, *Being and Event*, 25, 28.
44 Hallward, *Badiou*, 90.
45 Badiou, *Being and Event*, 24, 29.
46 Ibid., 24–5, 29.
47 Ibid., 56.
48 Badiou, *Manifesto*, 124; Badiou, *Being and Event*, 55–8, 93. In Badiou's own terms, '[t]he void is the name of being – of inconsistency – according to a

situation, inasmuch as presentation gives us therein an unpresentable access, thus non-access, to this access, in the mode of what is not-one, or composable of ones; thus what is qualifiable within the situation solely as the errancy of nothing' (ibid., 56).

49 Ibid., 93–4.

50 Ibid., 94; Brassier, *Nihil Unbound*, 102–4.

51 Badiou, *Logics of Worlds*, 118–20.

52 Hallward, Introduction, 2.

53 Badiou, 'Event as Trans-Being', 102; Badiou, *Being and Event*, 191, 198.

54 Badiou, 'Event as Trans-Being', 100–1.

55 Hallward, *Badiou*, 99.

56 Because the event cuts across being, but does not emerge from it, so to speak, he defines it as 'trans-ontological' ('Event as Trans-Being', 101).

57 Badiou, *Ethics*, 68–9; Badiou, 'Event as Trans-Being', 103.

58 An event is an 'originary disappearance supplementing the situation for the duration of a lightning flash; situated within it only in so far as nothing of it subsists' (Badiou, 'Truth', 124).

59 Badiou, *Manifesto*, 21–2, 81; Badiou, 'Eight Theses', 147-8; Hallward, *Badiou*, xxiii.

60 Badiou defines the subject as 'a *finite* moment of the generic procedure [of a truth]' (*Manifesto,* 108). Truth, as Badiou defines it, is neither a transcendental position to be accessed (Badiou, 'Truth', 128), nor a question of accurate correspondence between cause and effect. Rather, it is 'construct[ed], bit by bit' (*Ethics*, 67–8) – what Badiou terms a generic multiple – in the sense that it contains no single 'predicative trait' (Badiou, 'Truth', 123) that predetermines its content; (Badiou, 'Eight Theses', 154; Hallward, *Badiou*, xxiii), it is indiscernible from the objective perspective of an existential situation alone (ibid., xxvii; Badiou, 'Truth', 132), and must finally be recognized in terms of a decision and the commitment to which it gives rise (ibid., 124). Truth is infinite to the extent that its consequences are indefinite (*Manifesto*, 81), constitutively undecidable, and yet elicit the potential for infinite affirmation (Badiou, 'Eight Theses', 149–50). In this sense, truth reinvigorates the universal, presenting 'an incalculable emergence, rather than a describable structure' (ibid., 146), a 'universalizing diagonal' (ibid., 153) which is constitutively incomplete and open, for all time, and potentially for everyone capable of expressing their fidelity (ibid., 153–4; *Manifesto*, 81).

61 Badiou draws on the set-theoretical lineage of Dedekind, Cantor, Zermelo and Gödel, criticizing the logical (Frege and Russell) and formalist (Peano and Hilbert) reduction of numerical thought to protocol (*Number and Numbers*, 7–11).

62 Badiou, 'Platonism and Mathematical Ontology', 60.
63 Badiou, *Being and Event*, 55–8.
64 Ibid., 146.
65 Ibid., 96.
66 Badiou, 'Destruction, Negation, Subtraction'. http://www.lacan.com/badpas.htm (accessed 24 June 2017).
67 Rasch and Wolfe, Introduction, 14.
68 Donald Judd, *Untitled (Six boxes)*, 1974. National Gallery of Australia. http://artsearch.nga.gov.au/Detail-LRG.cfm?IRN=14962 (accessed 24 June 2017).
69 Frank Stella, *Empress of India*, 1965. Museum of Modern Art, New York. http://www.moma.org/collection/works/79806 (accessed 24 June 2017).
70 Fried, 'Three American Painters', 233.
71 Badiou, *Number and Numbers*, 2–3.
72 Ibid., 3.
73 Serres, *Genesis*, 6–7, 13–14; Badiou, 'The Subject of Art'. http://www.lacan.com/symptom6_articles/badiou.html (accessed 24 June 2017).
74 See Hegel, *Phenomenology of Spirit*, 69; Forster, 'Hegel's Dialectical Method', 132.
75 Husserl aims to clarify internality and externality by establishing the independence of the realm of empirical consciousness from the external world of spatial and temporal conditions: '[*w*]*e put out of action the general positing which belongs to the essence of the natural attitude;* we parenthesize everything which that positing encompasses with respect to being: *thus the whole natural world* which is continually "there for us"' (*Ideas*, 61).
76 Sim, *Manifesto for Silence*, 87.
77 Beckett, 'Sounds', 268.
78 Beckett, 'The Unnamable', *Three Novels*, 413.
79 Ibid.
80 Ibid.
81 Dauenhauer, *Silence*, 24.
82 Ibid.
83 Ibid., 21–3.
84 Serres, *Genesis*, 13.
85 See Richards and Kidd, 'Audition', 48–9.
86 Selective auditory attention refers to the 'process by which the perception of certain stimuli in the environment is enhanced relative to other concurrent stimuli of lesser immediate priority' (Waldorff, 'Auditory Attention', 50).
87 The phenomenon of masking is discussed by Richards and Kidd, 'Audition', 48.
88 Lippard, 'As Painting is to Sculpture', 120–9.
89 Strickland, *Minimalism: Origins*, 124.

90 As Strickland suggests, the work is more accurately described as monochordal than as monotonal (ibid., 35).

91 See Weitemeier, *Yves Klein*, 55.

92 Ibid., 11.

93 See Strickland, *Minimalism: Origins*, 139–40, 145, 157; Schwartz, *Minimalists*, 39; John Schaeffer, 'Who Is La Monte Young?', 31; Nyman, *Experimental Music*, 121.

94 Ibid., 157.

95 Potter, *Four Musical Minimalists*, 22.

96 See Nyman, *Experimental Music*, 119–21.

97 Meyer, *Minimalism: Art and Polemics*, 163.

98 Morris, 'Notes on Sculpture', 228.

99 Compare ibid., 226–8 and Fried's 'Art and Objecthood', 123–8.

100 Bernstein, *A Poetics*, 66.

101 Ibid., 25.

102 Ibid., 70.

103 Ibid., 64.

104 McCaffery, *Panopticon*, 39.

105 Ibid., 34.

106 Ibid.

107 Ibid., 35.

108 Ibid., 34.

109 Derrida, 'Ellipsis', 373.

110 Lora-Totino, 'FINITEINFINITE', 94–5.

111 It is worth noting the resonance of this sequence with a number of Beckett pieces, and especially 'Imagination Dead Imagine'.

112 McCaffery, *Panopticon*, 40.

113 Ibid.

114 Ibid.

115 Ibid., 39–40.

116 Nyman notes that in Young's music 'one is able to hear what is happening while it is happening (even if one is not aware of why it is happening)' (*Experimental Music*, 123).

117 Badiou, *Being and Event*, 23–4; 40–8

118 Ibid., 27.

119 Ibid., 25, 28.

120 Ibid., 24–5, 29.

121 Badiou, *Manifesto*, 124.

122 Badiou, *Being and Event*, 56–7.

123 Ibid., 93–4.

124 For a detailed discussion of some of these processes see Botha, 'Evental Distension', 261–88.

125 Fink, *Repeating Ourselves*, 20.

126 See ibid., 5; Mertens, *American Minimal Music*, 13–17; Miller, *Fiction and Repetition*, 7–8.

127 Ibid., 3.

128 Mertens, *American Minimal Music*, 17; Miller, *Fiction and Repetition*, 7–11.

129 Mertens, *American Minimal Music*, 17.

130 Fink, *Repeating Ourselves*, 44.

131 Ibid., 44–5.

132 Mertens, *American Minimal Music*, 17.

133 Fink, *Repeating Ourselves*, 43.

134 Ibid., 44–5.

135 Ibid., 46.

136 Botha, 'Evental Distension', 271–2.

137 Ibid., 272–3.

138 As a hypothetical example, we might take the sequence of notes, C-D-E-F.

139 For example, C-D-E-F-*G*, where *G* is clearly a single note supplement.

140 For example, C-D-E-F-*C-D-E-F-G*, where the italicized *C-D-E-F-G* is the supplement.

141 Using the example above, C-D-E-F-C-D-E-F-*G*, where *G* is added to the sequence C-D-E-F in order to constitute the sequences which supplement the original.

142 The subtractive version of what is still an additive sequence (in the sense that a sequence is still being added to the original) would be C-D-E-F-C-D-E, where *F* has been subtracted from the original sequence in order to constitute the sequence which supplements the original.

143 The repetition of C-D-E-F would be followed by C-D-E, and so forth. This should be distinguished from subtraction which still takes place in an added sequence, since the processual logic remains additive in such cases, as is predominantly the case in Glass' *Two Pages*.

144 Potter, *Four Musical Minimalists*, 287–8.

145 Page, Liner notes, n.p.

146 Beckett, 'what is the word', 129–34.

147 Ibid., 131.

148 Ibid., 131–2.

149 Ibid., 132.

150 On the 'resonance and density' of literary language as a mark of its facticity, see Fynsk, *Language and Relation*, 7.

151 Beckett, 'what is the word', 132.

152 Ibid., 132, 134.
153 On negative presentation, see Agamben, 'Messiah and the Sovereign', 172–4.
154 Lyotard, 'Sublime and the Avant-Garde', 92.
155 Ibid.
156 Lax, *word*, 9.
157 Derrida, 'Ellipsis', 378.
158 Badiou, *Being and Event*, 93–4.
159 Sol LeWitt, *Maquette for One, Two, Three*, 1979. Smithsonian American Art Museum. http://americanart.si.edu/collections/search/artwork/?id=14689 (accessed 24 June 2017).
160 Marzona, *Minimal Art*, 68.
161 Ibid.
162 Ibid.
163 Rorimer, 'Approaches to Seriality', 70.
164 Badiou, 'Truth', 129.
165 Badiou, *Being and Event*, 146. See also ibid., 267–75.
166 Dan Flavin, *the nominal three (to William of Ockham)*, 1964. Guggenheim Museum, New York. http://www.guggenheim.org/artwork/1294 (accessed 24 June 2017).
167 Govan, 'Irony and Light', 37.
168 Dan Flavin, qtd in ibid., 38.
169 Ibid., 37.
170 Kant, *Critique of Judgment*, 103. While the Kantian formulation of the sublime privileges an encounter with nature over artifice, it also recognizes that 'sublimity is contained not in any thing of nature, but only in our mind, insofar as we can become conscious of our superiority to nature within us, and thereby also to the nature outside us' (ibid., 123). More recent views, following an increasingly scientific understanding of the sublime feeling (see Shaw, *The Sublime*, 49–50) recognize that the sublime is distributed between natural, artificial and technological phenomena (Deguy, 'The Discourse of Exaltation', 12–13; Shaw, *The Sublime*, 7–8, 28, 124). Indeed, for Kant the distinction is not absolute, but relates to teleological judgment: '[g]iven that we find something purposelike in nature's products, let us call nature's procedure (causality) a technic' (Kant, *Critique of Judgment*, 271).
171 Burke, *Philosophical Enquiry*, 39.
172 Ibid., 107.
173 Ibid.
174 Ibid., 119–20.
175 Lyotard, *Lessons*, 90.
176 Ibid., 95.
177 Nico Muhly, email and recorded interview, 12–22 November 2011.

178 Beckett, 'Molloy', 70.
179 Ibid., 69–70.
180 Ibid., 30.
181 Ibid.
182 Ibid.
183 Beckett, 'A Piece of Monologue', 425.
184 Aragon, 'Suicide', qtd in Pegrum, *Challenging Modernity*, 265.
185 Drucker, 'Visual Performance of the Poetic Text', 147.
186 Ibid.
187 Andersen, 'I Have Confidence in You', n.p.

Chapter 6: Austerity: On the Lessness of Minimalism

1 Wyschogrod, 'Howl of Oedipus', 16.
2 Wimbush and Valantasis, Introduction, xix.
3 Ibid., xxviii.
4 Thurman, 'Tibetan Buddhist Perspectives', 108.
5 Harpham, *The Ascetic Imperative*, xi.
6 Thurman, 'Tibetan Buddhist Perspectives', 110–12.
7 Finn, *Asceticism*, 9–11.
8 Ware, 'Way of Ascetics', 2–3.
9 Wolf, *Poverty of Riches*, 57–64.
10 Wyschogrod, 'Howl of Oedipus', 18.
11 Ibid., 19.
12 Ibid., 22.
13 Ibid., 23.
14 Ibid.
15 Ware, 'Way of the Ascetics', 8.
16 Wyschogrod, 'Howl of Oedipus', 26.
17 Harpham, *Ascetic Imperative*, xiii.
18 Ibid.
19 Asceticism can be regarded in 'aesthetic terms because it is symbolic. Ascetic discipline … points beyond itself' (Harpham, *Ascetic Imperative*, xiv).
20 'Asceticism is not merely capable of assuming a multitude of forms; it is the form-producing agent itself' (ibid.).
21 Shui, *Austerity*, 6–9.
22 Ibid., 2.
23 Blyth, *Austerity*, 10.
24 'In sum, austerity is a dangerous idea for three reasons: it doesn't work in

practice, it relies on the poor paying for the mistakes of the rich, and it rests upon the absence of a rather large fallacy of composition [which mistakenly asserts that what is true of the whole is true for the parts] that is all too present in the modern world'. (ibid.)

25 Agamben identifies Aristotle as the classical source of what is often misdiagnosed as a predominantly Romantic phenomenon (Agamben, *Stanzas*, 12–13).

26 Ibid., 26.

27 According to the Carthusians – arguably the most austere religious order of the Western church, which, along with the Carmelites and Camaldolese Benedictines sought to revive the eremitic tradition of the early desert fathers within a broadly cenobitic or communal framework – silence and solitude are pivotal to the religious life for the way they 'enkindle [...] and nurture [...] in our hearts the fire of divine love, which is the bond of perfection' (*Statutes of the Carthusian Order*, Ch. 3, para. 5. http://www.chartreux.org/en/texts/statutes-book-1.php#haut [accessed 24 June 2017]). See Anonymous, *The Wound of Love*, 19–24, 61–90; Damian, *Language of Silence*, 16–21, 97–104.

28 See Ware, 'Way of the Ascetics', 4–9.

29 Hesiod, *Theogony*, 24.

30 Benedict, *Rule of Saint Benedict*, 49.

31 Raitt, 'European Reformations', 136.

32 Francis of Assisi, 'Salutation of the Virtues', 151–2.

33 Beckett, 'For to end yet again', 243.

34 El Greco, *Saint Francis Praying*, 1580–5. Joclyn Art Museum, Omaha. https://www.joslyn.org/collections-and-exhibitions/permanent-collections/european/el-greco-saint-francis-in-prayer/ (accessed 24 June 2017).

35 Although Foucault has little to say about the cell specifically, he draws several interesting structural parallels between the monastic and penitentiary systems (*Discipline and Punish*, 238, 243–4).

36 Ibid., 235. Foucault borrows this term from the writing of Baltard (ibid.).

37 *Statutes of the Carthusian Order*, Ch. 1, para. 1; Ch. 3, para. 1. http://www.chartreux.org/en/texts/statutes-prologue.php#haut and http://www.chartreux.org/en/texts/statutes-book-1.php#haut (accessed 24 June 2017).

38 Guenther, *Solitary Confinement*, xvi.

39 Ibid., 10–11.

40 Foucault, *Discipline and Punish*, 233.

41 Ibid. 234–5.

42 Foucault, *Discipline and Punish*, 231.

43 Guenther, *Solitary Confinement*, xxiii.

44 Ibid., xiii.

45 Ibid., 155–6.

46 Davis, *Mysticism and Space*, 46.
47 Ibid., 38–9.
48 Maguire, *Infinity of Little Hours*, 26.
49 Ibid., 64.
50 Ibid., 27. For illustrations of Carthusian monasteries, cells and the monastic life see http://www.chartreux.org/en/monks/diaporamas-monk.php (accessed 24 June 2017).
51 Rose, 'ABC Art', 296.
52 Rancière, 'The Surface of Design', 91.
53 Forrestall, 'Church in the Tridentine and Early Modern Eras', 100–1. See also Raitt, 'European Reformations', 133.
54 Ibid. See also Sim, *Manifesto for Silence*, 7–9.
55 Corrigan, 'Protestantism in the United States', 171.
56 These 'experiments typically had a religious or spiritual as well as a social animus' (Baker, *Minimalism*, 14).
57 Their official name, The United Society of Believers in Christ's Second Appearing, reflects their eschatological belief in 'the Holy Spirit … "shaking" the whole community in a kind of prophetic earthquake. The eschatological charity of the order produced an inward power which, they believed, would "shake" the world and prepare it for the millennial renewal' (Merton, *Seeking Paradise*, 55–6).
58 By viewing God as both paternal and maternal, the Shakers organized themselves into families which consisted of both brothers and sisters (Corrigan, 'Protestantism', 171). These families lived in single houses although, doubtless for practical reasons of maintaining their strict celibacy, maintained a certain practical distance.
59 Merton, *Seeking Paradise*, 76–7.
60 Baker, *Minimalism*, 14.
61 Corrigan, 'Protestantism', 171.
62 Most contemporary minimalism is functionless in an objective sense. However, it does not merely reverse functionalism, but in many cases instigates a critique of consumerism by offering itself as a parody of its own functionlessness (Lasch, *Minimal Self*, 31).
63 Merton, *Seeking Paradise*, 97.
64 Ibid., 63–4, 92–5.
65 Ibid., 79.
66 Baker, *Minimalism*, 14.
67 Merton, *Seeking Paradise*, 66.
68 Ibid., 85.
69 Roston, *Modernist Patterns*, 129.
70 See Cheviakoff, *Minimal Art*, 72–7.

71 Gerrit Rietveld, *Zig-Zag Chair*, 1934. Museum of Modern Art, New York. http://www.moma.org/collection/works/3477?locale=en (accessed 24 June 2017).
72 Donald Judd, *Chair 84/85*, 1991. Chinati Foundation, Marfa. http://juddfoundation.org/artist/furniture/wood-furniture/ (accessed 24 June 2017).
73 See Meyer, *Minimalism: Art and Polemics*, 7; Cheviakoff, *Minimal Art*, 110.
74 Roston, *Modernist Patterns*, 129.
75 Strickland, *Minimalism: Origins*, 20; Foster, *Return of the Real*, 52.
76 Merton, *Seeking Paradise*, 81.
77 Baker, *Minimalism*, 13.
78 Cheviakoff, *Minimal Art*, 80.
79 Adams, Liner notes, *Violin Concerto and Shaker Loops*, 6.
80 Merton, *Seeking Paradise*, 59.
81 Adams, Liner notes, *Violin Concerto and Shaker Loops*, 6.
82 Schwartz, 'Process vs. Intuition', 246–7.
83 Adams, 'Conversation', 78; Schwartz, *Minimalists*, 177.
84 Powell, 'Accessible Narratives', 405.
85 Ibid., 393.
86 Ibid., 401.
87 Powell refers to an 'over-saturation of tonal possibilities' (ibid.).
88 Ibid., 398.
89 Merton, *Seeking Paradise*, 80.
90 Strickland, *Minimalism: Origins*, 3. See also Colpitt, *Minimal Art*, 1; Schwartz, *Minimalists*, 10; and Meyer, *Minimalism: Art and Polemics*, 34.
91 Rose, 'ABC Art', 296.
92 Ibid.
93 Mertens, *American Minimal Music*, 12, 32, 44, 56, 67, 91–2.
94 Schwartz, *Minimalists*, 22–3; Mertens, *American Minimal Music*, 35.
95 Ibid., 44-5; Potter, *Four Musical Minimalists*, 19, 79–80, 103–4, 137. According to Rose, '[t]he 'continuum' of La Monte Young's *Dream music* is analogous in its endlessness to the Maya of Hindu cosmology' (Rose, 'ABC Art', 296).
96 Ibid, 259; Fink, *Repeating Ourselves*, 231; Schwartz, *Minimalists*, 117.
97 Ibid., 83–9.
98 Ibid., 88.
99 Monk, 'Mission Statement', 17
100 Siegel, 'Virgin Vessel', 36–9.
101 Sterritt, 'Notes', 108–9.
102 Brauneiss, 'Musical Archetypes', 52.
103 Ibid., 50.
104 Scholl, 'Arvo Pärt and Spirituality', 144–5; Botonia, 'Bells as Inspiration for Tintinnabulation', 129.

105 Ibid., 128.
106 Brauneiss, 'Musical Archetypes', 52.
107 Shenton, 'Pärt in His Own Words', 120.
108 Arvo Pärt, qtd in Brauneiss, 'Musical Archetypes', 52.
109 Scholl, 'Arvo Pärt and Spirituality', 142. An arpeggiated triad refers to a three-note chord where each note is sounded separately rather than together.
110 Brauneiss, 'Musical Archetypes', 51.
111 Ibid., 52.
112 Ibid., 62.
113 Ibid.
114 Scholl, Arvo Pärt and Spirituality', 143; Shenton, 'Pärt In His Own Words', 119–20.
115 Ibid., 120.
116 Rose, 'ABC Art', 285–6.
117 Meyer, *Minimalism*, 24.
118 Lyotard, 'Newman: The Instant', 84–7. Although, as Meyer notes, 'the Minimalists … rejected the metaphysical claims of the Abstract Expressionists … Even so, there were some artists associated with Minimalism who did not discount the expressive potential of pared-down abstraction' (Meyer, *Minimalism*, 24).
119 Agnes Martin, Interview with Chuck Smith and Sono Kuwayama, November 2007. http://vimeo.com/7127385 (accessed 24 June 2017).
120 Foster, 'Dan Flavin', 141–2.
121 Dan Flavin in Foster, 'Dan Flavin', 139.
122 Foster, 'Dan Flavin', 142.
123 Govan, 'Irony and Light', 100, 103.
124 Botha, 'Microfiction', 209–10.
125 Cage, *Conversing*, 65.
126 Hauff, *Line in Three Circles*, 134.
127 Beer, Introduction, xi–xii. For a more intimate view of this friendship it is necessary to examine the many letters exchanged between them, a selection of which were published in the journal *Voyages* (Merton and Lax, 'Catch of Anti-Letters', 44–56).
128 Hauff, *Line in Three Circles*, 48.
129 Beer, Introduction, xiv.
130 Here it is worth recalling that, for Lucretius, the laminar flow or downward fall of atoms constitutes the basic substance of the universe which is occasionally subject to a swerve within this fall – an event that brings a world into existence (Lucretius, *On the Nature*, 42–4). In this sense, Lax's poetry potentially opens a space of reading that mirrors the Lucretian generative event – the simultaneity of fall and swerve.

131 Lax, 'jacob & the angel', 129–33.

132 Hauff, *Line in Three Circles*, 48.

133 Karen Alexander describes Lax as a 'conceptual Minimalist' (*Minimalism in Twentieth Century*, 184). Beer, on the other hand, questions the habitual association of Lax with minimalism, although it should be noted that his definition of minimalism is considerably narrower than the one adopted in the present work (Introduction, xix).

134 Finlay, *Model of Order*, 44.

135 Ibid., 54.

136 Finlay, 'Arcady', 8.

137 Steiner, *Colour of Rhetoric*, 2–5. According to Bohn, Steiner traces the dissolution of not only 'the traditional barriers between the reader and text; it erases the boundaries between the text and the world' (Bohn, *Aesthetics of Visual Poetry*, 8).

138 Perloff and Dworkin, Introduction, 1.

139 Plato, 'Republic', 607b/1211.

140 See Plato, 'Phaedo', 103e/89. As Warren Montag notes: '[t]he current description of art and culture as simulacra are quite simply Platonic in the most traditional sense … Plato argued that the particular is a representation of the form and that art is a representation of the particular and thus a representation of a representation … His denunciation of art as mere appearance is not based on the hypothesis of its immateriality but precisely the opposite: its irreducible materiality' ('What is at Stake?' 98). See also Danto, *Transfiguration*, 7–9; 11–14; Deleuze, *Logic of Sense*, 253–9. In his epochal essay, 'The Art World', Danto begins from a similar position but reaches a different conclusion: distinguishing between the *imitation theory* of art, in which art is fundamentally mimetic, and the *reality theory* of art, in which art is fundamentally productive, he suggests that through the latter artists are 'to be understood not as unsuccessfully imitating real forms but as successfully creating new ones, quite as real as the forms which the older art has been thought … to be credibly imitating' (28).

141 Bowler, *The Word as Image*, 7–8, 119. Notable examples exist in almost all ancient cultures, and such talismans are by no means uncommon in the contemporary world (ibid).

142 Ibid.

143 Ibid., 9.

144 Simias of Rhodes's egg calligram is meant to be read from the outside towards the centre, making a semantic point on the nature of poetry, which, like the egg, is a self-contained form which carries within it the potential for production, or new life.

145 Ibid., 128.

146 Amuletic tughra, Iran. Date unspecified (ibid., 29). 'Tughra writings are the most

ingenious use of Arabic script. A sentence from the Koran or a common prayer is written in a way that the composition outlines a [form]' (ibid., 124). In this example, a face is composed of four words – Allah, Mohammed, Ali and Hassan – which mirror each other to make up the left and right halves of the face (ibid.).

147 Sloane, *The Visual in Metaphysical Poetry*, 24.

148 Bowler, *The Word as Image*, 129.

149 This impulse might be traced to ancient Dionysian and Orphic cults in Greece which emphasise *enthusiasm*, or, as it was then understood, the fusion of the human and the divine (Russell, *History*, 24–7, 30–1).

150 Steiner, *Colors of Rhetoric*, 14. See Wellek and Warren, *Theory of Literature*, 126.

151 Ibid., xiii.

152 Higgins, 'Points Towards a Taxonomy', 51.

153 Roubaud, 'Prelude: Poetry and Orality', 18.

154 Higgins proposes eight classes of sound poetry: 'folk varieties … onomatopoeic or mimetic pieces … nonsense poetries which trope their own languages' ('Points Towards a Taxonomy', 50) and the more contemporary expressions of 'works in an invented language … near-nonsense works … phatic poems [in which semantic meanings of sonic units are defamiliarized by various techniques of statement (ibid., 45–6)] … unwritten-out poems … notated ones' (ibid., 50).

155 McCaffery, 'Sound Poetry – A Survey', http://www.ubu.com/papers/mccaffery.html (accessed 24 June 2017).

156 Ibid.

157 Comotti, *Music in Greek and Roman Culture*, 16; West, *Ancient Greek Music*, 14–15; Aristotle, *Poetics*, 4. The most significant of these hymns are the *paean* and *dithyramb* – the former dedicated to Apollo, the latter to Dionysus – the same opposition from which arises the 'Dionysian madness … from which both the tragic and comic arts emerged' according to Nietzsche (*Birth of Tragedy*, 7).

158 Comotti, *Music in Greek and Roman Culture*, 6; West, *Ancient Greek Music*, 24–6.

159 Aristotle, *Poetics*, 9–11; 42–5.

160 West, *Ancient Greek Music*, 40–1; Calame, 'The Tragic Choral Group', 216.

161 Ibid., 217–18.

162 Ibid. See Aristotle, *Poetics*, 4; Plato, 'Ion', 532d/ 940.

163 West, *Ancient Greek Music*, 45. See also Comotti, *Music in Greek and Roman Culture*, 12.

164 Ibid., 2–3; West, *Ancient Greek Music*, 7.

165 Ibid., 4–6; Cole, *Sounds and Signs*, 7–8; Comotti, *Music in Greek and Roman Culture*, 2–3, 99.

166 Ibid., 12, 99–103; West, *Ancient Greek Music*, 7; Cole, *Sounds and Signs*, 7.

167 The comparative study of chant reveals four principal types: recitative, using a single tone for an entire text; syllabic, where each syllable is assigned a specific

tone to constitute a melody; neumatic, which includes occasional embellishments; and melismatic which involves elaborate melodic material and ornamentation.

168 O'Grady, *Last Troubadours*, 5; Donington, *Rise of Opera*, 19.

169 Ibid.

170 Stewart, 'Rhyme and Freedom', 36.

171 Donington, *Rise of Opera*, 19.

172 See Higgins, 'Points Towards a Taxonomy', 25.

173 Donington, *Rise of Opera*, 68.

174 *Sprechgesang* (and the later *Sprechstimme*) is a style between speech and song, similar to the recitative of earlier opera, although stylistically more punctuated than the verse of early opera and classical tragedy.

175 Ibid.

176 Perloff, *21st Century Modernism*, 131.

177 Butler, *Early Modernism*, 146.

178 Perloff, *21st Century Modernism*, 124–5.

179 Bök, 'When Cyborgs Versify', 130.

180 Alexey Kruchenykh, *zok zok zok*. Sound source undated. http://www.ubu.com/sound/phonetische.html (accessed 24 June 2017).

181 Nancy Perloff, 'Sound Poetry', 101–2, 104–5.

182 Perloff, *21st Century Modernism*, 143–4.

183 Ibid., 126.

184 Ibid.

185 Ibid., 124.

186 Ibid., 134.

187 Ibid., 125.

188 Khlebnikov, 'Incantation by Laughter', in Nancy Perloff, 'Sound Poetry', 101.

189 Perloff, *21st Century Modernism*, 141.

190 Khlebnikov and Kruchenykh, 'The Letter as Such', *Manifesto*, 237.

191 Perloff, *21st Century Modernism*, 127.

192 Pegrum, *Challenging Modernity*, 262; Bök, 'When Cyborgs Versify', 131.

193 Rothenberg and Joris, Introduction, xvii.

194 Dachy, *Dada*, 37–8.

195 Drucker, 'Visual Performance', 139.

196 Ibid., 31–2.

197 Attridge, *Poetic Rhythm*, 4.

198 Perloff, *21st Century Modernism*, 153.

199 Ibid., 4; Stewart, 'Rhyme and Freedom', 43.

200 Ibid., 41.

201 Agamben, *Coming Community*, 73.

202 With respect to the name, Agamben distinguishes between the synonym and the

homonym in terms of a tension between object, idea and concept. He suggests that objects are synonymous in relation to the concept through which their identity is amplified, which grants them 'the same name and the same definition' (*Coming Community*, 75). These 'become homonyms if considered with respect to the idea' (ibid.) and have 'the same name, but different definitions' (ibid.). The present suggestion is that there is a fruitful comparison to be drawn between the homonym and homophone, the name understood in this context as the imperfect sign for what is singular to a particular entity.

203 Agamben, *Signature of All Things*, 23, 32.
204 Stecopoulos, *Visceral Poetics*, 7.
205 Ibid.
206 Ibid., 9.
207 Menezes, 'Intersign Poetry', 262.
208 Isou, 'Manifesto of Lettrist Poetry', 545–6.
209 Ibid., 545.
210 Ibid., 546.
211 Agamben, 'Idea of Language', 42.
212 Mills, *Philosophy of Agamben*, 17.
213 Ibid.
214 Agamben, *Language and Death*, xiii. See de la Durantaye, *Giorgio Agamben*, 178.
215 Agamben, 'Idea of Language', 42.
216 Agamben, *Language and Death*, 86.
217 Ibid., 99.
218 Mills, *Philosophy of Agamben*, 21.
219 Agamben, *Language and Death*, 92.
220 Agamben, 'Idea of Language', 43.
221 Cage, 'Empty Words', 51.
222 Agamben, *Language and Death*, 95.
223 Ibid., 96. See Mills, *Philosophy of Agamben*, 12.
224 Monk, 'From Liner Notes', 167.
225 Nussbaum, *Upheavals of Thought*, 58.
226 Agamben, *Language and Death*, 96.
227 Monk, 'From Liner Notes', 168.
228 Ibid., 167.
229 Nussbaum, *Fragility of Goodness*, xii.
230 Despite the ubiquity of the technological mediation of the voice and its remarkable poetic potential, Bök notes that 'only a spartan coterie of sound poets have ever committed themselves to the use of such technology' ('When Cyborgs Versify', 132).
231 Connor, *Dumbstruck*, 35–6. See ibid., 127–35 regarding the technological mediation of the voice more generally.

232 Ibid., 35–6.

233 Bök, 'When Cyborgs Versify', 130.

Chapter 7: Minimum: On the Extremes of Minimalism

1 Reinhardt, 'Twelve Rules', 205–7.

2 Strickland, *Minimalism: Origins*, 45.

3 Ibid.

4 Ibid., 51.

5 Bois, 'Painting: The Task of Mourning', 230–1.

6 Reinhardt, 'Twelve Rules', 206.

7 Ibid., 205–7.

8 Ad Reinhardt, *Number 107*, 1950. Museum of Modern Art, New York. http://www.moma.org/collection/works/80269?locale=en (accessed 24 June 2017).

9 Ad Reinhardt, *Abstract Painting*, 1957. Museum of Modern Art, New York. http://www.moma.org/collection/works/79265?locale=en (accessed 24 June 2017).

10 Strickland, *Minimalism: Origins*, 44.

11 Lyotard, 'Sublime and the Avant-Garde', 90.

12 Ibid., 101.

13 Watten, *The Constructivist Moment*, 240.

14 See Chave, 'Minimalism and the Rhetoric of Power', 49–53.

15 Bruce Nauman, *Clown Torture*, 1987. Art Institute of Chicago. http://www.artic.edu/aic/collections/artwork/146989 (accessed 27 June 2017).

16 Schaffner, 'Circling Oblivion', 171.

17 Art Institute of Chicago. Notes. *Clown Torture Series*, Art Institute of Chicago. http://www.artic.edu/aic/collections/artwork/146989 (accessed 24 June 2017).

18 Danto, 'Bruce Nauman', 150.

19 Schaffner, 'Circling Oblivion', 170.

20 See Danto, 'Bruce Nauman', 151; Shaffer, 'Circling Oblivion', 172.

21 Ibid., 169.

22 It is worth recalling Agamben's remarkable formulation regarding the incompleteness of any act of testimony: 'language, in order to bear witness, must give way to a non-language…to show the impossibility of bearing witness. The language of testimony is a language that no longer signifies and that, in not signifying, advances into what is without language … To bear witness … [i]t is necessary that this senseless sound be, in turn, the voice of something or someone that, for entirely other reasons, cannot bear witness' (*Remnants of Auschwitz*, 39; also 33–4).

23 According to Agamben, the witness is 'a person who has lived through something

who has experienced an event from beginning to end and can therefore bear witness to it' (ibid., 17).

24 Benezra, 'Surveying Nauman', 140.
25 Adams, 'The Nauman Phenomenon', 78.
26 Schaffner, 'Circling Oblivion', 171.
27 Beckett, 'Endgame', 98, 107.
28 Schaffner, 'Circling Oblivion', 168.
29 Wall, *Radical Passivity*, 27.
30 Blanchot, 'The Essential Solitude', 64.
31 Robbe-Grillet, 'Some Outdated Notions', 71–2.
32 Meillassoux, *After Finitude*, 53–4.
33 See ibid., 63–5.
34 Ibid., 62.
35 Ibid., 60.
36 Ibid., 65. In absolutizing facticity, Meillassoux does not 'maintain that a determinate entity exists, but that it is absolutely necessary that every entity might not exist' (ibid., 60).
37 Weller, *Taste for the Negative*, 59.
38 Similar remarks might be made of artists working with as diverse materials and media as do Reinhardt, Nauman, Feldman and Blanchot (among many others).
39 According to Chieregin, '[i]n order to exist, something must be determinate: of the completely undetermined it is impossible to say or to know anything' ('Freedom and Thought', 62).
40 Ibid. In Hegel's own terms, entities are 'only determinate in so far as they *differentiate* themselves from one another, and *relate* themselves *to others* as to their opposite' (*Phenomenology of Spirit*, 69).
41 Ibid., 124.
42 Ibid., 21
43 Forster, 'Hegel's Dialectical Method', 132.
44 Chieregin, 'Freedom and Thought', 62.
45 Forster, 'Hegel's Dialectial Method', 133.
46 Badiou, *Being and Event*, 163.
47 Norris, *Badiou's Being and Event*, 144–7.
48 Ibid., 147.
49 Stein, 'Composition as Explanation', 23.
50 See Beckett, 'Texts for Nothing', 116.
51 Beckett, 'Endgame', 98, 107.
52 Beckett, 'Ill Seen Ill Said', 80, 84–5.
53 Ibid.
54 Ibid., 81.

55 Ibid., 64.
56 Beckett, 'Texts for Nothing', 116.
57 Mills, *Philosophy of Agamben*, 21.
58 Ibid.
59 According to Agamben, '[t]o exist in language without being called there by any voice, simply to die without being called by death, is, perhaps the most abysmal experience; but this is precisely, for man, also his most habitual experience' (*Language and Death*, 96).
60 Ibid., 56.
61 See Beckett, 'The Unnamable', 381–2.
62 Beckett, 'For to end yet again', 246.
63 Beckett, 'Heard in the Dark I', 147.
64 Beckett, 'Footfalls', 401.
65 Ibid., 403.
66 Agamben, *Coming Community*, 14–15.
67 Ibid., 15.
68 Ibid.
69 Richard Serra, *Gutter Corner Splash: Night Shift* (1969/1995). https://www.sfmoma.org/artwork/91.30 (accessed 24 June 2017).
70 Ibid.
71 Baker, *Minimalism*, 112.
72 Marzona, *Minimal Art*, 86.
73 Strickland, *Minimalism: Origins*, 290.
74 Chave, 'Minimalism and the Rhetoric of Power', 59. Chave's reference is to Serra's massive and often perilously balanced lead sheets and steel stacks, some of which are part of his ominously titled *Skullcracker* series of sculptures. The installation of Serra's sculptures has caused several injuries and even a death (ibid., 58–9; Strickland, *Minimalism: Origins*, 290). In Strickland's estimation, this perilous art connects it to a minimalist tradition of the sublime traceable to Barnett Newman (ibid., 270, 291). However, it is necessary to emphasize, with Kant, that if the feeling of the sublime arises from a 'momentary inhabitation of the vital forces' (Kant, *Critique of Judgment*, 98) it is affirmed when this is 'followed immediately by an outpouring of [these vital forces] … that is all the stronger' (ibid.), which cannot be the case if danger spills into destruction or death.
75 Mayer, 'fortführungen', 202.
76 Gappmayr, 'untitled', 39.
77 Weller, *Taste for the Negative*, 82.
78 Ibid., 83.
79 Ibid.
80 Meillassoux, *After Finitude*, 5.

81 Ibid., 4.
82 Agamben, *Coming Community*, 67.
83 Beckett, 'Texts for Nothing', 154.
84 Ibid.
85 Ibid.
86 Diken, *Nihilism*, 15.
87 Ibid.
88 Ibid.
89 See McInerny, 'Saint Thomas Aquinas', http://plato.stanford.edu/entries/aquinas/ (accessed 24 June 2017); Aquinas, *Selected Philosophical Writings*, 200–2.
90 Critchley, *Very Little*, 3–4.
91 Ibid., 5–6.
92 Nietzsche, *Nietzsche Reader*, 199.
93 Critchley, *Very Little*, 7.
94 Nietzsche, *Nietzsche Reader*, 209.
95 Vattimo, *End of Modernity*, 19.
96 Critchley, *Very Little*, 8.
97 Vattimo, *End of Modernity*, 22.
98 Ibid., 24.
99 Heidegger, 'What is Metaphysics?', 108; Stone, 'Heidegger and Carnap', 222, 239.
100 Priest, 'Chapter Introduction', 135.
101 Heidegger, 'What is Metaphysics?', 95–6.
102 Ibid., 96–9. On the relation of this point of logic to ontology, Heidegger might easily be misread, or judged to be inconsistent, as he is by Paul Edwards (*Heidegger's Confusion*, 108–11).
103 Heidegger, 'What is Metaphysics?', 99.
104 Ibid.
105 Ibid., 97.
106 Ibid.
107 Heidegger adopted and adapted this term from Kierkegaard.
108 'Only in the nothing of Dasein do beings as a whole, in accord with their most proper possibility – that is, in a finite way – come to themselves' (Heidegger, 'What is Metaphysics?', 108). In this way he seeks to address the very moment of entrapment in metaphysics which, he believes, Nietzsche fails to apprehend in seeking to overcome nihilism (Critchley, *Very Little*, 13–16).
109 Sartre, *Being and Nothingness*, 22.
110 Ibid., 7–9.
111 Heidegger, 'Hölderlin and the Essence of Poetry', 65.
112 Nancy, *Creation of the World*, 51.
113 Ibid.

114 Heidegger, 'What is Metaphysics?', 103. Heidegger writes, '*Das Nichts selbst nichtet*' (ibid.), retaining *nicht* at the root of both noun and verb, the latter which has been translated as *nothings* or *noths* in addition to *nihilates*.

115 Levinas, *Existence and Existents*, 52.

116 Levinas draws attention to the centrality of the *il y a* to his project as a whole (*Is It Righteous To Be?*, 47). With respect to the question of first philosophy, Levinas maintains that '[t]he comprehension of Being in general cannot *dominate* the relationship with the Other. The latter relationship commands the first. I cannot disentangle myself from society with the Other … this relation with an *existent* … precedes all ontology; it is the ultimate relation in Being' (*Totality and Infinity*, 47–8).

117 Levinas, *Time and the Other*, 48.

118 Ibid.

119 Levinas, *Existence and Existents*, 56.

120 Robbins, *Altered Reading*, 92.

121 Levinas, *Time and the Other*, 35–6, 75–6; Levinas, 'Reality and Its Shadow', 12; Davies, 'On Resorting to an Ethical Language', 96.

122 Levinas, *Existence and Existents*, 10–12, 55, 61; Hutchens, *Levinas*, 140; Wyschogrod, *Emmanuel Levinas*, 5.

123 Levinas, *Existence and Existents*, 5, 55–8; Levinas, *Is It Righteous To Be?*, 45; Robbins, *Altered Reading*, 92.

124 *Absolute existential anonymity* would refer to a situation in which no subject or object which exists has any effect in existence. The anonymity of the *il y a* – the counterpoint to identity, which marks the hypostasis of the subject – is a principal term in Levinas's writing. See Levinas, 'Reality and Its Shadow', 9; Levinas, *Existence and Existents*, 23, 37, 44, 52, 82, 88; Levinas, *Time and the Other*, 33, 47–8, 52, 62, 65–7. See Cohen, *Ethics, Exegesis and Philosophy*, 176 and Wall, *Radical Passivity*, 5.

125 It is towards a 'being in complete silence' (Levinas, *Is It Righteous To Be?*, 212) that the 'anonymous rumbling of existence' (Levinas, *Existence and Existents*, 23) seems to point us.

126 Levinas 'characterize[s] the *there is* … by a vigilance without possible recourse to sleep', (Levinas, *Time and the Other*, 48–9), where sleep is not a state of unconsciousness, but a 'modality of being' (Levinas, *Existence and Existents*, 84). See also ibid., 55, 64; Robbins, *Altered Reading*, 94.

127 Levinas, *Time and the Other*, 35, 62; Levinas, *Existence and Existents*, 51, 76; Levinas, *Is It Righteous To Be?*, 46. The unremitting presence of the *il y a* defines existential persistence in terms of 'an abyss between the present and death' … the strangeness of the future of death' (Levinas, *Time and the Other*, 81). See also ibid., 50–1, 69–73, 81–2; Levinas *Existence and Existents*, 56–7, 77; Levinas,

'Reality and Its Shadow', 11–12; Robbins, *Altered Reading*, 92, 96; Wyschogrod, *Emmanuel Levinas*, 9

128 Levinas, *Existence and Existents*, 53.

129 Ibid., 60.

130 Heidegger, 'Hölderlin and the Essence of Poetry', 65.

131 Levinas, *Existence and Existents*, 82.

132 Levinas, *Time and the Other*, 67.

133 Levinas, *Existence and Existents*, 54.

134 Ibid., 43.

135 Ibid., 83.

136 Ibid., 67.

137 Ibid. On Levinas's anthropocentric bias regarding hypostasis, see Harman, *Tool Being*, 242.

138 Ibid., 239.

139 Ibid.

140 Levinas, *Existence and Existents*, 27.

141 Levinas, *Time and the Other*, 63.

142 Levinas, *Existence and Existents*, 38.

143 Ibid., 30.

144 Harman, *Tool Being*, 237. Llewelyn identifies in Levinas's work a 'quest for concreteness' (*Emmanuel Levinas*, 22).

145 Ibid., 241. This conception is not dissimilar to idea of distributed cognition which aims 'to put cognition back into the social and cultural world' (Hutchins, *Cognition in the Wild*, xiv) by recognizing that it is distributed across social groups, between structures of internality and externality, and through time (Glenberg, 'Radical Changes in Cognitive Process', 76).

146 Harman, *Tool Being*, 241.

147 See Llewelyn, *Emmanuel Levinas*, 28.

148 Levinas, *Existence and Existents*, 57; Levinas, *Time and the Other*, 50. See Llewelyn, *Emmanuel Levinas*, 11.

149 For Levinas infinity is apparent not only in the introspective encounter with the *il y a*, but in the extroverted nature of intersubjective existence, and in the radical alterity at the heart of our encounter with the other.

150 Levinas, *Time and the Other*, 71.

151 Levinas, 'Reality and Its Shadow', 11. See Critchley, *Very Little*, 32, 70–2; Wall, *Radical Passivity*, 24.

152 Levinas, 'Reality and Its Shadow', 11.

153 Levinas, *Time and the Other*, 73. 'It is nothingness that would have left humankind the possibility of assuming death and snatching a supreme mastery from out of the servitude of existence' (ibid.).

154 Levinas, 'Reality and Its Shadow', 11. See also Levinas, *Time and the Other*, 50–1.
155 Critchley, *Very Little*, 73.
156 Motte, *Small Worlds*, 26.
157 In addition to its stylistic paucity, it is replete with '[m]oments of repetition, recurrence, or return' (Hill, *Blanchot*, 154), which are similarly deployed by, among others, Robbe-Grillet and Beckett.
158 Through a set of oppositions which tails off, perhaps not inappropriately, into ambiguity and vagueness, Hill suggests that for Blanchot death is 'both extreme possibility and extreme impossibility, finitude and infinity, limit and limitlessness, experience and anonymity, meaning and meaninglessness' (Hill, *Blanchot*, 151).
159 As Fynsk notes, this second death 'may not finish anything: her second death is offered only as a citation of the first' (Fynsk, *Language and Relation*, 248).
160 See ibid., 250.
161 Hill, *Blanchot*, 150.
162 Blanchot, 'Death Sentence', 142.
163 Blanchot, 'Literature and the Right to Death', 46.
164 Fynsk, *Language and Relation*, 233.
165 Blanchot, 'Literature and the Right to Death', 47.
166 Blanchot, 'Sleep, Night', 267.
167 Fynsk, *Language and Relation*, 234–5. This is '[n]ot a language full of images, but a language that has become the image of language, figuring by this nonreflection the dissimulation of being itself' (ibid., 236).
168 Blanchot, 'Literature and the Right to Death', 47.
169 LaBelle, *Background Noise*, 123.
170 Beckett, 'For to end yet again', 246.
171 Rabinovitz, 'The Self Contained', 51. According to Davies, these works – 'All Strange Away', 'Imagination Dead Imagine', 'Ping', 'Lessness', 'The Lost Ones' and 'For to End Yet Again' – should be assessed as a cycle (*Ideal Real*, 132–3, 137).
172 Finney, 'Assumption', 75.
173 This is also the opening line of the related piece, 'All Strange Away'.
174 Kenner, *Reader's Guide*, 176.
175 Beckett, 'All Strange Away', 169.
176 Ackerley and Gontarski, *Faber Companion*, 11.
177 Beckett, 'Imagination Dead Imagine', 184.
178 Ibid.
179 Ibid.
180 Davies, *Ideal Real*, 158.
181 Beckett, 'For to end yet again', 243.
182 Ackerley and Gontarski, *Faber Companion*, 325.
183 Ibid.

184 Beckett, 'Lessness', 198.
185 Ibid.
186 Ibid., 197.
187 See Ackerley and Gontarski, *Faber Companion*, 318.
188 Kearney, 'Imagination Wanted', 115-8.
189 Pilling, 'Shards of Ends and Odds', 175.
190 Beckett, 'Rockaby', 433.
191 Ibid., 435–6, 438, 440.
192 The woman herself is motionless, her feet on a footrest, and she exercises no physical force to set the chair in motion (ibid., 433–4).
193 Ibid., 436–7, 439, 440.
194 On this power of technology, we might recall how in *Krapp's Last Tape* authenticity is similarly granted by recordings of the voice of a faltering subject.
195 Ibid., 435–6, 438, 440.
196 See Connor, *Samuel Beckett*, 129, 131, 133.
197 Beckett, 'Rockaby', 435–6, 438, 440.
198 Connor, *Samuel Beckett*, 134.
199 Ibid., 442.
200 Ibid., 433.
201 As Connor notes, the 'tape seems to be caught in a series of self-recalling loops, each tending towards an end, but also stimulating an apparently infinite series of delays for recapitulation' (*Samuel Beckett*, 134).
202 Critchley, *Very Little*, 75.
203 Bastian, 'Since It Shouldn't', 17.
204 Barthes, 'Wisdom of Art', 18.
205 See Larsen, 'Cy Twombly', 20.
206 Ibid., 30; Dean, 'A Panegyric', 37–8, 40–1; Barthes, 'Wisdom of Art', 16–19.
207 Dean, 'A Panegyric', 36.
208 Bastian, 'Since It Shouldn't', 15.
209 Ibid., 23, 25.
210 Barthes, *Wisdom*, 12.
211 Ibid., 10.
212 Finlay, *The Present Order is the Disorder of the Future, Saint-Just*, 1983. Little Sparta, Dunsyre.
213 For a brief account of the philosophical and historical basis of this work see Botha, 'Precarious Present, Fragile Futures', 2–3. On Saint-Just and the French Revolution in Finlay's work see Bann, 'The Temple', 65; Scobie, *Earthquakes and Explorations*, 171–8; Hunt, *Nature Over Again*, 113–15; Abrioux, *Visual Primer*, 252–3.
214 Finlay, *Model of Order*, 22.

Bibliography

Abrams, Linsey. 'A Maximalist Novelist Looks at Some Minimalist Fiction'. *Minimalist Fiction*. Ed. Kim A. Herzinger. *Mississippi Review* 40/41, Special Issue (1985): 24–30.

Abrioux, Yves. *Ian Hamilton Finlay: A Visual Primer*. London: Reaktion, 1992.

Ackerley, C. J. and S. E. Gontarski. *The Faber Companion to Samuel Beckett*. London: Faber, 2006.

Adams, John. Liner notes. *Violin Concerto and Shaker Loops*. Nonesuch, 1996, 3–10.

Adams, Brooks. 'The Nauman Phenomenon'. *Bruce Nauman*. Ed. Robert C. Morgan. Baltimore: Johns Hopkins University Press, 2002, 78–85.

Adams, John. *Shaker Loops*, 1978/83.

Adams, John and Jonathan Sheffer. 'Conversation with John Adams'. *Perceptible Processes: Minimalism and the Baroque*'. Ed. Claudia Swan. New York: Eos, 1997, 76–82.

Ades, Dawn. *Dada and Surrealism*. London: Thames and Hudson, 1974.

Ades, Dawn. 'Dada and Surrealism'. *Concepts of Modern Art*. Ed. Nikos Stangos. London: Thames and Hudson, 1981, 110–37.

Adorno, Theodor W. *Negative Dialectics*. Trans. E .B. Ashton. London and New York: Routledge, 1973.

Adorno, Theodor W. 'Trying to Understand *Endgame*'. *Notes to Literature, Vol. 1*. Trans. Shierry Weber Nicholsen. New York: Columbia University Press, 1991, 241–77.

Agamben, Giorgio. 'Bartleby, or On Contingency'. *Potentialities: Collected Essays in Philosophy*. Trans. Daniel Heller-Roazen. Stanford: Stanford University Press, 1999, 243–71.

Agamben, Giorgio. 'Critique of the Instant and the Continuum'. *Infancy and History: The Destruction of Experience*. Trans. Liz Heron. London: Verso, 2007, 97–116.

Agamben, Giorgio. *Infancy and History: The Destruction of Experience*. Trans. Liz Heron. London and New York: Verso, 2007.

Agamben, Giorgio. *Language and Death: The Place of Negativity*. Trans. Karen E. Pinkus with Michael Hardt. Minneapolis and London: University of Minnesota Press, 1991.

Agamben, Giorgio. 'Movement'. *Uni.Nomade*. Seminar War and Democracy. Trans. Arianna Bove, 8 March 2005. Available online: http://www.generation-online.org/p/fpagamben3.htm (accessed 24 June 2017).

Agamben, Giorgio. 'On Potentiality'. *Potentialities: Collected Essays in Philosophy*. Trans. Daniel Heller-Roazen. Stanford: Stanford University Press, 1999, 177–84.

Agamben, Giorgio. *Remnants of Auschwitz: The Witness and the Archive*. Trans. Daniel Heller-Roazen. New York: Zone, 2002.

Agamben, Giorgio. *Stanzas: Word and Phantasm in Western Culture*. Minneapolis: University of Minnesota Press, 1993.

Agamben, Giorgio. *State of Exception*. Trans. Kevin Attell. Chicago and London: University of Chicago Press, 2005.

Agamben, Giorgio. *The Coming Community*. Trans. Michael Hardt. Minneapolis and London: University of Minnesota Press, 1993.

Agamben, Giorgio. 'The Idea of Language'. *Potentialities: Collected Essays in Philosophy*. Trans. Daniel Heller-Roazen. Stanford: Stanford University Press, 1999, 39–47.

Agamben, Giorgio. *The Idea of Prose*. Trans. Michael Sullivan and Sam Whitsitt. Albany: State University of New York Press, 1995.

Agamben, Giorgio. 'The Messiah and the Sovereign: The Problem of Law in Walter Benjamin'. *Potentialities: Collected Essays in Philosophy*. Trans. Daniel Heller-Roazen. Stanford: Stanford University Press, 1999, 160–74.

Agamben, Giorgio. *The Signature of All Things*. Trans. Luca D'Isanto with Kevin Attell. New York: Zone, 2009.

Albright, Daniel. *Modernism and Music: An Anthology of Sources*. Chicago and London: University of Chicago Press, 2004.

Alexander, Karen. *Minimalism in Twentieth Century American Writing*. Diss. University College London, 2005.

Althusser, Louis. *The Philosophy of the Encounter and Later Writings, 1978–87*. Trans. G. M. Goshgarian. London and New York: Verso, 2006.

Altieri, Charles. 'Frank Stella and Jacques Derrida: Toward a Postmodern Ethics of Singularity'. *Jacques Derrida*. Ed. Christopher Norris and David Roden, Vol. III. London: Sage, 2003, 190–210.

Andersen, Eric. *I Have Confidence in You*, 1965. *Notations*. Ed. John Cage. New York: Something Else, 1969, n.p.

Andre, Carl. *Cuts: Texts 1959–2004*. Ed. James Meyer. Cambridge, MA: MIT Press, 2005.

Andre, Carl. *Venus Forge*. 1980. Tate Modern, London. Available online: http://www.tate.org.uk/art/artworks/andre-venus-forge-t07149 (accessed 24 June 2017).

Anonymous. *Statutes of the Carthusian Order*. Available online: http://www.chartreux.org/en/texts/statutes-prologue.php (accessed 24 June 2017).

Anonymous. *The Wound of Love: A Carthusian Miscellany*. London: Darton, Longman and Todd, 1994.

Aragon, Louis. 'Suicide'. Mark A. Pegrum, *Challenging Modernity: Dada Between Modern and Postmodern*. New York and Oxford: Berghahn, 2000, 265.

Aquinas, Thomas. *Selected Philosophical Writings*. Trans. Timothy McDermott. Oxford: Oxford University Press, 1993.

Aristotle. *Metaphysics*. Trans. Hugh Lawson-Tancred. London: Penguin, 1998.

Aristotle. *Poetics*. Trans. John Warrington. London: J. M. Dent, 1963.

Aronson, Jerold L., Rom Harré and Eileen Cornell Way. *Realism Rescued: How Scientific Progress is Possible*. Chicago and La Salle, Illinois, Open Court, 1995.

Attridge, Derek. *Poetic Rhythm: An Introduction*. Cambridge: Cambridge University Press, 1995.

Attridge, Derek. *The Singularity of Literature*. London and New York: Routledge, 2004.

Azeredo, Ronaldo. 'Velocidade'. *An Anthology of Concrete Poetry*. Ed. Emmett Williams. New York: Something Else, 1967, 12.

Badiou, Alain. *Being and Event*. Trans. Oliver Feltham. London and New York: Continuum, 2005.

Badiou, Alain. *Destruction, Negation, Subtraction: on Pier Paolo Passolini*, Graduate Seminar, Art Center College of Design in Pasadena, 20 November 2011. Available online: http://www.lacan.com/badpas.htm (accessed 24 June 2017).

Badiou, Alain. 'Eight Theses on the Universal'. *Theoretical Writings*. Ed. and trans. Ray Brassier and Alberto Toscano. London and New York: Continuum, 2004, 145–54.

Badiou, Alain. *Ethics: An Essay on the Understanding of Evil*. Trans. Peter Hallward. London: Verso, 2001.

Badiou, Alain. 'Existence and Death'. Trans. Nina Power and Alberto Toscano. *Discourse* 24 (1) (2002): 63–73.

Badiou, Alain. *Handbook of Inaesthetics*. Trans. Alberto Toscano. Stanford: Stanford University Press, 2005.

Badiou, Alain. *Logics of Worlds: Being and Event 2*. Trans. Alberto Toscano. London and New York: Continuum, 2009.

Badiou, Alain. *Manifesto for Philosophy*. Trans. Norman Madarasz. Albany: State University of New York Press, 1999.

Badiou, Alain. 'Notes Toward a Thinking of Appearance'. *Theoretical Writings*. Ed. and trans. Ray Brassier and Alberto Toscano. London and New York: Continuum, 2004, 182–93.

Badiou, Alain. *Number and Numbers*. Trans. Robin Mackay. Cambridge: Polity, 2008.

Badiou, Alain. 'Philosophy and Mathematics: Infinity and the End of Romanticism'. *Theoretical Writings*. Ed. and trans. Ray Brassier and Alberto Toscano. London and New York: Continuum, 2004, 22–40.

Badiou, Alain. 'Platonism and Mathematical Ontology'. *Theoretical Writings*. Ed. and trans. Ray Brassier and Alberto Toscano. London and New York: Continuum, 2004, 51–60.

Badiou, Alain. *Second Manifesto for Philosophy*. Cambridge and Malden, MA: Polity, 2011.

Badiou, Alain. *The Century*. Trans. Alberto Toscano. Cambridge: Polity, 2007.

Badiou, Alain. 'The Event as Trans-Being'. *Theoretical Writings*. Ed. and trans. Ray Brassier and Alberto Toscano. London: Continuum, 2006, 99–104.

Badiou, Alain. 'The Question of Being Today'. *Theoretical Writings*. Ed. and trans. Ray Brassier and Alberto Toscano. London and New York: Continuum, 2004, 41–50.

Badiou, Alain. 'The Subject of Art'. Transcribed Lydia Kerr. *The Symptom*. 20 November 2011. Available online: http://www.lacan.com/symptom6_articles/badiou.html (accessed 24 June 2017).

Badiou, Alain. 'Truth: Forcing and the Unnameable'. *Theoretical Writings*. Ed. and trans. Ray Brassier and Alberto Toscano. London and New York: Continuum, 2004, 121–36.

Baker, Kenneth. *Minimalism: Art of Circumstance*. New York: Abbeville, 1988.

Bal, Mieke. *Travelling Concepts in the Humanities: A Rough Guide*. Toronto: University of Toronto Press, 2002.

Bann, Stephen. 'Concrete Poetry and the Recent Work of Robert Lax'. *Voyages: A National Literary Magazine* II (I–II) (1968): 80–1.

Bann, Stephen. 'From Place to Place: Traces of Transumption in Contemporary Visual Art'. *Mobility and Fantasy in Visual Culture*. Ed. Lewis Johnson. London and New York, Routledge, 2014, 31–43.

Bann, Stephen. Introduction. *Concrete Poetry: An International Anthology*. Ed. Stephen Bann. London: London Magazine Editions, 1967, 7–27.

Bann, Stephen. 'The Temple'. In Yves Abrioux, *Ian Hamilton Finlay: A Visual Primer*. London: Reaktion, 1992, 65.

Barry, Robert. '[This work has and continues to be refined since 1969]'. *The Ubuweb Anthology of Conceptual Writing*. Ed. Craig Dworkin. Available online: http://www.ubu.com/concept/barry_this.html (accessed 24 June 2017).

Barth, John. 'A Few Words About Minimalism'. *Further Fridays: Essays, Lectures, and Other Nonfiction 1984-94*. Boston: Little, Brown and Company, 1995, 64–74.

Barthes, Roland. 'The Wisdom of Art'. Trans. Annette Lavers. *Cy Twombly: Paintings and Drawings 1954–1977*. New York, Whitney Museum, 1979. *Works on Paper, Sculpture*. Ed. Harald Szeemann. Munich: Prestel-Verlag, 1987, 9–22.

Barthes, Roland. 'Introduction to the Structural Analysis of Narratives'. *Image, Music, Text*. Trans. Stephen Heath. London: Fontana, 1977, 79–124.

Bastian, Heiner. 'Since It Shouldn't Be, Since It Happens'. *Cy Twombly: Das Graphische Werk 1953–1984: A Catalogue Raisonné of the Printed Graphic Work*. Ed. Heiner Bastian. New York: New York University Press, 1985, 16–26.

Battcock, Gregory. *Constructivism and Minimal Art: Some Critical, Theoretical and Aesthetic Correlations*. Diss. New York University, 1979.

Battcock, Gregory. Introduction. *Minimal Art: A Critical Anthology*. Ed. Gregory Battcock. New York: E. P. Dutton, 1968, 19–36.

Batchelor, David. *Minimalism*. Cambridge: Cambridge University Press, 1997.

Baudrillard, Jean. 'Simulacra and Science Fiction'. *Simulacra and Simulation*. Trans. Sheila Faria Glaser. Ann Arbor: University of Michigan Press, 1994, 121–7.

Baudrillard, Jean. 'The Precession of Simulacra'. *Simulacra and Simulation*. Trans. by Sheila Faria Glaser. Ann Arbor: University of Michigan Press, 1994, 1–42.

Beckett, Samuel. 'A Piece of Monologue'. *The Complete Dramatic Works*. London: Faber, 1990, 423–9.

Beckett, Samuel. 'All Strange Away'. *The Complete Short Prose: 1929–1989*. Ed. S. E. Gontarski. New York: Grove, 1995, 169–81.

Beckett, Samuel. 'Fizzle 8: For to end yet again'. *The Complete Short Prose: 1929–1989*. Ed. S. E. Gontarski. New York: Grove, 1995, 243–6.

Beckett, Samuel. 'Company'. *Nohow On*. New York: Grove, 1996, 1–46.

Beckett, Samuel. 'Endgame'. *The Complete Dramatic Works*. London: Faber, 1990, 89–134.

Beckett, Samuel. 'Footfalls'. *The Complete Dramatic Works*. London: Faber, 1990, 397–403.

Beckett, Samuel. 'Heard in the Dark I'. *The Complete Short Prose: 1929–1989*. Ed. S. E. Gontarski. New York: Grove, 1995, 247–9.

Beckett, Samuel. 'Ill Seen Ill Said'. *Nohow On*. New York: Grove, 1996, 47–86.

Beckett, Samuel. 'Imagination Dead Imagine'. *The Complete Short Prose: 1929–1989*. Ed. S. E. Gontarski. New York: Grove, 1995, 182–5.

Beckett, Samuel. 'Lessness'. *The Complete Short Prose: 1929-1989*. Ed. S. E. Gontarski. New York: Grove, 1995, 197–201.

Beckett, Samuel. 'Molloy'. *Three Novels*. New York: Grove, 1958, 5–176.

Beckett, Samuel. 'Ping'. *The Complete Short Prose: 1929–1989*. Ed. S. E. Gontarski. New York: Grove, 1995, 193–6.

Beckett., Samuel. 'Rockaby'. *The Complete Dramatic Works*. London: Faber, 1990, 431–42.

Beckett, Samuel. 'Sounds'. *The Complete Short Prose: 1929–1989*. Ed. S. E. Gontarski. New York: Grove, 1995, 267–8.

Beckett, Samuel. 'Texts for Nothing'. *The Complete Short Prose: 1929–1989*. Ed. S. E. Gontarski. New York: Grove, 1995, 100–54.

Beckett, Samuel. 'The Lost Ones'. *The Complete Short Prose: 1929–1989*. Ed. S. E. Gontarski. New York: Grove, 1995, 202–23.

Beckett, Samuel. 'The Unnamable'. *The Beckett Trilogy*. London: Picador, 1979, 265–382.

Beckett, Samuel. 'what is the word'. *As the Story Was Told*. London: John Calder, 1990, 129–34.

Beer, Gillian. 'Wave Theory and the Rise of Literary Modernism'. *Realism and Representation: Essays on the Problem of Realism in Relation to Science, Literature, and Culture*. Ed. George Levine. Madison: University of Wisconsin Press, 1993, 193–213.

Beer, John. 'Introduction'. *Robert Lax: Poems (1962–1997)*. Ed. John Beer. Seattle and New York: Wave, 2013, xi–xxi.

Beistegui, Miguel de. 'The Ontological Dispute: Badiou, Heidegger and Deleuze'. Trans. Ray Brassier. *Alain Badiou: Philosophy and its Conditions*. Ed. Gabriel Riera. Albany: State University of New York Press, 2005, 45–58.

Belisle, Peter-Damian. *The Language of Silence: The Changing Face of Monastic Solitude*. Maryknoll, NY: Orbis, 2003.

Bell, Tiffany. 'Fluorescent Light as Art'. *Dan Flavin: A Retrospective*. Ed. Michael Govan and Tiffany Bell. New York: Dia Art Foundation, 2004, 109–28.

Bellamy, Joe David. 'A Downpour of Literary Republicanism'. *Minimalist Fiction*. Ed. Kim A. Herzinger. *Mississippi Review* 40/41, Special Issue (1985): 31–9.

Benedict. *The Rule of Saint Benedict*. Ed. Timothy Fry. Collegeville: Liturgical Press, 1981.

Benedikt, Michael. 'Sculpture as Architecture: New York Letter, 1966–67'. *Minimal Art: A Critical Anthology*. Ed. Gregory Battcock. New York: E. P. Dutton, 1968, 61–91.

Benezra, Neil. 'Surveying Nauman'. *Bruce Nauman*. Ed. Robert C. Morgan. Baltimore: Johns Hopkins University Press, 2002, 116–45.

Bennington, Geoffrey. *Lyotard: Writing the Event*. New York: Columbia University Press, 1988.

Berdini, Paolo. 'Similar Emotions/Dissimilar Objects: The Pilkington Paradigm and minimalist and baroque art'. *Perceptible Processes: Minimalism and the Baroque*. Ed. Clausia Swan. New York: EOS, 1997, 40–51.

Berger, Maurice. *Labyrinths: Robert Morris, Minimalism, and the 1960s*. New York: Icon, 1989.

Bergonzi, Bernard. *The Situation of the Novel*. Harmondsworth: Penguin, 1972.

Bernstein, Charles. *A Poetics*. Cambridge, MA and London: Harvard University Press, 1992.

Bhasksar, Roy. *Reclaiming Reality: A Critical Introduction to Contemporary Philosophy*. London and New York: Verso, 1989.

Bigeunet, John. 'Notes of a Disaffected Reader: The Origins of Minimalism'. *Minimalist Fiction*. Ed. Kim A. Herzinger. *Mississippi Review* 40/41 Special Issue (1985): 40–5.

Blanchot, Maurice. 'Death Sentence'. *The Station Hill Blanchot Reader: Fiction and Literary Essays*. Trans. Lydia Davis, Paul Auster and Robert Lamberton. Ed. George Quasha. Barrytown: Station Hill, 1999, 129–87.

Blanchot, Maurice. 'Literature and the Right to Death'. *The Gaze of Orpheus*. Trans. Lydia Davis. Barrytown: Station Hill, 1981, 21–62.

Blanchot, Maurice. 'Sleep, Night'. *The Space of Literature*. Trans. Ann Smock. Lincoln and London: University of Nebraska Press, 1982, 264–8.

Blanchot, Maurice. 'The Essential Solitude'. *The Gaze of Orpheus*. Trans. Lydia Davis. Barrytown: Station Hill, 1981, 63–77.

Blyth, Mark. *Austerity: The History of a Dangerous Idea*. Oxford and New York: Oxford University Press, 2013.

Bohn, Willard. *The Aesthetics of Visual Poetry, 1914–1928*. Cambridge: Cambridge University Press, 1986.

Bois, Yve-Alain. 'Painting: The Task of Mourning'. *Painting as a Model*. Cambridge, MA and London: MIT Press, 1990, 229–44.

Bök, Christian. 'When Cyborgs Versify'. *The Sound of Poetry/The Poetry of Sound*. Ed. Marjorie Perloff and Craig Dworkin. Chicago and London: University of Chicago Press, 2009, 129–41.

Bonet, Pilar. 'Minimalism: A Historical Reflection'. *Minimalism, Minimalist*. Ed. Sofía Cheviakoff. Köneman: Cologne, 2006, 24–33.

Botonia, Marguerite. 'Bells as Inspiration for Tintinnabulation'. *Cambridge Companion to Arvo Pärt*. Ed. Andrew Shenton. Cambridge: Cambridge University Press, 2012, 128–39

Botha, Marc. 'Evental Distension: Restless Simultaneity in Steve Reich's Piano Phase – Towards a Rehabilitation of the Real'. *Time: Limits and Constraints*. Ed. Jo Alyson Parker, Paul A. Harris and Christian Steineck. Leiden and Boston: Brill, 2010, 261–87.

Botha, Marc. 'Microfiction'. *The Cambridge Companion to the English Short Story*. Ed. Ann-Marie Einhaus. Cambridge, Cambridge University Press, 2016, 200–19.

Botha, Marc. 'Precarious Present, Fragile Future: Literature and Uncertainty in the Early Twenty-First Century'. *English Academy Review* 31 (2) (2014): 1–19.

Botha, Marc. 'The Poetics of Remoteness'. *Weeds and Viruses: Ecopolitics and the Demands of Theory*. Ed. Jennifer Wawrzinek and Cordula Lemke. Trier: WVT, 2015, 21–47.

Botha, Marc. 'Why minimalism matters: radical quantity and the representation of immanence'. *Textual Practice*. 29 (4) (2015): 745–72.

Bowler, Berjouhi. *The Word as Image*. London: Studio Vista, 1970.

Brassier, Ray. *Nihil Unbound: Enlightenment and Extinction*. London: Palgrave, 2007.

Brauneiss, Leopold. 'Musical Archetypes: The Basic Elements of the Tintinnabuli Style'. *Cambridge Companion to Arvo Pärt*. Ed. Andrew Shenton. Cambridge: Cambridge University Press, 2012, 49–75.

Brumbaugh, Robert S. *Plato on the One: The Hypotheses in the Parmenides*. New Haven: Yale University Press, 1961.

Bryant, Levi, Nick Srnicek and Graham Harman, eds. *The Speculative Turn: Continental Materialism and Realism*. Melbourne: re.press, 2011.

Burke, Edmund. *A Philosophical Enquiry into the Origin of our Ideas of the Sublime and Beautiful*. Oxford: Blackwell, 1987.

Butler, Christopher. *Early Modernism: Literature, Music, and Painting in Europe, 1900–1916*. Oxford: Clarendon, 1994.

Cage, John. 'Empty Words'. *Empty Words*. London and Boston: Marion Boyars, 1980, 11–77.

Cage, John. *Empty Words*. Wergo, 1991.

Cage, John. *Conversing with Cage*. Ed. Richard Kostelanetz. London and New York: Routledge, 2003.

Calame, Claude. 'The Tragic Choral Group: Dramatic Roles and Social Function'. Trans. Dan Edelstein. *A Companion to Tragedy*. Ed. Rebecca Bushnell. Oxford: Blackwell, 2005, 215–33.

Caputo, John D. *The Weakness of God: A Theology of the Event*. Bloomington and Indianapolis: Indiana University Press, 2006.

Carman, Taylor. *Maurice Merleau-Ponty*. London and New York: Routledge, 2008.

Carver, Raymond. 'On Writing'. *Fires: Essays, Poems, Stories*. New York: Vintage, 1989, 22–7.

Carver, Ramond, 'Fat'. *The Stories of Raymond Carver*. London: Picador, 1985, 13–16.

Carver, Raymond. 'The Bath'. *The Stories of Raymond Carver*. London: Picador, 1985, 214–20.

Caws, Mary Ann. 'Concretism'. *Manifesto: A Century of Isms*. Ed. Mary Ann Caws. Lincoln and London: University of Nebraska Press, 2001, 518–19.

Caws, Mary Ann. *The Poetry of Dada and Surrealism: Aragon, Breton, Tzara, Eluard and Desnos*. Princeton: Princeton University Press, 1970.

Chave, Anna C. 'Minimalism and the Rhetoric of Power'. *Arts Magazine*. January 1990: 44–63

Chave, Anna C. 'Revaluing Minimalism: Patronage, Aura, and Place'. *The Art Bulletin* 90 (3) (2008): 466–86.

Cheviakoff, Sofia. 'Minimal Art'. *Minimalism, Minimalist*. Ed. Sofía Cheviakoff. Köneman: Cologne, 2006, 35–114.

Chieregin, Franco. 'Freedom and Thought: Stoicism, Skepticism, and Unhappy Consciousness'. *The Blackwell Guide to Hegel's Phenomenology of Spirit*. Ed. Keneth R. Westphal. Oxford: Blackwell, 2009, 55–71.

Churchland, Paul. *The Engine of Reason, the Seat of the Soul: A Philosophical Journey into the Brain*. Cambridge, MA: MIT Press, 1995.

Clark, Robert C. *American Literary Minimalism*. Tuscaloosa: University of Alabama Press. 2014.

Clüver, Claus. 'Concrete Poetry: Critical Perspectives from the 90s'. *Experimental – Visual – Concrete: Avant-Garde Poetry Since the 1960s*. Ed. K. David Jackson, Eric Vos and Johanna Drucker. Amsterdam and Atlanta: Rodopi, 1996, 265–85.

Cohen, Richard A. *Ethics, Exegesis and Philosophy: Interpretation After Levinas*. Cambridge: Cambridge University Press, 2001.

Cole, Hugo. *Sounds and Signs: Aspects of Musical Notation*. London: Oxford University Press, 1974.

Cole, Teju. 'Seven Short Stories About Drones'. *The New Inquiry*, 14 January 2013. Available online: https://thenewinquiry.com/blog/seven-short-stories-about-drones/ (accessed 24 June 2017).

Colpitt, Frances. *Minimal Art: The Critical Perspective*. Seattle: University of Washington Press, 1990.

Comotti, Giovanni. *Music in Greek and Roman Culture*. Trans. Rosaria V. Munson. Baltimore and London: Johns Hopkins University Press, 1989.

Connor, Steven. *Dumbstruck: A Cultural History of Ventriloquism*. Oxford: Oxford University Press, 2000.

Connor, Steven. *Samuel Beckett: Repetition, Theory and Text*. Blackwell: Oxford, 1988.

Corrigan, John. 'Protestantism in the United States of America to the Present Day'. *The Blackwell Companion to Protestantism*. Ed. Alistair E. McGrath and Darren C. Marks. Oxford: Blackwell, 2004, 165–80.

Crace, Jim. *The Devil's Larder*. London: Penguin, 2002.
Critchley, Simon. *Very Little … Almost Nothing: Death, Philosophy, Literature*. London and New York: Routledge, 1997.
Critchley, Simon. *Infinite Demanding: Ethics of Resistance, Politics of Commitment*. London: Verso, 2007.
Crowther, Paul. *The Kantian Sublime: From Morality to Art*. Oxford and New York: Oxford University Press, 1991.
Culler, Jonathan. *Literary Theory: A Very Short Introduction*. Oxford: Oxford University Press, 1997.
Culler, Jonathan. 'Resisting Theory'. *The Literary in Theory*. Stanford: Stanford University Press, 2007, 73–96.
Culler, Jonathan. 'The Literary in Theory'. *The Literary in Theory*. Stanford: Stanford University Press, 2007, 23–42.
Dachy, Marc. *Dada: The Revolt of Art*. Trans. Liz Ash. London: Thames and Hudson, 2006.
Dachy, Marc. *The Dada Movement: 1915–1923*. Trans. Michael Taylor. New York: Rizzoli, 1990.
Damisch, Hubert. 'A Conversation with Hubert Damisch'. Interview with Yve-Alain Bois, Denis Hollier and Rosalind Krauss, *October* 85 (1998): 3–17.
Danto, Arthur C. 'Bruce Nauman'. *Bruce Nauman*. Ed. Robert C. Morgan. Baltimore: Johns Hopkins University Press, 2002, 146–54
Danto, Arthur C. 'Learning to Live with Pluralism'. *Beyond the Brillo Box: The Visual Arts in Post-Historical Perspective*. New York: Farrar, Straus & Giroux, 1992, 217–32.
Danto, Arthur C. 'Style and Narrative'. *Beyond the Brillo Box: The Visual Arts in Post-Historical Perspective*. New York: Farrar, Straus & Giroux, 1992, 233–48.
Danto, Arthur C. 'The Art World'. *Aesthetics and the Philosophy of Art: The Analytic Tradition: An Anthology*. Ed. Peter Lamarque and Stein Haugon Olsen. Oxford: Blackwell, 2004, 27–34.
Danto, Arthur C . 'The Art World Revisited: Comedies of Similarities'. *Beyond the Brillo Box: The Visual Arts in Post-Historical Perspective*. New York: Farrar, Straus & Giroux, 1992, 33–53.
Danto, Arthur C. 'The Philosophical Disenfranchisement of Art'. *The Philosophical Disenfranchisement of Art*. New York: Columbia University Press, 1986, 1–21.
Danto, Arthur C. *Transfiguration of the Commonplace: A Philosophy of Art*. Cambridge, MA. and London: Harvard University Press, 1981.
Dauenhauer, Bernard P. *Silence: The Phenomenon and Its Ontological Significance*. Bloomington: Indiana University Press, 1980.
Davies, Paul. 'On Resorting to an Ethical Language'. *Ethics as First Philosophy: The Significance of Emmanuel Levinas for Philosophy, Literature and Religion*. Ed. Adriaan T. Peperzak. New York and London: Routledge, 1995, 95–104.
Davies, Paul. *The Ideal Real: Beckett's Fiction and Imagination*. London and Toronto: Associated University Presses, 1994.

Davis, Carmel Bendon. *Mysticism and Space: Space and Spatiality in the Works of Richard Rolle,* The Cloud of Unkowing *Author, and Julian of Norwich*. Washington, DC: Catholic University of America Press, 2008.

Davis, Lydia. 'Index Entry'. *The Collected Stories of Lydia Davis*. London: Peguin, 2009, 713.

Dean, Tacita. 'A Panegyric'. *Cy Twombly: Cycles and Seasons*. Ed. Nicholas Serota. London: Tate, 2008, 33–41.

Deguy, Michel. 'The Discourse of Exaltation: Contributions to a Re-Reading of Pseudo-Longinus'. *Of the Sublime: Presence in Question*. Trans. Jeffrey S. Librett. Albany: State University of New York Press, 1993, 5–24.

Deleuze, Gilles. *The Logic of Sense*. Trans. Mark Lester with Charles Stivale. New York: Columbia University Press, 1990.

Derrida, Jacques. 'Before the Law'. *Acts of Literature*. Ed. Derek Attridge. London and New York: Routledge, 1992, 181–220.

Derrida, Jacques. 'Ellipsis'. *Writing and Difference*. Trans. Alan Bass. London and New York: Routledge, 2001, 371–8.

Derrida, Jacques. 'Force and Signification'. *Writing and Difference*. Trans. Alan Bass. London and New York: Routledge, 1–35.

Derrida, Jacques. *Monolingualism of the Other; or, The Prosthesis of Origin*. Trans. Patrick Mensah. Stanford: Stanford University Press, 1998.

Derrida, Jacques. *On the Name*. Trans. Thomas Dutoit. Stanford: Stanford University Press, 1995.

Derrida, Jacques. 'Otobiographies: The Teaching of Nietzsche and the Politics of the Proper Names'. *The Ear of the Other: Otobiography, Transference, Translation*. Trans. Peggy Kamuf and Avital Ronell. Lincoln: University of Nebraska Press, 1–38.

Derrida, Jacques. *Specters of Marx: The State of the Debt, the Work of Mourning and the New International*. Trans. Peggy Kamuf. London and New York: Routledge, 1994.

Didion, Joan. *Play It as It Lays*. Harmondsworth: Penguin, 1973.

Didion, Joan. *A Book of Common Prayer*. London: Penguin, 1977.

Donington, Robert. *The Rise of Opera*. London and Boston: Faber, 1981.

Diken, Bülent. *Nihilism*. London and New York: Routledge, 2009.

Drucker, Johanna. 'Experimental, Visual, and Concrete Poetry: A Note on Historical Context and Basic Concepts'. *Experimental – Visual – Concrete: Avant-Garde Poetry Since the 1960s*. Ed. K. David Jackson, Eric Vos and Johanna Drucker. Amsterdam and Atlanta: Rodopi, 1996, 39–61.

Drucker, Johanna. 'Visual Performance of the Poetic Text'. *Close Listening: Poetry and the Performed Word*. Ed. Charles Bernstein. Oxford and New York: Oxford University Press, 1998, 131–61.

Duckworth, William and Richard Fleming. 'Introduction'. *Bucknell Review* 40 (1) (1996): 13–18.

Dufrenne, Mikel. *The Phenomenology of Aesthetic Experience*. Trans. Edward S. Casey,

Albert A. Anderson, Willis Domingo and Leon Jacobson. Evanston: Northwestern University Press, 1973.

Durantaye, Leland de la. *Giorgio Agamben: A Critical Introduction*. Stanford: Stanford University Press, 2009.

Duve, Thierry de. *Pictorial Nominalism: On Marcel Duchamp's Passage from Painting to the Readymade*. Trans. Dana Polan with the author. Minneapolis: University of Minnesota Press, 1991.

Eagleton, Terry. *The Significance of Theory*. Oxford: Blackwell, 1990.

Edwards, Paul. *Heidegger's Confusion*. Amherst, NY: Prometheus, 2004.

Elden, Stuart. *Speaking Against Number: Heidegger, Language and the Politics of Calculation*. Edinburgh: Edinburgh University Press, 2006.

Elíasson, Olafur. *The Weather Project*. 2003. Tate Modern. Available online: http://olafureliasson.net/archive/artwork/WEK101003/the-weather-project (accessed 24 June 2017).

Epstein, Paul. 'Pattern Structure and Process in Steve Reich's *Piano Phase*'. *The Musical Quarterly* 72 (4) (1986): 494–502.

Falk, Eugene H. *The Poetics of Roman Ingarden*. Chapel Hill: University of North Carolina Press, 1981, 114–15.

Federman, Raymond. 'A Short Note on Minimalism'. *Minimalist Fiction*. Ed. Kim A. Herzinger. *Mississippi Review* 40/41, Special Issue (1985): 57.

Fer, Briony. 'Nocturama: Flavin's Light Diagrams'. *Dan Flavin: New Light*. Ed. Jeffrey Weiss. New Haven and London: Yale University Press, 2006, 25–48.

Feyerabend, Paul K. *Realism, Rationalism and Scientific Method: Philosophical Papers Volume 1*. Cambridge: Cambridge University Press, 1981.

Fink, Robert. *Repeating Ourselves: American Minimal Music as Cultural Practice*. Berkeley: University of California Press, 2005.

Finlay, Alec. Introduction. *Wood Notes Wild: Essays on the Poetry, Art and Gardens of Ian Hamilton Finlay*. Ed. Alec Finlay. Edinburgh: Polygon, 1997.

Finlay, Ian Hamilton. 'acrobats'. *Ian Hamilton Finlay: Selections*. Ed. Alec Finlay. Berkeley, University of California Press, 2012, 140.

Finlay, Ian Hamilton. *A Model of Order: Selected Letters on Poetry and Making*. Ed. Thomas A. Clark. Glasgow: WAX366, 2009.

Finlay, Ian Hamilton. 'Arcady'. *One Word Poems. Poor. Old. Tired. Horse.* 25 (1967): 8.

Finlay, Ian Hamilton. *The Present Order is the Disorder of the Future, Saint-Just*. Little Sparta, Dunsyre, Publisher, 1983.

Finn, Richard. *Asceticism in the Graeco-Roman World*. Cambridge: Cambridge University Press, 2009.

Finney, Brian. 'Assumption to Lessness: Beckett's shorter fiction'. *Beckett the Shape Changer*. Ed. Katherine Worth. London: Routledge, 1975, 63–83.

Flavin, Dan. *the nominal three (to William of Ockham)*. 1964. Guggenheim Museum, New York. Available online: http://www.guggenheim.org/artwork/1294 (accessed 24 June 2017).

Flavin, Dan. *monument 1 for V. Tatlin*, 1964, Museum of Modern Art, New York. Available online: http://www.moma.org/collection/object.php?object_id=81337 (accessed 24 June 2017).

Flavin, Dan. *untitled (to the real Dan Hill) 1b*, 1978. Museum of Modern Art, Antwerp. Available online: http://ensembles.mhka.be/items/untitled-to-the-real-dan-hill-1b?locale=en (accessed 24 June 2017).

Fluck, Winfried. 'Surface and Depth: Postmodernism and Neo-Realist Fiction'. *Neo-Realism in Contemporary American Fiction*. Ed. Kristiaan Versluys. Amsterdam and Atlanta: Rodopi, 1992, 65–85.

Foer, Joshua. 'A Minor History of Miniature Writing'. *Cabinet* 25 (2007). Available online: http://cabinetmagazine.org/issues/25/foer.php (accessed 24 June 2017).

Forrestall, Alison. 'The Church in the Tridentine and Early Modern Eras'. *The Routledge Companion to the Christian Church*. Ed. Gerard Mannion and Lewis S. Mudge. New York and London: Routledge, 2008, 85–105.

Forster, Michael. 'Hegel's Dialectical Method'. *The Cambridge Companion to Hegel*. Ed. Frederick C. Beiser. Cambridge: Cambridge University Press, 1993, 130–70.

Foster, Hal. 'Dan Flavin and the Catastrophe of Minimalism'. *Dan Flavin: New Light*. Ed. Jeffrey Weiss. New Haven and London: Yale University Press, 2006, 133–51.

Foster, Hal. *The Return of the Real: The Avant-Garde at the End of the Century*. Cambridge, MA and London: MIT Press, 1996.

Foucault, Michel. *Discipline and Punish: The Birth of the Prison*. Trans. Alan Sheridan. Harmondsworth: Penguin, 1977.

Francis of Assissi. 'The Salutation of the Virtues'. *Francis and Clare: The Complete Works*, trans. Regis J. Armstrong and Ignatius C. Brady. London: SPCK, 1982, 151–2.

Fraser, G. S. *The Modern Writer and His World*. Harmondsworth: Penguin, 1964.

Fried, Michael. 'Art and Objecthood'. *Minimal Art: A Critical Anthology*. Ed. Gregory Battcock. New York: E. P. Dutton, 1968, 116–47.

Fried, Michael. 'Three American Painters: Noland, Olitski, Stella'. *Art and Objecthood: Essays and Reviews*. Chicago and London: Chicago University Press, 1998, 213–68.

Friedman, Norman. 'What Makes a Short Story Short?' *Modern Fiction Studies* 4 (2) (1958): 103–17.

Fynsk, Christopher. *Language and Relation: … that there is language*. Stanford: Stanford University Press, 1996.

Gablik, Suzi. 'Minimalism'. *Concepts of Modern Art*. Ed. Nikos Stangos. London: Thames and Hudson, 1981, 244–55.

Gadamer, Hans-Georg. *Truth and Method*. Trans. Joel Weinsheimer and Donald G. Marshall. New York and London: Continuum, 2004.

Gappmayr, Heinz. Untitled. *The Chicago Review Anthology of Concretism*. Ed. Eugene Wildman. Chicago: Swallow, 1967, 39.

Garcia Cela, Carmen. 'Hearing in Robbe-Grillet'. Trans. Denise Pessah. *Poetics Today* 21 (2) (2000): 453–5.

Gasché, Rodoplhe. *The Idea of Form: Rethinking Kant's Aesthetics*. Stanford, Stanford University Press, 2003.

Gibson, Andrew. *Intermittency: The Concept of Historical Reason in Recent French Philosophy*. Edinburgh: Edinburgh University Press, 2012.

Gilmore, Jonathan. 'Between Philosophy and Art'. *The Cambridge Companion to Merleau-Ponty*. Ed. Taylor Carman and Mark B.N. Hansen. Cambridge: Cambridge University Press, 297–317.

Gillespie, Sam. *The Mathematics of Novelty: Badiou's Minimalist Metaphysics*. Melbourne: re.press, 2008.

Girard, René. *Deceit, Desire and the Novel: Self and Other in Literary Structure*. Trans. Yvonne Frecerro Baltimore and London: Johns Hopkins University Press, 1965.

Girard, René. *Violence and the Sacred*. Trans. Patrick Gregory. Baltimore and London, Johns Hopkins University Press, 1975.

Glaser, Bruce. 'Questions to Stella and Judd'. *Minimal Art: A Critical Anthology*. Ed. Gregory Battcock. New York: E. P. Dutton, 1968, 148–64.

Glass, Philip. *Opera on the Beach: Philip Glass on his New World of Music Theatre*. London and Boston: Faber, 1988.

Glass, Philip. *Einstein on the Beach*, London: Chester, 2013.

Glass, Philip. *Two Pages*, New York: Dunvagen, 1968.

Glenberg, Arthur M. 'Radical Changes in Cognitive Process Due to Technology: A Jaundiced View'. *Cognition Distributed: How Cognitive Technology Extends our Minds*. Ed. Itiel E. Dror and Steven Harnad. Amsterdam and Philadelphia: John Benjamins, 2008, 71–82.

Goodman, Nelson. *Languages of Art: An Approach to a Theory of Symbols*. Indianapolis: Bobs-Merill, 1968.

Goodman, Nelson. 'On Starmaking'. *Starmaking: Realism, Anti-Realism, and Irrealism*. Ed. Peter J. McCormick. Cambridge, MA and London: MIT Press, 1996, 143–50.

Goodman, Nelson. *Ways of Worldmaking*. Indianapolis: Hackett, 1978.

Govan, Michael. 'Irony and Light'. *Dan Flavin: A Retrospective*. Ed. Michael Govan and Tiffany Bell. New York: Dia Art Foundation, 2004, 19–107.

Greenberg, Clement. 'Avant-Garde and Kitsch'. *Art and Culture: Critical Essays*. Boston: Beacon Press, 1989, 3–21.

Greenberg, Clement. 'Recentness of Sculpture'. *Minimal Art: A Critical Anthology*. Ed. Gregory Battcock. New York: E. P. Dutton, 1968, 180–6.

Grumman, Bob. 'MNMLST POETRY', 1997. Available online: http://www.thing.net/~grist/l&d/grumman/egrumn.htm (accessed 24 June 2017).

Guenther, Lisa. *Solitary Confinement: Social Death and Its Afterlives*. Minneapolis: University of Minnesota Press, 2003.

Hall, James B. In 'Afterwords'. *Sudden Fiction: American Short-Short Stories*. Ed. Robert Shapard and James Thomas. Salt Lake City: Peregrine Smith, 1986, 225–58.

Hallet, Cythia Whitney. *Minimalism and the Short Story – Raymond Carver, Amy Hempel, and Mary Robison*. Lewiston, NY: Edwin Mellen, 1999.

Hallward, Peter. *Badiou: A Subject to Truth*. Minneapolis and London: University of Minnesota Press, 2003.

Hallward, Peter. 'Introduction: Consequences of Action'. *Think Again: Alain Badiou and the Future of Philosophy*. Ed. Peter Hallward. London and New York: Continuum, 2004, 1–20.

Harman, Graham. *Guerilla Metaphysics: Phenomenology and the Carpentry of Things*. Chicago and La Salle, IL: Open Court, 2005.

Harman, Graham. *Tool Being: Heidegger and the Metaphysics of Objects*. Chicago and La Salle, IL: Open Court, 2002.

Harman, Graham. 'Speculative Realism'. *Collapse* III (2007): 367–407.

Haskell, Barbara. *Blam! The Explosion of Pop, Minimalism, and Performance 1958–1964*. New York: Whitney Museum of American Art, 1984.

Harpham, Geoffrey Galt. *The Ascetic Imperative in Culture and Criticism*. Chicago and London: University of Chicago Press, 1987.

Harvey, David. *A Brief History of Neoliberalism*. Oxford and New York: Oxford University Press, 2005.

Hauff, Sigrid. *A Line in Three Circles: The Inner Biography of Robert Lax*. Herrsching: Waitawhile, 2007.

Hayles, N. Katherine. 'Intermediation: The Pursuit of a Vision'. *New Literary History* 38 (1) (2007): 99–125.

Hegel, Georg Wilhelm Friedrich. *Phenomenology of Spirit*. Trans. A. V. Miller. Oxford: Oxford University Press, 1977.

Hegel, Georg Wilhelm Friedrich. *The Science of Logic*. Trans. George di Giovanni. Cambridge: Cambridge University Press, 2010.

Heidegger, Martin. *Being and Time*. Trans. John Macquarrie and Edward Robinson. Oxford: Blackwell, 1973.

Heidegger, Martin. *The Fundamental Concepts of Metaphysics: World, Finitude, Solitude*. Trans. William McNeill and Nicholas Walker. Bloomington and Indianapolis: Indiana University Press, 1995.

Heidegger, Martin. 'Hölderlin and the Essence of Poetry'. *Elucidations of Hölderlin's Poetry*. Trans. Keith Hoeller. Amherst, NY: Humanity Books, 2000, 51–65.

Heidegger, Martin. 'The Question Concerning Technology'. *The Question Concerning Technology and Other Essays*. Trans. William Lovitt. New York and London: Garland, 1977, 3–35.

Heidegger, Martin. 'The Thing'. *Poetry, Language, Thought*. Trans. Alfred Hofstadter. New York: Harper & Row, 1971, 163–86.

Heidegger, Martin. 'What is Metaphysics?' *Basic Writings: Nine Essays, plus, the Introduction of* Being and Time. Ed. And trans. David Farrell Krell. London: Routledge, 1978, 91–112.

Herman, David. 'Storyworld'. *Routledge Encyclopedia of Narrative Theory*. Eds David Herman, Manfred Jahn and Marie-Laure Ryan. London; New York, Routledge, 2005: 569–70.

Herzinger, Kim A. 'Introduction: On the New Fiction'. *Minimalist Fiction*. Ed. Kim A. Herzinger. *Mississippi Review* 40/41, Special Issue (1985): 7–22.
Hesiod. *Theogony and Works and Days*. Trans. Catherine Schlegel and Henry Weinfield. Ann Arbor: University of Michigan Press, 2006.
Higgins, Dick. 'Points Towards a Taxonomy of Sound Poetry'. *Horizons: The Poetics and Theory of Intermedia*. Carbondale and Edwardsville: Southern Illinois University Press, 1984, 40–52.
Hilfer, Tony. *American Fiction Since 1940*. London: Longman, 1992.
Hill, Leslie. *Blanchot: Extreme Contemporary*. London and New York: Routledge, 1997.
Hooke, Robert. 'Micrographia: Some Physiological Descriptions of Minute Bodies Made by Magnifying Glasses with Observations and Inquiries Thereupon', 1665/2005. Available online: http://www.gutenberg.org/files/15491/15491-h/15491-h.htm (accessed 24 June 2017).
Horkheimer, Max and Theodor W. Adorno. *Dialectic of Enlightenment: Philosophical Fragments*. Trans. Edmund Jephcott and ed. Gunzelin Schmid Noerr. Stanford: Stanford University Press, 2002.
Howe, Irving. 'Introduction'. *Short Shorts: An Anthology of the Shortest Stories*. Ed. Irving Howe and Ilana Wiener Howe. New York: Bantam Books, 1983, ix–xv.
Hunt, John Dixon. *Nature Over Again: The Garden Art of Ian Hamilton Finlay*. London: Reaktion, 2008.
Husserl, Edmund. *Ideas Pertaining to a Pure Phenomenology and to a Phenomenological Philosophy. First Book: General Introduction to a Pure Phenomenology*. Trans F. Kersten. The Hague: Martinus Nijhoff, 1982.
Hutcheon, Linda. *A Poetics of Postmodernism: History, Theory, Fiction*. New York and London: Routledge, 1988.
Hutchens, Benjamin C. *Levinas: A Guide for the Perplexed*. London and New York: Continuum, 2004.
Hutchins, Edwin. *Cognition in the Wild*. Cambridge, MA and London: MIT Press, 1995.
Inwood, Michael. *A Heidegger Dictionary*. Oxford: Blackwell, 1999.
Iser, Wolfgang. *How to do Theory*. Oxford: Blackwell, 2006.
Isou, Isidore. 'Manifesto of Lettrist Poetry'. *Manifesto: A Century of Isms*. Ed. Mary Ann Caws. Lincoln and London: University of Nebraska Press, 2001, 545–6.
Ingarden, Roman. *Time and Modes of Being*. Trans. Helen R. Michejda. Springfield: Charles C. Thomas, 1964.
Jolley, Nicholas. *Leibniz*. London and New York: Routledge, 2005.
Jolley, Nicholas. 'Leibniz: Truth, Knowledge and Metaphysics'. *Routledge History of Philosophy, Vol. IV: The Renaissance and Seventeenth Century Rationalism*. Ed. G. H. R. Parkinson. London and New York: Routledge, 1993, 353–88.
Joselit, David. *Infinite Regress: Marcel Duchamp 1910–1941*. Cambridge, MA and London: MIT Press, 1998.

Josipovici, Gabriel. *The Inventory*. London: Michael Joseph, 1968.

Judd, Donald. *Chair 84/85*, 1991. Chinati Foundation, Marfa. Available online: http://juddfoundation.org/artist/furniture/wood-furniture/ (accessed 24 June 2017).

Judd, Donald. 'Complaints: Part I'. *Complete Writings 1959–1975*. Halifax and New York: Nova Scotia School of Art and Design, 1975, 197–9.

Judd, Donald. 'Specific Objects'. *Complete Writings 1959–1975*. Halifax and New York: Nova Scotia School of Art and Design, 1975, 181–9.

Judd, Donald. *Untitled (Six boxes)*, 1974. National Gallery of Australia. Available online: http://artsearch.nga.gov.au/Detail-LRG.cfm?IRN=14962 (accessed 24 June 2017).

Judd, Donald. *Untitled (Stack)*, 1967. Museum of Modern Art, New York. Availabel online; http://www.moma.org/collection/works/81324 (accessed 24 June 2017).

Judd, Donald. 'Young Artists at the Fair and at Lincoln Centre'. *Complete Writings 1959–1975*. Halifax and New York: Nova Scotia School of Art and Design, 1975, 130–1.

Just, Daniel. 'Is Less More? A Reinvention of Realism in Raymond Carver's Minimalist Short Story'. *Critique* 49 (3) (2008): 303–17.

Kant, Immanuel. *Critique of Judgment*. Trans. Werner S. Pluhar. Indianapolis: Hackett, 1987.

Kearney, Richard. 'Imagination Wanted: Dead or Alive'. *Samuel Beckett 100 Years: Centenary Essays*. Ed. Christopher Murray. New Island: RTE, 2006, 111–21.

Kelly, Ellsworth. *Spectrum IV*. 1967. New York: Museum of Modern Art. Available online: http://www.moma.org/collection/object.php?object_id=79739 (accessed 24 June 2017).

Kennedy, Douglas. 'Pierre, Prince of Dakrness'. *BBC Music* (March 1995): 28-31.

Kenner, Hugh. *A Reader's Guide to Samuel Beckett*. London: Thames and Hudson, 1973.

Khlebnikov, Velimir and Alexey Kruchenykh. 'The Letter as Such'. *Manifesto: A Century of Isms*. Ed. Mary Ann Caws. Lincoln and London: University of Nebraska Press, 2001, 236–7.

Khlebnikov, Velimir and Alexey Kruchenykh. 'The Words as Such'. *Manifesto: A Century of Isms*. Ed. Mary Ann Caws. Lincoln and London: University of Nebraska Press, 2001, 237–8.

Klein, Yves. *Monotone Symphony*, 1949. Available online: http://www.artep.net/kam/symphony.html (accessed 24 June 2017).

Knapp, Steven and Walter Benn Michaels. 'Against Theory'. *Critical Inquiry* 8 (1982): 723–42.

Kostelanetz, Richard. 'Microstories'. *Gander Press Review* 1 (2008): 93–4.

Krauss, Rosalind E. *Passages in Modern Sculpture*. New York: Viking, 1977.

Kruchenykh, Alexey. *zok zok zok*. Sound source undated. Available online: http://www.ubu.com/sound/phonetische.html (accessed 24 June 2017).

LaBelle, Brandon. *Background Noise: Perspectives on Sound Art*. London and New York: Continuum, 2008.

Lacoue-Labarthe, Philippe. *Typography: Mimesis, Philosophy, Politics*. Trans. and ed. Christopher Fynsk. Stanford: Stanford University Press, 1998.

Lacoue-Labarthe, Philippe and Jean-Luc Nancy. *The Literary Absolute: The Theory of Literature in German Romanticism*. Trans. Philip Barnard and Cheryl Lester. Albany: State University of New York Press, 1988.

Lailach, Michael. *Land Art*. Bonn: Taschen, 2007.

Lainsbury, G. P. *The Carver Chronotype: Inside the Life-World of Raymond Carver's Fiction*. London and New York: Routledge, 2004.

LaPorte, Joseph. 'Rigid Designator'. *Stanford Encyclopedia of Philosophy*, 20 September 2011. Available online: http://plato.stanford.edu/entries/rigid-designators/#NamOrdDesIdeSta (accessed 24 June 2017).

Larsen, Susan C. 'Cy Twombly: Works on Paper 1954–1976'. *Cy Twombly: Works on Paper 1954-1976: Newport Harbor Art Museum*. Newport Beach: Newport Harbor Art Museum, 1981, 16–50.

Lasch, Christopher. *The Minimal Self: Psychic Survival in Troubled Times*. London: Picador, 1984.

Latour, Bruno. *Reassembling the Social: An Introduction to Actor-Network Theory*. Oxford: Oxford University Press, 2005.

Lawson, Hilary. *Closure: A Story of Everything*. London and New York: Routledge, 2001.

Lax, Robert. 'is'. *New Poems 1962/1985*. London: Coracle, 1986, 13.

Lax, Robert. 'jacob & the angel'. *Robert Lax: Poems (1962–1997)*. Ed John Beer. Seattle and New York: Wave, 2013, 129–33.

Lax, Robert. 'things into words'. *New Poems 1962/1985*. London: Coracle, 1986, 42.

Lax, Robert. 'word'. *New Poems*. London: Coracle, 1986, 9.

Leach, David. 'Parallel Methods in Writing and Visual Arts'. *Generative Literature and Generative Art: New Essays*. Ed. David Leach. Fredericton: York Press, 1983, 11–16.

Leff, Gordon. *Medieval Thought: St Augustine to Ockham*. Harmondsworth: Penguin, 1958.

Lessing, Gotthold Ephraim. *Laocoon; or The Limits of Painting and Poetry*. Trans. William Ross. London: Ridgway, 1836.

Levinas, Emmanuel. *Existence and Existents*. Trans. Alphonso Lingis. Pittsburgh: Duquesne University Press, 1988.

Levinas, Emmanuel. *Is It Righteous To Be?: Interviews with Emmanuel Levinas*. Ed. Jill Robbins. Stanford: Stanford University Press, 2001.

Levinas, Emmanuel. 'Reality and Its Shadow'. *Collected Philosophical Papers*. Trans. Alphonso Lingis. Dordrecht: Martinus Nijhoff, 1987, 1–13.

Levinas, Emmanuel. *Time and the Other [and Additional Essays]*. Trans. Richard A. Cohen. Pittsburgh: Duquesne University Press, 1987.

Levinas, Emanuel. *Totality and Infinity*. Pittsburgh: Duquesne University Press, 1969.

LeWitt, Sol. *Incomplete Open Cubes*, 1974. San Francisco Museum of Modern Art, San Francisco. Available online: https://www.sfmoma.org/artwork/97.516.A-KKKKKKKKKK (accessed 24 June 2017).

LeWitt, Sol. *Maquette for One, Two, Three*. Smithsonian American Art Museum, 1979. Available online: http://americanart.si.edu/collections/search/artwork/?id=14689 (accessed 24 June 2017).

Leypoldt, Gunther. 'Raymond Carver's 'Epiphanic Moments'. *Style* 35 (3) (2001): 531–47.

Lippard, Lucy R. *Ad Reinhardt*. New York: Harry N. Abrams, 1981.

Lippard, Lucy R. 'As Painting is to Sculpture: A Changing Ratio'. *Changing: Essays in Art Criticism*. New York: Dutton, 1971, 120–9.

Lippard, Lucy R. 'The Structures, The Structures and the Wall Drawings, The Structures and the Wall Drawings and the Books'. *Sol LeWitt*. Ed. Alicia Legg. New York: Museum of Modern Art, 1978, 23–30.

Livingston, Paisley. 'Why Realism Matters: Literary Knowledge and the Philosophy of Science'. *Realism and Representation: Essays on the Problem of Realism in Relation to Science, Literature, and Culture*. Ed. George Levine. Madison: University of Wisconsin Press, 1993, 134–54.

Llewylyn, John. *Emmanuel Levinas: The Genealogy of Ethics*. London and New York: Routledge, 1995.

Lodge, David. 'Some Ping Understood.' *Critical Essays on Samuel Beckett*. Ed. Patrick A. McCarthy. Boston: G. K. Hall, 1986, 119–27.

Lora-Totino, Arrigo. 'FINITEINFINITE'. *The Chicago Review Anthology of Concretism*. Ed. Eugene Wildman. Chicago: Swallow Press, 1967, 94–5.

Losee, John. *A Historical Introduction to the Philosophy of Science*. Oxford and New York: Oxford University Press, 2001.

Lucier, Alvin. *I Am Sitting in a Room*. Libretto. Available online: http://www.ubu.com/sound/lucier.html (accessed 24 June 2017).

Lucier, Alvin. *I Am Sitting in a Room*. Lovely Music, 1990.

Lucretius, *On the Nature of the Universe*. Trans. R. E. Latham. London: Penguin, 1994, 42–4.

Lukács, Georg. *The Meaning of Contemporary Realism*. Trans. John and Necke Mander. London: Merlin, 1963.

Lyotard, Jean-François. 'Answering the Question What Is Postmodernism?' Trans. Régis Durand. *The Postmodern Condition*. Trans. Geoffrey Bennington and Brian Massumi. Manchester: Manchester University Press, 1984, 71–82.

Lyotard, Jean-François. *Duchamp's TRANS/formers*. Trans. Ian McLeod. Venice, CA: Lapis, 1990.

Lyotard, Jean-François. *Lessons on the Analytic of the Sublime*. Trans. Elizabeth Rottenberg. Stanford: Stanford University Press, 1994.

Lyotard, Jean-François. 'Newman: The Instant'. *The Inhuman: Reflections on Time*. Trans. Geoffrey Bennington and Rachel Bowlby. Cambridge: Polity, 1991, 78–88.

Lyotard, Jean-François. 'Presenting the Unpresentable: The Sublime'. Trans. Lisa Liebmann. *Artforum* 20 (8) (1982): 64–9.

Lyotard, Jean-François. 'Representation, Presentation, Unpresentable'. *The Inhuman: Reflections on Time*. Trans. Geoffrey Bennington and Rachel Bowlby. Cambridge: Polity Press, 1993, 119–28.

Lyotard, Jean-François. *The Differend: Phrases in Dispute*. Trans. Georges Van Den Abbeele. Manchester: Manchester University Press, 1988.

Lyotard, Jean-François. 'The Sublime and the Avant-Garde'. *The Inhuman: Reflections on Time*. Trans. Geoffrey Bennington and Rachel Bowlby. Cambridge: Polity Press, 1991, 89–107.

Madarasz, Norman. Introduction. *Manfiesto for Philsophy*, Alain Badiou. Trans. Norman Madarasz. Albany: State University of New York Press, 1999, 1–23.

Maguire, Nancy Klein. *An Infinity of Little Hours: Five Young Men and Their Trial of Faith in the Western World's Most Austere Monastic Order*. New York: PublicAffairs, 2006.

Man, Paul de. 'The Resistance to Theory'. *The Resistance to Theory*. Manchester: Manchester University Press, 1986, 3–20.

Maria, Walter de. *The Lighining Field*. Dia Art Foundation, Quemado, New Mexico, 1977.

Martin, Agnes. Interview with Chuck Smith and Sono Kuwayama. November 2007.

Marx, Karl. *Capital: A Critique of Political Economy. Volume 1*. Trans. Ben Fowkes. Harmondsworth: Penguin, 1976.

Marzona, Daniel. *Minimal Art*. Ed. Ute Grosenick. Köln: Taschen, 2004.

Maude, Ulrika. *Beckett, Technology and the Body*. Cambridge: Cambridge University Press, 2009.

Mayer, Hansjörg. From *fortführungen. An Anthology of Concrete Poetry*. Ed. Emmett Williams. New York: Something Else, 1967, 202.

McCaffery, Steve. *Panopticon*. Toronto: Bookthug, 2011.

McCaffery, Steve. 'Sound Poetry – A Survey'. *Sound Poetry: A Catalogue*. Ed. Steve McCaffery and bpNichol. Toronto: Underwich, 1978. Available online: http://www.ubu.com/papers/mccaffery.html (accessed 24 June 2017).

McDermott, James Dishon. *Austere Style in Twentieth Century Literature: Literary Minimalism*. Lewiston, NY: Edwin Mellen, 2006.

McGurl, Mark. *The Program Era: Postwar Fiction and the Rise of Creative Writing*. Cambridge, MA and London: Harvard University Press, 2009.

McInerny, Ralph. 'Saint Thomas Aquinas'. *The Stanford Encyclopedia of Philosophy*. Available online: http://plato.stanford.edu/entries/aquinas/ (accessed 24 June 2017).

McLuhan, Marshall. *Understanding Media: The Extensions of Man*. London: Abacus, 1964.

McTaggart, J. Ellis. 'The Unreality of Time'. *Mind* 17 (68), New Series (1908): 457–74.

Meillassoux, Quentin. *After Finitude: An Essay on the Necessity of Contingency*. Trans. Ray Brassier. London and New York: Continuum, 2008.

Meillassoux, Quentin. 'Speculative Realism'. *Collapse* III (2007): 408–49.

Melville, Stephen. 'What Was Postminimalism?' *Art and Thought*. Ed. Dana Arnold and Margaret Iversen. Oxford and Malden, MA: Blackwell, 2003, 156–73.

Menezes, Philadelpho. 'Intersign Poetry: Visual and Sound Poetics in the Technologizing of Culture'. *Experimental – Visual – Concrete: Avant-Garde Poetry Since the 1960s*. Ed. K. David Jackson, Eric Vos and Johanna Drucker. Amsterdam and Atlanta: Rodopi, 1996, 259–62.

Merleau-Ponty, Maurice. *Phenomenology of Perception*. Trans. Colin Smith. London: Routledge, 1962.

Mertens, Wim. *American Minimal Music: La Monte Young, Terry Riley, Steve Reich, Philip Glass*. Trans. J. Hautekiet. London: Kahn & Averill, 1983.

Merton, Thomas. *Seeking Paradise: The Spirit of the Shakers*. Ed. Paul M. Pearson. Maryknoll, NY: Orbis Books, 2003.

Merton, Thomas and Robert Lax. 'A Catch of Anti-Letters'. *Voyages: A National Literary Magazine* II (I–II) (1968): 44–56.

Meyer, James. *Minimalism*. London and New York: Phaedon, 2000.

Meyer, James. *Minimalism: Art and Polemics in the Sixties*. New Haven and London: Yale University Press, 2001.

Michaels, Walter Benn. 'Meaning and Affect: Phil Cahng's *Cache, Active*'. *nonsite.org*, 13 March 2012. Available online: http://nonsite.org/feature/meaning-and-affect-phil-changs-cache-active (accessed 24 June 2017).

Michaels, Walter Benn. *The Shape of the Signifier: 1967 to the End of History*. Princeton and Oxford: Princeton University Press, 2004.

Mills, Catherine. *The Philosophy of Agamben*. Stocksfield: Acumen, 2008.

Miller, J. Hillis. *Fiction and Repetition: Seven English Novels*. Cambridge, MA: Harvard University Press, 1982.

Miller, J. Hillis. *The Ethics of Reading: Kant, de Man, Eliot, Trollope, James and Benjamin*. New York: Columbia University Press, 1987.

Monk, Meredith. *Facing North*. ECM, 1992.

Monk, Meredith. 'From Liner Notes for *Facing North* Album, 1992'. *Meredith Monk*. Ed. Deborah Jowitt. Baltimore and London: Johns Hopkins University Press, 1997, 167–8.

Monk, Meredith. 'Mission Statement, 1983, Revised 1996'. *Meredith Monk*. Ed. Deborah Jowitt. Baltimore and London: Johns Hopkins University Press, 1997, 17.

Montag, Warren. 'What is at Stake in the Debate on Postmodernism?' *Postmodernism and its Discontents: Theories, Practices*. Ed. E. Ann Kaplan. London and New York: Verso, 1988, 88–103.

Morgan, Robert C. 'Bruce Nauman: An Introductory Survey'. *Bruce Nauman*. Ed. Robert C. Morgan. Baltimore: Johns Hopkins University Press, 2002, 1–17.

Morris, Pam. *Realism*. London and New York: Routledge, 2003.

Morris, Robert. 'Notes on Sculpture'. *Minimal Art: A Critical Anthology*. Ed. Gregory Battcock. New York: E. P. Dutton, 1968, 222–35.

Morris, Robert. *untitled (3 Ls)*, 1965/70. Whitney Museum of American Art, New York. Available online: http://collection.whitney.org/object/1774 (accessed 24 June 2017). Artwork.

Morrissette, Bruce. 'Generative Techniques in Robbe-Grillet and Ricardou. *Generative Literature and Generative Art: New Essays*. Ed. David Leach. Fredericton: York Press, 1983, 11–16.

Morton, Timothy. *Hyperobjects: Philosophy and Ecology After the End of the World*. Minneapolis and London: University of Minnesota Press, 2013.

Motte, Warren, *Small Worlds: Minimalism in Contemporary French Literature*. Lincoln: University of Nebraska Press, 1999.

Muhly, Nico. Email and recorded interview, 12–22 November 2011.

Muhly, Nico. *Mothertongue*. Bedroom Community, 2008.

Nancy, Jean-Luc. *The Creation of the World, or Globalization*. Trans. Francis Raffoul and David Pettigrew. Albany: State University of New York Press, 2007.

Nauman, Bruce. *Clown Torture*. 1987. Art Institute of Chicago. Available online: http://www.artic.edu/aic/collections/artwork/146989 (accessed 24 June 2017).

Neill, Ben. 'Pure Resonance'. *Bucknell Review* 40 (1) (1996): 191–4.

Nelles, William. 'Microfiction: What Makes a Very Short Story Very Short'. *Narrative* 20 (1) (2012): 87–104.

Nessett, Kirk. *The Stories of Raymond Carver: A Critical Study*. Athens, OH: Ohio University Press. 1995.

Newton-Smith, W. H. *The Rationality of Science*. London and New York: Routledge, 1981.

Nietzsche, Friedrich. *A Nietzsche Reader*. Trans. R. J. Hollindale. Oxford: Penguin, 1977.

Nietzsche, Friedrich. *The Anti-Christ, Ecce Homo, Twilight of the Idols, and Other Writings*. Trans. Judith Norman. Cambridge: Cambridge University Press, 2005.

Nietzsche, Friedrich. *The Birth of Tragedy and Other Writings*. Trans. Ronald Spears. Cambridge: Cambridge University Press, 1999.

Niiniluoto, Ilkka. *Critical Scientific Realism*. Oxford and New York: Oxford University Press, 1999.

Niiniluoto, Ilkka. *Truthlikeness*. Dordrecht: D. Reidel, 1987.

Noal, Robert and Gürol Irzik. *Philosophy, Science, Education and Culture*. Dordrecht: Springer, 2005.

Nochlin, Linda. *Realism*. Harmondsworth and New York: Penguin, 1971.

Norris, Christopher. *Badiou's Being and Event*. London and New York: Continuum, 2009.

Norris, Christopher. *New Idols of the Cave: On the Limits of Anti-realism*. Manchester and New York: Manchester University Press, 1997.

Norris, Christopher. 'Reply to Jeff Malpas: On Truth, Realism, Changing one's Mind about Davidson (not Heidegger), and Related Topics'. *International Journal of Philosophical Studies* 12 (3) (2004): 357–74.

Norris, Christopher. *Re-Thinking the Cogito: Naturalism, Reason and the Venture of Thought*. London and New York: Continuum, 2010.

Nussbaum, Martha C. *The Fragility of Goodness: Luck and Ethics in Greek Tragedy and Philosophy*. Cambridge: Cambridge University Press, 2001.

Nussbaum, Martha C. *Upheavals of Thought: The Intelligence of Emotions*. Cambridge: Cambridge University Press, 2001.

Nyman, Michael. *Experimental Music: Cage and Beyond*. New York: Schirmer, 1974.

Oates, Joyce Carol. In 'Afterwords'. *Sudden Fiction: American Short-Short Stories*. Ed. Robert Shapard and James Thomas. Salt Lake City: Peregrine Smith, 1986, 225–58.

O'Grady, Deirdre. *The Last Troubadours: Poetic Drama in Italian Opera 1597–1887*. London and New York: Routledge, 1991.

Page, Tim. Liner notes. Philip Glass. *Early Works*. Burbank: Elektra Nonesuch, 1994.

Parkinson, G. H. R. 'Philosophy and Logic'. *Cambridge Companion to Leibniz*. Ed. Nicholas Jolley. Cambridge: Cambridge University Press, 2005, 199–223.

Parmenides, 'Of Nature'. *Early Greek Philosophy*, trans. and ed. Jonathan Barnes. London: Penguin, 2001, 77–91.

Pegrum, Mark. A. *Challenging Modernity: Dada Between Modern and Postmodern*. New York and Oxford: Berghahn, 2000.

Perloff, Marjorie. *21st Century Modernism: The 'New' Poetics*. Oxford: Blackwell, 2002.

Perloff, Marjorie. 'Concrete Prose in the Nineties: Haroldo de Campos's *Galáxias* and After'. *Haroldo de Campos: A Dialogue with the Brazilian Concrete Poet*. Ed. K. David Jackson. Oxford: Centre for Brazilian Studies, 2005, 139–61.

Perloff, Marjorie. 'Minimalism'. *The Princeton Encyclopedia of Poetry and Poetics*, 4th edn. Ed. Roland Greene and Stephen Cushman. Princeton and Oxford: Princeton University Press, 2012, 886–7.

Perloff, Marjorie. *The Futurist Moment: Avant-Garde, Avant Guerre, and the Language of Rupture*. Chicago and London: University of Chicago Press, 1986.

Perloff, Marjorie. 'Writing as Re-Writing: Concrete Poetry as Arrière-Garde'. *CiberLetras* 17 (2007). Available online: http://www.lehman.cuny.edu/ciberletras/v17/perloff.htm (accessed 24 June 2017).

Perloff, Marjorie and Craig Dworkin. 'Introduction: The Sound of Poetry/The Poetry of Sound'. *The Sound of Poetry/The Poetry of Sound*. Ed. Marjorie Perloff and Craig Dworkin. Chicago and London: University of Chicago Press, 2009, 1–17.

Perloff, Nancy. 'Sound Poetry and the Musical Avant-Garde: A Musicologist's Perspective'. *The Sound of Poetry/The Poetry of Sound*. Ed. Marjorie Perloff and Craig Dworkin. Chicago and London: University of Chicago Press, 2009, 97–117.

Perreault, John. 'Minimal Abstracts'. *Minimal Art: A Critical Anthology*. Ed. Gregory Battcock. New York: E. P. Dutton, 1968, 256–62.

Pilling, John. 'Shards of Ends and Odds in Prose: From "Fizzles" to "The Lost Ones"'. *On Beckett: Essays and Criticism*. Ed. S. E. Gontarski. New York: Grove, 1986, 169–90.

Pincus-Witten, Robert. *Postminimalism into Maximalism: American Art, 1966–86*. Ann Arbor: UMI Research, 1987.

Plato. 'Ion'. Trans. Paul Woodruff. *Plato Complete Works*. Ed. John M. Cooper and D. S. Hutchinson. Indianapolis: Hackett, 1997, 937–49.

Plato. 'Parmenides'. Trans. Mary Louise Gill and Paul Ryan. *Plato Complete Works*. Ed. John M. Cooper and D.S. Hutchinson. Indianapolis: Hackett, 1997, 359–97.

Plato. 'Phaedo'. Trans. G. M. A. Grube. *Plato Complete Works*. Ed. John M. Cooper and D.S. Hutchinson. Indianapolis: Hackett, 1997, 49–100.

Plato. 'Republic'. Trans. G. M. A. Grube and C. D. C. Reeve. *Plato Complete Works*. Ed. John M. Cooper and D.S. Hutchinson. Indianapolis: Hackett, 1997, 971–1223.

Potter, Keith. *Four Musical Minimalists: La Monte Young, Terry Riley, Steve Reich, Philip Glass*. Cambridge: Cambridge University Press, 2000.

Potts, Alex. 'Dan Flavin "in Cool White" and "Infected with a Blank Magic"'. *Dan Flavin: New Light*. Ed. Jeffrey Weiss. New Haven and London: Yale University Press, 2006, 1–24.

Powers, Kevin. 'James Lee Byars (Memorial)'. *Third Text* 11 (39) (2007): 108–10.

Powell, Richard. 'Accessible Narratives: Continuity in the Music of John Adams'. *Contemporary Music Review* 33 (4) (2014): 390–407.

Priest, Stephen. Chapter Introduction. *Jean-Paul Sartre: Basic Writings*. Ed. Stephen Priest. London and New York: Routledge, 2001, 135–8.

Prigogine, Ilya and Isabelle Stengers. *Order out of Chaos: Man's New Dialogue with Nature*. London: Flamingo, 1985.

Psillos, Stathis. *Scientific Realism: How science tracks truth*. London and New York: Routledge, 1999.

Putnam, Hilary. *The Many Faces of Realism: The Paul Carus Lectures*. La Salle: Open Court, 1987.

Rabinovitz, Rubin. 'The Self Contained: Beckett's Fiction in the 1960s'. *Beckett's Later Fiction and Drama: Texts for Company*. Ed. James Acheson and Kateryna Arthur. Houndmills: Macmillan, 1987, 50–64.

Raitt, Jill. 'European Reformations of Christian Spirituality (1450-1700)'. *The Blackwell Companion to Christian Spirituality*. Ed. Arthur Holder. Oxford: Blackwell, 2005, 122–38.

Rancière, Jacques. 'Are Some Things Unrepresentable?' *The Future of the Image*. Trans. Gregory Elliott. London and New York: Verso, 2007, 109–38.

Rancière, Jacques. 'What Medium Can Mean'. Trans. Steve Corcoran. *Parrehsia* 11 (2011): 35-43.

Rancière, Jacques. 'The Surface of Design'. *The Future of the Image*. Trans. Gregory Elliott. London and New York: Verso, 2007, 91–107

Rasch, William and Cary Wolfe. Introduction. *Observing Complexity: Systems Theory and Postmodernity*. Minneapolis: University of Minnesota Press, 2000, 1–32.

Redfield, Marc. *Phantom Formations: Aesthetic Ideology and the Bildungsroman*. Ithaca: Cornell University Press, 1996.

Reich, Steve. 'Excerpts from an Interview in Art Forum'. *Writings on Music: 1965–2000*. Ed. Paul Hiller. Oxford: Oxford University Press, 2002, 33.

Reich, Steve. *Pendulum Music*. London: Universal Edition, 1980.

Reich, Steve. 'Pendulum Music'. *Writings on Music: 1965–2000*. Ed. Paul Hillier. Oxford: Oxford University Press, 2002, 31–2.

Reich, Steve. *Piano Phase (for two pianos or two marimbas)*. London: Universal Edition, 1980.

Reich, Steve. 'Music as a Gradual Process'. *Writings on Music: 1965–2000*. Ed. Paul Hillier. Oxford: Oxford University Press, 2002, 34–6.

Reich, Steve. 'Second Interview with Michael Nyman'. *Writings on Music: 1965–2000*. Ed. Paul Hillier. Oxford: Oxford University Press, 2002, 91–6.

Reinhardt, Ad. *Abstract Painting*, 1957. Museum of Modern Art, New York. Available online: http://www.moma.org/collection/works/79265?locale=en (accessed 24 June 2017).

Reinhardt, Ad. *Number 107*, 1950. Museum of Modern Art, New York. Available online: http://www.moma.org/collection/works/80269?locale=en (accessed 24 June 2017).

Reinhardt, Ad. 'Twelve Rules for a New Academy'. *Art-as-Art: The Selected Writing of Ad Reinhardt*. Ed. Barbara Rose. Berkeley and Los Angeles: University of California Press, 1975, 203–7.

Reinhardt, Ad. 'Writings'. *The New Art: A Critical Anthology*. Ed. Gregory Battcock. New York: E. P. Dutton, 1973, 167–77.

Richards, Virginia M. and Gerald D. Kidd, Jr. 'Audition'. *The MIT Encyclopedia of the Cognitive Sciences*. Ed. Robert A. Wilson and Frank. C. Keil. Cambridge, MA and London: MIT Press, 1999, 48–50.

Rietveld, Gerrit. *Zig-Zag Chair*, 1934. Museum of Modern Art, New York. Available online: http://www.moma.org/collection/works/3477?locale=en (accessed 24 June 2017).

Ridley, B.K. *On Science*. London and New York: Routledge, 2001.

Robbe-Grillet, Alain. 'A Path for the Future Novel'. *Snapshots* and *Towards a New Novel*. Trans. Barbara Wright. London: Calder and Boyars, 1965, 50–7.

Robbe-Grillet, Alain. 'From Realism to Reality'. *Snapshots* and *Towards a New Novel*. Trans. Barbara Wright. London: Calder and Boyars, 1965, 153–61.

Robbe-Grillet, Alain. 'In the Corridors of the Underground'. *Snapshots and Towards A New Novel*. Trans. Barbara Wright. London: Calder and Boyars, 1965, 27–34.

Robbe-Grillet, Alain. 'On Some Outdated Notions'. *Snapshots and Towards a New Novel*. Trans. Barbara Wright. London: Calder and Boyars, 1965, 59–74.

Robbins, Bruce. 'Modernism and Literary Realism: Response'. *Realism and Representation: Essays on the Problem of Realism in Relation to Science, Literature, and Culture*. Ed. George Levine. Madison: University of Wisconsin Press, 1993, 225–31.

Robbins, Jill. *Altered Reading: Levinas and Literature*. Chicago and London: University of Chicago Press, 1999.

Rorimer, Anne. 'Approaches to Servility: Sol LeWitt and his Contemporaries'. *Sol LeWitt: A Retrospective*. Ed. Gary Garrels. New Haven and London: Yale University Press, 2000, 60–71.

Rose, Barbara. 'A B C Art'. *Minimal Art: A Critical Anthology*. Ed. Gregory Battcock. New York: E. P. Dutton, 1968, 274–97.

Rosenbaum, S. P. *Aspects of Bloomsbury: Studies in Modern English Literary and Intellectual History*. London: MacMillan, 1998.

Roston, Murray. *Modernist Patterns in Literature and the Visual Arts*. New York: New York University Press, 2000.

Rothenberg, Jerome and Pierre Joris. 'Introduction'. *PPPPPP: Poems, Performance Pieces, Proses, Plays, Poetics*. By Kurt Schwitters. Ed. and trans. Jerome Rothenberg and Pierre Joris. Philadelphia: Temple University Press, 1993, xv–xxxiii.

Roubaud, Jacques. 'Prelude: Poetry and Orality'. Trans. Jean-Jacques Poucel. *The Sound of Poetry/The Poetry of Sound*. Ed. Marjorie Perloff and Craig Dworkin. Chicago and London: University of Chicago Press, 2009, 18–25.

Rugoff, Ralph. 'Homeopathic Strategies'. *At the Threshold of the Visible: Miniscule and Small-Scale Art, 1964–1996*. Ed. Ralph Rugoff. New York: Independent Curators Incorporated, 1997, 11–71.

Russell, Bertrand. *History of Western Philosophy*. London and New York: Routledge, 2007.

Rye, Jane. *Futurism*. London: E. P. Dutton, 1973.

Saltzman, Arthur M. *Understanding Raymond Carver*. Columbia: University of South Carolina Press, 1988.

Sanouillet, Michel. 'Dada: A Definition'. *Dada Spectrum: The Dialectic of Revolt*. Ed. Stephen C. Foster and Rudolf E. Kuenzli. Madison: Coda, 1979, 15–28.

Saroyan, Aram. 'Untitled poster-poem'. *Aram Saroyan: Complete Minimal Poems*. New York: Primary Information/Ugly Duckling Press, 2013, 28.

Sartre, Jean-Paul. *Being and Nothingness: An Essay in Phenomenological Ontology*. Trans. Hazel E. Barnes. London: Routledge, 1969.

Savitt, Steven F. 'On Absolute Becoming and the Myth of Passage'. *Time, Reality and Experience*. Ed. Craig Callender. Cambridge: Cambridge University Press, 2002, 153–67.

Schaeffer, John. 'Who Is La Monte Young?' *Bucknell Review* 40 (1) (1996): 25–43

Schaffner, Ingrid. 'Circling Oblivion/Bruce Nauman through Samuel Beckett'. *Bruce Nauman*. Ed. Robert C. Morgan. Baltimore: Johns Hopkins University Press, 2002, 163–73.

Schechner, Mark. 'American Realisms, American Realities'. *Neo-Realism in Contemporary American Fiction*. Ed. Kristiaan Versluys. Amsterdam and Atlanta: Rodopi, 1992, 27–50.

Schlegel, Friedrich. 'Athenaeum Fragment 51'. *Classic and Romantic German Aesthetics*. Ed. J. M. Bernstein. Cambridge: Cambridge University Press, 247.

Scholl, Robert. 'Arvo Pärt and Spirituality'. *Cambridge Companion to Arvo Pärt*. Ed. Andrew Shenton. Cambridge: Cambridge University Press, 2012, 140–58.

Schonberg, Harold C. 'Critic's Notebook: Plumbing the Shallows of Minimalism'. *New York Times*, 21 February 1986, online archive.

Schwartz, K. Robert. *Minimalists*. London: Phaedon, 1996.

Schwartz, K. Robert. 'Process vs. Intuition in the Works of Steve Reich and John Adams. *American Music* 8 (3) (1990): 245–73.

Scobie, Stephen. *Earthquakes and Explorations: Language and Painting from Cubism to Concrete Poetry*. Toronto: University of Toronto Press, 1997.

Serra, Richard. 'Art and Censorship'. *Ethics and the Visual Arts*. Ed. Alaine A. King and Gail Levin. New York: Allsworth Press, 2006, 185–94.

Serra, Richard. *Gutter Corner Splash: Night Shift* (1969/95). Available online: https://www.sfmoma.org/artwork/91.30 (accessed 24 June 2017).

Serres, Michel. *Genesis*. Trans. Geneviève James and James Nielson. Ann Arbor: University of Michigan Press, 1995.

Shaw, Philip. *The Sublime*. London and New York: Routledge, 2006.

Sheeler, Jessie. *Little Sparta: The Garden of Ian Hamilton Finlay*. London: Francis Lincoln, 2003.

Shenton, Andrew. 'Arvo Pärt in his own words'. *Cambridge Companion to Arvo Pärt*. Ed. Andrew Shenton. Cambridge: Cambridge University Press, 2012, 111–27.

Shui, Florian. *Asceticism: The Great Failure*. New Haven and London: Yale Universiy Press, 2014.

Siegel, Marcia B. 'Virgin Vessel'. *Meredith Monk*. Ed. Deborah Jowitt. Baltimore and London: Johns Hopkins University Press, 1997, 36–9.

Sim, Stuart. *Manifesto for Silence: Confronting the Politics and Culture of Noise*. Edinburgh: Edinburgh University Press, 2007.

Simmons, Philip E. *Deep Surfaces: Mass Culture and History in Postmodern American Fiction*. Athens and London: University of Georgia Press, 1997.

Sloane, Mary Cole. *The Visual in Metaphysical Poetry*. Atlantic Highlands, NJ: Humanities Press, 1981.

Smith, Brydon E. 'Recollections and Thoughts About Dan Flavin'. *Dan Flavin: A Retrospective*. Ed. Michael Govan and Tiffany Bell. New York: Dia Art Foundation, 2004, 131–44.

Smith, Daniel W. 'Badiou and Deleuze on the Ontology of Mathematics'. *Think Again: Alain Badiou and the Future of Philosophy*. Ed. Peter Hallward. London: Continuum, 2004, 77–93.

Sontag, Susan. 'Against Interpretation'. *Against Interpretation and Other Essays*. New York: Dell, 1964, 13–23.

Sörbom, Göran. 'The Classical Concept of Mimesis'. *A Companion to Art Theory*. Ed. Paul Smith and Carolyn Wilde. Oxford: Blackwell, 2002, 19–28.

Spade, Paul Vincent. 'William of Ockham'. *Stanford Encyclopedia of Philosophy*. Available online: http://plato.stanford.edu/entries/ockham/ (accessed 24 June 2017).

Stecopoulos, Eleni. *Visceral Poetics*. On Contemporary Practice; Oakland, CA: Publisher, 2016.

Steiner, Wendy. *The Colors of Rhetoric: Problems in the Relation between Modern Literature and Painting*. Chicago and London: University of Chicago Press, 1982.

Stella, Frank. *Arbeit Macht Frei*. 1967. Museum of Modern Art, New York. Available online: http://www.moma.org/collection/works/61219?locale=en (accessed 24 June 2017).

Stella, Frank. *Empress of India*, 1965. Museum of Modern Art, New York. Available online: http://www.moma.org/collection/works/79806 (accessed 24 June 2017).

Stella, Frank. *Tomlinson Court Park*. 1964. Museum of Modern Art, New York. Available online: http://www.moma.org/collection/works/61217?locale=en (accessed 24 June 2017).

Stein, Gertrude. 'Composition as Explanation'. *Look at Me Now and Here I Am: Writings and Lectures 1909–1945*. Ed. Patricia Meyerowitz. Harmondsworth: Penguin, 1967, 21–30.

Sterritt, David. 'Notes: Meredith Monk'. *Meredith Monk*. Ed. Deborah Jowitt. Baltimore and London: Johns Hopkins University Press, 1997, 106–12.

Stevenson, Diane. 'Minimalist Fiction and Critical Doctrine'. *Minimalist Fiction*. Ed. Kim A. Herzinger. *Mississippi Review* 40/41, Special Issue (1985): 83–9.

Stevick, Philip. In 'Afterwords'. *Sudden Fiction: American Short-Short Stories*. Ed. Robert Shapard and James Thomas. Salt Lake City: Peregrine Smith, 1986, 225–58.

Stewart, Garrett. *Bookwork: Medium to Object to Concept to Art*. Chicago and London: University of Chicago Press, 2011.

Stewart, Susan. 'At the Threshold of the Visible'. *At the Threshold of the Visible: Miniscule and Small-Scale Art, 1964–1996*. Ed. Ralph Rugoff. New York: Independent Curators Incorporated, 1997, 73–85.

Stewart, Susan. *On Longing: Narratives of the Miniature, the Gigantic, the Souvenir, the Collection*. Durham, NC and London: Duke University Press, 1993.

Stewart, Susan. 'Rhyme and Freedom'. *The Sound of Poetry/The Poetry of Sound*. Ed. Marjorie Perloff and Craig Dworkin. Chicago and London: University of Chicago Press, 2009, 29–48.

Stone, Abraham. 'Heidegger and Carnap on the Overcoming of Metaphysics'. *Martin Heidegger*. Ed. Stephen Mulhall. Aldershot and Burlington, VT: Ashgate, 2006, 217–44.

Strickland, Edward. *Minimalism: Origins*. Bloomington and Indianapolis: Indiana University Press, 1993.

Tallis, Raymond. *In Defence of Realism*. London: Edward Arnold, 1988.

Thomasson, Amie. 'Roman Ingarden'. *Stanford Encyclopedia of Philosophy*. Available online: http://plato.stanford.edu/entries/ingarden/ (accessed 24 June 2017).

Thurman, Robert A. F. 'Tibetan Buddhist Perspectives on Asceticism'. *Asceticism*. Ed. Vincent L. Wimbush and Richard Valantasis. Oxford and New York: Oxford University Press, 1998, 108–18.

Trieloff, Barbara. "Babel of Silence': Beckett's Post-Trilogy Prose Articulated'. *Rethinking Beckett: A Collection of Critical Essays*. Ed. Lance St John Butler and Robin J. Davis. Houndmills: Macmillan, 1990, 89–104.

Turrell, James. *Breathing Light*, 2013. Los Angeles County Museum of Art. Available online: http://www.lacma.org/art/exhibition/james-turrell-breathing-light (accessed 24 June 2017).

Twombly, Cy. *Arcadia*, 1958. Collection unspecified. Available online: http://www.cytwombly.info/twombly_gallery.htm (accessed).

Tymnieniecka, Anna-Teresa. 'Beyond Ingarden's Idealism/Realism Controversy with Husserl – The New Contextual Phase of Phenomenology'. *Ingardenia: A Spectrum of Specialized Studies Establishing the Field of Research*. Dordrecht and Boston: D. Reidel, 1976, 241–418.

Vanderlinde, Frans. 'Elimination/Incarnation'. *The Chicago Review Anthology of Concretism*. Ed. Eugene Wildman. Chicago: Swallow Press, 1967, 76–7.

Van Doren, Mark. 'Mark Van Doren on Robert Lax'. *Voyages: A National Literary Magazine* II (I–II) (1968): 62–4.

Vattimo, Gianni. *The End of Modernity: Nihilism and Hermeneutics in Post-modern Culture*. Trans. Jon R. Snyder. Cambridge: Polity Press, 1988.

Verhoeven, W. M. 'What We Talk About When We Talk About Raymond Carver: Or, Much Ado About Minimalism'. *Narrative Turns and Minor Genres in Postmodernism*. Ed. Theo D'haen and Hans Bertens. Amsterdam and Atlanta, GA: Rodopi, 1995, 41–60.

Waldorff, Marty G. 'Auditory Attention'. *The MIT Encyclopedia of the Cognitive Sciences*, ed. Robert A. Wilson and Frank. C. Keil. Cambridge, MA and London: MIT Press, 1999, 50–2.

Wall, Thomas Carl. *Radical Passivity: Levinas, Blanchot and Agamben*. Albany: State University of New York Press, 1999.

Ware, Kalistos. 'The Way of the Ascetics: Negative or Affirmative?' *Asceticism*. Ed. Vincent L. Wimbush and Richard Valantasis. Oxford and New York: Oxford University Press, 1998, 3–15.

Watten, Barrett. *The Constructivist Moment: From Material Text to Cultural Poetics*. Middletown: Wesleyan University Press, 2003.

Waugh, Patricia. 'Introduction: Criticism, Theory, and Anti-theory'. *Literary Theory and Criticism: An Oxford Guide*. Oxford: Oxford University Press, 2006, 1–34.

Weiss, Jeffrey. Preface. *Dan Flavin: A Retrospective*. Ed. Michael Govan and Tiffany Bell. New York: Dia Art Foundation, 2004, 10–11.

Welchman, John C. 'After the Wagnerian Bouillabaisse: Critical Theory and the Dada and Surrealist Word-Image'. *The Dada and Surrealist Word-Image*. Ed. Judi Freeman. Cambridge, MA and London: MIT Press, 1989, 57–96.

Wellek, René and Austin Warren. *Theory of Literature*. Harmondsworth: Penguin, 1963.

Weller, Shane. *A Taste for the Negative: Beckett and Nihilism*. London: Legenda, 2005.

Weitemeier, Hannah. *Yves Klein*. Köln: Taschen, 2001.

West, M. L. *Ancient Greek Music*. Oxford: Clarendon, 1992.

Wimbush, Vincent L. and Richard Valantasis. 'Introduction'. *Asceticism*. Ed. Vincent L. Wimbush and Richard Valantasis. Oxford and New York: Oxford University Press, 1998, xix–xxxiii.

Wolf, Kenneth Baxter. *The Poverty of Riches: St. Francis of Assisi Reconsidered*. Oxford and New York: Oxford University Press, 2003.

Wollheim, Richard. 'Minimal Art'. *Minimal Art: A Critical Anthology*. Ed. Gregory Battcock. New York: E. P. Dutton, 1968, 387–99.

Wyschogrod, Edith. *Emmanuel Levinas: The Problem of Ethical Metaphysics*. The Hague: Martinus Nijhoff, 1974.

Wyschogrod, Edith. 'The Art in Ethics: Aesthetics, Objectivity, and Alterity in the Philosophy of Emmanuel Levinas'. *Ethics as First Philosophy: The Significance of Emmanuel Levinas for Philosophy, Literature and Religion*. Ed. Adrian T. Peperzak. New York and London: Routledge, 1995, 137–48.

Wyschogrod, Edith. 'The Howl of Oedipus, the Cry of Héloïse: From Asceticism to Postmodern Ethics. *Asceticism*. Ed. Vincent L. Wimbush and Richard Valantasis. Oxford and New York: Oxford University Press, 1998, 16–30.

Yarmolinksy, Ben. 'Minimalism and the Baroque'. *Perceptible Processes: Minimalism and the Baroque*'. Ed. Claudia Swan. New York: Eos, 1997, 61–72.

York, Wes. 'Form and Process'. *Writings on Glass*. Ed. Richard Kostelanetz and Robert Fleming. Berkeley and Los Angeles: University of California Press, 1997, 60–79.

Young, La Monte and Marian Zazeela. 'Continuous Sound and Light Environments'. *Bucknell Review* 40 (1) (1996): 218–21.

Young, La Monte. *The Tortoise, His Dreams and Journeys*, 1964–present.

Young, La Monte. *Trio for Strings*, 1958.

Index

The letter *f* following an entry indicates a figure